AFTER SCIENCE AND RELIGION

The popular field of 'science and religion' is a lively and well-established area. It is, however, a domain which has long been characterised by certain traits. On one common model it tends towards an adversarial dialectic in which the separate disciplines, now conjoined, are forever locked in a kind of mortal combat. On a second, 'science and religion' move towards disentanglement, where 'science' does one sort of thing and 'religion' another. On a third, the duo are frequently pushed towards some sort of attempted synthesis, wherein their aims either coincide or are brought more closely together. In attempting something fresh and different, this volume tries to move beyond tried and tested tropes. Bringing philosophy and theology to the fore in a way rarely attempted before, the book shows how fruitful new conversations between science and religion can at last move beyond the increasingly tired options of either conflict or dialogue.

PETER HARRISON is Director of the Institute for Advanced Studies in the Humanities at the University of Queensland. He was formerly Andreas Idreos Professor of Science and Religion at the University of Oxford. His books include *The Bible, Protestantism and the Rise of Natural Science* (Cambridge University Press, 1998) and *The Territories of Science and Religion*. In addition, he edited *The Cambridge Companion to Science and Religion* (Cambridge University Press, 2010).

JOHN MILBANK is Emeritus Professor of Theology and Religious Studies at the University of Nottingham, where he is President of the Centre of Theology and Philosophy. His influential publications include *Theology and Social Theory* (1990) and *Radical Orthodoxy* (1999).

Praise for *After Science and Religion*

'This volume offers a set of historical studies that challenge naïve disciplinary distinctions between science and religion, combined with Anglo-Saxon theological and philosophical speculation. It's a book that can be expected to engage fans and critics alike of those who – as many in this book do – look back to pre-modern ways of wrestling with some vital issues.'

– *Willem B Drees, Professor of the Philosophy of the Humanities, Tilburg University*

'The starting point of this excellent volume could sound familiar: all sciences have built in theologies. If that is right, what then should come next in the study of science and religion? Harrison and Milbank have assembled a broad array of answers to that question, united as these are by an approach that might be characterised as *theology-engaged science*. It's a perspective that interrogates and deconstructs the basic categories of science and religion, telling the stories behind those terms by recounting moments at which the boundaries of each were in flux. This book offers a fresh and promising way of using history to challenge modernity's disciplinary boundaries by showing that scientific theories are already engaged in metaphysical and theological debates.'

– *John Perry, Senior Lecturer in Theological Ethics, University of St Andrews*

AFTER SCIENCE AND RELIGION

Fresh Perspectives from Philosophy and Theology

EDITED BY

PETER HARRISON

University of Queensland

JOHN MILBANK

University of Nottingham

with the assistance of

PAUL TYSON

University of Queensland

CAMBRIDGE
UNIVERSITY PRESS

CAMBRIDGE
UNIVERSITY PRESS

University Printing House, Cambridge CB2 8BS, United Kingdom

One Liberty Plaza, 20th Floor, New York, NY 10006, USA

477 Williamstown Road, Port Melbourne, VIC 3207, Australia

314–321, 3rd Floor, Plot 3, Splendor Forum, Jasola District Centre, New Delhi – 110025, India

103 Penang Road, #05–06/07, Visioncrest Commercial, Singapore 238467

Cambridge University Press is part of the University of Cambridge.

It furthers the University's mission by disseminating knowledge in the pursuit of education, learning, and research at the highest international levels of excellence.

www.cambridge.org
Information on this title: www.cambridge.org/9781316517925
DOI: 10.1017/9781009047968

First published 2022

A catalogue record for this publication is available from the British Library.

Library of Congress Cataloging-in-Publication Data
NAMES: Harrison, Peter, 1955- editor. | Milbank, John, editor.
TITLE: After science and religion : fresh perspectives from philosophy and theology / edited by Peter Harrison, University of Queensland, John Milbank, University of Nottingham.
DESCRIPTION: Cambridge, United Kingdom ; New York, NY, USA : Cambridge University Press, 2022. | Includes bibliographical references and index.
IDENTIFIERS: LCCN 2021044486 (print) | LCCN 2021044487 (ebook) | ISBN 9781316517925 (hardback) | ISBN 9781009048651 (paperback) | ISBN 9781009047968 (epub)
SUBJECTS: LCSH: Religion and science.
CLASSIFICATION: LCC BL241 .A49 2022 (print) | LCC BL241 (ebook) | DDC 215–dc23/eng/20211102
LC record available at https://lccn.loc.gov/2021044486
LC ebook record available at https://lccn.loc.gov/2021044487

ISBN 978-1-316-51792-5 Hardback

Contents

Contributors

SPIKE BUCKLOW is Professor of Material Culture at the Hamilton Kerr Institute, University of Cambridge. Bucklow's research interests fall into two broad categories: visual perception and artists' techniques. Research into visual perception includes work on formal connoisseurship of paintings to the classification of technical imagery. Research into artists' techniques includes theoretical and practical work on pigment recipes. Bucklow has a keen interest in the way in which material practices, science, art, and culturally situated meaning continually interact with each other. Some of his recent books are *The Alchemy of Paint* (2009), *The Riddle of the Image* (2014), and *The Anatomy of Riches* (2018).

MICHAEL HANBY is Associate Professor of Religion and Philosophy of Science, Pontifical John Paul II Institute, Washington, DC. Hanby is author of *No God, No Science?* (2013), which reassesses the relationship between the doctrine of creation, Darwinian evolutionary biology, and science more generally. He is also author of *Augustine and Modernity* (2003), which is simultaneously a re-reading of Augustine's Trinitarian theology and a protest against the contemporary argument for continuity between Augustine and Descartes.

PETER HARRISON is Director of the Institute for Advanced Studies of the Humanities, University of Queensland. An Australian Laureate Fellow who has published extensively in the field of intellectual history, Harrison is a Fellow of the Australian Academy of the Humanities and a corresponding member of the International Academy for the History of Science. His six books include *The Bible, Protestantism, and the Rise of Natural Science* (Cambridge University Press, 1998) and *The Territories of Science and Religion* (Cambridge University Press, 2015), based on his 2011 Gifford Lectures and winner of the Aldersgate Prize.

DAVID BENTLEY HART has most recently been a fellow of the Notre Dame Institute for Advanced Studies. Hart's specialties are philosophical theology, systematics, patristics, classical and continental philosophy, and Asian religion. His most recent work has concerned the genealogy of classical and Christian metaphysics, ontology, the metaphysics of the soul, and the philosophy of mind. Hart is a prolific author of articles and books, the latter including *Theological Territories* (2020), *The Experience of God* (2013), and *The Beauty of the Infinite* (2003).

PUI HIM IP is Tutor and Research Fellow at the Faraday Institute for Science and Religion and Affiliated Lecturer at the Faculty of Divinity, University of Cambridge. His research focuses on philosophical theology and Greek Patristics, currently centred on the works and reception of Origen of Alexandria. His book *Origen of Alexandria and the Emergence of Divine Simplicity before Nicaea* (forthcoming) offers the first genealogy of the doctrine of divine simplicity in early Christian thought. He is currently working on a second book on early Christian natural philosophy in the Origenian tradition. Ip has a MSci in Theoretical Physics.

BERNARD LIGHTMAN is Distinguished Research Professor of Humanities and Science and Technology Studies at York University, Canada. He is a Fellow of the Royal Society of Canada and past president of the History of Science Society. Lightman's research interests include nineteenth-century popular science and Victorian scientific naturalism. Among his most recent publications are the edited collections *Rethinking History, Science, and Religion* (2019), *Science Periodicals in Nineteenth Century Britain* (2020); and *Identity in a Secular World* (2020).

TOM MCLEISH is Professor of Natural Philosophy in the Department of Physics at the University of York. In 2011 he was elected a Fellow of the Royal Society where he has served as Chair of Education. McLeish's research interests are strongly interdisciplinary and include soft matter and biological physics, and issues of theology, ethics, and history of science, especially medieval science. He has published over 200 scientific articles and is regularly involved in science communication in writing and radio. Recent books include *Faith and Wisdom in Science* (2014), *The Poetry and Music of Science* (2019), and *Soft Matter – A Very Short Introduction* (2020). He was the 2021 Boyle Lecturer on Science and Religion.

JOHN MILBANK is President of the Centre of Theology and Philosophy at the University of Nottingham. He is a prolific author and wide-ranging thinker who has endeavoured to re-think the social theory, ethics, aesthetics, and politics of secular modernity with a sensitivity to its foundational assumptions, which he argues are problematically theological. He is best known for the classic *Theology and Social Theory* (1990, 2006), and more recent publications include *The Suspended Middle* (2005) and *Beyond Secular Order* (2013).

SIMON OLIVER is the Van Mildert Professor of Divinity at Durham University. Oliver's work centres on Christian theology and metaphysics, particularly the doctrine of creation within the Western history of ideas. He is particularly interested by the transition from a deeply teleological view of the cosmos and the associated doctrine of God up to the fourteenth century, to early modern natural philosophy and the alleged rejection of final causes. This was explored in his *Philosophy, God and Motion* (2005, 2013) and the Stanton Lectures at the University of Cambridge, delivered in 2017, to be developed as his next book entitled *Creation's Ends: Teleology, Ethics and the Natural.* He is the author of *Creation: A Guide for the Perplexed* (2017).

CATHERINE PICKSTOCK is the Norris-Hulse Professor of Divinity at the University of Cambridge. Pickstock is a philosophical theologian concerned with the application of linguistics to theories of religious language, analogy, and liturgy. Her work is critically engaged with postmodern philosophy in relation to the reinterpretation of premodern theology. Her current research centres on a reconsideration of the Platonic tradition in interaction with the biblically based faiths, in particular, the question of theurgy and understandings of the soul. She is well known for her 1997 book *After Writing.*

D. C. SCHINDLER is Professor of Metaphysics and Anthropology at the Pontifical John Paul II Institute, Washington, DC. He is currently working on a multi-volume critique of the modern concept of freedom as the power to choose in light of a metaphysics of freedom based on actuality. Schindler is a translator of French and German and has served as an editor of *Communio: International Catholic Review* since 2002. Among his acclaimed publications are *The Perfection of Freedom* (2012), *Plato's Critique of Impure Reason* (2008), and *Hans Urs von Balthasar and the Dramatic Structure of Truth* (2004).

JANET SOSKICE is Professor of Philosophical Theology, Emerita at the Jesus College, University of Cambridge, and the William K. Warren Distinguished Research Professor of Catholic Theology at Duke

Divinity School. Her book *Metaphor and Religious Language* (1984) was a pioneering work on models and metaphors in science and religion. She has been involved in four science and religion conferences at the Vatican Observatory and initiated their conference on creation ex nihilo, which resulted in the volume *Creation and the God of Abraham* (2010), a collection which examines the doctrine of creation from nothing in Jewish, Christian, and Muslim thought.

PAUL TYSON is a Senior Research Fellow at the Institute for Advanced Studies in the Humanities at the University of Queensland. Tyson's scholarship works across the sociology of knowledge and philosophical theology with a particular interest in applied theological metaphysics and applied theological epistemology in a contemporary Christian Neoplatonist register. His five books include *Returning to Reality* (2014), *Defragmenting Modernity* (2017), and *Seven Brief Lessons on Magic* (2019).

ROWAN WILLIAMS (Lord Williams of Oystermouth) was the Archbishop of Canterbury from 2002 to 2012, and Master of Magdalene College, University of Cambridge, from 2013 to 2020. In 1990, he was elected a Fellow of the British Academy. Williams is a noted linguist, poet, and translator of poetry, and has a particular interest in Eastern Orthodox theology. Questions concerning the relation of the Church to contemporary secular society, and the distinctive epistemic, metaphysical and pragmatic assumptions of its master knowledge discourse – modern science – are among the many matters to which he has given careful thought. Some of his recent books are *Faith in the Public Square* (2012), *Wrestling with Angels* (2007), and *Grace and Necessity* (2005).

Acknowledgements

The original idea for this volume came from Paul Tyson, who also recruited the participants and assisted with the planning for our meetings and discussions. We are deeply grateful for his formative contributions, without which this collection would not have happened. We received vital financial support from the Templeton World Charity Foundation and the Issachar Fund for which we also are most grateful. Special thanks to Pete Jordan and Andrew Briggs at the TWCF for their assistance and guidance, and to Kurt Berends and his support staff at Issachar. Thanks also to Karl Wiethoff and Jonathan Horton, who provided generous financial support that helped facilitate our gatherings. We were fortunate in being able to convene in Cambridge on two occasions and wish to express our gratitude to Catherine Pickstock and Andrew Davison for hosting us, respectively, at Emmanuel and Corpus Christi Colleges. Also participating in the project, but not represented in this volume, were Knut Alfsvåg, Andrew Davison, William Desmond, Keith Fox, Simone Kotva, Nathan Lyons, Sotiris Mitralexis, Michael Northcott, Charles Taylor, and David Wilkinson. We are grateful for their thoughtful commentary and critique. While not formally part of the project, John Perry, Michael Burdett, Mike Hamilton, and Jeff Bishop also attended our meetings, providing valuable input and advice. The fourth principal investigator on the TWCF grant, along with Peter Harrison, John Milbank, and Paul Tyson, was Tom McLeish, who from the beginning has been an inspiring and energetic presence, and we owe him a debt of gratitude for his participation. Mention should also be made of the administrative team at the University of Queensland's Institute for Advanced Studies in the Humanities – Narelle Jones, Lisa Gunders, Olivia Formby, and Beck Hurst, who provided their characteristically professional support for the project. Cambridge University Press kindly allowed us to publish, in revised form, material from Catherine Pickstock's *Aspects of Truth: A New Religious Metaphysics* (2020). Finally, we are most grateful to Katie Idle and the production team at Cambridge University Press, along with the Cambridge readers of the manuscript, with special thanks to Alex Wright for his support and sage advice.

Introduction
After Science and Religion?

Paul Tyson

The present literature on science and religion tends to be dominated by three genres: a conflict genre, according to which science and religion are locked into a relationship of perennial opposition; a disentangling genre, in which science does one sort of thing and religion does another; and a synthetic genre, in which science and religion are integrated, overlapped, or in some way related to each other in generally positive ways. While on the face of it these approaches could hardly be more divergent, in fact they share a common commitment to the idea that 'science' and 'religion' are valid, trans-historical categories that capture more or less perennial features of human culture. If it is true that science and religion, albeit in various guises, have been the chief lenses through which the world has been interpreted, then posing the question of how they relate to each other makes good sense. But what if it is not true? The guiding principle of the present collection is that we can initiate a much more fruitful discussion if we begin by questioning these two basic categories that frame and delimit the current conversation about how to interpret the world. *After Science and Religion* is thus an exploration of how the discussion might be changed if we were to relinquish, or at least critically examine, these two categories 'science' and 'religion'.

Historians of science have contended for some time now that the familiar concept of 'science' is a relatively recent one. They point out that while it is tempting to speak of ancient Greek science, medieval science, seventeenth-century science, and so on, in fact that terminology is deeply misleading, particularly if it is assumed that the activities in question are more or less analogous to the scientific enterprise as we presently understand it. The same is true for the 'sciences' of other cultures – Islamic science, Chinese science, Indian science.[1] The study of nature in the past

[1] See Peter Dear, 'What Is the History of Science the History of?', *Isis*, 96 (2005), 390–406; Andrew Cunningham, 'The Identity of Natural Philosophy', *Early Science and Medicine*, 5 (2000), 259–78;

was so often caught up with philosophical, ethical, and religious concerns that to regard it as a direct analogue to modern science is to seriously misunderstand what was going on. Scholars of religion have made similar claims for the putative object of their study: 'religion'. The idea of a generic 'religion', and of plural 'religions', understood as competing sets of beliefs and practices, is argued to be a product of the early modern West, arising as a consequence of both the religious reformations of the sixteenth century and the voyages of discovery and colonial projects that coincided with them.[2] In medieval Christendom, for example, we hardly ever encounter the expression 'religion'. Arguably, subsequent early modern attempts to understand and categorise 'other religions' in terms of propositional beliefs led only to a distorted view of the phenomena in question.

In *The Territories of Science and Religion* (2015), Peter Harrison brought these two scholarly developments together, showing how the historical processes that led to the reification of the two categories 'science' and 'religion' are connected, and offering glimpses of how the present conversation about science and religion might be radically reconfigured if we were to take seriously the historically contingent nature of the terms in which it is conducted. Harrison has been building bridges to both scientists and theologians for some time now, seeking to persuade them to move away from boundary and terrain disputes and to look at the entire landscape differently. His work suggests that a more historically informed and philosophically open attitude to first-order questions about the nature of natural knowledge and higher meaning, and an appreciation of where they cannot escape mutually entailing each other, would greatly improve the quality of investigation. Harrison is something of an ambassador for putting standard notions of conflict, demarcation, and limited synthesis between variously understood 'solid' notions of science and religion behind us. This message is starting to be heard outside the spheres of the history of science and religious history. In this volume a rather distinctive

Peter Harrison, Ronald L. Number, and Michael H. Shank (eds.), *Wrestling with Nature: From Omens to Science* (Chicago: University of Chicago Press, 2011).

2 The classic work here is Wilfred Cantwell Smith's *The Meaning and End of Religion* [1962] (London: SPCK, 1978). But see also Peter Harrison, *'Religion' and the Religions in the English Enlightenment* (Cambridge: Cambridge University Press, 1998); Guy Stroumsa, *A New Science: The Discovery of Religion in the Age of Reason* (Cambridge, MA: Harvard University Press, 2010); Brent Nongbri, *Before Religion: The History of a Modern Concept* (New Haven, CT: Yale University Press, 2012). On the interface of politics and religious studies, see Elizabeth Shakman Hurd, *Beyond Religious Freedom* (Princeton, NJ: Princeton University Press, 2015). In theology, see Nicholas Lash, *The Beginning and End of 'Religion'* (Cambridge: Cambridge University Press, 1996); William T. Cavanaugh, *The Myth of Religious Violence* (Oxford: Oxford University Press, 2009).

group of philosophical theologians and theologically interested philosophers and scientists take up Harrison's ideas and explore their implications for a new kind of discussion about science and religion.

What difference, then, does this historical analysis of the categories make, and how can it inform new and fruitful conversations? There is no single answer to this question, and our contributors offer a range of responses. But there is also a significant convergence in their perspectives. One thing that clearly emerges from the genealogy of the categories 'science' and 'religion' is just how historically contingent their appearance has been. In other words, the fact that we now tend to think in these terms – 'science' and 'religion' – is not necessarily a matter of finally having arrived at precise categories that describe discrete realms as they really are, but is rather the end product of specific historical developments that might well have given us different categories. It also follows that there was a *before* science and religion, as well as a possible *after* science and religion, and the former can help shed light on possibilities for the latter. When we abandon the attempt to impose our present concepts on the past, we are in a position to see how past actors entertained very different understandings of how the formal study of nature (our 'science') was related to the fundamental questions of meaning and value (our 'religion'). The category 'natural philosophy', which was in use from the time of the ancient Greeks until well into the nineteenth century, and which was the term most analogous to our modern 'science', offers a good example.[3] Natural philosophy was a branch of philosophy. It often included in its scope the activity of God and the angels, and was also intimately connected to the moral and religious formation of the person. Natural philosophy is thus very different from modern science if for no other reason than it includes these moral and religious components. How we get to naturalistic, value-free, modern science from this earlier, religiously inflected 'natural philosophy' is highly informative for our present thinking about how the realms of meaning and value should impinge upon the conduct and

[3] On the category 'natural philosophy', see John Gascoigne, 'Ideas of Nature: Natural Philosophy', in *The Cambridge History of Science*, vol. 4, ed. Roy Porter (Cambridge: Cambridge University Press, 2003), 285–304; John Heilbron, 'Natural Philosophy', in Harrison et al. (eds.), *Wrestling with Nature*, 173–99. On its religious connotations, see Andrew Cunningham, 'Getting the Game Right: Some Plain Words on the Identity and Invention of Science', *Studies in History and Philosophy of Science*, 19 (1998), 365–89; Peter Dear, 'Religion, Science, and Natural Philosophy: Thoughts on Cunningham's Thesis', *Studies in History and Philosophy of Science*, 32 (2001), 377–86. Peter Harrison 'Physico-Theology and the Mixed Sciences: The Role of Theology in Early Modern Natural Philosophy', in Peter Anstey and John Schuster (eds.), *The Science of Nature in the Seventeenth Century* (Dordrecht: Springer, 2005), 165–83.

content of the natural sciences and about the possibility for the future reconnection of these domains.

A second pay-off of close study of the emergence of the categories 'science' and 'religion', and indeed of simply attending more closely to the history of science, is that it reveals how the modern sciences, during their early modern incubation, drew strongly and explicitly on particular metaphysical and theological assumptions while at the same time rejecting others. Once we become aware of these (now largely implicit) foundations, we can ponder the extent to which modern science remains tacitly indebted to them. This, in turn, can inform our thinking about how different various sciences might look had they drawn upon alternative theological and metaphysical positions, and indeed whether they might in future be reshaped and redirected in fruitful ways by such alternatives.

Third, in addition to attending to the implicit philosophical commitments that continue to inform scientific practices from within, we are now in a position to see more clearly how and why a particular philosophical outlook – analytic philosophy – has tended to dominate contemporary Anglophone science–religion discussion from without. It is typically assumed that this mode of philosophising can bring clarity and precision to the discussion and provide a neutral bridging language that facilitates conversation between the two parties. But for this very reason, the approach of some analytic philosophers has the potential to exacerbate the distortions inherent in the categories themselves, often reducing 'religion' and 'science' to their propositional contents or their approaches to knowledge, and thereby disembedding them from their real-life contexts. Philosophy of science in the analytic mode is thus often indifferent (or even hostile) to the history of science and the sociology of science, both of which seek to attend closely to the messy reality of the actual practices of scientists in ways that resist abstraction and oversimplification. Moreover, because analytic philosophy is often self-consciously modelled on what science is imagined to be, it is usually accompanied by a commitment to naturalism, whether overt or not, which is in tension with its imagined neutrality.[4] It is no coincidence, then, that a number of the theological and philosophical thinkers engaging with Harrison in this volume are more representative of continental philosophy and sociological theory. Their

[4] The philosopher W. V. Quine (1908–2000) epitomises both tendencies. See, e.g., Sander Verfaegh, *The Nature and Development of Quine's Naturalism* (Oxford: Oxford University Press, 2018). For science as the model for philosophy, see Stephen Gaukroger, *The Failures of Philosophy: A Historical Essay* (Princeton, NJ: Princeton University Press, 2020), 261–82, 287.

theological influences are closer to Catholic and Orthodox approaches than Reformed thinking.[5] Of course, it is important not to overdraw the distinctions between 'analytic' and 'continental' philosophy, which in recent years have become less distinct. And the philosophy of science itself, particularly when historically inflected, has challenged narrow positivistic conceptions of science. That said, this volume seeks to introduce a new flavour of philosophical theology into the science and religion space. While the philosophical theologians contributing to this collection by no means represent a unified school, they do share a deep historically embedded theological awareness that has resisted the territorial boundaries of post-Victorian thinking. For this reason, they have never really been a part of discretely *religious* theology; they have never assumed that theology is defined by a distinctively religious domain.

Finally, awareness of the history of the categories 'science' and 'religion' sheds crucial light on their present power relations. A key part of the story of the emergence of the nineteenth-century categories of 'science', 'scientist', and 'scientific method' was their intended role as boundary-establishing devices. 'Science', at least in the Anglophone world, was self-consciously defined so as to exclude the theological, metaphysical, and moral.[6] Paralleling this, the promotion of the novel vocational identity 'the scientist' (a term first coined in the nineteenth century) had a significant professional dimension intended to set the practitioner of science apart from others, and especially the professions of 'clergyman', 'priest', and 'theologian'.[7] Advocates of science who promoted these new categories did so partly in order to carve out an expanding realm – nature or the natural world – in which the authority of the scientist could reign supreme. At the same time, a naturalistic scientific method was elevated to epistemic pre-eminence, setting the standard to which all knowledge claims thereafter were to aspire. This way of setting up the territories meant that theology – and indeed many of the disciplines in the humanities – needed to submit

[5] Participants in this project include representative of Roman Catholic, Anglican, Orthodox, and Lutheran philosophical theologies, which is to say the recent revival in small 'c' catholic philosophical theologies. These approaches have roots in classical patristic and medieval philosophical theology and transcend modern ecclesial and national categories. Neither is Reformed thinking inherently at odds with the small 'c' catholic outlook put forward in this volume. See, e.g., Lutheran philosophical theologian Knut Alfsvåg's *What No Mind Has Conceived* (Leuven: Peeters, 2010).

[6] See Harrison, *Territories*, 145–82, and Bernard Lightman's chapter in this collection.

[7] Frank Turner, 'The Victorian Conflict between Science and Religion: A Professional Dimension', *Isis*, 49 (1978), 356–76; Ruth Barton, '"An Influential Set of Chaps": The X-Club and Royal Society Politics, 1864–85', *British Journal for the History of Science*, 23 (1990), 53–81; Gowan Dawson and Bernard Lightman (eds.), *Victorian Scientific Naturalism* (Chicago: University of Chicago Press, 2014).

their claims to the new tribunal of 'the scientific method' or run the risk of being consigned to meaninglessness and irrelevancy. It is not a total exaggeration to say that scientism is built into the very category of 'science'. Certainly, the form of a good amount of contemporary science–religion dialogue is that of theology adjusting its claims to ensure their consistency with the latest deliverances of the natural sciences. This volume seeks to explore the possibility of a more balanced conversation – not one in which humanists seek to make illicit pronouncements in the sphere of the natural sciences, but in which the theological and philosophical assumptions of various scientific claims are brought to light and given their due and, equally, in which the theological and religious implications of scientific activities are assayed.

The book has four parts. In Part I, Peter Harrison and Bernard Lightman provide a historical introduction. Harrison's chapter pushes forward from his *Territories* book, beginning with questions about whether dialogue between science and religion is desirable or even possible, and if so under what conditions. What counts as dialogue, he suggests, often just amounts to theology and religion accommodating themselves to the sciences. Dialogue conducted in this mode can serve to reinforce unhelpful ways of categorising science and religion. Considering how, in the past, natural philosophy and religion were to a large extent formative practices (rather than proposition-generating activities), he speculates about what it would mean for thinking about the relations between science and religion if it were still the case. This leads him to make the case for understanding the sciences and religions as historical traditions, by way of a discussion of the problem of incommensuration, which draws upon insights from Thomas Kuhn, Paul Feyerabend, and Alasdair MacIntyre. Historical and sociological descriptions of scientific and religious practices, he concludes, should play a more prominent role in our understandings of sciences, religions, and their relations.

Lightman's chapter goes on to spell in out in careful detail just how the nineteenth-century drawing of boundaries around 'science' and 'religion' has decisively determined the shape of the present discussion. The key event of the nineteenth century turns out to be not the emergence of evolutionary theory and the so-called Darwinian Revolution, but the alignment of the newly defined 'science' with a naturalistic metaphysics. Lightman shows how this development, along with the growing prestige of the sciences, confronted theologians with an acute dilemma: either accept the authority of the naturalistic sciences, and thereafter place all substantive theological claims under their jurisdiction, or deny the sciences that overarching authority and risk being regarded as a reactionary advocate of science–religion conflict. Here again, it becomes clear just how much the present discussion of the relations between science and religion arises out of the historically conditioned terms in which the debate is conducted.

Part II, the most extensive part of the book, takes us into the territory of philosophical theology. David Bentley Hart leads off with the general question of how it might be possible to establish or discover consonance between science and theology. Here the older model of natural philosophy provides some resources, for it was clear to natural philosophers that their activities were grounded in metaphysical assumptions about the intelligibility of nature and the ultimate dependence of natural objects and processes on something more fundamental. This is no less true for modern science, although scientists may be less aware of it. When these hidden presuppositions of modern science are brought more clearly into view, Hart argues, there will be new opportunities for more fruitful conversations with theology which, in its broadest sense, also grapples with questions about ultimate reality. At the same time, this procedure also has the potential to expose inherent tensions between modern science and theology, at least insofar as modern science is identified with a simplistic, reductionist, and reverse-engineered mechanical world view which turns out to be inadequate to task of understanding even physical realities.

John Milbank's lengthy chapter offers the most extended and far-reaching first-order intervention of the collection. He proposes that instead of viewing Western modernity through the distorting lenses of 'science' and 'religion', we think instead in terms of competing philosophies or theologies of nature, understood in relation to two dimensions: 'enchantment' versus 'disenchantment' and transcendence versus immanence. The dominant model of science, from the time of Newton, has been a form of 'disenchanted transcendence'. But alternative approaches, which Milbank dubs 'enchanted immanentism' and 'enchanted transcendence', never really went away, and arguably are more consistent with contemporary physics than the traditional Newtonian assumption of disenchanted transcendence (although this is still what the modern sciences imagine themselves to be committed to, even if implicitly). Milbank also highlights the essentially 'magical' character of powers and causes, as preserved in the more enchanted models of nature, going on to suggest that 'magic', properly understood, can mediate between the practices of science and the theoretical claims of religion. In short, a thoroughgoing reconception of the basic categories we use to understand scientific and religious phenomena is in order if we are truly to reckon with what is going on in the natural world.

Janet Soskice begins her contribution by drawing attention to the fact that there is little empirical evidence for an acute tension between science and religion, at least in practice. Cambridge scientists, to take one of her examples, are just as likely to be religiously observant as anyone else in the university, if not more so.[8] Yet at the same time there is a familiar public narrative according to which modern science has displaced a now outmoded religion. This narrative, Soskice suggests, arises not out of anything to do with the actual practices of science, but from a set of metaphysical assumptions that have been attached to science. Like other contributors to this volume, Soskice identifies as one of the distinctive features of this tacit metaphysics the assumption that God exists as a being among other beings, and that divine agency operates in the same plane as natural agency. God, on this description, is indeed not a being who is the proper object of theology, but rather operates in the same plane as the agents and powers that comprise the objects of the natural sciences.

Michael Hanby runs a parallel argument in the chapter that follows, highlighting the general tendency of the modern sciences to reduce the ultimate truth about natural things to their utility. What matters about the objects of nature, on this view, is not what they are, but what can be done with them: science is true because it works.[9] For theology to seek dialogue with science on those terms is already to have capitulated to an impoverished view of nature. Hanby proposes that in place of this mechanistic and reductionist science we revive teleological and vitalistic elements of nature (which have never really gone away). A science that is ontologically enriched in this way will enable a richer dialogue, and one that is not compromised from the outset. Both Hanby and Soskice, in different ways, provide support for Milbank's critique of the dominant mode of disenchanted transcendence.

Catherine Pickstock offers us a fascinating account of an alternative modern metaphysics, focusing upon three key seventeenth-century

[8] For more general empirical evidence along these lines, see Elaine Howard Eckland, *Science vs Religion: What Scientists Really Think* (Oxford: Oxford University Press, 2010); and Eckland et al., *Secularity and Science: What Scientists around the World Really Think about Religion* (New York: Oxford University Press, 2019).

[9] For difficulties with this very common view, see, e.g., Mary Hesse, 'Truth and the Growth of Scientific Knowledge', *PSA*, 2 (1976), 261–80; Larry Laudan, 'A Confutation of Convergent Realism', *Philosophy of Science*, 48 (1981), 19–49; Peter Dear, *The Intelligibility of Nature* (Chicago: University of Chicago Press, 2006), 1–8; Kyle P. Stanford, 'An Antirealist Explanation for the Success of Science', *Philosophy of Science*, 67 (2002), 266–84.

English figures: Herbert of Cherbury, Robert Greville, and Anne Conway. While these thinkers have typically been relegated to the margins of the history of philosophy, Pickstock reinstates them as representatives of an important, if largely eclipsed tradition.[10] Indeed, they represent, along with the group characterised as 'the Cambridge Platonists', a kind of alternative trajectory for modern philosophy and natural philosophy, and one that would be firmly in the category identified in John Milbank's chapter as 'enchanted transcendence'.

Two of Pickstock's subjects – Herbert and Greville – wrote treatises on 'truth', and it is truth and its representation that is the key focus of Rowan Williams' chapter. The relations between science and religion are understood in terms of the respective truth claims of the two enterprises. The difficulty with this approach is that it often fails to appreciate the way in which truth claims are embedded in cultural practices. Williams proposes that it is not only in the religious traditions that knowledge is bound up in devotional practices; scientific practice, too, is an ascetic habit, albeit one that can lead to a narrowing of focus. To this extent, science, no less than religion, preserves some of the formative components that were associated with medieval notions of *scientia*. Understanding this helps us view the relationship between science and religion in a new light. Williams suggests that, on the one hand, the encounter can lead to new, self-critical questions being posed within each of the enterprises. On the other, it can help promote a broader a set of intellectual practices that help us confront some of the pressing existential questions that we presently face.

Part III looks at three traditional problems in science–religion discussions. Simon Oliver addresses what has been a major point of contention since the time of the scientific revolution: the problem of teleology (the purposefulness or directedness of natural processes). Pioneers of the modern sciences, such as René Descartes and Francis Bacon, insisted that Aristotle's so-called final causes that described the inherent purposefulness of natural things be banished from the formal study of nature. Teleology (notwithstanding that it should be distinguished from design) suffered a further setback with the inception of Darwinian evolution. Needless to say, perhaps, a world understood as entirely without purpose is not consistent with most religious traditions. But Oliver contends that it is not consistent with a comprehensive view of the natural world, either. Focusing on the key instance of the phenomenon of consciousness, he takes us back to the fundamental question of what kind of metaphysics

[10] As, too, Richard H. Popkin, *The Third Force in Seventeenth-Century Thought* (Leiden: Brill, 1991).

would enable a rehabilitation of teleology that was adequate to the purpose of giving a full account of what transpires in the natural world, including consciousness. Oliver's chapter again reminds us of the central relevance to science–religion matters of the implicit metaphysical underpinnings of modern scientific practices.

Scientism, which has often been to the fore of contemporary discussions of science and religion, is the central focus of David C. Schindler's contribution. A common strategy for resolving apparent tensions between science and religion is to distinguish 'genuine science' from 'scientism', where the latter is understood as acceding authority solely to the materialistic methods and theories of modern science in all of the realms of thought.[11] Abandonment of this over-reaching conception of science is typically understood as a prerequisite for arriving at a reconciliation between science and religion. Schindler contends, to the contrary, that modern science has tended to monopolise rational discourse not *in spite of* the restriction of its scope to the empirical, quantifiable, and so on, but precisely *because of* its apparently modest self-limitation. The argument is that, precisely by virtue of isolating itself from philosophy and theology, modern science has an inherent tendency to become 'scientistic' even for its most religiously sympathetic practitioners. Schindler proposes a radical alternative to the usual strategy for contending with scientism, proposing that science should *expand* rather than restrict its scope. In other words, it should seek to embrace some of the ambitions of its predecessor – natural philosophy. This path calls for a recognition that things in the world have natures that extend beyond the merely empirically available properties that modern science currently deals with.

Part IV, with contributors from authors trained in the natural sciences, sets out three different appropriations of the historical and theological insights developed by our other contributors. Tom McLeish looks to the period *before* science and religion – that is to say, before the emergence of these two modern categories – to reflect on lessons for the present conduct of science. The general question is: How did the great medieval thinkers approach the meaning and practice of natural knowledge understood as integral to both transcendent reality and the world of human meaning and daily practice? More specifically, McLeish looks closely at the thirteenth-century polymath Robert Grosseteste, who combined a theologically inspired metaphysics of light with the science of optics. Grosseteste thus offers an alternative model to a naturalistic modern science that explicitly

[11] See, e.g., Mikael Stenmark, *Scientism: Science, Ethics, and Religion* (London: Routledge, 2001).

eschews theological and metaphysical considerations and gestures towards the viability of Milbank's 'enchanted transcendence'.

Taking his cue from Pierre Hadot's celebrated account of philosophy as a form of spiritual exercises, Pui Him Ip asks us to reflect on physics as spiritual exercise.[12] He takes as his primary example the fourth-century Alexandrian polymath Origen. The Late Classical and Patristic thought world maintained deep mutually informing connections between nature, morality, and spirituality, offering a model for how we might think without the supposed wall of demarcation between science and religion. Ip thus sets out a clear historical precedent for Rowan Williams' suggestion that modern science is still a form of devotional practice.

In his contribution, Spike Bucklow considers the relationship between science and religion in terms of the self-image that is encouraged by everyday interactions with a technological society. He contrasts the modern and medieval experiences of work, as extrapolated from the documented processes and extant products of that work (in particular, medieval works of art). Bucklow points out how the self-image indirectly generated by modern science devalues many aspects of lived experience in comparison with the self-image indirectly generated by Neoplatonic and Aristotelian informed sciences. Bucklow concludes that modern science's implicit operational redefinition of human nature has important consequences for how we understand the relationship between science and religion.

Peter Harrison rounds out the volume with some concluding reflections about the collection as a whole, and what it means for the future direction of science–religion discourse.

[12] Pierre Hadot, *Philosophy as a Way of Life*, trans. Michael Chase (Oxford: Blackwell, 1995); Pierre Hadot, *What Is Ancient Philosophy?*, trans. Michael Chase (Cambridge, MA: Harvard University Press, 2004).

PART I

Modern Historians on 'Science' and 'Religion'

CHAPTER 1

Science and Religion as Historical Traditions

Peter Harrison

The year 2016 saw the publication of *Science and Religion: An Impossible Dialogue* by French-Canadian sociologist Yves Gingras.[1] The book, it must said, does not constitute a particularly helpful intervention, and against the grain of virtually all recent scholarship presents a reactionary reassertion of the discredited notion of an enduring historical conflict between science and religion.[2] But it does offer an interesting challenge, evident in its title, in that it enquires after the conditions of possibility for a dialogue between science and religion, and raises the normative issue of whether such a dialogue is desirable. By way of contrast, much contemporary science–religion discussion has tended to assume, to some degree uncritically, both the possibility and the desirability of dialogue between science and religion.[3] This chapter begins with the question posed by Gingras's book, asking what must be true of 'science' and 'religion' for dialogue between them to be possible. One obvious response to this question is that they must in some sense be commensurable, that is, be the kinds of entities that can be in conversation with each other. My suggestion will be that understanding them in these terms can perpetuate an illicit reification in which they come to be understood primarily as enterprises that deliver propositions about the world. The chapter explores two main alternatives: science and religion as formative practices, and science and religion as historical traditions. The latter argument proceeds by way of a discussion of the problem of incommensurability, and potential solutions to it. In

[1] Yves Gingras, *L'Impossible dialogue: Sciences et religions* (Paris: Éditions du Boréal, 2016); English translation, *Science and Religion: An Impossible Dialogue* (Cambridge: Polity, 2017).

[2] For assessment of the book, see the book symposium in *Metascience*, 28 (2019), 203–48; Peter Harrison, 'From Conflict to Dialogue and All the Way Back', *LA Review of Books*, December 27, 2017.

[3] The prominence of the terminology of 'dialogue' is likely owing to its deployment by one of the pioneers of the science-and-religion subfield, Ian Barbour, as one of four types of relationship: conflict, independence, dialogue, integration. *Religion and Science: Historical and Contemporary Issues* (London: SCM Press, 1998), ch. 4.

both cases, some form of historically informed philosophy turns out to be vital for an understanding of the relations between science and religion.

1.1 The History of 'Science' and 'Religion'

Much historical work in the field over the past thirty years has focused on critique of the conflict narrative – the notion that the history of Western science has been characterised by unremitting conflict with religion, and that the decline of religion and its baleful influence is a precondition for the success of science. This myth-busting mission had to be undertaken and continues to be important, although its lessons still seem to be routinely ignored.[4] Thus, the conflict myth has persisted in the popular imagination despite the weight of evidence against it, and its very persistence has itself become a historical phenomenon that is worthy of further analysis.

Part of the reason for the persistence of the conflict narratives is that historians have sought to challenge the conflict myth simply by pointing to the complexity of history and illustrating this with repeated examples.[5] This 'complexity thesis' has been a hard sell, however, and seems to have made little headway, not only with non-specialist audiences, but even in other academic disciplines and especially the social sciences. The complexity thesis, it has been said, has little to commend it except its truth.[6] So there is the question of whether there might be a more compelling counter-narrative about the history of science and religion and, if so, what it is. More generally, we can ask where historians who remain interested in the science–religion relations, yet wish to move on from myth-busting, might now direct their efforts.

One possibility is to expand the focus of investigations to explore how the conflict thesis relates to broader accounts of modernity such as

[4] Jeff Hardin, Ronald L. Numbers, and Ronald A. Binzley (eds.), *The Warfare between Science and Religion: The Idea That Wouldn't Die* (Baltimore: Johns Hopkins University Press, 2018).

[5] For examples, see John Hedley Brooke, *Science and Religion: Some Historical Perspectives* (Cambridge: Cambridge University Press, 1991); David Lindberg and Ronald Numbers (eds.), *God and Nature: Historical Essays on the Encounter between Christianity and Science* (Berkeley: University of California Press, 1986); David Lindberg and Ronald Numbers (eds.), *When Science and Christianity Meet* (Chicago: University of Chicago Press, 2003); Ronald Numbers (ed.), *Galileo Goes to Jail, and Other Myths in the History of Science and Religion* (Cambridge, MA: Harvard University Press, 2009).

[6] Ronald Numbers, 'Simplifying Complexity: Patterns in the History of Science and Religion', in Thomas Dixon, Geoffrey Cantor, and Stephen Pumfrey (eds.), *Science and Religion: New Historical Perspectives* (Cambridge: Cambridge University Press, 2010), pp. 500–39. On the fortunes of the 'complexity thesis', see the recent collection edited by Bernard Lightman, *Rethinking History, Science, Religion* (Pittsburgh: University of Pittsburgh Press, 2019), 221–34.

secularisation theory, or more general notions that link science and human progress. Part of the explanation for the resilience of the conflict narrative and its resistance to falsification may lie in the fact that it is a corollary of a more general myth about Western modernity that underpins and sustains contemporary, often incipiently scientistic, world views. Stories about the march of reason and scientific progress, along with the accompanying narratives about the inevitable decline of religion, may play an important part in self-understanding of modern individuals. While these narratives continue to play a role in the identity and self-understanding of such individuals, they will be difficult to dislodge.

Another approach – basically that adopted in *The Territories of Science and Religion* – is to concentrate on the categories that frame the debate and study the history of their evolution. It is significant that the categories 'science' and 'religion' emerged only during the modern period, and (at least as I have argued) it is possible that both the general 'problem' of science–religion interactions and the range of solutions to the problem are already predetermined by the way in which these categories divide up aspects of our intellectual and religious lives. According to this analysis, the history of the emergence of the categories is vital for an understanding of the specific character of modern discussions. Crucially, this is relevant not only to the conflict model but to the dialogue model as well. While these are typically understood to be competing viewpoints, this disguises the fact that they share a common commitment to the validity of the categories in terms of which the interactions are understood. Once we understand the historically contingent nature of these categories, though, we can ask whether the modern concept 'religion' accurately captures what it purports to represent. There are numerous instances of both religious 'insiders' and those devoted to the academic study of religion who think not. The situation with 'science' is a little different. There have certainly been 'outsiders' who have challenged the coherence of the *idea* of science – and it is important to understand that this is very different from questioning the findings of the various sciences – but for the most part scientific insiders, if they give any thought to the issue at all, have been comfortable with the category. This is not surprising, since the historical emergence of the concept 'science', along with ideas of 'the scientific method' and 'the scientist', was central to establishing the social legitimacy and epistemic authority of the natural sciences. Indeed, this is part of what predetermines the present relations of 'science' and 'religion', since from the late nineteenth century the natural sciences, like the social sciences, have often been shaped as alternatives to religious and moral interpretations of the natural and social worlds, consciously or otherwise. This situation means that there an asymmetry of incentives, with scientific insiders having less reason to question the categories than those insiders who are identified by the label 'religion'.

What follows from this? For a start, it is possible to imagine alternative historical trajectories in which these concepts did not take hold, and in which the division of intellectual territories and methods of inquiry came to be understood in quite different ways. Some of these imagined alternatives remain live options. John Milbank's proposals about 'enchanted transcendence' take us in this direction, as do the contributions of Catherine Pickstock, Simon Oliver, Michael Hanby, and others. Much of this volume is about attempting to think outside these categories and imagine fruitful alternatives.

There are two further lines of inquiry that I would like to explore briefly in the rest of this chapter, both of which are suggested by the history of the categories in question and which move us beyond historical description. One is to reflect on the significance of the older connotations of *religio* and *scientia*, which relate, respectively, to religious and intellectual formation. This is a theme that Pui Ip takes up explicitly in his chapter, and upon which Rowan Williams's chapter offers a number of illuminating observations.[7] Tom McLeish's contribution similarly asks us to rethink science in terms of the *contemplation* of nature, and the notion of contemplation is referenced in a number of other chapters. The other line of inquiry is to focus on the roles played by philosophy – philosophy of religion and philosophy of science – both in fortifying the categories of science and religion and in helping to liberate us from them.

1.2 Religion, Science, and Intellectual Formation

Before the seventeenth century, both *religio* and *scientia* were regarded as virtues. During the modern period, for a variety of reasons, both were reified into sets of beliefs and practices. As already intimated, for the case of *religio*, there may be normative implications for what 'religion' should now be. Understanding the history might prompt us to rethink the present category, whether it adequately captures the religious life, and if not what this could mean for religious practice and belief. In the case of 'science' my

[7] For another very recent exploration along similar lines, but drawing upon the cognitive science of religion, see Sara Lane Richie, 'Integrated Physicality and the Absence of God: Spiritual Technologies in Theological Context', *Modern Theology* 37 (2021), 296–315.

working hypothesis is that some of the traditional formative aspects of philosophy – philosophy as 'a way of life' if you will – have survived into the contemporary natural sciences (which are the distant descendants of the enterprise of natural *philosophy*).[8] The suggestion here is that the putative objectivity of the natural sciences has masked the fact that scientific training involves, in part, a formative process designed to inculcate what we might call a lack of attention to certain features of reality. This is a matter of focusing on very limited features of the world, with the success of some of the sciences being predicated upon the asking of small questions. On this hypothesis, training involves a process of habituation aimed, inter alia, at the suspension of specific modes of disbelief. The fact that physicists seem relatively at ease working with quantum field theory, with many following the 'shut up and calculate' approach, offers an obvious example. Consider this statement about the 'Standard Model':

> The 'Standard Model' of elementary particle physics tells us that to understand the interactions between the twelve particles and four forces that it postulates we need to invoke some twenty free parameters which have values that no theory can predict, and 'constants' – including the number of special dimensions, the ratio of fundamental energies, the cosmological constant, the number of electrons and protons in the observable universe – which we are unable to derive from any mathematics or principles of physics, and which are quite contingent features of the universe. At the same time, these features depend on their being more matter than antimatter in the universe, but we have no idea why there is this imbalance. In fact, even if the Standard Model were successful, it could at best describe just under five percent of the matter–energy content of the universe, given the amounts of dark matter and dark energy.[9]

I rehearse this statement not as a criticism of physics. But I am interested in how professional physicists get to be comfortable with this level of theoretical messiness and uncertainty (the experimental successes of the

8 See especially Pierre Hadot, *Philosophy as a Way of Life: Spiritual Exercises from Socrates to Foucault* (Oxford: Wiley-Blackwell, 1995). See also *What Is Ancient Philosophy?*, tr. Michael Chase (Cambridge, MA: Harvard University Press, 2004). Hadot's *formes de vie* has significant and acknowledged parallels with Wittgenstein's *Lebensformen*. See *Philosophy as a Way of Life*, 17f., 280; *Wittgenstein et les limites du langage* (Paris: Vrin, 2004). See also Beroald Thomassen, *Metaphysik als Lebensform: Untersuchungen zur Grundlegung der Metaphysik im Metaphysikkommentar Alberts des Grossen* (Münster: Aschendorff, 1985); Michel Foucault, *The Care of the Self*, vol. 3 of *The History of Sexuality*, trans. Robert Hurley (New York: Vintage, 1986), esp. 39–68.

9 Stephen Gaukroger, *The Failures of Philosophy: A Historical Essay* (Princeton, NJ: Princeton University Press, 2020), 286.

model notwithstanding). This, I think, has at least something to do with being initiated into a set of inter-related rituals, practices and beliefs.

This is likely true for most of the natural sciences, and we can imagine gaps or assumptions that would be quite startling to the uninitiated, but which formal scientific training eventually helps initiates move beyond. The history of science has an important role to play in this kind of analysis, since our knowledge of historical resistance to features of new theories (Newtonian action at a distance, natural selection, the measurement problem, fine-tuning, for example) can help identify counter-intuitive doctrines that in present practice are overcome through the desensitising aspects of scientific formation. (Counterfactually, we might also try to imagine which features of our present science future generations will find deeply puzzling and, from their perspective, plain wrong.)

The implications for science-and-religion go beyond simply addressing our attention to the respective roles of formation in each. Beyond such generic comparisons are specific aspects of formation that have visible surface affects at the substantive level. The stance of methodological naturalism, for example, seems to produce good science, and need generate no particular difficulties for theistic scientists. Indeed the very concept of 'methodological naturalism' was invented and promoted by Christian scientists.[10] But it is reasonable to inquire whether the regular adoption of such a heuristic has a habituating effect that precludes seeing the world in a non-naturalistic, non-reductive way. It is a question of whether scientific habits of mind and inquiry, which admittedly seem optimal for our present scientific endeavours, can be left at the door of the laboratory on the way out.

The idea, then, is that while the content of natural philosophy/science has obviously changed radically since the scientific revolution, elements of the formative practices of natural philosophy may have survived in various guises. Thus, in addition to helping gloss over some of the deeply counterintuitive commitments that the contemporary sciences require – such as the measurement problem, dark energy, action at a distance, quantum entanglement, apparent design by largely blind evolutionary processes, and so on – scientific training can also crowd out the posing of fundamental philosophical and theological questions about the foundations of the

[10] See, e.g., Edgar Brightman, 'An Empirical Approach to God', *The Philosophical Review*, 46 (1937), 157–8. Paul De Vries, 'Naturalism in the Natural Sciences', *Christian Scholar's Review*, 15 (1986), 388–96. Also Peter Harrison, 'Naturalism and the Success of Science', *Religious Studies* 56 (2020), 274–91.

scientific enterprise: the intelligibility of cosmos, laws of nature, the basis of experimentation, the success of mathematics, and so on. While such questions may be irrelevant to the mundane performance of science and to its undeniable practical successes, the very possibility of conducting science depends on these questions having answers. Perhaps, ultimately, the social legitimacy of science depends upon this too.

When in the past, science was conducted as part of 'natural philosophy', these issues were more integral to the project.[11] By that I mean that moral, theological, and philosophical questions were admitted as part of the enterprise. In the nineteenth-century transition from natural philosophy to the natural sciences, these broader considerations were set aside. If we bear this in mind when we think about science–religion conflict, it may be that superficial conflicts are not so much to do with substantive matters of fact that arise out of scientific investigation, but are the by-products of a scientific formation that has simply rendered a whole set of questions invisible. Perhaps this is why, in a kind of disciplinary Dunning–Kruger effect, some celebrity spokespersons for science just don't seem to get the point of philosophy and theology. It is significant in this context that the claim that science has rendered religion unnecessary is now often extended to philosophy. (Lawrence Krauss: philosophy is 'a waste of time'. Stephen Hawking: 'Philosophy is dead.' Neil deGrasse Tyson: philosophy is useless – 'too much question asking', apparently.)

It is entirely possible that, for some, the consideration of foundational issues is just a distraction, much as blinkers on a racehorse help it focus on what is ahead and run the course, albeit at the cost of broader vision. And there is nothing wrong with focusing on a narrow sliver of reality and adopting a particular heuristic to do so, particularly if it has proven success in that sphere. But to insist on a universal applicability of such an approach seems misguided. This rejection of philosophy is also quite new, as should be evident from the change in terminology from natural *philosophy* to natural *science*. It contrasts in interesting ways with the attitude of many leading physicists in the late nineteenth and early twentieth centuries.

11 On the category 'natural philosophy', see, e.g., Andrew Cunningham, 'Getting the Game Right: Some Plain Words on the Identity and Invention of Science', *Studies in the History and Philosophy of Science*, 19 (1988), 365–89; Margaret J. Osler, 'Mixing Metaphors: Science and Religion or Natural Philosophy and Theology in Early Modern Europe', *History of Science*, 35 (1997), 91–113 (91); William A. Wallace, 'Traditional Natural Philosophy', in Charles Schmitt and Quentin Skinner (eds.), *The Cambridge History of Renaissance Philosophy* (Cambridge: Cambridge University Press, 1988), 201–35; Peter Harrison, 'Physico-Theology and the Mixed Sciences: The Role of Theology in Early Modern Natural Philosophy', in Peter Anstey and John Schuster (eds.), *The Science of Nature in the Seventeenth Century* (Dordrecht: Springer, 2005), 165–83.

Arguably, it was their broader vision, both philosophical and religious, that led to the remarkable theoretical breakthroughs that characterised the period. But to return to the main point, the history of the development of scientific disciplines can be illuminative of the processes that render religious and philosophical questions no longer askable. To be clear, the claim is not that all scientists are necessarily so constrained in their thinking. The participation of scientists in this book project is clear evidence to the contrary. But it remains true that *qua scientists*, on the current understanding of the disciplines, certain broad conceptions and avenues of investigation seem to be off-limits.

If there is anything to this line of investigation, the relations between science and religion, and indeed among the sciences themselves, may turn on differences in disciplinary formation. Such differences can be masked by the fact that science–religion discussion takes place, by proxy, at the level of competing truth claims or differing epistemological commitments. My proposal is that aspects of these debates can be thought of as the epiphenomenal manifestation of differences that arise out formative processes associated with different forms of life.

We can express this in an alternative, albeit more simplistic, way. What science and religion share is the fact that coming to believe or know certain things requires that a certain prior work be performed on the self, or that certain disciplinary practices be undertaken, in order to access the relevant knowledge. Michel Foucault spoke in this context of 'technologies of the self'. While Foucault's style of thinking is often regarded with suspicion in both religious and scientific circles, religious history had a major influence on his thinking. It is not too much of a stretch to say the idea of technologies of the self is a kind of echo of the Christian principle *lex orandi, lex credenda* (the 'law of praying establishes the law of believing').[12] In the seventeenth century Blaise Pascal offered this (much misunderstood) recommendation on acquiring faith that draws upon a similar principle:

[12] Foucault describes them as permitting 'individuals to effect by their own means or with the help of others a certain number of operations on their own bodies and souls, thoughts, conduct, and way of being, so as to transform themselves in order to attain a certain state of happiness, purity, wisdom, perfection, or immortality'. *Technologies of the Self* (Amherst: University of Massachusetts Press, 1988), 18. On *lex orandi*, Prosper of Aquitaine: 'obsecrationum quoque sacerdotalium sacramenta respiciamus, quae ab apostolis tradita, in toto mundo atque in omni catholica Ecclesia uniformiter celebrantur, ut legem credendi lex statuat supplicandi'. *Patrologia cursus completes*, series Latina, ed. J.-P. Migne, 1844–1905, vol. 51, cols. 209–10 ('let the rule of prayer determine the rule of belief').

> You would like to attain faith, and do not know the way; you would like to cure yourself of unbelief, and ask the remedy for it. Learn of those who have been bound like you.... Follow the way by which they began; by acting as if they believed, taking the holy water, having masses said, etc.[13]

This is not so distant from the observations of contemporary anthropologist Tanya Luhrman on the commitments of American evangelicals: 'coming to a committed belief in God was more like learning *to do* something than *to think* something ... These practices work. They change people.'[14] Some religious practices enable the faithful to see things that others are unable to. But scientific habituation can function in a similar way. Training enables the expert to 'read' a microscope slide, an X-ray plate, or an ultrasound, and to see things that the uninitiated cannot. Again, these examples suggest that apparent conflict between respective beliefs might arise out divergent modes of disciplinary formation. Focusing on propositional or doctrinal differences alone not only can lead to pointless disputes (or, what is just as significant, pointless agreements) but can mask where it is that the genuine differences lie.

The history of science, broadly conceived, can be helpful in illuminating all of this. It can track, for example, how disciplinary formation in the various sciences came to move away from the ideal of 'the natural philosopher' to various and plural forms of 'scientist'. To take two specific cases, consider the manner in which during the seventeenth century features of an existing 'experimental religion' were transferred into the new category of 'experimental natural philosophy'. 'Experiment' had once referred primarily to forms of religious experience, and only belatedly was it transferred to the scientific context in which specific experiences (or 'experiments') yielded a special kind of knowledge to the experimenter.[15] Or consider the way in which over the course of the eighteenth and nineteenth centuries the category of the 'religious virtuoso' became the 'man of science', which in turn become 'the scientist'.[16] In the English

[13] Pascal, 'The Wager', *Pensées*, tr. W. F. Potter (London: Dent, 1910), §233.

[14] Tanya Luhrman, *When God Talks Back* (New York: Vintage, 2012), xxi, xxii.

[15] Peter Harrison, 'Experimental Religion and Experimental Science in Early Modern England', *Intellectual History Review*, 21 (2011), 413–33.

[16] On the notion 'man of science', see Bernard Lightman, 'Fashioning the Victorian Man of Science: Tyndall's Shifting Strategies', *Journal of Dialectics of Nature*, 38 (2015), 25–38; Paul White, 'The Man of Science', in Bernard Lightman (ed.), *A Companion to the History of Science* (Chichester: Wiley Blackwell, 2016), 153–63; and Paul White, *Thomas Huxley: Making the 'Man of Science'* (Cambridge: Cambridge University Press, 2002), 4–5. On the notion of scientific identities as 'personae', see Lorraine Daston and H. Otto Sibum, 'Scientific Personae and Their Histories', *Science in Context*, 16 (2003), 1–8; Ruth Barton, '"Men of Science": Language, Identity and Professionalization in the Mid-Victorian Scientific Community', *History of Science*, 41 (2003),

context at least, these earlier categories had significant moral and religious dimensions. But 'the scientist' came to be regarded as an individual who is morally and religiously neutral or disinterested, at least in the performance of their scientific activities. Weber famously remarked on this in 'Science as a Vocation' (1917) and Robert Merton spoke similarly of 'moral equivalence'.[17] These are just two examples of the ways in which the history of science/intellectual history can continue to be instructive on central science/religion questions.

1.3 History, Philosophy, and the Problem of Commensuration

To the person with the hammer, as the saying goes, everything looks like a nail. When applied to science and religion, the powerful tools of analytic philosophy, focusing as they tend to do on propositions, can promote the impression that the real level of interaction takes place at the level of the propositional.[18] Such philosophical approaches work in concert with modern understandings of the categories of science and religion, and assist in the constructing and maintenance of their boundaries. Oversimplifying the position somewhat, both the sciences and the religions are thought to generate propositions about the world, and whether these propositions are commensurate determines whether there is conflict or congruence. The fundamental assumption here is that there is a common measure – this, related to the literal meaning of 'commensuration' – and that the respective propositions can be placed in some meaningful relation to each other.

Part of what drives this approach is a worry that if there is no common measure, not only is genuine interaction or comparison ruled out, but the rationality of one or both of the enterprises is called into question. For some proponents of the conflict model, this does not constitute a problem, since 'religion' comes to be understood as inherently irrational or non-rational. Here the conflict arises not out of contradictory propositional assertions, but the failure of religion even to reach the threshold of generating propositions that bear comparison to scientific claims. This is the 'not even wrong' suggestion that was characteristic of twentieth-century positivistic critiques of religious language, and which is still

73–119; Frank Turner, 'Victorian Scientific Naturalism and Thomas Carlyle', in Frank M. Turner, *Contesting Cultural Authority* (Cambridge: Cambridge University Press, 1993), 131–50. I am grateful to Ian Hesketh for these references.

17 But cf. Steven Shapin, *The Scientific Life* (Chicago: University of Chicago Press, 2008), ch 3.

18 There are signs that this is changing, however, the emergence of virtue epistemology being one instance.

encountered in popular writing of a certain kind.[19] On the other side, the concern is a challenge to the cognitive status of scientific claims. This is often associated with the notion of *in*commensurability, famously articulated by Thomas Kuhn in his account of theory change in the natural sciences. Basically, Kuhn seems to suggest that when paradigm shifts occur, as from a Ptolemaic to a Copernican world view, for example, there is no Archimedean point from which the relative merits of each paradigm can be appraised. As we will see, it is more complicated than this. While Kuhn had focused on scientific theory, broader application of his views has been thought to posit dangers to the respective truth claims and rationality of both science and religion.[20]

Among those interested in asserting the possibility of positive relations between science and religion, then, there have been two powerful forces militating against an appropriation of the historical insights of Kuhn and other philosophically engaged historians of science. (These insights, incidentally, informed some of the arguments of *The Territories of Science and Religion*.) On the positive side, there has been a selection effect that naturally produces a science–religion community that shares an investment in upholding the cognitive status of both scientific and religion claims. Without this, the conversation has seemed not worth pursuing. On the negative side is a fear of relativism and a vaguely defined 'postmodernism'.[21] This has motivated a strong animus against historical approaches that invite what seem to be relativistic interpretations, along with a corresponding endorsement of philosophical approaches that are imagined to shore up the rational foundations of the respective enterprises.

In what follows I will offer a more sympathetic interpretation of supposedly relativist alternatives – particularly as articulated by historically informed philosophers of science such as Thomas Kuhn and Paul Feyerabend – and see if they are as undesirable as has commonly been argued. This involves consideration of the initial philosophical reception of the ideas of Kuhn and Feyerabend, and their subsequent fortunes in science–religion discourse. The latter largely followed the dominant, and negative, philosophical interpretation. The suggestion will be that the fear

19 For a recent example, consider Jerry Coyne, *Faith versus Fact: Why Science and Religion Are Not Compatible* (New York: Viking Press, 2015).

20 T. S. Kuhn, *The Structure of Scientific Revolutions* (Chicago: University of Chicago Press, 1962)

21 For such fears, see, e.g., Roger Trigg, *Beyond Matter: Why Science Needs Metaphysics* (Philadelphia: Templeton Foundation Press, 2017), 18–21, and passim. Also Ian Barbour, on the 'strong programme' in sociology of science. *Religion in an Age of Science* (San Francisco: Harper and Rowe, 1990), 74.

of 'irrationality' turns out to be reliant upon an idealised conception of rationality that does not map well onto the actual practices that it purports to characterise – which is to say mostly science, but also religion. This will lead us back to the question of how formative practices within communities are related to beliefs, how rationality might be understood in ways that do not distort the historical traditions that generate beliefs and practices, and how this does not necessarily lead towards some self-defeating relativism.

Thomas Kuhn began *The Structure of Scientific Revolutions* (1962) with an announcement of his own revolutionary ambitions: 'History, if viewed as a repository for more than anecdote and chronology, could produce a decisive transformation of the image of science by which we are now possessed.'[22] Despite the impact of Kuhn's *Structure*, which is one of the most widely cited books of all time, it is fair to say that the transformation of the image of science foreshadowed in the opening lines of his classic work has only partially eventuated. It is certainly not prominent in science–religion discussions. That this is so, I would suggest, is largely owing to Kuhn's account of paradigm shifts and the concomitant claim that paradigms were incommensurable. At the time, this led to accusations that Kuhn was relativist and that his historical take condemns science to irrationality. That view persists to the present and has been a barrier to the wider uptake of the ideas of figures such as Kuhn and Feyerabend, and the image of science that they promoted.

Kuhn's *Structure* provoked an almost uniformly hostile response from the philosophical community, beginning with Dudley Shapere's influential critique in *The Philosophical Review*. This became the Ur-text for a tradition that condemned Kuhn (and Paul Feyerabend) for the putatively irrationalist image of science in their work. We get some sense of the general reception from the fact that Shapere's original review and his 1966 paper on the topic attracted well over 700 citations. Many respected philosophers either directly adopted his reading or arrived at it on their own.[23] For Imre Lakatos, Kuhn's position is equivalent to saying that

[22] Thomas Kuhn, *The Structure of Scientific Revolutions*, 2nd ed. (Chicago: University of Chicago Press, 1970), 1.

[23] See, e.g., J. Giedymin, 'The Paradox of Meaning Invariance', *British Journal for the Philosophy of Science*, 21 (1970), 257–68; Larry Laudan, *Progress and Its Problems* (Berkeley: University of California Press, 1977), 141f.; K. P. Parsons, 'A Criterion for Meaning Change', *Philosophical Studies*, 28 (1975); I. Szumilewicz, 'Incommensurability and the Rationality of the Development of Science', *British Journal for the Philosophy of Science*, 28 (1977), 345–50; Thomas Nagel, 'The Sleep of Reason', *The New Republic*, October 12, 1998, 32–8. For an overview of the history of Kuhn's

'scientific revolution is irrational, a matter for mob psychology'.[24] C. R. Kordig similarly maintained that the views of Kuhn and his fellow travellers were 'tantamount to denying that science is an empirical and cognitive enterprise'.[25] In *Relativism Refuted* (1987) Harvey Siegel agreed that Kuhn's 'irrationalist portrayal of theory choice makes scientific knowledge relative'.[26] Rachel and Larry Laudan also stressed the 'irrationality' of the Kuhnian position, maintaining that in the end Kuhn was reduced to talking the 'psycho-babble' of 'Gestalt switches' and 'conversion experiences'.[27]

The concept of incommensurability was typically identified as the chief obstacle to an acceptance of Kuhnian understandings of scientific change, and in time Feyerabend's version incommensurability came to be included in the standard critique. Summing up the common philosophical understanding of incommensurability and its implications, Canadian philosopher W. H. Newton-Smith declared in *The Rationality of Science* (1981): 'The thought that theories are incommensurable is the thought that theories simply cannot be compared and consequently there cannot be any rationally justifiable reason for thinking that one theory is better than another.... It suggests that I could never have rationally justified grounds for holding any belief whatsoever.'[28]

Not surprisingly, perhaps, the scientific community was not particularly enamoured of the way in which Kuhn and Feyerabend portrayed their activities, either. An impassioned 1987 article in *Nature* issued a call to arms to scientists, urging them to 'reassert the pre-eminence of the concepts of objectivity and truth'. Those who uphold the complete equivalence of all paradigms were deemed to be 'absolute relativists'. While

reception, see Fred D'Agostino, 'Verballed? Incommensurability 50 Years On', *Synthese*, 191 (2013), 517–38.

24 Imre Lakatos, 'Falsification and the Methodology of Scientific Research Programmes', in Imre Lakatos and Alan Musgrave (eds.), *Criticism and the Growth of Knowledge*, 91–196 (Cambridge: Cambridge University Press, 1970), 178.

25 C. R. Kordig, 'The Theory-Ladenness of Observation', *Review of Metaphysics*, 24 (1971), 448–84 (477).

26 Harvey Seigel, *Relativism Refuted: A Critique of Contemporary Epistemological Relativism* (Dordrecht: D. Reidel, 1987), 54.

27 Rachel Laudan and Larry Laudan, 'Dominance and the Disunity of Method', *Philosophy of Science*, 56 (1989), 221–37 (222).

28 W. H. Newton-Smith, *The Rationality of Science* (Boston: Routledge and Kegan Paul, 1981), 148. See also a number of the essays in Lakatos and Musgrave (eds.), *Criticism and the Growth of Knowledge*; D. Davidson, 'The Very Idea of a Conceptual Scheme', *Proceedings and Addresses of the American Philosophical Association*, 47 (1973), 5–20; F. Suppe (ed.), *The Structure of Scientific Theories*, 2nd ed. (Urbana: University of Illinois Press, 1977), 135–51; James Robert Brown, *The Rational and the Social* (London: Routledge, 1989), 11, 5.

Feyerabend's 'monstrous ideas' were singled out for special attention, Popper, Kuhn, Lakatos, and Feyerabend were all indiscriminately labelled 'betrayers of the truth'.[29] Curiously, these assessments have recently been replayed in recent claims that complicity with these 'postmodern' approaches has contributed to the present post-truth age.

Pioneers of the science–religion dialogue tended to follow suit. Ian Barbour offered a sympathetic account of Kuhn and even deployed his notion of paradigms.[30] But he could never fully reconcile himself to the idea of incommensurability. 'Kuhn has overemphasized *the arbitrary nature of paradigm shifts*', he observed. As a consequence, Kuhn was said to have given undue weight to the 'subjective, relativistic, and communal features' of scientific change.[31] Another distinguished progenitor of the science–religion field, John Polkinghorne, offered a sharp critique of Kuhn and Feyerabend: 'Kuhn's revolutionary incommensurability, if true, would undermine the idea that science can claim our rational, as opposed to rhetorical, assent.' Paul Feyerabend was identified as an even greater threat. Polkinghorne concluded that 'what in Kuhn was simply preposterous becomes in Feyerabend the Theatre of the Absurd'.[32] Kuhn and Feyerabend, Polkinghorne concludes, 'open the door to irrationality'.[33] Arthur Peacocke, yet another seminal figure in the field, expressed similar reservations.[34]

Not surprisingly, there was little initial uptake of the ideas of Kuhn and Feyerabend in canonical works on science-and-religion. In time, Nancey Murphy offered an insightful analysis of Kuhn, Feyerabend, and, especially Imre Lakatos. Murphy saw in Kuhn what many of his philosophical critics had missed: Kuhn does not so much present an irrationalist account of science as show that the actual practices of scientists do not conform to an artificially imposed, positivistic version of rationality.[35] In this she agrees with Kuhn. But again, the problem of incommensurability rears its head. Murphy, possibly reflecting Kuhn's own ambivalence on this issue, argues

[29] T. Theocharis and M. Psimopoulos, 'Where Science Has Gone Wrong', *Nature*, 329 (1987), 595–8.

[30] Ian Barbour, *Myths, Models and Paradigms* (New York: Harper and Rowe, 1974).

[31] Ian Barbour, *Issues in Science and Religion* (London: Harper Torchbooks, 1966), 155f.

[32] John Polkinghorne, *One World; The Interaction of Science and Theology* (Philadelphia: Templeton Foundation Press, 2007), 19. Cf. Polkinghorne, *Rochester Roundabout* (Essex: Longman, 1985), 162–7; *Science and Theology* (Philadelphia: Fortress Press, 1998), 11.

[33] Polkinghorne, *One World*, 21.

[34] Arthur Peacocke, *Creation and the World of Science*, 2nd ed. (Oxford: Oxford University Press, 2004), 34, 123, 17–18.

[35] Nancey Murphy, *Theology in the Age of Scientific Reasoning* (Ithaca, NY: Cornell University Press, 1990), 56, 106.

that he lacked a 'normative methodology – a theory about what kinds of theories *ought* to be accepted'.[36] Murphy saw more mileage in the account of science offered by Imre Lakatos, who was fiercely opposed to what he saw as the relativism of Kuhn's ideas. Lakatos focused not on paradigms but rival 'research programmes', which preserved some of Kuhn's key insights while at the same time upholding a version of scientific rationality that could specify scientifically relevant criteria for preferring one research programme over another.[37] Others, such as Robert J. Russell, have been similarly persuaded by Lakatos's more conservative understanding of scientific change.[38] The intellectual authority of these figures, which was entirely justified, means that their suspicions cast a long shadow over subsequent discussions.

The only significant uptake of the ideas of Kuhn and Feyerabend in the field, aside from the generally non-normative work of historians, is the very recent monograph by Josh Reeves. Reeves proposes that much science–religion discourse has been devoted to establishing the scientific status of theology. This was in order to persuade the academy to take theology seriously, while at the same time being a necessary prerequisite for engaging in dialogue. However, this approach has a tendency to adopt and promote an essentialist view of science and its methods, which, as Reeves points out, is at odds with the clear trend in history of science scholarship and, to a degree, recent philosophy of science scholarship as well.[39] Reeves's work offers an insightful application of some of the ideas of *Territories* to the science–religion field, along with helpful references to the relevance of Kuhn, Feyerabend, and Lakatos.

My own take on the relevance of Kuhn and Feyerabend, in summary, is this. Neither Kuhn nor Feyerabend held to the understanding of incommensurability routinely ascribed to them. More specifically, they did not hold to an irrationalist view of scientific change, and neither were they strong cultural relativists. Their account of incommensurability yields important lessons for the respective roles played by philosophy and history in science–theology discussions. One lesson is that philosophical analysis

[36] Ibid., 58. [37] Ibid., 205.

[38] Robert J. Russell, *Cosmology: From Alpha to Omega: The Creative Mutual Interaction of Theology and Science, Theology and the Sciences* (Minneapolis, MN: Fortress Press, 2008). For an excellent critical overview of the deployment of Lakatos in science–religion discourse, see Josh Reeves, 'After Lakatos', *Theology and Science*, 9 (2011), 395–409.

[39] See Josh Reeves, *Against Methodology in Science and Religion* (London: Routledge, 2020). For an excellent discussion of its implications, see the book forum in *Vision* , with contributions from Paul Allen, Peter N. Jordan, J. B. Stump, Jaime Wright, Victoria Lorrimar, and a response from Reeves.

may not be the optimal way to seek consonance between science and theology/religion. Another is the instability of 'science' as a historical category.

On philosophers' misinterpretation of his views of incommensurability, for example, Kuhn maintained that philosophers had misconstrued his argument on account of their preconceived notions of what scientific rationality consisted in. These did not match the historical reality: 'If history or any other empirical discipline leads us to believe that the development of science depends essentially on behaviour that we have previously thought to be irrational, then we should conclude not that science is irrational but that our notion of rationality needs adjustment here and there.'[40] Kuhn specifically pointed to 'philosophers' as the ones who had systematically misunderstood and misrepresented his position. Beyond this, he identified the philosophical analysis of science as the true generator of its apparent irrationality: incommensurability is what you end up with if you insist on reading science through a particular philosophical lens.

Paul Feyerabend responded to his critics in much the same way: 'Incommensurability only shows that scientific discourse, *which contains detailed and highly sophisticated discussions concerning the comparative advantages of paradigms*, obeys laws and standards that have little in common with the naïve models that philosophers of science have constructed for that purpose.'[41] This might be, as Feyerabend archly remarked, 'the end of the world for philosophers', but not so for historians or, indeed, scientists themselves. The real failure, Feyerabend maintained, has not to do with the possibility of theory comparison, which happens in real life, but with 'a rather simpleminded theory of explanation.'[42] As for Feyerabend's notorious assertion that 'anything goes', this was not a normative recommendation, but rather what science looks like when read through a preconceived grid of philosophical expectations: anything goes is 'the terrified exclamation of a rationalist who takes a closer look at

[40] Kuhn, *Structure*, 2nd ed., 188–9; Kuhn, 'Notes on Lakatos', *PSA: Proceedings of the Biennial Meeting of the Philosophy of Science Association 1970* (1970), 137–46 (144).

[41] Paul Feyerabend, *Reason, Rationalism and Scientific Method, Philosophical Papers*, vol. 1 (Cambridge: Cambridge University Press, 2003), 16. And later: 'what fails is not the process of theory comparison; it is a rather simpleminded theory of explanation' (238). This explanation was repeated in the second appendix to Feyerabend's *Against Method*: 'I never said ... that *any two* rival theories are incommensurable.... What I *did* say was that *certain* rival theories, so-called "universal" theories, or "non-instantial" theories, *if interpreted in a certain way*, could not be compared easily.' *Against Method* (New York: Verso, 1975), 114.

[42] Paul Feyerabend, *Philosophical Papers*, vol. 1, 238.

history'.[43] History reveals science to be not the outworking of some preconceived philosophical principle. Rather, '*scientific practice*, even the practice of the natural sciences, *is a tightly woven net of historical traditions*'.[44] Applying heteronomous philosophical theories to scientific practices, then, does not provide very good insights into the relations among competing scientific accounts. And, I would argue, they are even less helpful when it comes to analysis of religious activities, and their comparison with science.

Three things follow: first, it is not obvious that a thoroughgoing relativism necessarily follows from adoption of the perspectives of Kuhn and Feyerabend. Second, if we agree with their analyses, it looks as if history might give us better understanding of science and scientific change than philosophy. Third, the historically informed views of science expressed by Kuhn and Feyerabend, and their understanding of the role played by the scientific community in scientific change, comport to some degree with the image of science and religion as formative processes that I set out in the first section. Kuhn spoke of 'conversion' in relation to paradigm change. Wittgenstein has similar remarks about conversion in *Philosophical Investigations* and *On Certainty*. Feyerabend, interestingly, makes reference to both thinkers on this point.[45]

My overall conclusion is that philosophy, despite its superficial promise, is the wrong instrument for commensuration. In the case of the relations among scientific theories, it leads to puzzles about how scientific change might be rational, and indeed, how it takes place at all. While Kuhn and Feyerabend were clearly talking about competing scientific theories, and not relations between science and religion, I wish to offer some (admittedly speculative) suggestions about how these ideas might be applied to that latter sphere. Feyerabend's suggestion that the sciences be thought of 'a tightly woven net of historical traditions' provides a good starting point. By this he meant that we have plural activities, which may or may not have a common goal, and which resist comparison when understood in philosophical terms. Philosophy might seek to render them into a form that enables comparison, but any failure to do so is a failure of the philosophical starting point. By the same token, the success of philosophy at this task could come only at the cost of distortion and mistranslation. How else might we get them talking to each other, or is the only alternative mutual

[43] Paul Feyerabend, *Against Method*, vii. [44] Paul Feyerabend, *Philosophical Papers*, vol. 1, 4.

[45] Antonia Soulez, 'Conversion in Philosophy: Wittgenstein's "Saving Word"', *Hypatia*, 15 (2000), 127–50.

incomprehension and strong incommensurability? Much the same question can be posed about religious traditions. Indeed, religious traditions, understood as such, offer a good historical model for thinking about the modern sciences.

Alasdair MacIntyre has spoken in a similar way about 'traditions', and it is not surprising that to some extent his ideas about this are indebted to the insights of Kuhn and Feyerabend:

> dramatic narrative is the crucial form for the understanding of human action and I shall want to argue that natural science can be a rational form of enquiry if and only if the writing of a true dramatic narrative – that is, of history understood in a particular way – can be a rational activity. Scientific reason turns out to be subordinate to, and intelligible only in terms of, historical reason. And, if this is true of the natural sciences, a fortiori it will be true also for the social sciences.... Kuhn's work criticized provides an illuminating application for the ideas which I have been defending.[46]

It is not surprising that MacIntyre has himself been accused of relativism.[47] But what he cautions against is the assumption that our current standards of rationality – which inform a range of philosophical stances – are somehow natural and universal, whereas they are demonstrably the product of the European Enlightenment. This is the more general version of the objections of Kuhn and Feyerabend to the uses of philosophy to judge competing scientific theories.[48]

Unless we get inside the language games/paradigms of the respective traditions – and this necessarily requires their construction as concrete historical practices rather than as abstract philosophical traditions – the resulting conflict or consonance will be a contrived artefact of the tools of analysis and translation. As MacIntyre puts it, 'dramatic narrative' and 'historical reason' provide us with a means of negotiating between apparently incommensurable traditions. Such a reconstruction of historical

[46] Alasdair MacIntyre, 'Epistemological Crises and Dramatic Narrative', in *The Tasks of Philosophy* (Cambridge: Cambridge University Press, 2006), 15.

[47] Thus, elsewhere: 'what historical enquiry discloses is the situatedness of all enquiry, the extent to which what are taken to be the standards of truth and of rational justification in the contexts of practice vary from one time to another'. *After Virtue*, 3rd ed. (Notre Dame, IN: University of Notre Dame Press, 2007), preface. Again: 'There is no theoretically neutral, pretheoretical ground from which the adjudication of competing claims can proceed.' *Three Rival Versions of Moral Enquiry* (Notre Dame, IN: University of Notre Dame Press, 1994), 173.

[48] Nancey Murphey has also recently drawn attention to the significance of MacIntyre's thinking about 'traditions' in this context. See her excellent tribute to the work of Ian Barbour: 'Religion, Theology, and the Philosophy of Science: An Appreciation of the Work of Ian Barbour', *Theology and Science* 15 (2017), 42–52.

practices was part of the task of my *Territories of Science and Religion*, albeit partially and imperfectly realised.

This is not the place to rehearse MacIntyre's views about competing moral traditions and how a partial reconciliation of them might be attempted. What a connection to science-and-religion discourse might look like in this connection bears an analogy to MacIntyre's distinction between a liberal university based on Enlightenment principles ('encyclopedia'), and one based on his idea of 'tradition'. The liberal university 'aspired to be a place of unrestrained agreements'. The alternative, which takes tradition seriously, is 'a place of constrained disagreements, of imposed participation in conflicts' in which participants are initiated into conflict.[49] So in the absence of some Archimedean philosophical principle of commensuration, we might instead resign ourselves to, or possibly even embrace, the possibility of ongoing tension. But MacIntyre also suggests one possibility for overcoming what look like irresolvable conflicts, and that is to see how one tradition, albeit viewed from the inside, might successfully manage some of the internal tensions of competing traditions, while maintaining its own coherence. Perhaps that tradition could be historical theology?

Appealing to MacIntyre does not immediately solve all the problems. But it does suggest a way forward. Rather than seeking to accommodate historical religious traditions to a model of the natural sciences, we might explore the possibilities of moving in the other direction, that is, understanding the sciences as akin to living religious traditions. The natural sciences were never exemplifications of operations of pure reason, somehow able to operate untethered from the realities of history. Yet idealised philosophical analysis sometimes led to the impression that they were. Seeking to correct this vision by appealing to the empirical facts of history – telling the truth about science, in other words – should not be a threat to the rationality of the enterprise, but may shed important light on our understandings of human rationality, and how it operates in a variety of cultural practices.

1.4 Conclusion

In this chapter I have sought both to extend some of the arguments that were implicit in *The Territories of Science and Religion* and to provide some tentative connections to a number of the other chapters in this volume.

[49] MacIntyre, *Three Rival Versions of Moral Inquiry*, 230–1.

The two main sections developed parallel arguments, one pointing to significance of understanding both science and religion as formative activities, without which their more obvious propositional content cannot fully be understood. The second chief argument moved from the problem of commensuration to the suggestion that both science and religion can profitably be thought of as historical traditions. Both approaches move the science–religion discussion more into what is home ground of religion, rather than the 'away game' of either philosophy or some idealised 'science'. Ludwig Wittgenstein once remarked, 'I am not a religious man, but I cannot help seeing every problem from a religious point of view.'[50] In taking up the related ideas of formative practices and historical traditions, my proposal is that the question of the relation between science and religion is best looked at from what is essentially a 'a religious point of view' – a perspective that can do justice to the truth of both activities.

[50] M. O'C. Drury, 'Notes on Conversations with Wittgenstein', in Rush Rhees (ed.), *Ludwig Wittgenstein – Personal Recollections* (Totowa, NJ: Rowman and Littlefield, 1981), 94.

CHAPTER 2

The Nineteenth-Century Origins of the Problem

Naturalistic Metaphysics and the Dead Ends of Victorian Theology

Bernard Lightman

> With the benefit of hindsight, we can now see that over the course of the past 150 years a remarkable reversal has taken place. Whereas once the investigation of nature had derived status from its intimate connections with the more elevated disciplines of ethics and theology, increasingly during the twentieth century these latter disciplines have humbly sought associations with science in order to bask in its reflected glory – whence bioethics and science-and-religion.
>
> —Peter Harrison[1]

On January 11, 1876, T. H. Huxley presented a provocative paper titled 'The Evidence of the Miracle of the Resurrection'.[2] Huxley acknowledged that his handling of the Resurrection could upset the Christian believers who were in attendance. In grappling with a 'particular case of an alleged miracle' he feared that he might 'let slip phrases that may needlessly wound some of my hearers; or, what would be still worse, fail in expressing my own profound reverence for the subject of the alleged miracle of which I propose to treat'. However, although he was neither a theologian nor a biblical scholar, he believed that he had some expertise that could be brought to bear on the issue. Huxley claimed that his training as physiologist and biologist gave him the authority to determine if Christ had actually died on the cross. Whether an organism 'said to be dead was really dead or not so, is a question of biology', and therefore the matter fell within the 'range of those questions with which it is my ordinary business to concern myself'. He proposed to treat the matter as if he were being called as an expert witness before a medical-legal tribunal.

1 Peter Harrison, '"Science" and "Religion": Constructing the Boundaries', *Journal of Religion*, 86 (2006), 81–106 (87).

2 T. H. Huxley, 'The Evidence of the Miracle of the Resurrection', in Catherine Marshall, Bernard Lightman, and Richard England (eds.), *The Papers of the Metaphysical Society 1869–1880: A Critical Edition* (Oxford: Oxford University Press, 2015), vol. 2, 366–72.

He then summed up the facts of the case, based on the evidence contained in the Gospels and the data provided by modern medical science. The key physiological question was whether Christ was somatically or molecularly dead before the alleged resurrection took place. If he were merely somatically dead, then the Resurrection was no miracle. Huxley gave examples of animals, such as the common 'wheel animalcules' (rotifers), that could be fully revived after being dried and reduced to a condition of apparently lifeless matter for weeks or even months. Their somatic death did not prevent a perfectly natural 'resurrection'. Like other living beings in the natural world, Christ could have been somatically dead but not molecularly dead. For a miracle to take place, Christ would have had to be molecularly dead. But determining molecular death was extremely difficult. None of the disciples was trained a physiologist, so they would have been unable to confirm that Christ was molecularly dead. Therefore, the question of whether Christ died could never be answered with certainty.[3] Although Huxley ends up professing ignorance – an appropriate position for the man who had coined the term 'agnostic' – he nevertheless established that the reality of miracles was best determined by using scientific expertise. A religious belief was brought before the bar of scientific judgement.

Huxley's paper was delivered at a meeting of the Metaphysical Society, a unique debating club that lasted for eleven years, from 1869 to 1880. The sixty-two members produced ninety-five papers. These debaters came from every sphere of intellectual endeavour. To name but a few, William Gladstone, John Morley, and Arthur James Balfour were among the Society's political figures. The men of science included John Tyndall, Henry Acland, G. Croom Robertson, J. J. Sylvester, William Kingdon Clifford, and St. George Mivart. Religion had its defenders: the Catholic Archbishop of Westminster, Henry Edward Manning; the Catholic theologian Father J. D. Dalgairns; liberal Anglicans Frederick Denison Maurice and Arthur Stanley; the Bishop of Peterborough, William Connor Magee; the Bishop of Gloucester and Bristol, C. J. Ellicott; and the Unitarian reverend James Martineau. Philosophers included Henry Sidgwick, Shadworth Hodgson, and Mathew Boulton. There were also literary lights such as Alfred Tennyson, James Anthony Froude, the positivist Frederic Harrison, John Ruskin, Leslie Stephen, Sir James Fitzjames Stephen, Walter Bagehot, James Knowles, Richard Holt Hutton, and many more. The roster of members includes many of the English intellectual superstars

[3] Ibid., 366, 369–72.

of the period.[4] It was set up as a private club in order to allow members to speak frankly about controversial issues. Huxley took advantage of the tolerant atmosphere to be more honest about his beliefs than he was in public. His paper on the resurrection never appeared in a periodical. Although his friends wanted him to publish it in the ultra-liberal *Fortnightly Review* as a contribution to an important debate, he decided not to.[5] It was just too sensitive a topic to be aired in public.

Nevertheless, Huxley's controversial paper is extremely revealing. It represents a sea change in the second half of the nineteenth century in the relationship between science and religion. The principle behind Huxley's notion that the legitimacy of religious beliefs had to be tested using the scientific method led to the origins of the 'remarkable reversal' in the early twentieth century pointed to by Peter Harrison in the epigraph at the beginning of this paper. Science came to be seen as the providing the model for seeking truth, and even ethicists and theologians had to bring their insights to the scientist for validation. In his *Territories of Science and Religion*, Harrison observes that Huxley established the exclusivity of science while making claims for the wide applicability of its methods. As Harrison shows, Huxley asserted that the scientific method was the only method by which truth could be ascertained. Harrison concludes, 'the scientific method, thus understood, entails the view that underlying the various scientific disciplines there is a single unified and generic "science", and that this science offers us a unique and privileged access to truth'.[6] The success of science in the second half of the nineteenth century, generally regarded by historians as the age of the worship of science, led to a reorganisation of all of the disciplines, including theology.

A historical understanding of the evolving relationship between science and religion is an essential component of any attempt to rethink our current situation. Historians can open up new ways of thinking by showing the paths not taken that were live options at one point, before new assumptions constrained and narrowed thinking. Historians can also point to the intellectual dead ends that resulted when intellectuals accepted these new assumptions. One of those dead ends was the adoption of the

4 For more on the Metaphysical Society, see Marshall et al. (eds.), *The Metaphysical Society*.

5 Leonard Huxley, *Life and Letters of Thomas Henry Huxley*, 2 vols. (New York: D. Appleton and Company, 1900), vol. 1, 491. Desmond asserts that the paper was 'too hot to handle' and that Morley told Huxley that it was for scholars to discuss, not the crowd. See Adrian Desmond, *Huxley: From Devil's Disciple to Evolution's High Priest* (Reading, MA: Addison-Wesley, 1997), 466.

6 Peter Harrison, *The Territories of Science and Religion* (Chicago: University of Chicago Press, 2015), 169–70.

conflict thesis as an influential way of viewing the present and historical relationship between science and religion. But there were others. In this chapter I will examine how scientific naturalists like T. H. Huxley attempted to constrain thinking about science and religion, how those constraints shaped debates as well as previous scholarship, and how important Christian theologians of the period responded to this development. Surprisingly, some influential Christian theologians were willing to accept Huxley and his colleagues as legitimate scientific authorities who also had valuable insights into the religious implications of modern scientific thought.

2.1 Huxley and Scientific Naturalism

Harrison treats the nineteenth century as a pivotal turning point in the historical relationship between science and religion. He argues that it is in the nineteenth century that modern science was born. Whereas pre-modern science had been associated with the personal qualities of those who practiced it, during the nineteenth century it was redefined so as to be 'linked to a putatively unified set of practices ("the scientific method"), associated with a distinct group of individuals ("scientists"), and purged of elements that had once been regarded as integral to its status and operations (the theological and the metaphysical)'.[7] In its new configuration science now became a competitor to religion – and potentially in conflict with it – since both claimed the same territory, and scientists like Huxley demanded that religious beliefs be subjected to scientific judgement. Historians have referred to the group of intellectuals who pushed for the redefinition of science in the second half of the nineteenth century, and who advocated that scientific thought should play a larger role in British culture, as the scientific naturalists.

Scientific naturalists were those men who put forward new interpretations of nature, society, and humanity derived from the theories, methods, and categories of empirical science. They were naturalistic in the sense that they ruled out recourse to causes not present in empirically observed nature and they were scientific in that they interpreted nature in accordance with three major mid-century scientific theories, the atomic theory of matter, the conservation of energy, and evolution. According to the intellectual historian Frank Turner, the leading scientific naturalists included biologists T. H. Huxley and E. Ray Lankester, physicist John

[7] Ibid., 147.

Tyndall, mathematician William Kingdon Clifford, founder of eugenics Francis Galton, statistician Karl Pearson, anthropologist Edward Tylor, doctor Henry Maudsley, philosopher of evolution Herbert Spencer, and a group of journalists, editors, and writers, such as Leslie Stephen, G. H. Lewes, John Morley, Grant Allen, and Edward Clodd. Although Turner does not include Charles Darwin in the list, he should. Not only was Darwin's naturalistic approach to science an inspiration to many of the scientific naturalists; he encouraged Huxley and his other allies to engage Christian figures who attacked his theory of evolution, although he liked to remain above the fray himself. Turner argued that these were the men who were engaged in a contest for cultural authority with the Anglican clergy in the second half of the nineteenth century.[8] Whereas early Victorian scientists like William Whewell and John Herschel were products of Cambridge University, an Anglican institution that was saturated with the ethos of natural theology, the scientific naturalists (with some exceptions) came from outside the Oxbridge system and wanted to secularise science. They not only claimed to have scientific authority; they also attempted to parlay their scientific authority into cultural authority. That is, they demanded the right to be considered experts on social, political, and even religious issues by virtue of their scientific knowledge. They insisted that only they had special insights into how to interpret the broader metaphysical significance of modern science, not Christian theologians. If Turner's notion of a contest for cultural authority between the scientific naturalists and the Anglican clergy is added to Harrison's idea of a 'remarkable reversal', we can begin to see the explosive dynamic at play in the period after the publication of Darwin's *Origin of Species* (1859).

For the purposes of this essay I will focus on Huxley's views on science and religion as representative of the scientific naturalists, though these men were not always in full agreement on this and other issues.[9] Huxley's position is complicated – to say the least – as he does not adhere to a

[8] Frank Miller Turner, *Between Science and Religion: The Reaction to Scientific Naturalism in Late Victorian England* (New Haven, CT: Yale University Press, 1974); Frank M. Turner, *Contesting Cultural Authority: Essays in Victorian Intellectual Life* (Cambridge: Cambridge University Press, 1993). Recent work on scientific naturalism has offered new perspectives on this important group by focusing on issues of community, identity, and continuity. Retaining Turner's term 'scientific naturalism', scholars nevertheless now recognise that this category is more fluid and mutable than hitherto acknowledged. See Gowan Dawson and Bernard Lightman, 'Introduction', in Gowan Dawson and Bernard Lightman (eds.), *Victorian Scientific Naturalism: Community, Identity, Continuity* (Chicago: University of Chicago Press, 2014), 20.

[9] For recent scholarship on scientific naturalism, see Michael S. Reidy and Bernard Lightman (eds.), *The Age of Scientific Naturalism: Tyndall and His Contemporaries* (London: Pickering and Chatto, 2014); Dawson and Lightman (eds.), *Victorian Scientific Naturalism.*

traditional version of the conflict thesis. Despite his negative attitude towards the Christian Church as the chief obstacle to scientific progress, Huxley retained a deep respect for religion. He explicitly rejected the notion that science and religion were necessarily in conflict. Science and religion could exist in peaceful harmony as they belonged to two separate, fully autonomous spheres. Rightly conceived, Huxley believed, science and religion could never come into conflict because each realm was distinct and without authority outside its proper sphere of interest. In 1859, the year of the publication of Darwin's *Origin of Species*, Huxley was asserting that science and religion were not opposed to each other; rather, 'true science and true religion are twin-sisters'.[10] Religion, to Huxley, involved the sphere of feeling and emotion, and was expressed in art and poetry. Huxley, then, adopted a version of what the biologist Stephen Jay Gould later referred to in his *Rock of Ages* (1999) as the notion of non-overlapping magisteria. But there was a twist in how Huxley thought about theology, which he distinguished from religion. Conflict arose when theology was confused with religion. Theology operated in the scientific world of intellect because of its attempt to embody religious feelings in concrete facts. When religion and theology were mixed up, the potential for conflict became possible.[11] Huxley declared that 'the antagonism between science and religion about which we hear so much, appears to me to be purely factitious – fabricated, on the one hand, by short-sighted religious people who confound a certain branch of science, theology, with religion; and, on the other, by equally short-sighted scientific people who forget that science takes for its province only that which is susceptible of clear intellectual comprehension'.[12] There are two points to make about this quote. First, according to Huxley, theology is a 'branch of science', and therefore required legitimation from valid scientific theories.[13] Second, Huxley referred to the 'province' of science, making this very much, as Harrison has argued, a matter of territories, or of carving up the intellectual map of modernity to give science greater autonomy and prominence.

By holding to the separation of science and religion, while placing theology, carefully distinguished from religion, within the province of

[10] [T. H. Huxley,] "Science and Religion," *The Builder*, 18 (1859), 35.

[11] Imperial College, Huxley Papers, Huxley to James Creelman, June 11, 1894, vol. 12, 343.

[12] T. H. Huxley, *Science and Hebrew Tradition* (London: Macmillan, 1893), 160–1.

[13] The potential for constructing a scientific theology was explored by the scientific naturalists. See Bernard Lightman, 'The Theology of Victorian Scientific Naturalists', in Peter Harrison and Jon H. Roberts (eds.), *Science without God? Rethinking the History of Scientific Naturalism* (Oxford: Oxford University Press, 2019), 235–53.

science, Huxley and his fellow scientific naturalists were aggressively pushing for a significant shift in the metaphysical presuppositions of Western culture. It was a shift that went far beyond the acceptance or rejection of a specific scientific theory, such as evolution. It should be recalled that Huxley was never an enthusiastic convert to Darwin's theory of natural selection. What he, and the other scientific naturalists, liked about Darwin's theory was its naturalistic approach to doing science. To refer to the change in thinking taking place in the nineteenth century as the Darwinian revolution is to miss the point. We must go beyond disputes over specific scientific theories like evolution and explore a deeper level of intellectual change. What actually happened had more to do with the new naturalistic metaphysics that began to ground modern science in general. The fundamental questions in the second half of the nineteenth century debated in the Metaphysical Society and in British culture at large were: How should science be defined? What are the limits of science, if any? To what extent does science provide the sole path to truth? What is the role of religion and theology once these questions are answered? And, finally, who has the authority to interpret the religious significance of modern scientific ideas?

I am arguing that the scientific naturalists were able to set the agenda for discussion of the relationship between science and religion long after they were gone by persuading their contemporaries to accept their scientific, and in some cases even their religious, authority. This allowed them to frame the issues in such a way that it gave the upper hand to naturalistic metaphysics. The end result is that theologians in this period, and afterwards, were forced to choose between several dead ends. They could accept the authority of science, as defined by the scientific naturalists, in order to be seen as being in line with modernity. But this meant that they had to defer to scientists by bringing religious beliefs, such as the reality of miracles, to the bar of scientific judgement. They had to adapt Christian theology to whatever scientific theories were currently accepted by the scientific community. Theologians also had to put less stock in natural theology, since scientific naturalists wanted to remove theological concepts and language from the study of nature. If they rejected the authority of science, or its autonomy, they risked being marginalised as medieval relics of the past whose theology was not based on current knowledge. Whichever option they chose, theologians and religious thinkers in the second half of the nineteenth century were constrained as both led to equally untenable positions in which the cultural status of theology and religion was seriously compromised.

2.2 Previous Scholarship and Naturalistic Metaphysics

In the past, scholars who have examined theological and religious thought in the latter half of the nineteenth century have focused their discussion on the responses to specific scientific theories, such as evolution. They have largely ignored the underlying metaphysical shift represented in the 'remarkable reversal' in the disciplinary status of both theology and science pointed to by Harrison. In his *Development of English Theology in the Later Nineteenth Century* (1952), L. E. Elliott-Binns includes a chapter titled 'The Impact of Science and Philosophy'. Here he observed that 'in England as elsewhere our period was marked by an enormous expansion of scientific knowledge, not only through the accumulation of new facts, but also by the emergence of new theories'.[14] The focus is on these new theories and how they were opposed or accepted by religious thinkers. Elliott-Binns maintains, like Huxley, that there was no real opposition between genuine science and genuine theology – the conflicts were due to misunderstandings.[15] Bernard Reardon's *From Coleridge to Gore: A Century of Religious Thought in Britain* (1971) also remains on the level of scientific theories in the chapter titled 'Religion, Science and Philosophy'.[16] Like Elliott-Binns he hives off science from other issues, rather than seeing scientific naturalism as a pervasive influence that affects the very metaphysics of all thinking, including theological thinking.

In the more sophisticated *Religious Thought in the Victorian Age: Challenges and Reconceptions* (2007), James C. Livingston argued that this period constituted a 'watershed in British religious and theological history'. It was not 'simply a time of secularization'; it was also a time of religious change that 'had profound and enduring influence'.[17] Livingston explores the controversies surrounding such issues as the reign of law and miracle (design, providence, teleology, evil, theodicy), humanity's place in nature (human origins, the fall, sin, mind, free will, morality), and the new science of religion. Although Livingston does not segregate the impact of science on theology in one chapter, like Elliott-Binns and Reardon, he focuses primarily on how various scientific theories affected assorted

14 L. E. Elliott-Binns, *The Development of English Theology in the Later Nineteenth Century* (Hamden, CT: Archon Books, 1971), 23.

15 Ibid., 32.

16 Bernard M. G. Reardon, *From Coleridge to Gore: A Century of Religious Thought in Britain* (London: Longman Group, 1971), 285–320.

17 James C. Livingston, *Religious Thought in the Victorian Age: Challenges and Reconceptions* (New York: Continuum, 2007), 2.

religious doctrines, though at one point he examines how theological presuppositions and concerns remained 'constitutive in the work of important scientists', such as Owen, Wallace, Carpenter, Mivart, and many more.[18] As valuable as this point is, Harrison's approach suggests a very different tack: analysing how scientific assumptions became constitutive in the work of theologians.

While Livingston recognised that a turning point in the history of the relationship between science and religion took place in the second half of the nineteenth century, and that the impact of science has to be dealt with across all of theological thought, Cashdollar, in his *The Transformation of Theology, 1830–1890: Positivism and Protestant Thought in Britain in America* (1989), pushed these insights even further. Positivism, Cashdollar argues, questioned the ability of human beings to engage in any meaningful theological discussion at all. Seen by nineteenth-century intellectuals as inextricably associated with both Darwinism and the Higher Criticism, positivism came to signify the whole of modern thought. To Cashdollar, positivism subsumes scientific naturalism. Christian thinkers in both Britain and the United States were forced to respond to positivism from 1840 to 1890, and in the process they reconstructed theology. Even those who opposed Comte 'changed themselves'.[19] The 'judicious conservatives' took their agenda from orthodox Christianity 'and adjusted it to fit the demands of the age', while the liberals, who called for a 'New Theology', tried to shape the age 'into a Christian form'. In sum, 'the judicious conservatives, therefore, preferred the minimum change possible, the liberals the maximum allowable'.[20] On the British side, Cashdollar includes moderate Scottish writers and English Congregationalists (e.g., Robert Flint, Henry Calderwood, Henry Drummond, and John Blackie) among the judicious conservatives, and Oxford Hegelians, Cambridge social theologians, and Scottish figures (e.g., Benjamin Jowett, Andrew Martin Fairbairn, Edward Caird, and F. D. Maurice) among the liberals. In the epilogue to the book Cashdollar acknowledges his sympathies with 'those who sought reconciliation between the traditional and the modern and who worked to transform theology in that spirit. I do not think they conceded too much.'[21] Cashdollar recognises that there was a significant transformation in the

[18] Ibid., 5.

[19] Charles D. Cashdollar, *The Transformation of Theology, 1830–1890: Positivism and Protestant Thought in Britain and America* (Princeton, NJ: Princeton University Press, 1989), 14.

[20] Ibid., 373–4. [21] Ibid., 447.

second half of the nineteenth century but does not see the constraints it placed upon theology.

2.3 Granting Authority to Scientific Naturalism

Neither Livingston nor Cashdollar, two of the more sophisticated scholars who have published important books on Victorian theology in the last few decades, attempted to grapple directly with the constraints placed upon religious thinkers by the challenge of scientific naturalism. I would like to develop Harrison's suggestion that we move the discussion of Victorian science and religion to a different, and deeper, level of analysis that allows us to fully investigate the 'remarkable reversal' he discusses in *Territories of Science and Religion*. To move in that direction, it is important to explore the diverse positions taken by Victorian theologians on how much, if any, authority to grant to scientific naturalists, and what type of authority was involved. The specific scientific naturalists who were discussed most in the theological literature were Darwin, Huxley, Spencer, and Tyndall. Some Victorian theologians were not willing to grant authority of any kind to these men. Others acknowledged their authority on scientific matters, but not on religious issues. Still others believed that scientific naturalists possessed authority in discussions concerning both scientific and religious questions. In short, a debate took place within the Victorian theologian community on the nature of authority when scientific and religious matters were being discussed that affected the status of theology. At stake was not only the authority of scientific naturalists in religious controversies but also the authority of theologians in scientific controversies.

The older scholarship, with its emphasis on the conflict thesis, drew attention to those theologians who rejected evolution and denied authority to the scientific naturalists in scientific as well as religious issues. Figures like Samuel Wilberforce, Fellow of the Royal Society, Bishop of Oxford, and a committed high churchman, immediately leap to mind. In his anonymous review of the *Origin of Species* in the *Quarterly Review* he ridiculed Darwin's reasoning abilities, refused to accept the validity of evolutionary theory, and rejected the religious and moral lessons that seemed to arise out of it.[22] Wilberforce was just one of many theologians who rejected both the scientific and religious authority of the scientific naturalists. The Reverend Francis Orpen Morris, a prolific author of natural history books with high church leanings, launched an aggressive

[22] [Samuel Wilberforce], 'Darwin's *Origin of Species*', *Quarterly Review*, 108 (July 1860), 225–64.

criticism of Darwin, Huxley, and Tyndall in his *All the Articles of the Darwin Faith* (1875). Here he offered a series of quotes and paraphrases intended as representative of the views of these three men on scientific and religious issues. He sarcastically commented, 'It is really difficult to say whether Huxley or Tyndall talks and writes the most senseless maundering.' Huxley's views on human evolution contained assumption without proof and went against all evidence, while Darwin's analysis in the *Descent of Man* (1871) of how reason, language, and religion were acquired was wildly speculative. 'It is really an abuse of language', Morris declared, 'to call such writing "scientific": to mistake the "Arabian Nights" for history would be far more excusable.'[23]

In his *Modern Physical Fatalism and the Doctrine of Evolution* (1876), Thomas Rawson Birks, a leading evangelical anti-Darwinian and Knightbridge Professor of Moral Philosophy at Cambridge, was more concerned with rejecting the scientific and religious authority of Herbert Spencer. Despite the wide praise it had received, Spencer's *First Principles* (1862), the cornerstone of his System of Synthetic Philosophy, was 'wholly fallacious and misleading in its reasoning, and completely antichristian in its whole spirit and tone'. Spencer's concept of the Unknowable, Birks warned, was really 'Atheism under a disguised name', and he really didn't understand a scientific theory as essential as Newton's law of gravitation.[24] Even liberal Nonconformists challenged the scientific and religious authority of scientific naturalists. James Martineau, a leading Unitarian theologian, charged Darwin with going beyond the evidence to reach his grand conclusions on evolution. Moreover, Darwin ignored the religious implications of his own theory. 'It is a matter for regret and surprise', Martineau asserted, 'that Mr. Darwin himself should have set forth his hypothesis as excluding the action of a higher intelligence.'[25] Leading Catholics firmly denied the scientific and religious authority of scientific naturalists. Henry Manning, St. George Jackson Mivart, and William Ward, respectively, a cardinal, a scientist, and a theologian-philosopher, all argued that the study of nature was still in the domain of the Catholic Church and that scientific naturalists did not speak on behalf of science. They claimed to be more

[23] F. O. Morris, *All the Articles of the Darwin Faith* (London: Moffatt, Paige, 1875), 26, 40, 43.
[24] Thomas Rawson Birks, *Modern Physical Fatalism and the Doctrine of Evolution* (London: Macmillan, 1876), 3, 9, 46.
[25] James Martineau, *Essays, Reviews and Addresses* (London: Longmans, Green, 1891), vol. 3, 162.

trustworthy guides to understanding the religious significance of modern science.[26]

But there were other theological voices that accepted evolutionary theory and granted scientific authority to scientific naturalists while denying them religious authority. The philosopher and theologian Robert Flint, who held the divinity chair of Edinburgh University from 1876 to 1903, was willing to accept the scientific theories of Huxley and Darwin in his *Theism* (1877) while objecting to their theology. Throughout *Theism* he engages with leading scientific naturalists, focusing especially on their evolutionary theory. For Flint, evolution provided scientific support for the design in nature. Huxley, Flint pointed out, admitted that evolution 'cannot touch' the 'higher teleology, the general designs', but he inconsistently argued that the 'lower teleology' led the scientist to discard the notion of 'special designs'. Though Flint had no reservations about Huxley's science, he could be trusted only so far as a guide to understanding the religious implications of evolutionary theory. Flint's attitude towards Darwin was similar. 'I have challenged the theology of Mr Darwin', Flint declared, 'and those who follow his guidance in theology. I have no wish to dispute his science.' Flint was willing to assent to the scientific validity of the theory of natural selection and the 'privation, pain, and conflict' that Darwin saw in the evolutionary process. But he was critical of Darwin's inability to realise that evolution's final result was 'order and beauty' and that through natural selection 'design may be realized'. Whatever Darwin's views on the religious implications of his theories, Flint was confident that 'the works of Mr. Darwin are invaluable to the theologian, owing to the multitude of "beautiful contrivances" and "marvellous adjustments" admirably described in them'. Paley's *Natural Theology* was out of date not because Darwin and his followers had refuted it, 'but because they have brought so much to light which confirms its argument'.[27]

Flint wasn't the only one to take this position. Another Scottish theologian, James Iverach, adopted a similar standpoint. Starting in 1887 Iverach was appointed to chairs in apologetics, dogmatic theology, and New Testament exegesis at the Free Church College, Aberdeen. From 1905 to 1907 he was principal of the College.[28] In his *Theism in the Light of Present Science and Philosophy* (1899), Iverach expressed his gratitude to

[26] Bernard Lightman, 'Catholics and the Metaphysical Basis of Science', in Marshall et al. (eds.), *The Metaphysical Society*, 252–69.

[27] Robert Flint, *Theism*, 9th ed. (Edinburgh: William Blackwood and Sons, 1895), 198, 204, 208–9.

[28] James R. Moore, *The Post-Darwinian Controversies: A Study of the Protestant Struggle to Come to Terms with Darwin in Great Britain and America 1870–1900* (Cambridge: Cambridge University Press, 1979), 253.

the evolutionists for showing that everywhere there is 'method, order, law' that implies intelligence, though they did not understand that this was the upshot of their work. 'We take their results, and leave their philosophy on one side', Iverach insisted. Despite Huxley's well-known views on the machine-like qualities of the human body, Iverach offered his readers a quote from him about the distinctive properties of living matter. 'Huxley, speaking when he was not on the war-path, uses words which concede all that we need for the great distinction between living and lifeless matter'. An anti-materialist position could be drawn out of Huxley's science. Although Spencer did not believe in a traditional Christian god, nevertheless he did acknowledge that there is a 'power that works according to a plan, and produces intelligible results'.[29] In sum, trust Spencer and Huxley's science, but not the philosophical, metaphysical, or religious conclusions that they draw from it.

An important distinction can be made between Flint and Iverach and another group of Christian theologians, who accepted the science of scientific naturalists while going further in granting Huxley and his allies some measure of authority to interpret the religious significance of modern scientific thought. Congregational minister and principal of Mansfield College, a Congregational theological college in Oxford, Andrew Martin Fairbairn advocated cooperation between the theologian and the scientist. In his *Studies in the Philosophy of Religion and History* (1876) he argued that science had become far more speculative in the previous twenty years and held Darwin and Spencer responsible for the change. Fairbairn had grave reservations about Spencer, who was inconsistent in his emphasis on the limits of knowledge while at the same time asserting the existence of an Unknowable being. Spencer's God was unacceptable to Fairbairn; far too abstract and bloodless, it was 'like a dead mask concealing a living face, a ghastly eye-socket without the eye'. Darwin, Fairbairn believed, was more cautious, 'hardly ever adventuring into the exhausting atmosphere of pure speculation', while Spencer was 'bolder and more speculative' in his attempt to build 'a science of the universe on a philosophy of the Unknowable'. Fairbairn praised Darwin's conception of evolution as a process filled with 'subtle complexity'. Darwin exalted 'our sense of the infinite sufficiency, the universal activity and inexhaustible energy of the Cause'. Fairbairn had mixed feelings about John Tyndall. He referred to Tyndall's 'Belfast Address' (1874), widely condemned for its supposed

[29] James Iverach, *Theism in the Light of Present Science and Philosophy* (New York: Macmillan, 1899), 30–2, 46, 93.

materialism, as 'memorable enough, were it only as an instance of sweet simplicity in things historical, and the most high-flying metaphysics disguised in scientific terms'. But later in the book, when Fairbairn quotes from the final paragraph of the *Origin of Species*, he draws on Tyndall's language in the 'Belfast Address' to explain and praise the richness of Darwin's tangled bank metaphor. Fairbairn maintains that Darwin refers to the few forms at the beginning of the evolutionary process as simple, but 'if they are regarded as the parents of the future, containing 'the promise and potency' of the 'endless forms' that have been and are to be, then they are exceedingly wonderful'.[30] Fairbairn echoes Tyndall's assertion near the end of the 'Belfast Address' that it is possible to discern in matter 'the promise and potency of all terrestrial Life'.[31] But instead of seeing in it a statement of materialism, he offers it as a way to reconcile Darwin's conception of the evolutionary process with Christian modes of thought. Both Darwin and Tyndall provide valuable insight into the religious significance of modern scientific theory.

Fairbairn's position is analogous to the one put forward by Frederick Temple, a liberal Anglican who eventually became archbishop of Canterbury in 1897. In his *The Relation between Religion and Science* (1884), which aimed at reconciliation, Temple argued that 'the doctrine of Evolution does not affect the substance of Paley's argument at all. The marks of design which he has pointed out remain marks of design still even if we accept the doctrine of Evolution to the full.' The science in Darwin and Spencer's evolutionary works could be accepted by committed Christians. However, like Fairbairn, he preferred Darwin to Spencer when it came to their attempts to draw philosophical and religious significance out of evolution. He was critical of Spencer's very 'weak chapter' on personal identity in his otherwise 'remarkable volume of First Principles' and is, in general, opposed to the thrust of Spencer's defence of the relativity of knowledge. But there is nothing but praise for Darwin in the book. Darwin's investigations had made it 'exceedingly probable that the vast variety of plants and animals have sprung from a much smaller number of original forms'. Temple was also willing to accept Darwin's statements about the immense destruction and waste in nature. However, Temple did not hesitate to draw on Darwin to demonstrate how evolution

30 A. M. Fairbairn, *Studies in the Philosophy of Religion and History* (London: Strahan, 1876), 64–5, 93, 104.

31 John Tyndall, *Fragments of Science*, 8th ed., 2 vols. (London: Longmans, Green, 1892), vol. 2, 191.

was consistent with Revelation.[32] Temple and Fairbairn represent those theologians who not only accepted the scientific authority of the scientific naturalists, but were also prepared to grant them limited authority in determining the religious significance of modern scientific theories.

2.4 Providing Scientific Credibility for Religion (I): Kingsley and Matheson

In the second edition of the *Origin of Species*, Darwin added some material intended to assure his readers that there was 'no good reason why the views given in this volume should shock the religious feelings of any one'. He referred to a letter he had received from a 'celebrated author and divine' that stated he had '"gradually learnt to see that it is just as noble a conception of the Deity to believe that He created a few original forms capable of self-development into other and needful forms, as to believe that he required a fresh act of creation to supply the voids caused by the action of His laws"'.[33] The unnamed author of the letter was none other than Charles Kingsley, Christian socialist, novelist, and liberal Anglican cleric.

While Darwin drew on Kingsley's letter to defuse religious hostility to evolution, Kingsley was devoting his time to using Darwin's theories to modernise Christian theology. He wrote in 1863 to fellow liberal Anglican Frederick Denison Maurice, 'I am very busy working out points of Natural Theology, by the strange light of Huxley, Darwin, and Lyell. I think I shall come to something worth having before I have done.'[34] Kingsley was part of a diverse group of theologians who not only deferred to the scientific authority of the scientific naturalists; they also looked to them for clues on how to interpret the larger metaphysical and theological meaning of modern science. In addition to Kingsley, the group included George Matheson, Henry Drummond, and Aubrey Moore. Some even quoted from the works of scientific naturalists to provide their theology with more credibility. In effect, this gave scientific naturalists religious as well as scientific authority.

The results of Kingsley's attempt to update natural theology with the help of scientific naturalists were presented in a public lecture at Sion

32 Frederick Temple, *The Relation between Religion and Science* (London: Macmillan 1884), 43, 113, 164–5, 188.

33 Charles Darwin, *The Origin of Species by Means of Natural Selection*, 6th ed. (London: John Murray, 1873), 421–2.

34 Fanny Kingsley, *Charles Kingsley: His Letters and Memories of His Life*, 2 vols. (London: Henry S. King, 1877), vol. 2, 171.

College on January 10, 1871. Kingsley used this lecture as the 'Preface' to his *Westminster Sermons* (1874), and then later included it among his *Scientific Lectures and Essays* (1880) under the title 'The Natural Theology of the Future'. Kingsley's main point in the lecture was that those who worked within each of the separate territories of science and religion had to respect the boundaries between them. Scientists had no business with final causes, but only with 'the How of things', whereas the duty of natural theologians was to 'find out the Why'. Whether or not a new scientific theory like evolution really operated in nature as the 'how' was to be determined by scientists, not by theologians. 'As for the theory being impossible', Kingsley insisted, 'we must leave the discussion of that to physical students.' Scientists had full authority within their territory.[35]

But, Kingsley reminded his audience, evolution dealt only with the 'how'. It was the role of the theologian to study the 'why'. By dividing science and natural theology into two spheres of authority, Kingsley hoped to put an end to the notion of a conflict between science and religion and to define a specific role for natural theologians in the post-Darwinian era. Kingsley denied that the theory of evolution – or any scientific theory for that matter – did away with final causes or with natural theology itself. However, a new scientific conception of natural processes required that the theologian undertake a readjustment in how the 'why' was to be conceived. 'We might accept all that Mr. Darwin, all that Professor Huxley, all that other most able men, have so learnedly and so acutely written on physical science', Kingsley declared, 'and yet preserve our natural Theology on exactly the same basis as that on which Butler and Paley left it. That we should have to develop it, I do not deny. That we should have to relinquish it, I do.' The principle of the old natural theology could be summed up as: if there be design in nature there must be a designer. The principle of the new natural theology that took evolution into account was encapsulated in the sentence: 'If there be evolution, there must be an evolver.'[36]

As proof that the theory of evolution did not destroy 'the old theory of design, contrivance, and adaptation, nay, with the fullest admission of benevolent final causes', Kingsley recommended a study of Darwin's *Fertilization of Orchids*, 'a book which, whether his main theory be true or not, will still remain a most valuable addition to natural Theology'. Despite Kingsley's insistence that the spheres of science and religion be

35 Charles Kingsley, 'Preface', in *Westminster Sermons* (London: Macmillan, 1874), xxi, xxiv.
36 Ibid., xxii–xxiii.

kept separate, Darwin's book dealt with both the how and the why. Kingsley then quoted directly from Darwin's *Origin of Species* on how natural selection was daily and hourly throughout the world scrutinising every variation and preserving what is good so as to improve every organic being. Lifting passages from the *Origin* provided scientific support for the theological notion of providence and helped Kingsley to explain the religious implications of evolutionary theory. Kingsley added that in comparison to older depictions of nature prevalent in the eighteenth century, evolution moved science away from an emphasis on mechanism and a tendency towards deism.[37]

George Matheson, another representative of liberal theology, had been influenced by John Caird, the Hegelian philosopher, while at Glasgow University from 1857 to 1862, where he obtained a BA and an MA. Appointed minister of Innellan church in 1868, and then minister of St Bernard's parish church in Edinburgh in 1886, Matheson was a prolific author. His *Can the Old Faith Live with the New? or, The Problem of Evolution and Revelation* (1885) focused directly on the implications of modern science for religion. Matheson's main question in the book was: What should a Christian theologian do in a period when scientists are debating the validity of evolution, a theory with tremendous implications for religion? The theologian cannot intervene in the discussions as the determination of the truth of scientific statement of fact is 'beyond him, and investigation in this sphere is therefore to him impossible'. Scientists, Matheson affirms, are the sole arbiters in scientific matters. But the theologian can ask: What effect will the establishment of these conclusions exert upon the old belief? To what extent will it modify, in what measure shall it overthrow, the religious conclusions of the past? Matheson, then, asks: What are the repercussions for religion, if evolution is proven to be scientifically valid?[38]

To answer that question Matheson systematically examines every aspect of traditional Christian theology in light of evolutionary theory – issues of Divine knowledge, creation, the origin of life, providence, the work of the Spirit, Divine communion, and immortality. Throughout the book he returns again and again to the thought of one scientific naturalist in particular: Herbert Spencer. Spencer becomes his chief ally in his attempt to make the larger religious implications of evolutionary theory clear to his

37 Ibid., xxiii, xxv.

38 Rev. George Matheson, *Can the Old Faith Live with the New? or, The Problem of Evolution and Revelation* (Edinburgh: William Blackwood & Sons, 1885), 18.

readers. Spencer is the perfect guide according to Matheson because he is the 'chief apostle' of the doctrine of evolution. Matheson's preference for Spencer is not intended, he claims, as a criticism of Darwin. Matheson is 'not arguing against the principles of Darwinism'. But Darwin merely accepts aspects of the evolutionary process such as variation as a 'fact of nature' without explaining them. In so doing Darwin is 'perfectly scientific'. Spencer is better for Matheson's purposes because as a philosopher he calls in the 'aid of the inscrutable' to explain Darwin and evolutionary theory.[39]

Spencer has shown that 'led by the hand of the evolutionary theory itself' we must acknowledge the existence of the Unknowable, 'a Power which transcends nature'. Although Spencer does not see the Unknowable as an object of worship, its transcendence is in common with the God of theism. The Unknowable becomes a foundation for building upon the continuities between Spencerian evolutionism and Christian theology. There are parallels between 'the two most representative systems of creationism and evolutionism – the system of the Book of Genesis and the system of Mr. Herbert Spencer'. If Spencer's grand conception of cosmic evolution is verified by science – and Matheson leaves 'the determination of that to the judgement of the specialists' – then the doctrine of special creation would have a scientific basis. Spencer, though somewhat 'unconsciously', reconciled evolution and special creation since he traced everything back to a 'fire-cloud' which is 'the shadow of a Power which is perfectly transcendental'. Matheson again turns to the philosopher of evolution to show how the intelligent Will that Spencer sees in nature is indicative of the operation of a divine providence. After having gone through all of the points of contact between modern evolution and 'the revelations of the old faith', Matheson concludes that even if the truth of Spencer's assertions was established, Christianity had nothing to fear. 'The only effect which the universal acceptance of evolution would produce upon the Christian claim to empire', Matheson believed, 'would be to rest upon a basis of science what has hitherto reposed only on a system of faith.'[40] Strikingly, it is Spencerian evolution that provides the scientific justification for the central tenets of Christian theology.

2.5 Providing Scientific Credibility for Religion (II): Drummond and Moore

Matheson singled out two books that stimulated him to write *Can the Old Faith Live with the New?* One was Henry Drummond's *Natural Law in the*

[39] Ibid., 168, 170–1. [40] Ibid, 88, 90–1, 107, 132, 165, 235, 377, 387.

Spiritual World (1883). However, Matheson pointed to a significant difference between his work and Drummond's. Matheson's purpose was to inquire: If evolutionary theory be true, what then? He expressed no opinion on the scientific accuracy of the theory. That had to be left to the scientific experts. But Drummond's book aimed to build faith on the acceptance of the modern doctrine of evolution. Drummond did not question the scientific validity of evolution. According to Matheson, Drummond's goal was constructive, while his purpose was 'purely analytic'.[41]

Henry Drummond, natural science lecturer and theology professor at the Free Church college, Glasgow, participated in the Edinburgh campaign of the American evangelists Dwight L. Moody and Ira D. Sankey in 1874 and 1875. His *Natural Law in the Spiritual World* was a Victorian best seller. In only five years after it first appeared, it sold about 70,000 copies.[42] Compare that with the 56,000 copies of Darwin's *Origin of Species* that sold from 1859 up until the end of the nineteenth century.[43] Drummond's main point in the book was that 'many of the Laws of the Spiritual World, hitherto regarded as occupying an entirely separate province, are simply the Laws of the Natural World'. This insight, which allowed him to bring together science and religion, ended up changing the latter more than the former. 'The subject-matter Religion had taken on the method and expression of Science, and I discovered myself enunciating Spiritual Law in the exact terms of Biology and Physics.' However, if natural law could be traced in the spiritual world, 'it would offer Religion a new credential' and allow the production of a 'truly scientific theology'. Science could not only 'corroborate Theology'; it could also 'purify it'. Drummond supported his conception of a scientific theology by quoting from Huxley: If anyone is able to assert 'that his theology rests upon valid evidence and sound reasoning then it appears to me that such theology must take its place as a part of science'. Drummond believed that a characteristic of the current age was the demand 'that all that concerns life and conduct shall be placed on a scientific basis'. One of the advantages of his entire approach was that this demand 'will be satisfied'.[44]

41 Ibid., vi–vii.

42 D. W. Bebbington, "Henry Drummond," in *Oxford Dictionary of National Biography*. https://doi-org.ezproxy.library.yorku.ca/10.1093/ref:odnb/8068.

43 R. B. Freeman, *The Works of Charles Darwin: An Annotated Bibliographical Handlist* (London: Dawsons of Pall Mall, 1965), 45.

44 Henry Drummond, *Natural Law in the Spiritual World* (London: Hodder and Stoughton, 1883), vi–vii, ix, xviii, 23–4.

Throughout the entire book Drummond draws on quotes and references to scientific naturalists to present his vision of the continuity between the physical and the spiritual worlds. The scientific naturalists are not only treated as scientific authorities; Drummond also grants them religious authority as their works contain important insights into religious issues. He quotes from Spencer's *First Principles* on how religion's central position is impregnable. A Huxley quote is brought to bear on how the immaterial world is on firmer reality than the material. Tyndall is referenced and Huxley is quoted on how spontaneous generation has been disproven by science. Traditional religious and theological concepts are translated into contemporary scientific terms in chapters with titles such as 'Biogenesis', 'Degeneration', 'Growth', 'Death', 'Eternal Life', 'Environment', 'Conformity to Type', and 'Parasitism'. The reader is directed to sections on physical degeneration in Darwin's *Origin of Species* for an understanding of the scientific basis of the spiritual law of degeneration. Spencer's discussion of biological death is used to guide an examination of the 'parallel phenomenon of Death in the spiritual world'. In the chapter titled 'Conformity to Type', Drummond strikingly draws on Huxley's concept of protoplasm, which, when it was originally used by the biologist in his essay 'The Physical Basis of Life' (1868), led to accusations of materialism. Drummond not only accepts Huxley's analysis of protoplasm as the basic material composing all life; he uses it to ground his entire discussion of the religious implications of modern biology. Just as Huxley peers through the lens of a microscope to study how protoplasm is sculpted according to a plan determined by the law of conformity to type, so too is there a sculpting in spiritual life that is described in the New Testament when humans are reborn by coming into contact with Christ's teachings.[45]

Drummond's heavy reliance on the scientific naturalists to frame his reconstruction of Christianity is echoed by Aubrey Lackington Moore, a theologian, philosopher, and historian. Moore's impeccable ecclesiastical credentials derive from the close relationship he had with Oxford Anglicanism. He graduated with a BA in 1871 and an MA in 1874 from Oxford, and became a fellow of St John's College, Oxford, from 1872 to 1876. He served as tutor at St John's until 1876, and at Magdalen and Keble Colleges from 1881 until his death. At Oxford, Moore lectured on philosophy and the history of the Reformation. But his greatest contribution to the intellectual life of Oxford was his exploration of the impact of

[45] Ibid., 29, 56, 63–4, 120, 152, 290, 295.

modern philosophical and scientific thought on traditional theology. A liberal high-churchman, he was one of the contributors to *Lux mundi* (1889), a manifesto of progressive Anglo-Catholicism. Here he argued that new philosophical and scientific ideas could enrich and confirm theological doctrine. Moore's contemporaries, including biologists such as E. B. Poulton, W. H. Flower, E. R. Lankester, and G. J. Romanes, were impressed by his broad knowledge of current scientific thought.[46]

In 'Darwinism and the Christian Faith', one of the key chapters in Aubrey Moore's *Science and the Faith* (1889), he reflects on the challenges to Christianity coming from Darwinism. Moore's piece was originally written in response to the publication of Darwin's *Life and Letters* in 1887, which, he declared, provided an opportunity to 'face the question how far Darwinism affects Christian faith, and what are the points of traditional interpretation or apology which are modified by it'.[47] Moore asserted that Christian theology had no reason to fear new scientific theories. This fear was 'as unreasonable as the attempt to base the eternal truth of religion on what may eventually prove to be a transient phase of scientific belief'.[48] In the case of evolution, however, he held that this was an established doctrine. The question, then, for Moore, was: Given a churchman who accepted the dogmatic positions of the English Church and who believed that the 'doctrine of evolution' was the truest solution yet discovered by science, 'what reconstruction of traditionally accepted views and arguments is necessary and possible?'[49] What follows is Moore's attempt to remove the difficulties generated by Darwin's evolutionary theory by re-examining three Christian doctrines: (1) the theory of special creation, (2) the old argument from design, and (3) the old view of humanity's place in nature. For Moore, then, the reconstruction of Christian beliefs is driven by new developments in science, in this case, evolution.

Moore argues that the doctrine of special creation, which depends on the notion of the immutability of species, can safely be rejected since it is not intrinsic to Christianity. Adopting the role of the historian, Moore establishes that this doctrine was 'unknown to Bacon and unauthorised by S. Thomas', and therefore 'is not likely to be essential either to science or religion'. The historical origins, Moore asserts, actually lie in Milton's

46 Richard England, "Moore, Aubrey Lackington," in *Oxford Dictionary of National Biography*. https://doi-org.ezproxy.library.yorku.ca/10.1093/ref:odnb/19097.

47 Aubrey L. Moore, *Science and the Faith: Essays on Apologetic Subjects* (London: Kegan Paul, Trench, 1889), 162.

48 Ibid., 162. 49 Ibid., 166.

'Paradise Lost', which came to be seen, erroneously, as a 'sort of inspired gloss on the early chapters of Genesis'. Moore insisted that evolution was 'infinitely more Christian than the theory of "special creation"', as it implied the immanence of God in nature, whereas special creation had more in common with deism.[50] It is notable that Moore conceives of special creation as a religious 'doctrine' that was in competition with the scientific doctrine of evolution. It is also significant that Moore quotes Huxley to support his notion that in destroying the dogma of special creation, evolution presented no real difficulties for theism.[51] Huxley's expert opinion is considered by Moore to be decisive.

Moore then proceeds to investigate how the 'doctrine of natural selection' is said to have destroyed the argument from design. He remarks that 'that is a much more serious matter'.[52] Although Moore acknowledges that Darwin destroyed the old teleological doctrine based on Paley's emphasis on design, he also 'unconsciously introduced a new teleology'. Again, Moore quotes Huxley for support. Besides, Moore points out, Kant had destroyed the old design argument long ago – metaphysicians already knew that.[53] Finally, Moore reflects on how Darwin required a new view of man's place in nature. Christian theologians had protested that Darwin's theory degraded humanity. But, Moore asked, was that really true? Moore responds by turning to Darwin rather than Huxley. In tracing human descent Darwin had chronicled 'his rise from the lowest origin to the highest order of being of which science has any knowledge'.[54] Moore again defers to a scientist to corroborate his views on the proper interpretation of evolutionary theory. Throughout the chapter he turns time and time again to Darwin for confirmation, drawing on the *Life and Letters* for evidence as to the late evolutionist's more reverent views.[55] In the end, Moore brings three Christian doctrines to the bar of science, rejects them, and reconstructs Christianity with the guidance of Darwin and Huxley.

2.6 Reconfiguring Territory: Some Concluding Thoughts

British theologians from diverse Christian traditions grappled with the onslaught of metaphysical naturalism that was championed by influential scientific naturalists in the second half of the nineteenth century. Huxley

[50] Ibid., 177–9, 184. [51] Ibid., 186. [52] Ibid., 186. [53] Ibid., 191–4.
[54] Ibid., 207. See also 213–14.
[55] Moore prefers Darwin to Huxley. At one point, after referring to Huxley's "anti-theological *animus*," he admits that "it is refreshing to turn to the cautious and reverent utterances of Charles Darwin." Ibid., 188.

and his allies had set a clever trap for Victorian theologians. They leveraged their scientific authority so as to force theologians to make choices that could only lead them into dead ends. Scientific naturalists like Huxley fought to establish the autonomy of science; they wanted the fate of important theories – evolution, for example – to be determined on scientific grounds alone, without interference from theologians. But this position led to the notion that scientific knowledge was privileged and that all theories, concepts, and ideas, including religious ones, required the imprimatur, the blessing, of scientific authority. Some theologians chose to deny scientific authority to the scientific naturalists. Since Huxley and his friends claimed that they alone spoke for science, figures like Wilberforce, Morris, and Birks risked the possibility that they would be considered anti-scientific and obsolete in their thinking. Indeed, Wilberforce and the others who took this position are often depicted as the great losers in the debate, both then and now. Their opinions seemed to lack legitimacy as they were not based on science. They have been marginalised.

For those theologians who chose to accept the scientific authority of the scientific naturalists, there was a further decision to make: whether or not to confer religious authority on them as well. Kingsley, Matheson, Drummond, and Moore, men from diverse traditions within Christianity, all opted to grant both scientific and religious authority to Huxley and his friends. Scientific naturalists, they argued, did have insight into religious issues based on their scientific expertise. Their views on the religious significance of modern science could be used to support an updated vision of Christianity. But it also gave science a privileged status. This position was a dead end in the sense that the validity of religious belief was to be judged using scientific criteria. The result is the remarkable reversal to which Harrison draws our attention. Then there were the positions in between. Flint and Iverach grant scientific, but not religious, authority to the scientific naturalists. But the challenge for those who held to this position was maintaining parity between theology and science in an age when the status of the latter was growing significantly. Why was Huxley trustworthy as a scientist but not as a religious thinker? The other 'in between' position, advanced by Fairbairn and Temple, was that some scientists could be religious authorities. But whereas Temple trusted Spencer when he ventured into religious territory, Fairbairn was suspicious of Spencer and preferred Darwin and Tyndall. However, if Fairbairn and Temple could not agree on which scientific naturalists merited a degree of religious authority, it raised questions about whether any scientific naturalists could be trusted and about the judgement of Christian theologians on these issues.

Today we are still enmeshed in the coils of the shift in metaphysical presuppositions grounding Western culture. The remarkable reversal in the positions of science and theology, which flipped their cultural authority, remains a serious problem for contemporary theology. Although Huxley declared that religion still had value and a territory of its own, as did Stephen Jay Gould, it was the scientist who determined the size and boundaries of that territory. The origins of our contemporary situation can be traced back to the Victorian period, when the territories assigned to science and religion were deeply problematic, and ultimately disastrous for theology. If we attempt to re-think the way in which we conceive of science and religion, and their respective territories, we must recognise that there may even be a problem with the very notion of territories, whether they are seen to be overlapping or non-overlapping. The preoccupation with magisteria, or in Harrison's terms, territories, may preclude any effort to escape how the scientific naturalists framed the issues around a privileged naturalistic metaphysics, and it may indicate that Huxley and his allies still dictate the parameters of the debate.

PART II

Beyond 'Science and Religion'

CHAPTER 3

Science and Theology

Where the Consonance Really Lies

David Bentley Hart

When we ask, as some of us occasionally do, whether it is possible to discover or establish a true consonance between the modern sciences and theology, we are asking a question prompted first of all by nostalgia. We are casting a perhaps somewhat forlorn glance back, on the one hand, to a period four or five centuries ago, before any estrangement had begun to take shape between 'natural philosophy' and theology, and before mechanistic models of the physical order had begun to evolve into a metaphysical naturalism (the firm philosophical conviction, that is to say, that there can be no reality beyond the closed continuum of physical exchanges of matter and energy); but also, and much more essentially, we are looking back to an almost timeless moment of innocence, at once immemorial and yet intimately known to each of us, when we were as yet unaware of any distinctions between different spheres of inquiry, let alone any dissonances among them. We all remember, without being able quite to recall it with any immediacy, the first dawn of wonder within us: that instant when the infinitely open question of everything posed itself to us all at once, but when it had not yet become a specific question about anything as such. Every attempt to know the truth of the world in later life – empirical, theoretical, hermeneutical, critical, speculative, spiritual – begins for all of us in an instant of naïve surprise before the mystery of being, an unanticipated experience of the sheer fortuity and givenness of the world, a sudden fleeting moment of limpid awareness when one knows simultaneously the utter strangeness of everything familiar and the utter contingency of everything presumed. This is the existential amazement that, as Plato and Aristotle both affirmed, first awakens us to the love of wisdom: an aboriginal summons to which, so long as we recall even the faintest shimmering trace of its uncanniness, we must remain faithful all our lives. And, at first, this primordial vocation is the same for everyone, as are the first stirrings of a response; no alienations are yet possible. But the initial moment passes: boundless possibility contracts into a multitude of finite and divergent actual paths; habits of thought and decisions of the will make the luminous simplicity of the original experience ever more difficult to recollect; and at the last the mystery is lost somewhere amid the tangles of our methods and our prejudices. The day is long; the light of dawn soon fades from memory.

If we persist in asking the question long enough to allow that initial wistfulness to dissipate, however, and begin to pose it in more concrete terms, we all at once conjure up a host of ancillary questions, the most obvious of which is what precisely we think our words really mean. 'Science', even more than 'theology', is an abstraction, however disposed we may be today to imagine that it names a clearly defined realm of practices, comprising exact rules of method and comprehensive principles of evidence. Moreover, 'modern science', in particular, is a distinct culture, with all the historical, linguistic, and conceptual conditionality that this entails; and every culture incubates within itself, even if only tacitly and tenuously, certain metaphysical presuppositions: what, for instance, constitutes reason; what the limits of knowledge are; what questions ought to be asked; which methods of inquiry should be presumed to reflect reality and which should be regarded only as useful fictions. And it is here, at the level of culture, that the truly irreconcilable conflicts between scientific and theological thinking are inevitably found; for in most circumstances it is not what we can prove, but what we presuppose, that determines what we think we know or imagine we have discovered. Before we can pose the question of the consonance between theology and the sciences, therefore, we must first make sure that we know what territories these cultures properly encompass, and whether there are still any to which both at once might be able to lay some legitimate claim. Otherwise, we are likely to careen across boundaries we do not even know exist.

For what it is worth, these days the most inept incursions and encroachments tend to come more often from the side of the sciences. Perhaps theologians have by now been sufficiently chastened by the memories of theology's past trespasses and so can see the lines of demarcation with greater clarity. At least, it would be a very poorly trained theologian indeed who produced anything as philosophically confused or as engorged with category errors as Lawrence Krauss's *A Universe from Nothing* (2013), or who exhibited a comparable ignorance of the difference between aetiological queries about our universe's origin from an antecedent physical state and modal queries about the possibility of physical existence as such – between, that is, cosmology and ontology. Nor can one imagine any serious theologian venturing interventions in the sciences as reckless as

Richard Dawkins's maladroit attempts to master Thomas Aquinas's *quinque viæ* (at which one can only wince in pity and then look away). From whichever side the interlopers come, however, our first impulse when confronted by the conceptual disasters they perpetrate is, naturally enough, simply to reassert proper boundaries. To avoid the ghastly spectacle of Richard Dawkins attempting to philosophise, we are all too happy to adopt something like Stephen Jay Gould's strict discrimination between two 'non-overlapping magisteria', one concerned with facts, the other with values. But this achieves only the consonance of segregation – and at the cost of intolerably reductive accounts of both spheres. After all, the sciences invoke questions not only of physical origins, properties, and processes, but also (even if only indirectly) of their intrinsic intelligibility, rational coherence, and even modal plausibility, which inevitably touch upon questions that classical theology asks as well. Yes, quite obviously, the physical sciences have nothing to say about *dogmatic* theology – say, Trinitarian doctrine or Chalcedonian Christology – which concern hermeneutical approaches to particular historical events, social practices, personal and communal experiences of salvation, or allegedly revealed truths. But there is also theology in the wider sense, as delineated by, say, Proclus or the Pseudo-Dionysius or Shankara or Nicholas of Cusa or Mulla Sadra, which embraces a set of logical and speculative claims about reality as a whole, and about an ultimate coincidence between its rational structure and its actual existence. And each of these claims entails still further deductive claims regarding the divine ground of all that is: that, when reduced to its deepest source or most irreducible ontological premise, nature proves to be contingent ultimately not on some material substrate or order, but much more originally upon something analogous to mind, spirit, Geist – something, moreover, that is not simply yet another force among forces or being among beings, but the infinite plenitude of both being and rational order, in which all finite things participate. And in regard to these deductions, curiously enough, the sciences are not irrelevant, even if they are in some sense only preliminary. (But I shall return to this below.)

Rather, then, than discrete magisteria absorbed in absolutely discontinuous regions of concern, it might then seem better to adopt something closer to Thomas Aquinas's distinction between theology and philosophy (including natural philosophy), and say that we are concerned here with two autonomous practices of understanding, each of which encompasses vast areas of investigation concerning which the other has no competence, but both of which occasionally converge upon the same area, albeit each according to its own idiom and constraints. Thus, for Aquinas, both natural philosophy and theology may have a great deal to say about God (for instance), though the former might do so chiefly in terms of a Prime Mover or primary causality while the latter might do so chiefly in terms of the creator of heaven and earth or the Father of Christ. Even here, though, we risk making the issue of consonance too easy, if for no other reason than that a solution drawn from the high Middle Ages presumes a unified intellectual culture that, for better or worse, no longer exists. In a sense, the 'scientistic' polemicist who stumbles across unseen disciplinary boundaries in an ultracrepidarian stupor is not always entirely in the wrong; there are now in fact contested territories where the dissonances are quite real. Certainly, before all else there can be no accord reached between any theistic logic and the tacit mechanistic or physicalist or emergentist materialist metaphysics that so deeply informs much of the culture of the sciences today. And if we are seeking a consonance that consists in more than a few sporadic embassies between two otherwise alien realms, we have to interrogate precisely those cultural premises that now truly divide us. This is a rather delicate matter, naturally, because it involves a confrontation at a level that many in the sciences do not even acknowledge exists: that of their own metaphysical presuppositions. The first task, then, is to make the hidden metaphysical horizon of the modern sciences appear to view, and then perhaps to call it into question: not of course by simplistically conflating the cosmological and the ontological, as Krauss and Dawkins do, but rather by asking whether that essentially mechanistic picture of reality is adequate even to the realm of the physical. And I suspect that the best way to do this is to consider and reconsider the language of causality.

3.1 Excluding 'Higher Causes'

The extraordinary fruitfulness of modern scientific method was achieved, before all else, by a severe narrowing of investigative focus; and this involved the wilful shedding of an older language of causality that possessed great richness, but that also seemed to resist empirical investigation. The first principle of the new organon was a negative one: the exclusion of any consideration of formal and final causes, and even of any distinct principle of 'life', in favour of an ideally inductive method purged of metaphysical prejudices, allowing all natural systems to be conceived as mere machine processes, and all real causality as an exchange of energy through antecedent forces working upon material mass. Everything physical became, in a sense, reducible to the mechanics of local motion; even complex organic order came to be understood as the emergent result of physical forces moving through time from past to future as if through Newtonian space, producing consequences that were all mathematically calculable, with all discrete physical causes ultimately reducible to the most basic level of material existence. And while, at first, many of the thinkers of early modernity were content to draw brackets around physical nature, and to allow for the existence of realities beyond the physical – mind, soul, disembodied spirits, God – they necessarily imagined these latter as being essentially extrinsic to the purely mechanical order that they animated, inhabited, or created. Thus, in place of classical theism's metaphysics of participation in a God of infinite being and rationality, they granted room only for the adventitious and finite Cosmic Mechanic or Supreme Being of Deism or (as it is called today) Intelligent Design Theory. But, of course, this ontological liberality was unsustainable. Reason abhors a dualism. Any ultimate ground of explanation must be one that unites all dimensions of being in a simpler, more conceptually parsimonious principle. Thus, inevitably, what began as method soon metastasised into a metaphysics, almost by inadvertence. For a truly scientific view of reality, it came to be believed, everything – even mind – must be reducible to one and the same mechanics of motion. Those methodological brackets that had been so helpfully drawn around the physical order now became the very shape of reality itself.

It was always something of a fantasy, of course. For one thing, even as a method, the mechanical model extends only so far. Pure induction is an impossible ideal. In the life sciences, for instance, organisms can only very rarely be investigated without any hypothetical appeals to purpose whatsoever, or without treating organic structures as intentional systems; and it is only a metaphysical prejudice that dictates that explanations referring to purpose are no more than a useful and dispensable fiction. Moreover, before 'higher causes' like form and finality could be excised from the grammar of the sciences, they had first to be radically misconstrued. Even such residual Aristotelian terminology as remained in the sciences had already, by the late sixteenth century, been mechanised, so to speak. One need only read Francis Bacon to confirm this. Form and finality had come to be seen as physical forces or influences extrinsic to a material substrate that in itself was not the pure potentiality of 'prime matter' but merely a universal, subtle, ductile, unarticulated physical substance. The elements of nature were not imagined, as they had been in the classical and medieval synthesis, as having an intrinsic disposition toward order or vital integrity;

they were seen simply as inert ingredients upon which formal determinations were adventitiously impressed, under the external guidance of final causes that operated merely as factitious designs. And so, seen thus, form and finality soon came to seem not only superfluous suppositions, but little more than features of an inferior and obsolete mechanical model.

But, of course, one cannot really reject something one does not understand. Neither Aristotle's concept of an *aition* nor any scholastic concept of a *causa* actually corresponds to what we – following our early modern predecessors – mean when we speak of a 'cause'. A better rendering of *aitia* or *causae*, in the ancient or medieval sense, might be 'explanations', 'rationales', 'logical descriptions', or (still better) 'rational relations'. The older fourfold nexus of causality (Aristotle's material, efficient, formal, and final causes) was not, that is to say, a defective attempt at modern physical science, but was instead chiefly a grammar of predication, describing the inherent logical structure of anything that exists insofar as it exists, and reflecting a world in which things and events are at once discretely identifiable and yet part of the larger dynamic continuum of the whole. It was a simple logical picture of a reality in which both stability and change can be recognised and described. And these *aitia* or *causae* were intrinsic and indiscerptibly integral relations, distinct dimensions of a single causal logic, not separated forces in only accidental alliance. A final cause, for instance, was an inherent natural end, not an extrinsically imposed design, and this was true even when teleology involved external uses rather than merely internal perfections (as in the case of human artifacts); it was at once a thing's intrinsic fullness and its external participation in the totality of nature. Thus, in the *Liber de causis* (that mysterious digest and theological synthesis of the metaphysics of Proclus that entered Western scholasticism from the Islamic philosophical world) one of the principal 'causes' of any isolated substance is the taxonomic category in which that thing subsists, the more 'eminent' rational structure to which it belongs. In a sense, a causal *relation* in this scheme is less like a physical interaction or exchange of energy than like a mathematical equation, or like the syntax of a coherent sentence. Admittedly, this is a picture of reality that comes from ages in which it was assumed that the structure of the world was analogous to the structure of rational thought. But then again, this was an eminently logical assumption – if only because there appears to be a more than illusory or accidental reciprocal openness between mind and world, and because the mind appears genuinely able to penetrate the physical order by way of irreducibly noetic practices like mathematics and logic.

In any event, perhaps it really was necessary to impose the discipline of this impoverished causal language upon the scientific intellect, if only to direct its attention to the finest and humblest of empirical details. But even so, as Hegel so brilliantly demonstrated, one can never really reason purely from the particular. Once the notion of causality has been reduced from an integral system of rationales to a single kind of local physical efficiency, it becomes a mere brute fact, something of a logical black box; description flourishes, but only because explanation has been left to wither. So it was that Hume, having seen the spectral causal agencies of the schoolmen chased away, found causality itself now to be imponderable, logically reducible to nothing but an arbitrary sequence of regular phenomenal juxtapositions; even mathematical descriptions of events now became nothing more than reiterations of an episodic narrative without clear logical necessity. And this is indeed where we remain. Wherever induction fails to provide us with a clear physicalist narrative for especially complex or exceptional phenomena (like life or consciousness), we now must simply *presume* the existence and force of physico-mechanical laws sufficient to account for the emergence of such phenomena; and we must, moreover, do so no less casually and vaguely than those schoolmen of old supposedly presumed 'obscure' or 'occult' formal and final causes. We are no less dogmatic than our ancestors; we merely have fewer clear reasons for the dogmas we embrace. The older physical logic was coherent, though speculative; the newer is incoherent, though empirical. When mechanistic method became a metaphysics, and the tinted filter through which it viewed nature was mistaken for an unveiling of its deepest principles, all explanations became tales of emergence, even in cases of realities – life, consciousness, even existence itself – where such tales seemed difficult to distinguish from stories of magic.

3.2 A False Model of Nature

Nowhere is the essential arbitrariness of this picture of reality more obvious than in the alleged principle of the 'causal closure of the physical' – the principle that there simply cannot be any kind of 'causality' in nature other than brute material forces – which is so often invoked as a scientifically established truth, on the rather thin basis of the fixed proportionality of matter and energy in the universe, but which is merely a metaphysical dogma, and one that even otherwise sophisticated theorists often translate into the crudest kind of physical determinism. I have known learned physicists who still talk as if something like Laplace's fantasy holds true: a demon of superlative intelligence, knowing at a given instant the precise location and momentum of every atomic particle in existence, could both reconstruct the entire physical history of the universe and foresee its entire future. True, these physicists might all have granted that statistical thermodynamics probably dictates that this would not be literally possible; but still they spoke as if, in principle, all events at higher levels of physical organisation must be reducible – without remainder – to lower, more particulate causal moments. Hence, if our demon could somehow account for irreversibility or quantum indeterminacies – maybe by a perfect grasp of maximum entropy thermodynamics or by an occult knowledge of quantum hidden variables – he could, from the dispositions of all the atoms and molecules composing me and my environment last Wednesday at noon, have infallibly predicted my presence here today, because everything we do is the inevitable macroscopic result of the ensemble of impersonal physical forces underlying our formal existence.

And yet we know this to be false. This is the special absurdity of allowing an artificial method appropriate to an isolated perspective upon reality – nature considered as a machine, which is to say nature considered as though devoid of anything analogous to purposive intellect – to hypertrophy into a universal judgement on all of reality, including those of its aspects – such as, obviously, those instances of purposive intellect that actually exist – to which such a method cannot possibly apply. To whatever degree I am a physical system, I am also an intentional 'system' whose mental events take the forms of semiotic (symbolic, interpretive, 'meaningful') determinations, and whose actions are usually the consequences of intentions that are irreducibly teleological. As such, these intentions could appear nowhere within a reductive account of the discrete processes that constitute my actions as physical events; for final causes are not visible within any inventory of the impersonal antecedent physical events composing me. Simply said, I have reasons for being here, and reasons are qualitatively unlike mechanical forces, even when inseparably allied to them. Any good phenomenological description of my choice to be here would be one that could never be collapsed into a physical description of atomic, molecular, or even brain events. Yes, of course, at the level of the exchanges of matter and energy – or of their inter-changeable mathematical values – the natural order may always have to even out into an inflexible equation. But the movement of those material and energetic forces is also directed by causal (or rational) relations of a different kind, which impose upon the flow of physical events formal and final determinations that are not merely the phenomenal residue of those events, and that are not visible to those aforementioned physical inventories. The obvious physicalist riposte to this, of course, is to claim that all intentionality is in some sense illusory or reducible to complex electrochemical brain events, which are in turn reducible to molecular description, and then to atomic description, and so on. But that too is obviously false. Not that I have the time here to argue the point comprehensively (even if I thought it necessary). I will simply note that, over the past few years of my research in philosophy and science of mind, I have become more than convinced that every attempt to fit mental phenomena – qualitative consciousness, unity of apprehension, intentionality, reasoning, and so forth – into a physicalist narrative must prove a total failure. If nothing else, mental intentionality – in the full philosophical sense of determinations not only of the will but of every act of the mind in orienting itself toward specific ends, meanings, aspects of reality, and so on – is clearly a part of nature, and yet one whose irreducibly teleological structure is entirely contrary to the mechanical picture. This is why, among devout philosophical physicalists, such wild extremes as eliminativism and materialist panpsychism (with or without the supplement of the currently fashionable pseudoscience of 'Integrated Information Theory') are ever more in vogue. The mental, it turns out, is no more reconcilable to the modern picture of material nature than it was in Descartes's day.

Nor need we confine ourselves to the realm of the mental to call the mechanistic picture into question. It may well be that a conception of causality richer than what materialist orthodoxy can provide will ultimately prove just as necessary for molecular and evolutionary biology. At least, this is where a more diverse causal language seems constantly to be attempting to assert itself – top-down causation, circular causality, epigenetic information, symbiogenesis, teleonomy, convergent evolution, systems biology – even as traditional genetocentric neo-Darwinism strives to contain that language within its more linear narrative. And this is not simply on account of the failure of the human genome project to yield the master key to the entire mystery of life, from protein-folding to my love of Glenn Gould or Ella Fitzgerald. Life appears to be structurally hierarchical not only because evolution is a cumulative process, in which more complex levels are gradually superposed upon lower, self-sufficient levels, but because every discrete organism possesses a causal architecture in which there can be no single, privileged level of causation; each level depends on levels both above and below it, and none of these levels can be intelligibly isolated from the others as a kind of causal 'base'. At least, such is the contention of Denis Noble, perhaps the subtlest champion of systems biology or (as he also calls it) 'biological relativity'. Maybe there was a time when one could innocently think in terms of a master ground or centre of life, with the DNA molecule as the primordial genetic repository of information (whatever that means). And perhaps it seemed to make sense to understand life in terms of a very simple dichotomy between replicators and vehicles (those clever selfish genes and the organic 'robots' they program for their survival). Now though, argues Noble, we can scarcely even define a gene, let alone identify any genetic explanation of the entirety of living systems; nor can we ignore the degree to which DNA sequences are passive causes, variously informed and given expression as determined by the organism and its environment. And for Noble there is a special kind of beauty in the exquisite complexity of organic life; he positively delights in the interdependent simultaneity of all of life's functions, the way in which each level at once assembles the components of an immediately lower level while itself constituting a component of an immediately higher level: atoms, molecules, networks, organelles, cells, tissues, organs, holosomatic systems, complete organisms, populations, species, clades, the physical environment ... He even, daringly enough, talks freely of natural teleology – in part, because he understands that such teleology, properly understood, is an intrinsic rational determination within a complex system, not a factitious purpose extrinsically imposed by some detached designing intelligence; but in larger part because there clearly are levels of explanation at which purpose constitutes not just an illusory epiphenomenon of inherently purposeless material processes, but a real causal power. An organ, no matter how stochastic its phylogenetic history, exists within an organism *because* of the purpose it serves, apart from which it would not exist. And these levels are not reducible to one another, but exist only as a totality. Within the hierarchy of relations, there may be *discrete levels* of organisation, but no independent causal functions. The entire structure is a profoundly logical and purposive whole.

Now, maybe this intentional structure somehow emerges – biochemically and phylogenetically – from very primitive causes, which then become ingredients in a recursive system of interactions that were originally random or chaotic, and is therefore still reducible to a state prior to 'purpose'. But unless we are using the word 'emergence' as a synonym for 'miracle' or 'magic', we are still obliged to assume that the formal determinations of organic complexity – or, as we now call it, 'information' – are already present in those causes in at least latent or virtual form, awaiting explication in developed phenotypes (and other 'molar' or 'macroscopic' forms); and so we are also obliged to assume that whatever rational relations may exist in organisms (including form and finality) are already present in those seemingly random states. That is to say, we need not assume that, prior to the complex unity of a living system, some extrinsic 'design' existed within its material substrate like a kind of algorithm programmed by an intelligent designer; but we cannot doubt that everything that enters into the structure of a living system is already constituted by those rational causal relations that cause discrete purposive systems to arise. Even if we cannot say how life began, or how self-replicating organisms became available for natural selection, we can certainly doubt that those 'higher' causal relations are accidental accretions upon some single isolated aspect of their relations. 'Irreducible emergence' is a logical nonsense; whatever properties appear in an effect, unless imposed adventitiously, are already implicit in its 'lower' causes, even if only in a kind of virtual state. Perhaps even matter, then, in its barest constitution, already has something of the character of mind.

Even Noble, I should note, does not appreciate quite how radical the consequences of a hierarchical view of life might prove. At one point in his book *Dance to the Music of Life*, he invokes the old experiment of placing, say, a dozen metronomes on a wooden table and setting each in motion independently; over time, the initially asynchronous oscillations of the metronomes will become perfectly synchronised, solely as the result of the chaotic interactions of the vibrations passing between them through the resonant material of the table. This, he argues, is a splendid example of an 'initial disorder becoming highly ordered by interaction'. But this is wrong. Actually, it is a case of an initial complexity, stochastically but intricately syncopated, reduced over time to uniformity – which is to say, maximal equilibrium achieved by subsidence to a minimal expenditure of energy. This is not the emergence of order, but a descent into an entropic state, which preserves only such order as it cannot entirely eliminate (though in time, if left undisturbed, even this order will vanish, as table and metronomes alike resolve into dust). To fit the picture that Noble's account of life adumbrates, the oscillations of the metronomes would have to arrive not at perfect synchrony, but at something like the contrapuntal intricacies of a Buddy Rich cadenza or of Javanese and Balinese gamelan.

Then again, perhaps one need not look either to molecular and evolutionary biology or to the phenomena of mental life to see that the mechanical model of nature is defective. Really, perhaps, it is enough simply to consider the seemingly indivisible relation that exists between them in the very encounter between nature and mind: the intelligibility of the world and the power of thought to lay hold of it. Perhaps all we need consider is how the inherently formal and intentional structure of rational thought seems to correspond so fruitfully to the rational structure of the world. This by itself invites us to reconsider something at least like the causal language proposed in the Aristotelian tradition, in which (again) nature's deepest rational relations are more like the syntax of a sentence, or mathematical equations, than like mere accidental concrescences of physical forces. Perhaps modern prejudice has the matter backwards; perhaps it is mechanism that should be regarded as the dispensable methodological fiction, while the purposive language we use to isolate specific organic functions is the true reflection of reality. Perhaps mechanistic models never were anything more than artificial constraints, by which discrete processes might be prescinded from a whole that, in itself, has something like the structure of intentional thought. After all, it is absurd to think that a model created by the wilful exclusion of all mental properties from our picture of nature could then be used to account for the mental itself; and yet the mental is quite real, and quite at home within the natural order. If, then, one presumes a reductively physicalist model of all reality, but is then confronted by *any aspect* of nature that, as in the case of consciousness or intentionality, proves utterly resistant to mechanical description, the only responsible course of action is to abandon or suspend the model in regard to the *whole* of nature. If the phenomenon cannot be eliminated, the model is false.

Nor can we stop there. Once again, a certain principle of logical parsimony asserts itself here, and then invites or even obliges us completely to reverse our original supposition. Reason abhors a dualism, as I have said; ideally, all phenomena should be reducible to a single, simpler, more capacious model of reality. Far from continuing to banish mind from our picture of nature, then, perhaps we should reconsider the ancient intuition that nature and mind are not alien to one another precisely because nature already possesses a rational structure analogous to thought. Perhaps the ground of the possibility of regular physical causation, in the energetic and mechanical sense, is a deeper logical co-inherence of rational relations underlying all reality; and hence mind inhabits physical nature not as an anomaly but as a revelation of the deepest essence of everything that exists. The intentionality of mind, then, is neither a ghostly agency inexplicably haunting a machine nor an illusion reducible to non-intentional and impersonal forces, but instead the most intense and luminous expression of those formal and teleological determinations that give actuality to all nature. What makes us believe we should – or, for that matter, can – think otherwise?

3.3 The Limits of Inquiry

What difference might all this make for the sciences, practically speaking? Little or none, really. The sciences need not aspire to total exhaustive explanation; they are often most powerful when they consist largely in local and narrow investigations, and then in theoretical interpretations of very particular discoveries. For the *culture* of the sciences, however, as well as for a true consonance (rather than a mere amicable segregation) between the sciences and theology, it could scarcely be more consequential. For one thing, it is always salubrious to be reminded of the limits of our methods; and, for anyone committed to the search for truth, it is always wise to think about the universal frame of reality within which one's investigations take place. If one does this, one may approach a place where the deepest aspirations of the sciences and the most essential affirmations of theology prove to be both irresistibly apposite. When we think seriously about the complex rational structure of reality and the way in which it seems to be reflected in the structure of rational mind, we enter the realm of spirit, of intellect, of a formal and final logic in nature already analogous to mind or rational thought. Perhaps only for this reason can the veil of Isis be lifted, and nature be revealed to mind, and perhaps it is also only for this reason that mind can inhabit nature. Here the physical sciences themselves urge us toward a certain metaphysical supposition. It may be that, pursued to its logical terminus, the very enterprise of scientific reasoning suggests or even secretly presumes that the being of the world – the ontological horizon within which it takes shape and exists – is something like an act of thought. Here the questions of science and those of theology converge upon the same mysteries, not through some maladroit confusion of two incompatible kinds of causal narrative (the cosmological and the ontological, say), but quite naturally, because the very concept of causality itself still demands for itself the full richness of all its possible logical acceptations. No physical science can answer or explain away the mysteries that here come into view – neither can any theology – but both would do well to recognise the threshold upon which they stand.

All the labours of the scientific intellect are undertaken within the embrace of a structure of intelligibility that the sciences need not pretend to understand, penetrate, or encompass, but that nevertheless sustains them in all their labours. That intelligibility is the transcendental horizon toward which they necessarily strive, even when they hew faithfully to the limits of their proper remit. It shows itself to be nothing other than that original experience of the radiant mystery of being that first awakens the desire for truth, but now translated into a fixed orientation of the rational will. The sciences venture all their energies upon the reality of this ultimate rational intelligibility – upon the wager that the world's being and its structure of rational order are one and the same event. Thus they undertake their perpetual journey toward an end that perhaps, in principle, they cannot reach: to disclose a perfect reciprocal transparency between mind and world, and hence an ultimate reality where existence and perfect intelligibility are convertible with one another because both subsist in a single unrestricted act of spiritual intelligence. This, in theological terms, is one of the paths of the mind's journey into God. And this is also, at least in its ultimate intentions, a place where the consonance of scientific and theological reasoning is restored, on the far side of a provisional separation that at times has become an alienation. Both pursuits set out originally upon their different paths from the same innocent instant of existential amazement, and both together end, after all their several peregrinations, at a place where description fails, but where that primordial wonder finds its final consummation in wisdom: the threshold of that mystery – the cause of causes, the explanation of explanations, the holy of holies – toward which both are forever turned. And however different the paths by which they have reached this sanctuary, each approaches it at the end ideally not as a stranger in a far country but as a pilgrim entering a long-sought holy land.

CHAPTER 4

Religion, Science and Magic
Rewriting the Agenda

John Milbank

4.1 Introduction: A New Intellectual Programme

The aim of the new 'After Science and Religion' project is to call into question an entire existing intellectual discourse and to try to forge a new one in its place. In what follows, I shall try to describe the outlines of this new programme, its historical and theoretical contentions, and some key points of authorial reference, in a preliminary schematic fashion.

The existing discourse tends to assume that there have more or less always, or for a very long time, existed discrete realms called 'science' and 'religion'. These are sometimes seen as locked in inevitable conflict, or at least tension. Thus, for example, one can sometimes read that, in biology, doctrines of epigenesis were held back by theological doctrines of preformation.[1] Yet, in reality, a belief in divine creative power often just as much favoured the former, while a rationalistic immanentism has sometimes favoured the latter.

Where it is, by contrast, merely a case of perceived rather than inevitable tension between religion and science, then apologetic arguments tend to develop in order to meet anti-religious hostility on the part of some scientists. Characteristically, these try to show how a more rigorous, usually Christian monotheism, by further disenchanting a pagan universe, first gave rise to modern science.[2]

In addition to this, or in complement to it, one has hybrid discourses which try to show either how modern scientific outlooks favour belief, or how and why belief must be adapted in order to assimilate modern discoveries about nature.

[1] See Edward Dolnick, *The Seeds of Life* (New York: Basic Books, 2017).

[2] See, for example, Stanley L. Jaki, *The Origin of Science and the Science of Its Origin* (Edinburgh: Scottish Academic Press, 1979).

4.2 The History of 'Science'

As Peter Harrison and others have shown, the trouble with this set of approaches is that the modern distribution of academic disciplines and cultural spheres is very recent indeed. The phrase 'experimentall science' was first used in English in the seventeenth century by the occult philosopher John Dee, who borrowed it from Nicholas of Cusa's Latin: *scientia experimentalis.*[3] And specific textual treatments of topics in mechanics, optics, magnetism or astronomy were sometimes entitled 'new science' in the early modern period. But overall, the treatment of nature fell within 'natural philosophy', which was not totally divorced from metaphysics and theology.

'Science' as a specifically recognised field of knowledge is no older than William Whewell in the nineteenth century and belongs to specifically Anglo-Saxon culture.[4] Its emergence had to do with an attempt to promote a unity of disparate fields of enquiry into nature, a Baconian re-insistence on their technological usefulness, a drive for public funding for them and eventually an attempt to separate science from natural theology as the previous overarching discourse concerning nature, with an accompanying segregation of lay, professional and male from clerical, amateur and female practitioners. Only in the wake of these developments did notions of a 'perennial' conflict between science and religion first arise. It was accentuated when attempts were made to revive, beyond Enlightenment neo-humanism, the application of 'exact' understanding also to human realities – something that had been present (contrary to much received opinion) already in the seventeenth century 'scientific revolution': for example, with Hobbes and Locke.[5]

The more inchoate human sciences of the eighteenth century, often linked to a new sense that 'sentiment' gives a prior access to reality, cannot really be regarded, as Stephen Gaukroger argues, as the prime origin of our contemporary notion of a single unified and uniquely prestigious scientific field. He is on much stronger ground in claiming that the idea of such a field is in reality an illusion: that now, as in the past, experimental and mathematical approaches do not always cohere, and that much of what we

[3] Richard J. Oosterhoff, *Making Mathematical Culture: University and Print in the Circle of Lefèvre D'Étaples* (Oxford: Oxford University Press, 2018), 212.

[4] Peter Harrison, *The Territories of Science and Religion* (Chicago: University of Chicago Press, 2015).

[5] See, for example, Ethan H. Shagan, *The Birth of Modern Belief* (Princeton, NJ: Princeton University Press, 2018), 232.

think of as science is driven by engineering and medical practice, and not by the application of prior existing theory.[6]

Meanwhile, on the Continent, in the early nineteenth century, the 'science' of nature often continued to mean vaguely just one mode of knowledge that could also still be described as 'philosophy of nature'. In the case of Germany, *Naturphilosophie* was practised not just by philosophers but by those we would today think of as 'scientists'.[7] And it may be wholly significant that the physics that has eventually triumphed in the twentieth century in many ways derives as much from this, often romantically rooted current, as from British 'science' grounded in both a Baconian and a Newtonian legacy.

For example, Bernhard Riemann's discovery of non-Euclidean geometry physicalises geometry, where Descartes had done the reverse, and thereby thinks of three-dimensionality as a contingency, held together by vital, occult forces.[8] Without this effectively mystical reconception, Einstein could not have thought of the whole of space as a curved surface, and developed his subversions of Newton, apparently removing the need to think of gravity as a 'force', and of motion as operating against a fixed background which it does not reciprocally alter – even if his suppression of the originally vitalist and so forceful assumption behind this conception has profound links to his later problematic relationship to quantum mechanics. How, after all, can space be considered 'curved', which is an inherently relative term, if it is also claimed to be absolute space-time as such?[9]

Insofar as the British made a contribution to modern physics, it was often in terms of an honest negativity concerning the failure of the Newtonian vision, besides their own versions of a post-Newtonian exploration of irreducibly non-mechanical forces, as with James Clerk Maxwell's supremely important integration of electricity, magnetism and light.[10]

However, both in public mythology and to an extraordinary extent amongst scientists themselves, 'science' is nowadays understood in terms of certain supposedly crucial historical episodes which are used to support

6 Stephen Gaukroger, *Civilization and the Culture of Science: Science and the Shaping of Modernity, 1795–1935* (Oxford: Oxford University Press, 2020), 423–35.

7 Bruce Rosenstock, *Transfinite Life: Oskar Goldberg and the Vitalist Imagination* (Bloomington: Indiana University Press, 2017), 1–75.

8 Ibid., 47–8.

9 See Edward Feser, *Aristotle's Revenge: The Metaphysical Foundations of Physical and Biological Science* (Neunkirchen-Seelscheid: Editiones Scholasticae, 2019), 279.

10 Gaukroger, *Civilisation and the Culture of Science*, 104–21.

a myth of progress and the debatable notion that 'science', unlike philosophy, art and religion, has a uniquely cumulative character, never needing to revert to abandoned styles and models, nor to refer to 'classic' texts and paradigms of the past. These historical episodes are above all (1) Galilean and Newtonian physics of the seventeenth century, (2) Darwinian evolution and (3) Einsteinian relativity, with quantum physics as a problematic footnote.

The first episode is seen as a 'revolutionary' and irreversible overthrowing of older cosmologies and accounts of physics, the second of an older natural history and the third as evidence that science is a process of *continuous* revolution: of a permanently sustained counter-intuitive disturbing of anthropocentric illusions.

Yet if one attends to the historical fluctuation of disciplinary boundaries, then these three ruptures, and the supposed underlying continuity of 'science', appear in a very different light. The seventeenth-century physics that is celebrated as most of all paradigmatic belonged to a hybrid physico-theological discourse, and triumphed for essentially theological reasons to do with both the banishing of immanent enchantment and a primarily *religious* shift towards basing belief upon evidence.[11] It was by no means perfectly integrated with chemical, medicinal and natural historical disciplines that flourished within the same era.[12] Often, indeed, the most crucial founders of 'experimental science' like Boyle and Newton were themselves caught within the resulting tensions, which they never satisfactorily resolved.[13]

Darwinianism, after Thomas Huxley, was promoted for essentially atheist or at least agnostic reasons, and remained in tension with other, often more vitalistic and teleological biological theories – especially, but not exclusively, on the Continent.[14] Charles Darwin's doubtful dogmatism about natural selection as the sole motor of evolution derived largely from a mistaken desire to apply a Newtonian 'covering law' model inappropriately to the natural historical sphere.[15]

[11] Shagan, *The Birth of Modern Belief*, 227–36.

[12] See E. A. Burtt, *The Metaphysical Foundations of Modern Science* [1925] (New York: Anchor Books, 1954), 163–7; Amos Funkenstein, *Theology and the Scientific Imagination: From the Middle Ages to the Seventeenth Century* (Princeton, NJ: Princeton University Press, 1986); Charles Webster, *From Paracelsus to Newton: Magic and the Making of Modern Science* (New York: Dover, 2013).

[13] Michael Hunter, *Boyle: Between God and Science* (New Haven, CT: Yale University Press, 2010); Michael White, *Isaac Newton: The Last Sorcerer* (London: Fourth Estate, 1997).

[14] I am indebted here to discussions with Rupert Sheldrake.

[15] David J. Depew and Bruce H. Weber, *Darwinism Evolving: Systems Dynamics and the Genealogy of Natural Selection* (Cambridge, MA: MIT Press, 1995); Conor Cunningham, *Darwin's Pious Idea: Why the Ultra-Darwinists and Creationists Both Get It Wrong* (Grand Rapids, MI: Eerdmans, 2011).

Einstein, who largely inaugurated quantum physics as well as relativity, stood at the culmination of a long process of the defeat of a certain physico-theology, and in this respect his affinity with both the scepticism of Hume and the non-dualist theology of Spinoza is significant.[16] However, his hesitations about the direction taken by quantum physics are much to do with the continuing lure of the myth of Newton and a desire after all somehow to rescue the now 'classical' physical model, with its claimed completeness of predictive power; its absolutising of space, time and motion; and equivalent removal of all real potential, force and change in the real and radical sense.[17] Even today, many popular guides to physics try as far as possible to suppress the unavoidable fact of a quite drastic break with this legacy which preceded quantum physics but is consummated by it.

4.3 The Three Different Visions of Physical Reality

If there is any overall continuity in the history of 'science' in relation to 'religion', then, it does not lie in the sphere of disciplinary confinements and consequent interdisciplinary unease. Instead, with all due qualifications and nuancing, one can speak instead of tensions and conflicts, existing ever since the twelfth century, between three different visions of physical reality.

The first is one of a 'disenchanted transcendence' which tends to regard symbolic realism, or what Michel Foucault called 'the prose of the world' – the whole idea that Creation has been variously 'signed' by its creator – with suspicion, both as harbouring too many shadows of demi-gods and as impugning the freedom of the God of the Bible. In consequence, this vision eventually proved hospitable to a de-equivocation of dialectic and of being, to a denial of emanative flux as describing the process of Creation, and to a denial also of the reality of universals and relations as opposed to isolated particulars. Eventually, this mentality encouraged the re-emergence of antique atomism.

In addition, any qualitative difference between the celestial and the terrestrial within the cosmic order was rebutted. Because God was now seen as an almighty infinite being nonetheless lying within the same

[16] Albert Einstein, *Autobiographical Notes*, trans. P. A. Schillp (Chicago: Open Court, 1979), 51; G. S. Viereck, *Glimpses of the Great* (New York: Macauley, 1930), 372–3.

[17] John Gribbin, *Six Impossible Things: The 'Quanta of Solace' and the Mysteries of the Subatomic World* (London: Icon, 2019).

univocal ontological plane as created beings, Creation itself, by the time of the seventeenth century, came to be regarded as a kind of container separate from God. It was also regarded as an inherently empty container, since God is free to determine its contents as he likes. Partly in consequence, space and time became abstracted and absolutised, with motion being thought of as belonging essentially and questionably to the kinetic rather than dynamic trajectories of discrete individual items against this neutral background.[18] Such a picture was reinforced from the opposite direction, insofar as focus on the kinetic allowed a positivist bracketing of the questions of the ultimate forces that might be at work – a bracketing itself linked to a pious agnosticism in the face of a God conceived in terms of an inscrutable will.[19]

There was no unquestionable 'progress' involved in this re-construal of motion and of cosmology. Galileo's attack on terrestrial fixity required inconvenient empirical observations to be glossed in terms of new 'natural interpretations' that were themselves altogether unproven: in this case the relativity of all motion and 'the law of circular inertia'. Similarly inconvenient observations were sidelined in relation to Copernicus's heliocentrism, by the insinuation of a new common sense, for which the observations made through a telescope would be 'obviously' more reliable than those made by the naked eye.[20] But there is nothing obvious here, for a rival supposition could be that our eyes as themselves natural may, at least in some crucial respects, be better adapted to observe how nature really is. Experiment and the use of observational prostheses are always ambiguous: they can reveal genuine hidden realities and provide clues to hidden causes, yet by always inevitably altering (which does not, however, necessarily mean distorting) what is being dealt with or regarded, they also always risk concealing other realities or not, after all, accounting for ordinary appearances, which are themselves fully real.

Given the onticisation of God and the increasingly zero-sum or 'concursive' and potentially competitive view of his interaction with finite causes, divine proximity and omnipresence got redefined more in terms of a literal 'closeness' of God to a separate, created reality, which sometimes took the form of the notion that God is nearer to a certain dimension of the Cosmos than another: to space in the case of Henry More, to time in

[18] Funkenstein, *Science and the Theological Imagination*, 57–70, 117–202; Stephen Gaukroger, *The Emergence of a Scientific Culture: Science and the Shaping of Modernity 1210–1685* (Oxford: Oxford University Press, 2006), 49–86.

[19] Burtt, *The Metaphysical Foundations*, 98–104.

[20] Paul Feyerabend, *Against Method* (New York: Verso, 1975), 49–72.

the case of Isaac Barrow, to both in the case of Barrow's pupil, Isaac Newton.[21]

A crucial problem for contemporary theology is that, on the whole, it regards this sort of disenchanted outlook as a historical disaster, and yet it is just this outlook which undergirded what, in the popular and even much of the scientific mind, is the very epitome of successful science.

One can only dissipate this quandary by trying to undermine an entire scientistic mythology: by suggesting that things might have originally gone otherwise and that they eventually did, in such a way that later, post-Newtonian physics in some ways echoes earlier theological approaches to the physical world, as Thomas Torrance argued (albeit rather imperfectly), in relation to the work of Robert Grosseteste in the twelfth century,[22] or as others have argued in relation to the radical and 'magical' animistic immanentism or semi-immanentism of, respectively, Giordano Bruno and Tommaso Campanella.[23]

The second historical vision, in extreme tension with the first, is, as in the case of Bruno, 'enchanted immanence'. This refers to different modes of immanentist naturalism, which can be variously neo-stoic, neoplatonic or Aristotelian. Right back in the twelfth century, it would seem, there were pantheistic exacerbations of the thought of Eriugena put forward by Amalric of Bène and David of Dinant (though we cannot be sure that they were not simply misunderstood by officialdom). Later, one has the different naturalisms put forward by both Latin Avicennians and Latin Averroists, all the way to Pietro Pomponazzi in the Renaissance, and following that the revival of neo-stoic visions in the work of Telesio and others, eventually perpetuated in different ways by Bruno, Baruch de Spinoza and still later John Toland.[24]

[21] Funkenstein, *Science and the Theological Imagination*, 23–20; Gaukroger, *The Emergence of a Scientific Culture*, 129–53; Burtt, *The Metaphysical Foundations*, 135–61. For *concursus* versus *influentia*, see John Milbank, *Beyond Secular Order: The Representation of Being and the Representation of the People* (Oxford: Wiley-Blackwell, 2013), 99–105.

[22] Thomas Torrance, 'Creation and Science', in *The Ground and Grammar of Theology* (Charlottesville: University of Virginia Press, 1980), 144–75. One can also note here that the natural philosophical interests of the Albertine lineage in German Scholasticism – Dietrich of Freiburg, Ulrich of Strasbourg, etc. – in optics, especially, represented a more neoplatonic approach than that favoured by the Merton school in Oxford.

[23] Hilary Gatti, *Giordano Bruno and Renaissance Science* (Ithaca, NY: Cornell University Press, 1999); Brian P. Copenhaver and Charles B. Schmitt, *Renaissance Philosophy* (Oxford: Oxford University Press, 1992), 303–28.

[24] Funkenstein, *Theology and the Scientific Imagination*, 42–7; Gaukroger, *The Emergence of a Scientific Culture*, 101–16; Copenhaver and Schmitt, *Renaissance Philosophy*, 60–126.

One of the most crucial things to grasp is that the historical triumph of the first vision, of disenchanted transcendence, far from being a subversive advance, is really the result of a series of attempts to head off the real naturalistic radicals: these being, respectively, the early modern pantheists, and those who had already in the Middle Ages developed an Aristotelianism within the Liberal Arts Faculty that makes no reference to Creation – so seeming to allow both the eternity of the world and of matter.[25] The long route to Galileo, Descartes and Newton arises after the papal and episcopal condemnations of 1270–7 designed to head off perceived Aristotelian and (to a much lesser degree) neoplatonic excesses.[26]

Similarly, after the later triumphs of Reformation and Counter-Reformation, Renaissance naturalism was refused and seventeenth-century physics was in some ways articulated against the outright paganism of Giordano Bruno, or even supposed lesser compromises with such paganism, besides mystical Judaism. One sees this especially with the entirely instrumentalist and technological nominalism and voluntarism of Marin Mersenne. Even scholastic 'form' now started to be seen as too animistic, particularly with Descartes.[27] Mersenne and Gassendi articulated their position partly in opposition to the Anglican Hermeticist Robert Fludd, and in their case one can argue that they saw themselves as opposing a kind of rival Protestant 'pan-sacramentalism', even though a recently previous Catholic establishment had been more prepared to see parallels between, for example, alchemical and sacramental transmutations – just as the Medieval Church had effectively mixed the liturgical with the magical in terms of the blessing of crops and so forth.[28]

As Stephen Toulmin argued and Bruno Latour now seconds, the 'counter-renaissance' reaction against 'animated matter', after roughly 1610, was partly driven by its association with the political 'animation' of popular forces and with sceptical uncertainty. The new search for natural philosophical (what we think of as 'scientific') certainty was not

[25] See François-Xavier Putallaz, *Insolente liberté: Controverses et condemnations au XIIIe siècle* (Paris: Cerf, 1995), 15–45; Claude Lafleur and Joanne Carrier, *L'Enseignement de la philosophie au XIIIe siècle: Autour du 'Guide de L'étudiant du Ms Ripoli 109'* (Quebec: Brepols, 1997).

[26] Lesser, because in fact an Albertine, neoplatonic route is sustained and even revived beyond this date, as by Meister Eckhart. But obviously his fate showed that this very influential current could still be ambivalently regarded.

[27] Robert Lenoble, *Histoire de l'idée de nature* (Paris: Albin Michel, 1969); Henri Gouhier, *Les premièr pensées de Descartes: contribution à l'histoire de l'anti-renaissance* (Paris: Vrin, 1979).

[28] Morris Berman, *The Reenchantment of the World* (Ithaca, NY: Cornell University Press, 1981), 69–132; Carolyn Merchant, *The Death of Nature: Women, Ecology and the Scientific Revolution* (New York: HarperCollins, 1989).

in tension, but rather fused, with a renewed search for religious certainty after humanist attempts at mediating compromise were deemed to have failed.[29] A greater turn now ensued to 'extrinsic', founding authority, either for Catholics in magisterial authority or for Protestants in Scripture alone, whose well-attested, rational evidence, or at least high degree of probability, could elicit 'justified belief'. Such evidence applied both to God's ultimate causation of nature and to his revealing of now reductively propositional truths. It follows that search for secure 'belief' did not divide, but rather united religion and natural philosophy.[30] What we think of as the 'absolute' authority of science itself emerges from a new attempt in a hysterically insecure age to give a more absolute authority to Christianity, itself now construed more narrowly and rigidly. Thereby, it becomes apparent that in the long term the eventual imperialist focussing of Western culture around the claims of its 'science' is a successor project to the universalising claims of Christianity, later mutated in this more absolutist and foundationalist direction.

And yet we now know that the triumph of mechanical theology was not final nor determinative for the whole subsequent history of 'science'. Brunonian radicalism revived with figures like John Toland in the later seventeenth century, and once Ralph Cudworth had correctly qualified Isaac Casaubon to show that the Hermetic writings were not, after all, outright forgeries, and might indeed preserve some elements of ancient and so perhaps also (as he supposed) Mosaic wisdom, an entire 'esoteric' current of thought enjoyed a new lease of life from Newton onwards into the eighteenth century, and did not have to wait upon Romantic revival.[31]

The most crucial point here is that the radicals like Toland tended to embrace occult affinities, hidden sympathies and ultimately explanatory vital forces, and often, in consequence, the continued possibility of natural magic, however named or renamed.[32] The cognitive 'left wing', as it were, was not therefore characterised by an embrace of dead mechanism: far

[29] Stephen Toulmin, *Cosmopolis: The Hidden Agenda of Modernity* (Chicago: University of Chicago Press, 1992); Bruno Latour, *Facing Gaia: Eight Lectures on the New Climatic Regime*, trans. Catherine Porter (Cambridge: Polity, 2017), 186–90.

[30] Shagan, *The Birth of Modern Belief*, 65–249; Michel de Certeau, *The Mystic Fable*, trans. Michael Smith (Chicago: University of Chicago Press, 1992).

[31] Jan Assmann, *Moses the Egyptian: The Memory of Egypt in Western Monotheism* (Cambridge, MA: Harvard University Press, 1997), 20; Margaret Jacob, *The Radical Enlightenment: Pantheists, Freemasons and Republicans* (Lafayette, LA: Cornerstone, 2006); White, *Isaac Newton*.

[32] Paul Kléber Monod, *Solomon's Secret Arts: The Occult in the Age of the Enlightenment* (New Haven, CT: Yale University Press, 2013); John V. Fleming, *The Dark Side of the Enlightenment: Wizards, Alchemists and Spiritual Seekers in the Age of Reason* (New York: W. W. Norton, 2013).

from it, as we see in the case of the anti-Christian Denis Diderot or the non-Christian Goethe in the eighteenth century.[33] And this variegated faction is as much a part of the 'history of science' as is 'disenchanted transcendence'.

The third historically descended vision is 'enchanted transcendence': a more traditional view that was sustained, albeit in variously mutated forms, within the modern area and in the hinterland of 'science'. Here, the Cambridge Platonists can be offered as, to some degree, revealing representatives. On the one hand, as moderate Puritan Anglicans, they had become alert to the eventually atheistic dangers of disenchanted transcendence. A dead world might eventually dispense with the living God. Or else the God of such a world appeared to be simply a tyrant, or the most ultimately powerful material force, as with Thomas Hobbes. A disenchanted world, without either life or 'magic' as Cudworth specifically and literally says, is also a world without goodness and beauty, or natural human fellowship.

On the other hand, the Cambridge thinkers (and their associates beyond Cambridge) equally opposed the so-called hylozoists, the Spinozists and the Hermetic left, advocates of a purely immanentist vitalism. Cudworth and More already realised that if everything is equally alive and cognitive, then nothing is especially so, and therefore one is faced with another mode of reduction. Moreover, if every single thing is self-moving and responsive, how does everything hold together?[34] The immanentist answer can only be in terms of the entire whole, as for Spinoza. But that results in a determinism and a subordination of the reality of the particular and the relational.[35]

[33] See Stephen Gaukroger, *The Collapse of Mechanism and the Rise of Sensibility: Science and the Shaping of Modernity 1680–1760* (Oxford: Oxford University Press, 2010).

[34] Funkenstein, *Theology and the Scientific Imagination*, 77–80.

[35] Frequently, as in the case of both Newton and Robert Boyle, natural philosophers in the seventeenth century tried to blend, or oscillated between, disenchanted and enchanted versions of monotheism. Boyle variously combined a voluntarist mechanism with elements of vitalism, including a vitalist mode of atomism and theories of a spiritual 'spring' in the air, besides alchemical notions derived from J. B. Van Helmont of Flanders and perpetuated by the earliest prominent American scientist George Starkey, with whom Boyle was in communication. Associations of experiment with the revelation of wonders could contribute to rationalist materialists like Thomas Hobbes being disparaging about them, as in the case of his dispute with Boyle. See William R. Newman and Lawrence M. Principe, *Alchemy Tried in the Fire: Starkey, Boyle and the Fate of Helmontian Chemistry* (Chicago: University of Chicago Press, 2005); Stephen Shapin and Simon Schaffer, *Leviathan and the Air-Pump: Hobbes, Boyle and the Experimental Life* (Princeton, NJ: Princeton University Press, 2011).

In these ways, the Cambridge Platonists to an extent (and with varying degrees of authenticity) tried to renew a Patristic, High Medieval and early Renaissance mode of enchanted transcendence. For this perspective, in the most general terms, Creation is also emanation and theophany. The world is in consequence the symbolic book of nature. As fallen, it must be read through the other revealed book of the Bible, which uniquely, by way of the inspiration of the human spirit, evokes, and in words remotely repeats (as the Kabbalists, who strongly influenced More, had thought) the lost gesture of divine creation, just as it recalls the hidden cosmic rupture of the Fall and invites, eventually elicits, and records the Incarnation of God into the world by which he restores and renews it.

Yet the biblical book is merely a key: by recoding natural reality it asks us to read that reality again in its light, in order to realise the world's true amplitude of disclosure. Only by doing this – by seeing that the two books are interleaved, do not exist merely in mutually confirming parallel, as a more disenchanted transcendence supposes – do we then perceive the deeper allegorical meanings of scripture: the way it always points to the original and renewable creation, to each individual spiritual life and to the final consummation. Or rather, only from the interaction of both texts do we see that therein lies the full scope of their conjoined meaning.[36]

Thus Wordsworth in *The Prelude*, which invokes More's and Cudworth's 'plasticity' both in nature and in his own imaginative power,[37] reflects that in his lapsed era he has been better instructed by northern nature than by the decadent (post-Platonic) learning of southern Cambridge, fallen away from its once ascetic central focus on Scripture, as Wordsworth thinks pertained in both the Middle Ages and (notably) the early Reformation.[38] At one point in the poem he celebrates a Cumbrian old lady's 'clear though shallow stream of piety' whose 'fresher course' on Sunday afternoons involved the reading of her Bible. The poet 'loved when she has dropped asleep / And made of it a pillow for her head'.[39] Surely, this is a figure of the nestling of the one great book in the lap of the other – the 'naturalisation' of the Bible itself.

[36] Henri de Lubac, *Scripture in the Tradition*, trans. Luke O'Neill (Chicago: Crossroad, 2001).

[37] William Wordsworth, *The Prelude* (1805), Book II, lines 380–419, and Book IV, lines 150–61, in *The Prelude: The Four Texts (1798, 1799, 1805, 1850)* (London: Penguin, 1995), 94–6, 148.

[38] *The Prelude* (1805), Book III, lines 459–91, p. 128.

[39] *The Prelude* (1805), Book IV, lines 207–21, p. 152.

4.4 Enchanted Transcendence

In terms of its outlook on the cosmos, enchanted transcendence embraces a vision which is analogical, participatory and hierarchical. It does not debase the high to the low, like a purely mechanical philosophy, but neither does it elevate the low to the high like pure vitalism, thereby risking the obliteration of qualitative difference.[40] Somewhat like Cudworth and More, it tends to allow, for example, a relatively mechanical play of the more local and isolated, and yet to see shaping and unifying forces everywhere at work, and to read even atoms as more like lesser forms of life and cognition, than reading life and mind as infinitely complex modes of atomic interaction. There is a hierarchy, but lesser is generously read in terms of more rather than vice versa, precisely because the more is seen as more instigating.

Cudworth and More still, however, offered too much dualism between atomism and vitalism, and between body and mind, rendering their work in one respect, after all, but a version of disenchanted transcendence. More, especially, but to a degree also Cudworth, far too much accepted a self-sufficient mechanism as 'regionally' entirely true, requiring qualification only in terms of inexplicable 'exceptions', including the overall framework of moving reality, which in More's case got attributed both to a direct and literal presence of God and to a 'spirit of nature', regarded too much as his 'underworker', at a supplementary distance from his entire providential control.[41] The route to Newton's metaphysical Arianism, for which Christ's spiritual body upholds the operation of strange forces acting at a distance, is all too apparent here. By contrast, the Quaker philosopher Anne Conway later showed how one could import more Spinozism and alchemical vitalism into the Cambridge Platonic vision, without denying divine transcendence.[42] For her (as indeed once for Church Fathers like Maximus and Augustine), the most basic elements of reality are suffused with vital energy.

For enchanted transcendence there also tends to be less of a distinction between physics and metaphysics. Motion was by Aristotle granted a

[40] For an account of this vision in general, see Paul Tyson, *Returning to Reality: Christian Platonism for Our Times* (Eugene, OR: Wipf and Stock, 2014). For its application to natural science, see Michael Hanby, *No God, No Science: Theology, Cosmology, Biology* (Oxford: Wiley-Blackwell, 2016).

[41] Burtt, *The Metaphysical Foundations*, 135–50.

[42] Anne Conway, *The Principles of the Most Ancient and the Most Modern Philosophy* (Cambridge: Cambridge University Press 1996); Merchant, *The Death of Nature*, 253–74. And see Chapter 7 of this volume by Catherine Pickstock.

qualified ontological status as intermediate between potency and act. Power as potential also has ontological weight, though it is inherently orientated to act of which it is a privation: totally unlike the basically amoral primacy of power in the later theological model of disenchanted transcendence. Causality as formal, final and material, in a fused integration with efficiency, belongs to the very structure of being: the way things 'account for themselves' in order to exist at all.[43]

Thus mere physical motion could, for the Aristotelian-influenced Aquinas, point all the way to God, whereas being, taken in abstraction from motion, modality and perfection (all implying orders of causation), did not for him do so, in his apparent refusal of the Anselmian mode of argumentation to divine existence (ST. I. q.1.a.3)[44]

In his combination of Aristotle with Proclus, Aquinas sought to do justice to both horizontal and vertically generative processes of motion, and at the culmination of the metaphysical hierarchy, horizontal procession is given a kind of eminent ultimacy within the Divine Trinity. His recognition of rising degrees of more and more intimate and so constitutive emanative relation in the cosmos (in the *Compendium* and at SCG 4.11) returns him at depth to a kind of 'trans-physics' of the kind that was earlier articulated by Eriugena. The latter saw even God as falling within 'nature' rather than the metaphysical, which actually for Aquinas delineates most primarily merely immanent existence.[45]

Aquinas's cosmos, like that of his teacher Albert the Great, was one of inevitably obscure analogical linkages between incommensurate ontological levels, and of a holding of everything together within a 'convenient' order aesthetically appreciable, rather than rationally surveyable with complete surety. He also cautiously recognised, in a preserved letter, the 'occult' properties of things, which are the result of invisible substantive forms and which we can to a degree deploy legitimately to our (strictly) natural advantage in sympathetic invocation of natural, including angelic, forces.[46] Thus the use of unmarked amulets and other charms is allowed, but not of 'magical' marked or signed stones and amulets – which, since

[43] See David Hart's chapter in the present volume.

[44] In reality, *Anselm's argument assumes a Platonic causal order of rising perfections.*

[45] See John Milbank, 'Manifestation and Procedure: Trinitarian Metaphysics after Albert the Great and Thomas Aquinas', in *Tomismo Creativo: Letture Contemporanee del* Doctor Communis, ed. Marco Salvioli OP (Bologna: Edizioni Studio Domenicano, 2015), 41–117.

[46] Thomas Aquinas, *De occultis operibus naturae ad quemdem militem ultramontanum*, in Joseph B. McAllister, *The Letter of Thomas Aquinas* De occultis (Washington, DC: Catholic University of America Press, 1939).

they involve language, must be invocations beyond nature as ordinarily known, to preternatural beings. They can only be illicit appeals to demons, rather than licit ones to angels; otherwise, they would be made in terms of the ordinary and prescribed Catholic liturgical forms (ST II.II. q. 96 aa 1–4; SCG III cc 103–7).[47]

One can nonetheless question Aquinas's general view that metaphysics is focused more directly on Being than on God, and his linked and novel division between a 'metaphysical theology', on the one hand, and a *sacra doctrina* reflecting on a discrete and unified 'revelation' (a usage which Aquinas almost seems to have invented), on the other.[48] He thereby displaced an older, Boethian and more outrightly neoplatonic view that metaphysics was primarily about God and was virtually at one with the discourse of faith.[49]

Some historians of science, notably, Stephen Gaukroger, view the emergence of a less theological metaphysics (whose independence of theology they also exaggerate) as crucial to the allowance of an autonomous cognitive space in which science can eventually flourish – even if this autonomy was for a while compromised by the physico-theology of the seventeenth century.[50] Yet this is to ignore the notable strength of interest in nature, focussed around Plato's *Timaeus,* and tendencies to bring mathematics and physics closer together under the auspices of the *Quadrivium*, under the influence both of that text and of Boethius, in a way that would seem *more* to anticipate early modern mathematicised physics than is the case with Aristotelian naturalism.[51] And all this happened within the scope, not of any secularisation, but rather of a *greater* degree of integration

[47] Brian P. Copenhaver, *Magic in Western Culture: From Antiquity to the Enlightenment* (Cambridge: Cambridge University Press, 2015), 119–26; Lynn Thorndike, 'Some Medieval Conceptions of Magic', *The Monist,* 25, no. 1 (January 1915), 107–39.

[48] Jean-Luc Marion, *D'Ailleurs, La Révélation* (Paris: Grasset, 2020), 65–84.

[49] Andreas Speer, 'The Hidden Heritage: Boethian Metaphysics and Its Medieval Tradition', *Quaestio* 5 (2005), 163–81; 'The Division of Metaphysical Discourses: Boethius, Thomas Aquinas and Meister Eckhart', in Kent Emery Jr (ed.), *Philosophy and Theology in the Long Middle Ages* (Leiden: Brill, 2011), 91–115.

[50] Stephen Gaukroger, *The Emergence of a Scientific Culture: Science and the Shaping of Modernity, 1210–1685* (Oxford: Oxford University Press, 2006), 47–86; *Civilisation and the Culture of Science,* 426–8. Gaukroger's account of Aquinas (unlike much of his excellent reading and analysis of many later thinkers) is particularly odd: he denies that he thought that metaphysics was primarily about Being (he thought it was) and claims he considered it to be primarily about rational mediation between theology and natural philosophy (he did not).

[51] It is important also to be aware of the fact that prior to the re-discovery of Aristotle's *Metaphysics* and *Physics,* Christian thinkers were already familiar, through many channels, as in the case of Boethius, with his categorial scheme, his hylomorphism and distinction between substance and accident.

of the metaphysical with the scriptural. This same integration was revived in the fifteenth century by Nicholas of Cusa, who specifically re-invoked many theses of the twelfth-century Boethian Thierry of Chartres, and was then sustained by the university circles around Lefèvre d'Étaples in sixteenth-century France: Lefèvre notably refused the category of 'natural theology' and insisted on the primacy of faith for all modes of understanding.[52]

A fusion of the scriptural and the metaphysical tended to encourage further integrations of the theological with the mathematical and the physical: the tripartite Aristotelian division of knowledge with which Boethius operated.[53] The God of the Bible who created by 'number, weight and measure' was equated with the mathematising demiurge of the *Timaeus*, and our more limited, human mathematics was seen as offering some approximate equivalent to, and insight into, his working, while mathematical models were applied with great subtlety and apophatic nuance to Trinitarian and Christological theology themselves.[54] Equally, within these currents of thought which early modernity revived, there tended to be echoes of Eriugena's neoplatonic view that God and intelligent spirits are in some eminent sense as much in motion as at rest, besides being as much eminently plural as one, and so, in this sense, belong also to the 'physical' or the 'natural'.[55]

By contrast, Aristotelianism, especially if purged of any neoplatonic gloss, promotes a more absolute gulf between the physical as the moving and the metaphysical as without motion. It is, indeed, in this sense true that Aristotelianism helped to promote a more autonomous physics in modern times, and yet this does not amount, for reasons just seen, to any unequivocal shift towards the 'more scientific' in our sense, just because it was thereby *less* amenable (though with many variations) to the closing of the gap between the physical and the mathematical. An increased distance from physics from the theological-metaphysical suggested also more sundering from the mathematical, since this was taken to be the mediator of degrees of abstraction from matter. Thus, different, apparently proto-modern currents were, in reality, here in competition. There was no single, straightforward vector of 'progress'.

52 Oosterhoff, *Making Mathematical Culture*, esp. 25–55; David Albertson, *Mathematical Theologies: Nicholas of Cusa and the Legacy of Thierry of Chartres* (Oxford: Oxford University Press, 2014).

53 Boethius, *De trinitate*, II.5–60.

54 Albertson, *Mathematical Theologies*.

55 See John Milbank, 'One in Three and Two in One: the Double Coincidence of Opposites in Nicholas of Cusa' (forthcoming).

Nevertheless, to complicate matters further, the lack of any account of original derivation of physical reality from God in Aristotle, and the consequently deficient account of generative causality and radical change within immanence, could *of itself* nurture a shift towards promotion of a dead and mechanical nature, in the work of some early modern Catholic philosophers like Marin Mersenne.[56] Concomitantly, the Aristotelian denial that mere induction from observational or experimental moving particulars could engender universal and so 'scientific' certainty in terms of deduction of particulars from immanently universal essences (whereas a more Platonic thinker like Cusa saw mere 'conjecture' as truly intimating transcendent and unknown ultimate forms in the mind of God) tended to encourage, amongst Jesuit neo-scholastics, the mathematisation of these results, such that they could be re-understood after all as deductions from intuitive first principles.[57] Descartes himself stood within this lineage. Optics, astronomy and mechanics tended to be approached by Jesuits in such a fashion, even if they retained a reserve about understanding all of 'physics' proper in this manner, unlike Galileo, Descartes and Newton. All the same, large regions of the physical world became thereby mathematised, and so approximated to an Aristotelian criterion of 'science', sometimes with accompanying agnosticism (as in the case of Mersenne), as to the ultimate forces at work behind the deduced and inductively confirmed operation of mathematical principles. For it was still not usually allowed by the Jesuits that mathematics could universally penetrate to the level of real universal essences.[58]

Analogous ambivalences of a neo-scholastic Aristotelianism are today seen in the work of a neo-scholastic like Edward Feser, who criticises the claim of modern physics exhaustively to describe nature and yet fervently resists any imputations of 'vitalism'.[59] This requires him to see Aristotelian *morphe* as 'entirely physical', whereas, if it is added to matter, according to hylomorphism, its nature is inherently *spiritual*. Given this kind of outlook, Feser proves able, anti-climactically, fully to accept Newton's inertial

56 Peter Dear, *Mersenne and the Learning of the Schools* (Ithaca, NY: Cornell University Press, 1988).

57 Peter Dear, *Discipline and Experience: the Mathematical Way in the Scientific Revolution* (Chicago: University of Chicago Press, 1995), 11–62.

58 Nonetheless, some Jesuits, especially those based in Rome, where natural magic lingered on into the eighteenth century, in particular Athanasius Kircher, embraced a more Hermeticist view of occult forces. They notably tended to blend sympathetic magic with Scholastic accounts of natural properties. See Mark A. Waddell, *Jesuit Science and the End of Nature's Secrets* (London: Ashgate, 2017), 47–50, 164–86.

59 Feser, *Aristotle's Revenge*, 375–83.

account of ordinary local motion (only conceding that a non-realist view of inertia might be 'possible'), thereby abandoning the Aristotelian view – *at once* physical and metaphysical – that all motion as such, as somehow halfway between potentiality and actuality, is always inherently tending to something actual.[60] Each thing, for Aristotle, seeks its place in terms of its natural, non-accidental motion, just because, in the physical realm that is defined in general by the presence of the moving, there would *be* no stable places if some things were not tending towards them and thereby co-constituting them, even though they are of themselves 'at rest', since they 'draw' things towards themselves. When a thing is accidentally propelled, as in the various cases of local motion, then it is caught up in the natural teleology of the moving agent, or the most ultimate moving agent.[61]

Given this surrender to modern ontology at the level of the physical, Feser then (for all his many crucial insights) restricts, like Bernard McGinn, the role of Aristotelian metaphysics to describing what must in general be the case for modern physics to be possible.[62] Yet this has too Kantian and transcendentalist a ring: it does not sufficiently allow that, if the physical is co-composed of form as well as matter, then, to the degree that forms can be considered in general apart from motion ('mathematically') and possess a kinship with forms that can exist in abstraction from matter altogether (gods, angels and God), it follows that there is an area for Aristotle in which physics and metaphysics combined are *directly* describing physical reality and not just its conditions of (albeit) ontological possibility.

The danger then, of a purged 'Aristotelianism' (probably not Aristotle's own philosophy)[63] is that it sometimes historically proved, and sometimes continues to prove, all too *complicit* with a reduced and mechanised physics, just because it has no sense (as found in Maximus, Augustine, Eriugena and even Aquinas) of the vital and shaping power of obscurely intimated forms as participating in the divine creative power that continuously brings them into being.

[60] Ibid., 216–29.

[61] Aristotle, *Physics*, 192b8–193b22. Feser does, however, rightly note that one can defend Aristotle's notion that a projectile is in part moved by surrounding air disturbed by the initial thrower, in terms of modern understandings of surrounding 'field'.

[62] Feser, *Aristotle's Revenge*, 222–4.

[63] The evidence we have of Aristotle's lost texts and some of his more marginal surviving ones, like *De Caelo*, suggest that he was ultimately more in continuity with Plato than his main extant texts might lead us to think. See A. P. Bos, *Cosmic and Meta-Cosmic Theology in Aristotle's Lost Dialogues* (Leiden: Brill, 1989).

4.5 Disenchanted Transcendence: Genealogy and Deconstruction

In order to understand further how the first vision, of disenchanted transcendence, eventually and to a large degree triumphed, and continues overwhelmingly to shape a popular and ideologically controlling view of 'science', we need to grasp some quite complex shifts in the economy of knowledge from the late medieval through to the early modern period.

Originally, metaphysics was aporetically poised between God and Being. For the neoplatonic Boethian tradition, as we have seen, it was about both, but primarily about God, who is supreme Unity and *esse*, beyond mere individual 'existence', from which all else emanates.[64] For Aquinas it was rather about Being, but remotely pointed to God as the cause of 'common' created Being, without providing any very solid knowledge of this cause, which was, rather, recovered by attention to inspired scripture and tradition. But later, in the wake of Avicenna and Duns Scotus, God was taken to fall within the scope of being, now understood to be univocal. Eventually, this discipline got renamed 'ontology' or 'general metaphysics'. 'Special metaphysics', concerning more specifically God, the soul and providence, was now a merely regional science within this ontological space.

This regional science got named 'natural theology' by Nicolas Bonet in the fourteenth century. Such a naming has to be seen as the reverse face of the later eventual naming of the general metaphysical science as 'ontology' in the sixteenth. Strictly speaking, to speak of either is to have obliterated the aporetic 'metaphysical' space within which Boethius's, Albert's, Aquinas's and Bonaventure's purely 'rational' discourses about God belonged, though with differing construals.[65] Within their older perspective, it was clear that no merely rational, rather than intellectually intuitive and faith-imbued discourse, gives an adequate account of Being (or of 'ontology'), never mind of God, not subject to revision in the light of revelation – as in the case of what I have already described as Aquinas's 'trans-physics', his Trinitarian ontology. For the Boethian tradition prior to Aquinas (to which Bonaventure to a degree still cleaved), intellectual intuition had been indistinguishably fused with faith at the apex of a metaphysical philosophy identical with theology, itself at once rational and revealed.

64 See Speer, 'The Hidden Heritage'.

65 Olivier Boulnois, *Métaphysiques rebelles: Gènese et structures d'une science au Moyen Ăge* (Paris: PUF, 2013).

But the novel and dubious notion of a 'natural theology', something specifically modern, as many scholars, including Peter Harrison, have now stressed, was originally one of the most encompassing terms for what we now call 'science'. How did there come to be such a close linkage between natural theology and physics?

As Simon Oliver has argued, one effect of the early modern emergence of 'ontology' is to further loosen the links between physics and metaphysics, which Aristotle's partial (at least) separation of the two already encouraged.[66] For univocity and nominalism meagrely nurture a merely minimal metaphysics, according to which every truly substantial existing thing is isolated, self-standing and disconnected. This tends to leave more work for a purely physical discourse to do on its own. Reality is no longer inherently connected in terms of substantive relations, universals, shared forms, hylomorphic unities and vertically emanating causes. It is, rather, accidentally connected in terms of mere efficiency, often linked to counterfactually paradigmatic understandings of the behaviour of isolated bodies in a void, vacuum or absolute space.

And given that the being of finite things is no longer seen as inherently their created, participatory reality, the creative and sustaining motions of God are now also in effect shifted from a metaphysical to a physical plane – in a very different and onticised sense from that of Eriugena (for whom divine motion was ontological, qualitatively different and incommensurable with created motion.) The latter is now closed off within itself, no longer involving an analogically open sense of motion, such as characterised Eriugena or Aquinas's 'trans-physics'.

One eventually gets the strange hybridisation of physics and theology that is often predominate in the seventeenth century, as described by Amos Funkenstein, for which divine causality supplies and completes what is lacking in sheerly intra-cosmic explanations – losing the medieval sense of the incommensurable levels of primary and secondary causality. Despite the new bracketing of the metaphysical, which might (for reasons we have seen) imply, as with Aristotelian modes of naturalism, a removal of the physical also from the mathematical, in fact, by a new mode of short-circuiting, the mathematical was now directly conflated with the theological and with a directly involved, univocal deity, operating with the same numbers as our numbers, though with infinitely greater power. Of course, all this was seen as heading off a more radical immanentist naturalism (the spectre raised by currents of the Renaissance) in a supposedly more

[66] Simon Oliver, *Philosophy, God and Motion* (London: Routledge, 2005).

experimental and demonstrative way than could be achieved by an enchanted transcendence.

As already mentioned, a disenchanting flattening of the material world was reinforced by an emphasis on the inscrutable power of God, which encouraged the reduction of natural philosophy to positivistic and pragmatic truths, at once refusing an arrogant insight into the purposes of God and promoting processes that potentially had practical value. Such a predominating trajectory can be traced from Mersenne and Gassendi through Boyle to Newton, who still saw geometry as ultimately a branch of mechanics and rejected all theoretical hypotheses extraneous to the construction of experiments, as any intrinsic part of science.[67]

Such positivism, however, belied its own agnosticism to the extent that the very idea of an area of physical reality that can be isolated, supposedly without theoretical conjecturing, from the realms of the unknown, of itself necessarily implies that there is, indeed, a region of physical reality that is sheerly mechanical, sheerly equivalent to our own processes of calculable operation – as if nature's 'artful modelling' was *here*, at least, confined to that, and as if the repeatability of our fictions guaranteed their 'purifying' of at least this region of the real.[68]

In this sense any (after all) metaphysically dogmatic positivism, as E. A. Burtt argued, necessarily projects its method as a regional ontology.[69] But things typically went much further than that in the seventeenth century. The method was often projected to its maximum conceivable reach. In consequence, the minimal realities assumed by a quantifiably repeatable experiment were vastly extended into all of physical being: nature itself must be constructed according to *our* numbers for Galileo (and no longer hidden divine numbers, as for the older tradition still surviving in Cusa and Lefèvre). It must consist only in actual and factual items like those we observe (and soon through microscopes) and so must be both atomic and free of any mysterious 'potential', as for Aristotle and scholasticism.

This time thoroughly to agree with Edward Feser, the upshot is effectively a return to pre-Socratic naiveté.[70] Aristotle had argued that all change is from potential to actuality, just in order to avoid the

[67] Burtt, *The Metaphysical Foundations*, 207–302.

[68] Nancy Cartwright, *Nature, the Artful Modeller: Lectures on Laws, Science, How Nature Arranges the World and How We Can Arrange It Better* (Chicago: Open Court, 2019); Isabelle Stengers, *The Invention of Modern Science*, trans. Daniel W. Smith (Minneapolis: University of Minnesota Press, 2000), 161–7.

[69] Burtt, *Metaphysical Foundations*, 98–104, 203–6, 215–20, 303–25.

[70] Feser, *Aristotle's Revenge*, 3–64.

Parmenidean conclusion that all is one and unchanging, or the Heraclitean one that all is in uninterrupted flux, which amounts to the same thing. If all is now in principle immanently calculable according to our mathematics (returning to the pre-Socratic version of Pythagoreanism), then the implication has to be that space is all one; time is absolute and free of motion, which is really always already over; while motion itself is a mere rearrangement of coordinates.

It was Descartes who most of all carried through this strong programme of projection of the positivistic, and even if his project manifestly failed, it continues to define the implicit reach of science as ideology. His collapsing of geometric space into number via algebraic equivalence indeed already opened the possibility of a relativistic coordination of space with time in the case of Einstein, while significantly precluding from view those aspects of geometry (and so of physical reality) not so readily reducible.[71]

Of course, this opening also went the other way: time as either pure flow or a sequence of infinitesimal isolated nows (the two alternatives both entertained by Newton)[72] implied already an entire spatialisation of time. Just as 'algebraic' capitalism (intimately linked to the mathematico-mechanical programme) is at once about the massification of land and about the conversion of wealth into abstract number, so also the Cartesian collapse of magnitude and multiplicity into each other went equally in both directions. It was really a sacralised algebra, as it were the ultimate voluntarist-nominalist caricature of Kabbalah, that here triumphed.

And yet, notoriously, this total projection could never be complete. Within physics, anomalies remained: How to account for the 'occult' forces of magnetism, electricity and gravity – to which later in the twentieth century came to be added the 'strong' and 'weak' forces of nuclear energy operating between protons and electrons? Beyond physics, how to account for mysterious chemical processes of transmutation and all of the complex phenomena studied by biology and medicine? In truth, the mathematisation of reality as confirmed by experiment never reached all that far.

And ultimately, how to account for overall mobility at all and for the relative cohesion of planetary systems within the cosmos? In order to sustain loyalty to the positivistic vision of mechanism, two ruses had to be resorted to. The first was Descartes's supposition of an ether, or of a

[71] Ibid., 277; Sophie Roux, 'Forms of Mathematization', *Early Science and Medicine*, 15, nos. 4–5 (2010), 319–37.

[72] Burtt, *Metaphysical Foundations*, 244–5.

different kind of much more refined matter which he imagined as eddying in ultimately controlling vortices, directly moved by the hand of God. Both More and Newton sustained this supposition, while tending to add to it the operation of occult forces: the more the latter allowed that the ether was in fact, rather, the direct presence of God, or some sort of subordinate God, eventually indeed the spiritual body of Christ (reflecting his Arianism), the more also he allowed that these forces might be really acting at an otherwise unmediated distance.[73] Explanatory recourse to such unexplained powers was the second ruse. It had been avoided by Galileo to the degree that he was prepared more exhaustively to mathematise dynamic and gravitational realities, but this still deliberately left their operative forces unaccounted for.[74]

Today, in effect, hypotheses of 'dark matter' as constituting most of the universe are surely updates of the 'ether', since they attempt to account for enormous gravitational anomalies and once more to explain just why planetary systems do not simply fly apart.[75] Thereby, we see that the undeniable, because operationally confirmed, progress of mathematical physics has also *much more* revealed the limits of its understanding, which continues (as with Newton's dabbling in the dark with alchemy)[76] to pose the uneasy question of whether we are pursuing the *right* kind of understanding, if we wish to delve further into nature's ultimate secrets. Is it an accident that the assumption of our alienation within the cosmos comes up against such increasing limits? Of course, quantum physics seems most acutely to confront us with that issue – on which see further below.

The alternative possibility of avoiding any projection of method as ontology, even in the regional sense, crucially involves, as Feser also argues, recovering the role of *substance* and *essence* as the originally observed 'things' and 'natures' (with more or less crucially defining properties and family resemblances) which alone allows us to make specific observations and undertake specific experiments in the first place.[77] If we do that, then there will always be an interchange between experiment and theorising about experiment that goes beyond experiment, in order to know what questions to ask, what to test and how to interpret evidence, in a fashion

[73] Michael Hunter, *Isaac Newton: The Last Sorcerer* (London: Fourth Estate, 1997), 350.
[74] Burtt, *Metaphysical Foundations*, 72–124, 135–50, 264–9.
[75] Stephen Gaukroger, *The Failures of Philosophy: A Historical Essay* (Princeton, NJ: Princeton University Press, 2020), 286–7.
[76] B. J. T. Dobbs, *The Janus Faces of Genius: The Role of Alchemy in Newton's Thought* (Cambridge: Cambridge University Press, 2002).
[77] Feser, *Aristotle's Revenge*, 23–37 and passim.

that involves a constant to and fro between 'experimental science' and 'natural philosophy', and which corresponds with *what must really happen in scientific practice, even today.*[78]

However, the ontological projection of the positive requires the contradictory obliteration of the original holistic entities or substances that it must nonetheless continue to work with. In consequence, as both Burtt and Feser have detailed, these everyday realities get split between an assumed atomic substructure of objective reality, on the one hand, and an assumed projection by our mind of 'secondary qualities', like heat and cold and colour, on the other, rendering entirely mysterious the correlation between the two. Somehow, physical reality itself has vanished down the middle, leaving human subjectivity implausibly isolated and anomalous within the world that it inhabits. And yet 'science' *itself* is manifest only to this unexplained subjectivity.

One can contrast this obliteration of the human with its centrality for a more enchanted transcendence and enchanted immanence, and note the way that their linked espousals of both humanism and vitalism returned to view in the eighteenth century.[79] The barbarism of disenchanted monotheism does not therefore in any way imply the barbarism of 'science', but it does imply the barbarism of what we too often take to be science. Genealogically disinterred and deconstructed, the core of this bleakest of secularities turns out to be simply bad theology.

4.6 The Early Modern Survival of Enchanted Transcendence

It would be wrong to suppose that enchanted transcendence was ever simply defeated – as the example of the Cambridge Platonists indicates. To the contrary, as Philipp Rosemann has shown, within Medieval scholasticism itself and before or coinciding with the Humanist Renaissance, there was, amongst some in the fifteenth century, an anti-nominalist reaction, especially within the sustained Albertine current, that was often fused, as with Meister Eckhart and later the Flemish theologian Heimeric da Campo, with the Boethian legacy of Thierry of Chartres, besides the maverick thought of the picaresque Majorcan, Ramon Lull.[80] It was felt that theology had become too much a matter of mere logic-chopping, losing sight of vivid immediacy (which Lull and then Heimeric and

[78] See Stengers, *Invention of Science.* [79] Gaukroger, *Collapse of Mechanism.*

[80] Philipp W. Rosemann, *The Story of a Great Medieval Book: Peter Lombard's* Sentences (Peterborough: Broadview, 2007).

eventually Nicholas of Cusa in their wake tried to address in terms of an immediate language and pictography of concepts)[81] with little attention paid to its coherence or even its main subject matter, and that philosophy and theology were coming dangerously adrift from each other. Denys the Carthusian tried instead to go back to Peter Lombard's Patristic synthesis, and to unite the insights of High Medieval thinkers like Aquinas and Bonaventure, but in a way that more explicitly stresses an ultimately mystical purpose and unity, as for both Augustine and the first Denis, the Areopagite.

The second Denys was not a very original thinker, but his friend and collaborator Nicholas of Cusa was. In the case of the latter, one sees perhaps an implicit worry that Aquinas's over-focus on being, compromising of the simplicity of God in terms of absolute/ordained power, dividing of metaphysical from revealed theology, and Aristotelian distinction of physics from metaphysics, helped unintentionally to usher in a disintegration of a unifying theological/metaphysical vision.

Thus God as Good and One and Intellect is now stressed by Cusanus as much or more as God as *esse*. In his case, and later in that of Marsilio Ficino,[82] Pico della Mirandola and Giles of Viterbo, the higher neoplatonic view of *kinesis*, beyond Aristotle, is recovered, such that even God, as with Cusanus, is seen as the infinite coincidence of motion with rest.[83]

As already mentioned, the Stagirite had seen motion as hovering between potential and actuality is its own aporetic infinite subset.[84] He had additionally thought, as also discussed, that every motion, as inherently of its very nature *tending* towards the actual, is teleological, else it is not motion. If, instead of this aporetic hovering, every motion is regarded as only half potential and half actual, down to an infinitesimal division, then there would be no motion as transition at all, only various modes of *stasis* and inexplicable 'jumpings'.[85] This is why, as we have seen, it is

[81] Especially as enabled by printing, this had much influence on the formation of 'science', but was later reduced to a more rationally calculative logic of automatic computation of reality by Peter Ramus and eventually Leibniz.

[82] So far from being ecclesially marginal, Ficino was responsible for the adoption of the doctrine of the immortality of the soul as official Church teaching, precisely against Pomponazzi's excessively Aristotelian view of the soul's nature.

[83] On Cusa, see John Milbank, '*Mathesis* and *Mathexis*: The Post-Nominalist Realism of Nicholas of Cusa', in Isabelle Moulin (ed.), *Participation et vision de Dieu chez Nicolas de Cues* (Paris: Vrin, 2017), 143–69, and 'One in Three and Two in One'.

[84] I have learnt much from Victor Emma-Adamah of Cambridge University here.

[85] This is why Leibniz's 'monadology' gets rid of motion in favour of the infinitesimal actuality of discrete entities in pre-established harmony with each other. But one should surely, after Aristotle,

correct to say that Newton, after Galileo, abolishes motion.[86] Yet Aristotle already arguably risked such a reduction. He effectively dissolved *kinesis* into infinitesimal instances of potency and act and could not quite allow for the full reality of 'transition' as Plotinus later did, just because the Alexandrian neoplatonist did not so distinctly elevate rest over motion.[87] It is in part for this reason that neoplatonism did not have the clear Aristotelean metaphysics/physics divide.

The neoplatonists considered even thought to be a more unperturbed, faster motion and not a mere completed 'act' (*energeia*), as for Aristotle. It is rest that is more inhibiting and finitising, even if it also expresses in its own degree eternal truth; thus the One for Plotinus is as equally beyond rest as it is beyond motion.[88] Likewise, for Plotinus, since every act remains in motion, there is no clear distinction, as for Aristotle, between internal 'doing' and external making'.[89]

Cusa and the Renaissance neoplatonists generally returned to this more elevated view of transitional motion which renders everything physical and transphysical, everything 'natural' or kinetic, as for Eriugena, who, as we saw, included even God within his *Divisio Naturae* (*natura* = *physis* = moving reality). It also allowed them to rethink and intensify the Trinitarian ontologies of Augustine, Boethius, Thierry of Chartres, Achard of St Victor and Aquinas.[90] It is characteristic of this current that the figure of perfection becomes less one of rest than of completed motion which is circular – a thought which had an impact upon Copernicus.[91]

It can be argued, therefore, that an enchanted transcendence sometimes renewed itself in early modern times, through both innovation and a sustained continuity with perennial tradition. Cusa embraced much that anticipated later seventeenth-century physics and mathematics: a unified cosmos (though in his case based on traditional macro-microcosmic correspondence); the relativity of motion, space and time only to the infinite; a decentred and infinitised universe (though without the 'container view');

trust the (on reflection) fantastic implications of appearances, more than a metaphysical fantasy which denies their pertinence? The Platonic allowance of the full reality of motion goes along with its recognition of the ineffable 'suddenness' (*exaiphnes*), and so discontinuity of alteration, from the *Parmenides* onwards. See Florian Marion, 'The *exaiphnes* in the Platonic Tradition: From Kinematics to Dynamics' (forthcoming).

86 Oliver, *Philosophy, God and Motion*; Feyerabend, *Against Method.*

87 Rémi Brague, *Aristote et la question du monde* (Paris: PUF, 1988), 38–67; Milbank, 'Confession of Time in Augustine'. And see further in the main text.

88 Plotinus, *Enneads*, II.6.1; VI.3.27–8.

89 Ibid., VI.1.15–16.

90 See Milbank, '*Mathexis* and *Mathesis*' and 'Three in One and One in Two'.

91 Dilwyn Knox, 'Ficino, Copernicus and Bruno on the Motion of the Earth', *Brunoniana and Campelliana*, 5, no. 2 (1999), 333–66.

and a reckoning with the infinite in mathematics — but in a more Platonic and aporetic fashion that does not embrace the flattening and formalising of mathematics that is usually assumed by modern physics.

Elsewhere, I have argued, after Jacob Klein, that mathematics itself underwent thoroughly debatable changes in the early modern period and that seventeenth-century physics does not just 'apply' a perennially inherited maths.[92] The 'new science' on the whole operated with a new 'disenchanted' mathematics that substituted Zero for One as the 'transcendental' number, levelled prime numbers with negatives and fractions, algebraically abolished the distinction between arithmetic multitude and geometric magnitude in terms of a univocal account of their shared proportions or ratios, and sought, as with 'calculus', to rationalise the paradoxes of the infinite–finite relation which Cusa regarded as symbolic mysteries.[93]

These shifts were again linked to a disenchanting and voluntarist theology, not wanting to see in number anything special and mystical, or nor as belonging to its own peculiar ontological domain, halfway between theology and physics, as for Aristotle and Boethius. Yet Nicholas still held to such a view, and was nonetheless able to offer in these terms his own rival mathematised physics – and also without seeing it as an all-vaunting and conquering discourse.[94]

This remained true of the French sixteenth-century 'Fabrists', so-called because of a pun on the Latinisation of Lefèvre's name and with deliberate reference to Cusanus's exaltation of the knowledge gained through making by his exemplary figure of the 'idiot' spoonmaker. Recent scholarship has stressed the influence of this current on William Gilbert, the father of magnetism and other English Baconians. Lefèvre himself and Charles de Bouelles certainly put pressure on the inherited divisions of mathematics and the Aristotelian opinions that 'amount' (like fiveness) is not subject to degrees, and that there can be no maximum and minimum of quantity. In the first instance Lefèvre engaged with the 'intension and remission of forms' of the fourteenth-century Merton *calculatores*, who had thereby explored the margins of confusion between quantity and quality, as in phenomena like acceleration and temperature. Yet he rebuked the

92 John Milbank, 'Writing and the Order of Learning', *Philosophy, Theology and the Sciences*, 4, no. 1 (2017), 46–73; Jacob Klein, *Greek Mathematical Thought and the Origin of Algebra*, trans. Eva Brann (New York: Dover, 1992), 150–224.

93 See also Oosterhoff, *Making Mathematical Culture*, 180–213.

94 See Johannes Hoff, *Kontingenz, Berührung, Überschreitung: Zur philosophischen Propädutik christlicher Mystik nach Nikolaus von Kues* (Freiburg: Karl Alber, 2007), 88–196, 301–9.

nominalist Oxonians for their confinement to *ratio* rather than intuitive *intelligentia*, and understood the tending of quantity to quality as linked with the Cusan coincidence of the maximal and minimal opposites. His modification of Aristotle remained committed to the Aristotelian categories (as with Cusa) and he regarded the proportionate comparison of geometric magnitude with arithmetic multitude as still strictly analogical.[95]

Most significantly of all, the Fabrist marginal closing of the gap between physics and mathematics (implied by the allowance of pole and degree to quantity) did not so much imply the later Vietian, Ramist and Cartesian approximation of the physical to the mathematical, and so the moving to the static, as the *very reverse*. After Proclus (and ultimately the Stoics) and Cusa, it is rather that mathematics is physicalised, to the degree that it is thought of itself in terms of motion – as when a line is taken to emanate or 'unfold' from a point, or the later number sequence forms the generative one. It is in these terms that a single quantity like a point can be seen to expand latitudinally into a line, plane and volume, or reversely to shrink back into a point. Moreover, the possibly non-Aristotelian allowance of maxima and minima of the same amount is only instanced by Lefèvre in the case of actually physical realities like heating and freezing.[96] Such a closer alignment of the mathematical with the physical naturally tends to fuse with the Fabrist espousal also of animism and natural magic, which they had imbibed from the Italians Pico and Ficino.[97]

In this way, we can see how the stronger role of mathematics in physics did not necessarily imply either a disenchanted transcendence (as with Mersenne) or a total break with Aristotle (still less so than with Mersenne).

Perhaps the real mystery (to which I do not know the answer) is just why, with Galileo, a neoplatonic and symbolic Pythagoreanism evolved into a more dogmatic, again 'pre-Socratic' one, once more claiming that the world was constructed literally from *our* construal of number and shape, which is the same as God's, if finitely restricted as to scope of

95 Oosterhoff, *Making Mathematical Culture*. One can note here that Aquinas, unlike Aristotle and Boethius, significantly omits mathematical abstraction from *motion* in his commentary on the latter's *De trinitate*, at Q.5, a.1 resp., mentioning only abstraction from real particular instances of quantity.

96 Possibly, since Aristotle seems to anticipate this at *De caelo* I.1.

97 Lefèvre later retreated from magic, not because he came to doubt its reality, but because his fears increased as to its real dangers: Oosterhoff, *Making Mathematical Culture*, 83 and 30–7, 89–90, 211–13.

application.[98] Such enchanted dogmatism (worthy of Prospero, before his chastening), one can suppose, could readily start to merge with the newly disenchanted nominalist mathematics, itself more suited to envisage shape or number as a literal and univocal 'thing', thereby facilitating the equation of physical reality with extension, and extension itself with algebraic quantification. Given this double reduction, it was not surprising that Henry More sought to overcome Cartesian dualism by supposing mind as such to be more 'subtly' extended.[99]

4.7 The 'New Science' as Ergetic Knowledge

As many scholars have now insisted, alongside the dramatic shifts in seventeenth-century physics, there were also 'scientific revolutions' in medicine, chemistry, natural history, political theory (Hobbes) and economics (the Baconian William Petty), besides the less mechanically kinetic realms of physics, like optics and magnetics. No single detailed method or approach fused all these disciplines and practices, even if mechanical physics became the most prestigious after Newton, ironically at the same time that this prestige almost immediately started to be challenged.

Does nothing then link all these discourses in novelty? It surely does, but in terms, as scholars like Paulo Rossi and Amos Funkenstein have argued, of the new favouring of 'ergetic knowledge', or the notion that we can only fully know what we can make, rendering both experiment and technological application absolutely central – with, indeed, experiment usually being thought of as itself already a technological operation: not so much (as one sees indeed with Bacon himself) the testing of a hypothesis, but itself a performative hypothesis.[100]

It is just this priority of experiment and technology (the two being almost inseparable in people's minds at this period) which tends to bring the non-mathematical also within the 'scientific' purview, and much later,

[98] Is this really the influence of Giordano Bruno, who specifically elevated Pythagoras above Plato, returning his thought to pre-Socratic immanence? See Gatti, *Giordano Bruno*, 24. One could then see Galileo's Pythagorean identification of God's numbers with ours as a point of mediation between Bruno's enchanted immanence and Cartesian disenchanted transcendence. For Descartes, univocal *mathesis* is stripped of any eternal mystical resonance because its rules, which we take to be inexorable, are but contingently determined by the ultimately unknown divine simplicity (rather than divine 'will', to be perfectly accurate).

[99] Burtt, *Metaphysical Foundations*, 135–40.

[100] Funkenstein, *Theology and the Scientific Imagination*, 290–345; Paolo Rossi, *The Birth of Modern Science* (Oxford: Blackwell, 2001). American pragmatism is therefore much more authentically Baconian than is English empiricism.

with the work of Michael Faraday and François Geoffroy and many others, this becomes still more apparent. Not every observable regularity or reproducible effect can be quantified. At the same time, quantification, when achievable, much exalts the prestige of experiment. Inversely, much of the rise in prestige of mathematics owed a great deal to the construction of new machines and engines based upon its application: it is thus false to align more mathematical science mainly with speculation and grand theory. Furthermore, it is clear from Cusanus, as with Bacon's materialist pupil Hobbes (for whom numbers were literally atoms in motion) that mathematics itself was seen as the supremely successful experiment: the most extreme example for human beings of a complete 'maker's knowledge', since here we simultaneously see what we construct and construct what we see (as God had been held to do for all of reality).

For these reasons, a new and initially Humanist devotion to 'technology' was truly the most ultimate and inclusive horizon of the 'Scientific Revolution'. We now realise, after the work of Mary Carruthers, that this was not altogether novel: if the Fabrists had begun much more to exalt even the liberal arts as 'craft', then it turns out that the craft analogy was already quite strongly present back in the twelfth century, somewhat qualifying the traditional despising of the 'mechanical', which was even sometimes included and respected as part of learning, as by Hugh of St Victor.[101] The community of scholars itself could be later seen in the Renaissance as a 'republican' work of participating friends, and the unity of ultimately divine contemplation with charitable practice and application was simply natural within the Christian legacy.[102] It is in the end arguable that this is the real and most simple explanation of why science (a particular kind of science) was most cultivated and sustained within a Christian civilisation.

Nevertheless, the advent of printing clearly much boosted this sense, with the Fabrists and others, that learning is in part a technical process (as today for us with computers), just as the novel 'immutable mobility' of the book exalted a sense of shared objective, and communicable 'facts' – intimately linked with *facta*, fabrications (whereas our digital 'information' at once extends that sense and yet so multiplies it by 'mobile immutability', as one could say, that facts seem to dissolve in the virtual ether).[103]

[101] Mary Carruthers, *The Craft of Thought: Meditation, Rhetoric and the Making of Images, 400–1200* (Cambridge: Cambridge University Press, 2008).

[102] Oosterhoff, *Making Mathematical Culture*, 181–90.

[103] Bruno Latour, 'Visualisation and Cognition: Drawing Things Together', in M. Lynch and S. Woolgar (eds.), *Representation in Scientific Activity* (Cambridge, MA: MIT Press, 1990), 19–68.

Many commentators are nonetheless misled by Bacon's distinction between 'experiments of light' and 'experiments of fruit' into thinking that he drew a sharp distinction between discovery and invention, or advocated the primacy of a sheerly theoretical inquiry over practical orientation and application. The priority of light over fruit is advocated only in the interests of a greater eventual fruitfulness: 'fruits and works are as it were sponsors and sureties for the truth of philosophies'.[104] Bacon is advocating a much more systematic development of artisanal method or 'art' beyond the merely ad hoc procedure of mechanics, alchemists and investigators of magnetism: 'For axioms rightly discovered and established supply practice with its instruments not one by one, but in clusters, and draw after them trains and troops of works.'[105] The 'true causes and axioms' are themselves 'rightly discovered' through experimental performance, which is in effect a kind of 'meta-technology' involving a much wider and more general achievement of regular control, and the production of regular effects. No specific applications are indeed at first envisaged, but the whole point is that a much greater range of applications – improving man's fallen natural state – will then ensue. The causes sought are effective powers, whose inherent nature may be but vaguely known or construed. Thus the analogy that Bacon here appeals to is of God creating light before he created substances – *not* the divine light that God first sees, but the created light that is *also* something produced, as a precondition of all the lesser works that will follow.

And Bacon proved to be indeed prophetic. Human beings have been empiricists and technologists since the Stone Age: witness, for example, Stonehenge itself. The difference involved in modern technological 'take-off' is exactly the reflexive systematisation and compounding of the artisanal. Given that a 'scientific' bent of human beings belongs to the species as such, but that a religious bent does so equally, why should we imagine that they are in competition? And since there has therefore *been no* 'rise of science' (we have never been modern because we have always been modern), neither has it caused a 'decline of religion'. Insofar as there is any linkage, it is much more to do with the misuse of science by atheistic scientism, which is surely at one with the capture of the real Baconian 'artisanal' revolution by the capitalist exploitation of labour. Its disenchanting as well as abuse of labour (removing its creativity and integration with

[104] Francis Bacon, *The New Organon* [*Novum Organon*] (Cambridge: Cambridge University Press, 2000), Book I, LXIII, pp. 60–1.

[105] Ibid., Book I, LXX, pp. 57–8; see also LXIII, pp. 60–1.

the rest of life) is at one with its disenchantment of natural philosophy, leaving us with a 'natural science' also not integrated with the rest of human life, including the religious imperative.[106]

It is true that Bacon himself (as if he were in this respect also a dark prophet of utilitarianism and state technocracy) disallowed the symbolic aspect both of the natural world and of human works and workings, but these were fully restored by the great Bohemian (and religiously a member of the Reformed communion) and Baconian Jan Amos Comenius, who returned this vision to the earlier perspective of Nicholas of Cusa and his view that all the processes and upshots of reality, including our human working and results of working, participate in the Trinitarian and Creative operations of God.[107] This vision sustains a unity of the pragmatic with the contemplative and includes our artificial additions to reality within teleology by demanding that they be appropriate additions, lured forwards to further true goals by the authenticity of their own inspiration. And this vision also assumes that our more restricted, if exact, mathematical and technological contrivances are included within a wider and more conjectural *poesis*, concerned with the aesthetic and the ethical, besides the religiously contemplative, with more profundity as to substantive content, if less exactitude as to formality. For this reason Cusanus, Lefèvre and Comenius retain a crucial exemplarity for the future reintegration of Christianity, metaphysics, art, science and technology. And one can also see just how, in terms of the thematic of participation in the Divine Trinity and the Divine Creation (besides eschatological anticipation, as described below), the pragmatic-experimental side of modern science is no less linked to the religious than is its more theoretical aspect, even though this is sometimes overlooked.

Ergetic knowledge in general was, as Funkenstein stated, neither inherently an idealism, nor an empiricism, nor a utilitarianism, nor a Prometheanism, though it can become all these things. It is in a sense of itself neutral: the simple core of 'science' being a maximisation of the consensus that results when, if one does *a*, then *b* follows: as when one drops a glass on a stone floor, it shatters. This neutrality, as D. C. Schindler points out in this volume, has of itself had a sinister upshot:

[106] This is how to be religiously more Marxist than Marx. See Eugene McCarraher, *The Enchantments of Mammon: How Capitalism Became the Religion of Modernity* (Cambridge, MA: Harvard University Press, 2019).

[107] See Simon J. G. Burton, '"Squaring the Circle": Cusan Metaphysics and the Pansophic Vision of Jan Amos Comenius', in Simon J. G. Burton et al. (eds.), *Nicholas of Cusa and the Making of the Early Modern World* (Leiden: Brill, 2019), 417–49.

we have built societies around an empty core of mere 'success' and the 'growth' of this success, just as we have built them round the empty core of liberal formal agreement, without any consensus as to substance.

For this reason, ergetic knowledge, though in its bare self seemingly innocent, requires an 'embedding' in something deeper: theoretically in the philosophy and theology of nature, practically in a discernment of which outcomes and effects are truly good, revelatory and desirable. Otherwise, science indeed encourages a degeneration into the reign of mere rational control according to a system, or else into a utilitarian worship of 'achievement' as sufficient in itself.

Beyond a certain level, even the pragmatic innocence of the experimental is nonetheless not so certain. Science must always be haunted by the thought of the experiments it has not carried out, once 'successful' ones have launched it upon certain trajectories — experiments which might seem to disconfirm what we thought we already knew, as has come to pass in the case of quantum physics. Furthermore, the replication of an experiment (today becoming ever more inadequate, due to the pressures of market funding that favour 'novelty') is always biased towards reproducing also the specific equipment that produced a certain result, as Simon Schaffer and others have contended, even though slight modifications of this equipment might bring about modified outcomes. Schaffer specifically argued that Newton's prism experiment, which he took to prove that coloured rays 'pre-existed' within white light (tending to suggest that their appearance as 'coloured' was illusory), actually depended upon the use of overly specified and specific modes of equipment (including English, not Continental, prisms).[108] Furthermore, once a certain experimental result has become canonical, the 'black box' phenomenon tends to define a 'successful' reiteration of this experiment as one that arrives at the presupposed 'correct result'.[109]

David Wootton's outraged protest against Schaffer that a huge number of technologies, from reflector telescopes to colour televisions, depend upon Newton having been right, spectacularly misses the historical and philosophical point.[110] For of course what 'works' in a specified way can be

[108] Simon Schaffer, 'Glass Works: Newton's Prisms and the Uses of Experiment', in D. Gooding et al. (eds.), *The Uses of Experiment: Studies in the Natural Sciences* (Cambridge: Cambridge University Press, 1989), 67–104.

[109] Trevor J. Pinch, 'Opening Black Boxes: Science, Technology and Society', *Social Studies of Science* 22 (1992), 487–510.

[110] David Wootton, *The Invention of Science: A New History of the Scientific Revolution* (London: Penguin, 2016), 521–2.

reproducible *ad nauseam*, and its mode of working may well turn out to enable other and extended modes of working. Not an empiricist notion of truth 'out there, without us' is thereby confirmed, but indeed a strictly ergetic mode of truth, as many in the seventeenth century themselves realised, even if they chose to interpret this in many different ways: empiricist, rationalist, sceptical, utilitarian and metaphysically realist and teleological, as with Cusa, Comenius and Vico (see below). We can never be sure that somewhat different or altogether different experiments might not engender somewhat different or altogether different technologies. But this is not an outright relativism designed to shock more conventionally English sensibilities; it is simple a recognition, as Bruno Latour argues, that experimentation involves a *real* interaction between active things, active equipment and active people, societies and institutions: *this* 'networked' reality is the reality from which it is unrealistic to prescind. But such a *more* realistic account of things, if it does not beckon us towards a nihilistic relativism (which it need not), tends to imply that our decisions about experiments and their application always involve elements of wider, 'non-scientific', ethical, aesthetic and metaphysical judgement about appropriate questions to be posed, usages and applications of results. Perhaps this is to restore the original ergetic dimension in its full Cusan and Comenian scope.

But for all the dangers of fantasising an exaggerated experimental objectivity, once the potential of the ergetic has been realised, and we have seen the possibilities opened up by the Baconian call to learn more systematically from artisanal success by professionally generalising what were once taken to be merely humble means, it is an illusion to think that one can just return to a re-pristinated sense of more securely pre-given and unalterable 'natures'. The task is instead to relate the ergetic itself to an older inheritance of metaphysical realism and natural law.

Already, the 'natures' of things had been understood in the High Middle Ages to mean how things 'should be' and so indeed normally are, as participating in the Mind of God. But the early modern realisation of an unexpected fluidity and alterability of things (later vastly extended by the discovery of natural evolution)[111] now places a still higher premium upon a true valuation of things and of their genuine flourishing, if their eternal natures are to be glimpsed within the relative consistencies of time.

[111] Feser rightly says that the fact that the dinosaurs evolved and eventually vanished does not at all mean that they lack a specific essence: without that they would never have stayed in being for an epoch at all: *Aristotle's Revenge*, 400–6.

The neo-scholastic alternative, abandoning the neoplatonic dimension, can be to have recourse to a supposed purely rational observation of given instanced essences as though these were immanently unalterable 'facts'. Yet this strangely and ironically coincides with the disenchanted scientific tendency, according to its new 'empirical language game', to think of nature as just factually 'there' before us (like the immovable mobility of a printed book, which has in reality been once produced), yet in terms of an also evaporated factuality reducible to a manipulable minimum of algebraicised geometric extension and quantifiable mechanical effects, assuming a 'more real' atomised sub-structure.[112] As reconceived in this all too modern guise, the neo-scholastic approach to essence was bound to lose out, as in the case of the compromising Jesuits, to a more consistent modernity.

By contrast, the more Early to High Medieval scholastic approach to holistic essence and substance can be expanded (as already with Cusa) to take more account of the mutable and generative, often under more neoplatonic influences in the traditions of Maximus, Boethius and Eriugena, which had absorbed and integrated elements of Stoic vitalism.[113] The key point here is that only the eternal really guarantees stability, such that the only genuine theological sense of a 'nature' prior to time and alteration is in terms of a partial sharing in this eternal reality. It is clear that, even for Aquinas's understanding of 'eminence', the only fully true and perfect chestnut tree blooms in the mind of God in his perpetual spring. Our sense of the proper nature of the chestnut tree here below, of how it 'should be' and how it 'should be sustained in being' therefore

[112] Shapin and Schaffer, *Leviathan and the Air-Pump*, 67. It is clear that pre-modern realism was not like this empiricism, as it included an ideal element in reality, inherently linked to our mental responses. Nor does such empiricism necessarily involve any realism: it has always proved vulnerable to positivist, pragmatist and idealist reductions. It is therefore simply question-begging for David Wootton to roundly declare (*The Invention of Science*, 539): 'The peculiar feature of science is that it claims not simply to cooperate with nature (as gardeners, cooks and naval architects do), but to discover a truth that existed before that cooperation began.' One is perplexed: many philosophers have claimed to know such a truth, and indeed we ordinarily assume it. On the other hand, whether such assumptions are entirely true remains philosophically debatable in the case of both these assumptions and their scientific equivalents. And the Baconian-Mertonian view that 'science' is precisely the systematisation of the work of gardeners and others is a more plausible one than the 'capitalising' expropriation of their labours by such blandly free-floating theoretical assertions.

[113] It is wholly significant here that Cusa and those influenced by him returned to the Boethian preoccupations of the twelfth-century Renaissance. See Albertson, *Mathematical Theologies: Nicholas of Cusa and the Legacy of Thierry of Chartres* (New York: Oxford University Press, 2014); Richard J. Oosterhoff, 'Cusanus and Boethian Theology in the Early French Reform', in *Nicholas of Cusa and the Making of the Modern World*, 339–66. Oosterhoff discusses how Lefèvre sustained Nicholas's Boethian and Chartrian interest in mathematical models of the Trinity.

involves our entire existential stance as creatures standing alongside other creatures under providence. It arises not merely from regarding how the tree is, however holistically, but also from our appreciation of its beauty, its inherent worth within the Created order and its role in a wider ecology.

4.8 The Genealogy of Ergetic Knowledge

With respect to the relationship of the ergetic to the essential, the genealogy of ergetic knowledge is relevant. It is complex, but one can note three decisive things.

(1) The notion that the perfectly knowable is *factibilitas* was first most decisively articulated by Nicholas of Cusa in his *Idiota de mente*. For him the idea is both participatory and Trinitarian. God the Father's knowledge is only theoretically 'given' as simultaneously willed through the Spirit and expressed in the Son, his *Verbum*.[114] This is a strict thinking-through of the consequences of doctrinal orthodoxy, and it also ultimately echoes John Scottus Eriugena, for whom God knows himself only by creating, both externally and internally (both Eriugena and Cusa describe the generation of the Son and Procession of the Spirit as a kind of divine 'self-creation').[115]

Our human knowledge echoes this situation in one sense most perfectly in the case of mathematics, where we produce realities that nonetheless fully compel the shape of our productions. We do not find a triangle lying around on a pavement, yet we cannot just make a shape any old how for it to be recognisable as a triangle, nor improvise as to its inherent properties which we indeed discover, albeit usually through further acts of construction and not just observation.

Nevertheless, this little world of numbers and figures that we fully create or generate is a very meagre world, which can only *symbolise* God's real *mathesis*, his knowing/making of himself in the Trinity and the world in creation in a mostly rather *formal* way.[116] Only to some degree (unlike for Galileo) does it allow us to comprehend nature. To approach a fuller grasp of the unknown divine *mathesis* that coincides with the ability to create everything out of nothing, we must engage 'conjecturally' in less certain crafts and symbolic utterances (including 'experiments' and 'technologies', 'games' and 'works of art', all of which are invoked by Nicholas), which,

[114] Nicholas of Cusa, *Idiota: De mente*, II, 59; XI, 133. And see again Milbank, '*Mathexis* and *Mathesis*'.
[115] See Milbank, 'One in Three'. [116] Ibid.

however, are more existentially engaging than numbers. Yet like numbers (and like the Son 'reacting' from the outset upon the Paternal source), they also to a degree and more freely 'compel' us, such that one might say our artefacts make us as much as we the artefacts, and, as already argued, lure us towards their 'proper' (and even natural) finality, as much as we shape them through our planning intentions.

Thus, in another sense, this less certain mode of making, which also involves contemplative attention to all that we have not made in nature, is more perfectly imitative of the divine act of creation. It should also be made clear that, for Nicholas, such wider conjecture fully assumes that our basic modes of understanding somehow 'correspond' to perceived natural realities that we do not construct, such that the forms of natural realities are primarily in things and not in our minds. (Nicholas was in no sense an Idealist.)[117]

It is then possible to read later versions of the so-called *verum-factum* axiom, and so most of 'Baconianism', as debasements of an inclusion of technological aspiration within a Trinitarian ontology, which includes for Cusa the idea that *all* of finite reality, not just the human, exists by trying conjecturally to 'express' itself in an imperfect attempt to manifest the divine.[118] This ontology was somewhat sustained, as we have seen, by the Fabrists in France and later recovered, not just by Comenius, but also (through whatever route of influence) by Giambattista Vico in his early *Liber metaphysicus* (the *De antiquissima italorum sapientia*) where he provides the historically most explicit version of the *verum-factum* axiom, whose Vichian form as also *verum-factum-bonum* explicitly reveals that it is conceived as a Trinitarian revision of the traditional doctrine of the transcendentals. This text also tried to articulate an anti-Cartesian, neo-Proclean version of modern natural philosophy and mathematics, undoing the algebraicisation of the geometric and the supposed de-mystification of mathematical unity and generative power.[119]

As I have already indicated, one can additionally say that, since mathematics was taken to be the most paradigmatic ergetic knowledge, then, at least on Cusa's and Vico's Proclean-Boethian understanding – which refuses to reduce maths either to the a priori rational or the a posteriori

[117] Ibid. [118] Milbank, '*Methexis* to *Mathesis*'.

[119] Giambattista Vico, *On the Most Ancient Wisdom of the Italians*, trans. Jason Taylor (New Haven, CT: Yale University Press, 2010), ch. 1, pp. 17–29. An insistence on the irreducibility of geometry was also characteristic of Scottish Enlightenment thinking, including Hume. See George Davie, *The Scotch Metaphysics: A Century of Enlightenment in Scotland* [1952] (London: Routledge, 2001), 10–40.

empirical – it follows that mathematics was also understood to be perfect experimentation.[120]

This casts in a somewhat different light the usual expressions today of wonder that it should turn out for physics that the natural world happens to coincide or correlate with our supposedly 'private' mathematical reasonings. For to the contrary, the 'little world' of numbers and geometric shapes that we both perfectly make and yet perfectly discover is just that *superficial and 'stoppable'* aspect of always dynamic nature that we are able fully to penetrate and to co-produce with some exactitude – even if, as Cusanus noted with fascination, the real unity, point, line, circle, triangle and so on eludes, us, since they are aporetically at once spaceless and yet as such no longer distinguishable from different and even opposite numbers and configurations. Even mathematical exactitude is problematic at the margins.

Nevertheless, a wider experimentation linked to maths, but always to a rougher extension of *mathesis*, is evidence that there is no total gulf between this relatively exact penetration and a more problematic, wider and deeper probing. What that circumstance then suggests is that there is indeed a real and natural linkage between the in-themselves natural processes of our thinking and the processes of nature in general.[121] But mathematics of itself *already* confirms this linkage, at once in an extreme and yet also a very 'thin' and confined sort of way, just insofar as it both exceeds through idealisation and yet altogether depends upon its informing of the spatial, as both Aristotle and Boethius in his wake realised, in their articulation of the division of theoretical knowledge in general into the physical, mathematical and theological, according to respective degrees of abstraction first from motion, and then from matter itself.

What all this suggests is that there is, indeed, an affinity, incoherently sidelined by disenchanted monotheism, between our minds and the natural world (unsurprisingly, since all of our thoughts and feelings are also part of nature, as Alfred North Whitehead insisted)[122] but that the latter implies a higher and unreachable mentality of origin that eludes us, as argued against both German idealism and English empiricism by the Scottish nineteenth-century Presbyterian philosopher James Ferrier.[123]

120 Proclus understood mathematical realities as *probolai*, or 'projections'. See Albertson, *Mathematical Theologies*, 66.

121 Cartwright, *Nature: The Artful Modeller*.

122 Alfred North Whitehead, *The Concept of Nature* (Cambridge: Cambridge University Press, 2015).

123 James Ferrier, *Institutes of Metaphysics: The Theory of Knowing and Being* (Edinburgh: Blackwood, 1854); George Davie, *Scotch Metaphysics*, 117–235.

Vico was not however in every respect historically eccentric: he belonged to an entire 'neo-Renaissance' in the late seventeenth and early eighteenth century, including Leibniz, that variously, if imperfectly, tried to restore more relational, connected, eidetic and vitalist understandings of reality – partly, indeed, because Newton himself had ultimately conceded that 'action at a distance' was irreducible and that purely mechanical hypotheses of an all-pervasive ether and so forth did not work. Sheer mechanism and sheer materialism, it turned out, simply would not co-conjugate. Just for this reason, the Baconian (but more ultimately Cusan) defining of science by 'experiment' became eventually ever more important.[124]

Thus the deeper irony regarding Newton is that he himself can be seen as both the culmination of a disenchanted monotheism and the beginnings of the return of enchantment in somewhat modified idioms. Not the last of the magicians after all, but the first of a new wave.

(2) The second thing to be said about maker's knowledge is that it already existed in the realms of optics and alchemy, stretching back to Roger Bacon in the twelfth century and behind him and above all to Arabic learning, giving the lie to the claims of counter-revisionists like David Wootton that a totally new thing which we call 'science' arose with a revolutionary break in the seventeenth century.[125] Most experiments before early modernity were carried out in order to confirm or to slightly extend existing observations, adopting only 'slight variations', as Bacon noted, and after isolated problems were considered solved, experimental interest tended to lapse.[126] Modern experiments, by contrast, attempt drastically, systematically and often counter-intuitively to alter reality in order to isolate and bring to the fore some hidden forces and effects.

[124] Gaukroger, *Collapse of Mechanism*, 83–94.

[125] See Oliver, *Philosophy, God and Motion*, 75–84. Wootton's claim that the discovery of the New World legitimated the notion of radical novelty does not seem entirely convincing. It was not, after all, new to know that there were undiscovered parts of the Earth. Moreover, right up to Newton and beyond, the 'new science' was presented as a recovery of ancient knowledge. This could be a perpetuation of an originally Patristic sense of a unified perennial understanding (typically uniting Israel, Egypt and Greece) still retaining a stronger echo of our lost innocence, or else (or also) a usually Protestant repudiation of a supposedly excessive Greek pagan legacy, strangely favouring an imagined earlier Mesopotamian wisdom. And we have already seen how the stimuli to novelty were more primarily religious than natural philosophical. Wootton argues (*The Invention of Science*, 50) against Burtt and others that only 'new experiences' and 'new sense-perceptions' could have inaugurated the 'Scientific Revolution', since 'if all that was required for [it] was *new thinking*, then it would be impossible to explain why it did not take place long before the seventeenth century'. To which the obvious riposte is that millennia elapsed before anyone thought like Confucius, Plato, or the Buddha.

[126] Gaukroger, *Civilisation and the Culture of Science*, 424.

Optics and alchemy already to some extent did this, however, in their attempt to discover, control and adapt concealed powers: in consequence, chemists and natural magicians tended already to identify a more complete knowledge and penetrative knowledge with construction and reproduction. Given his post-Renaissance campaign for disenchantment and the rationalising of natural magic Bacon perhaps rather underestimated this achievement.

And it was made, as already with Roger Bacon, against an eschatological background. As Peter Harrison has emphasised after Charles Webster (and ultimately Joseph Needham and Benjamin Farrington), the focus on experimentation and technology in early modernity belonged to a desire to reverse the effects of the fall in anticipation of the eschaton, or even to help usher it in by engendering a knowledge that will transfigure human life on earth.[127] The Protestant sense of our total depravity may have reinforced this, as Harrison argues, though in actual fact the Baconian theorists and practitioners tended to qualify the sternness of Protestant doctrine in Renaissance-inherited ways.

What is more, the same theologically restorative project was found in contemporary Catholic Italy (Tommaso Campanella and others), even in Descartes, and much earlier in the case of Roger Bacon and then with thinkers like Ficino and Lefèvre in the Renaissance – in close linkage with, though with neoplatonic mollification of, the apocalyptic prophecies of the Dominican Savanarola in the Florentine prophetic tradition, which were much more material and incarnational in character than those of Franciscan Joachitism.[128]

Do we indeed fully understand the exact modes of millenarianism that were associated with the rise of 'science'? Were they in the tradition of the Joachite and spiritual Franciscan notions of a new 'age of the Spirit' beyond that of the Son, in which case one has the paradoxical and, as Eric Voegelin suggested, 'gnostic' notion of an age to come in time that will be somehow 'less material', less Christologically 'incarnated' than the current era? The danger of this perspective, as Bruno Latour argues, is that

[127] Peter Harrison, *The Fall of Man and the Foundations of Science* (Cambridge: Cambridge University Press, 2007). Cusanus also had eschatological interests: see his *Coniectura de ultimis diebus*, trans. Jasper Hopkins (2008) from *Nicolai de Cusa Opera Omnia*, vol. IV (Opuscula I), ed. Paul Wilpert (Hamburg: Felix Meiner, 1959), 91–100.

[128] See Amos Edelheit, *Ficino, Pico and Savanarola: The Evolution of Humanist Theology 1461/2–1498* (Leiden: Brill, 2008); Henri de Lubac, *La Posterité spirituelle de Joachim de Flore* (Paris: Cerf, 2014). There is evidence that both Descartes and Hobbes were 'secularising' their earlier interests in Rosicrucian currents of alchemical and eschatological thinking. See Michael Allen Gillespie, *The Theological Origins of Modernity* (Chicago: University of Chicago Press, 2008).

it associated science and technology with a false definite knowledge of the correct 'progressive' shape of the future – a millenarianism which liberalism oddly shares with fundamentalists. In this way, as he says, it denies the real vagaries of the actual immanent earth with which we have to deal.[129]

On the other hand, perhaps elements, at the very least, of alchemical, Paracelsian and Baconian apocalyptic still lay, like that of Savanarola, within a basically Augustinian perspective on the end of time: before that end, beyond which lies the real, eternal apocalyptic disclosure, the conflict of good and evil will intensify: the earth will suffer a further fallen decline, but the counter-mission of the ecclesial minority will shine out all the more. Paracelsian-Baconian themes of the improvement of practical knowledge in anticipation of the end might be seen as more lying within this trajectory, rather than as Joachite 'utopian' projects, linked to a worldly reign of the saints in time, even though these schemes undoubtedly, especially with the Puritans, got mixed up with that thematic. Furthermore, the very materiality of the alchemical and post-alchemical salvific projects meant that they were still conceived within a Christological, incarnational and eucharistic purview, rather than the Joachite and Franciscan 'spiritualising' one.[130]

One can also note that, if it is true that Baconianism is really a secularisation of the doctor and chemist Paracelsus's Lutheran apocalypticism, then, all the same, Paracelsus was very heterodox in Lutheran terms – he saw justifying faith in a 'magical' light (despite his rejection of key alchemical theses) as being none other than transformative imagination, and regarded Mary, to which he was devoted, as an incarnation of the divine Sophia.[131]

(3) The third point in relation to maker's knowledge concerns its indeed continued possible relation to magic. Exactly because it was essentially pragmatic and even sometimes 'poetic' – looking for truth in a made outcome that is revealed solely through the making process – links of ergetic knowledge to inscrutable magical processes of affinity and forceful power were almost inevitable.

[129] Latour, *Facing Gaia*, 184–254. Clearly, David Wootton still supports this dangerous secularised millenarianism.

[130] Even the non-spiritual Franciscans like Bonaventure were semi-Joachites, as Joseph Ratzinger long ago showed.

[131] See Andrew Weeks, *Paracelsus: Speculative Theory and the Crisis of the Early Reformation* (Albany: State University of New York Press, 1997), 82–5, 98, 101–28, 144; Charles Webster, *Paracelsus: Medicine, Magic and the Mission at the End of Time* (New Haven, CT: Yale University Press, 2008).

This applies to Marsilio Ficino, whose concern with natural magic remained within quite conceptually tight bounds. He was careful to make it tally with the thought of Aquinas, even if this sometimes meant some extension of the latter's meanings. Specifically, he argued that while Aquinas differentiated between an artificial figure that forms matter – like a table or a painted depiction – and an amulet merely encrusted with words or signs, he also thought, entirely in line with both Aquinas and Aristotle, that the former, more than the engraved sign, approximated to the natural form of a material thing, without entirely acquiring that status. Ficino took this proximity to be a justification for the invocatory use of figured images, while still regarding the magical use of inscribed amulets as demonic and forbidden.[132]

What is at issue here, as Brian Copenhaver has understood, is not a distinction between occult and natural – since for Aquinas also 'occult' powers (simply hidden powers whose effect is manifest, but source unknown) are perfectly natural,[133] but rather between occult powers and those of *noesis*. Only where language, and so explicit understanding, is involved, does a question of an illicit attempt to coerce and manipulate the demonic and angelic arise. In line still with Aquinas and other scholastics, Ficino endorsed only natural attempts at influence via similitude and affinity, which are assumed to operate through a shared 'life' or 'spirit' operating at different analogical levels, yet holding together and in unity all of physical reality.[134] However, he extended the scholastics' latitude by drawing on his greater knowledge of the ultimate neoplatonic sources to which they were already in these respects ultimately indebted. Consequently, he allowed that artificial figures, regarded (again in keeping with Aristotle) as fully bound together by form, even though such form cannot keep its matter alive or reproduce itself, may also be engaged for the transformational 'eliciting' of new effects from immanently more elevated metaphysical strata.

The high scholastics had already entertained this elicitation in a more restricted guise, that crucially had not permitted the Ficinian mingling of artificial with natural process. But Ficino's much more direct Renaissance acquaintance with texts by Iamblichus and others allowed him to argue for a naturally 'automatic' influence also of signs, without any attempt at noetic and linguistic coercion of spiritual entities, or 'stimulus from our

[132] Copenhaver, *Magic in Western Culture*, 102126. [133] Aquinas, *De occultis operibus naturae*.
[134] Copenhaver, *Magic in Western Culture*, 123. Copenhaver claims that 'similitude' and 'life' are Platonic categories; 'spirit' Stoic, though integrated within the neoplatonic synthesis.

thinking', as Iamblichus put it.[135] Precisely the need for an incantatory reiteration of signs beyond our intentional mastery ensures that all magic is retained within a 'natural' scope and does *not* involve any hubristic attempt deliberately to manipulate hidden or transcendent forces.

Just this mingling of natural change with artificial procedure, as has frequently been observed, is *centrally germane* to all later 'scientific' experimental practice, whether still (or once more) 'natural magical', or merely mechanical.[136] And one can say that every time an experimental or technical operation is able reliably to summon and channel a not entirely decipherable natural force or process, it acts in *precisely* the manner of a magical ritual.[137] Of course this does not mean that anything more than the 'natural' is involved, nor necessarily anything that we cannot to a degree rationally account for, but then Ficino insisted on these restrictions also. To invoke anything preternatural in magic was still for him inevitably to involve oneself in a 'Goetic' darkness, unless strictly related to prescribed religious ritual, in which case it sustains an allowable theurgy.

All the same, we can note here, given our modern sense that even nature is inscribed with signs yielding 'information', that today we might be logically compelled to extend the bounds of 'natural magic' still further – to include also the operation of a (still nonetheless) automatic *noesis* which clearly involves for us a hybridity of natural and artificial sign *in excess* of Ficino's mere hybridity of artificial and natural *figure*. How exactly, one might ask, in the long-term wake of C. S. Lewis, do we suppose that we are *not* involved in conjuration, which may well turn anonymously dark just to the degree (which is usually absolute) that we try to deny it?

One can also significantly argue here that the natural magical version of the fusion of the artificial with the natural, insofar as it stresses the primacy of the experimental in the face of the inscrutable and non-mathematically reducible, is more primarily 'scientific' than the mechanical version of this fusion. What is more, even though such operative fusion in its magical version was to a degree novel, it was actually in continuity with the ancient mediation exercised by the category of form in Platonic-Aristotelian philosophy between physical reality, mind and artificial productions. Because the form in things is identical with the forms of things understood, for this philosophy, it remained within the scope of what Owen Barfield referred

[135] Ibid., 124.
[136] Copenhaver, for all his admirable scholarly sophistication, oddly seems still to assume the uncontested defeat of natural magic after the seventeenth century: ibid., 153.
[137] I am grateful for this insight to a private communication from David Bentley Hart.

to as 'original participation' whereby our minds are in a real and sympathetic resonance with the external world.[138] Additionally, *both* a tree and a table are instances of formed substances possessed of a defined essence: indeed, for Aristotle, as for Plato, the insertion of form into matter by a craftsman is clearly a crucial paradigm for his hylomorphic account of physical reality in general.[139]

Thus a contemporary neo-scholastic like Edward Feser is simply wrong to claim that artefacts had no essential form for premodern philosophy. This involves a confusion of the definition of form with the definition of natural rather than artificial form as able to self-move and to generate.[140] In consequence, he exaggerates the degree to which the error of modern scientism and of the mechanical philosophy was to confuse the natural with the artificial. This exaggeration is in part witnessed by the fact that for quite a long time machines themselves were thought of as vital (since to a degree self-sustaining through currents of force) and magical.[141] The shift was not really towards the mechanical, but towards 'disenchanted machines', now seen as entirely dead things empowered by alienated minds, just as the universe came to be thought of as a vast dead machine set in motion by God.

Indeed, this shift suggests that mechanical metaphysics *overly separated* the natural and the artificial, and was thus not fully true to their operative blending which is at once to some extent traditional (as we have seen) and yet characteristic of the 'magical' core of modern science. Bruno Latour has most strongly argued that the modern scientistic and capitalist mentality is crucially characterised by a duality of nature and culture; but this duality involves also a duality of the natural and the artificial. Thus, as Latour contends (in his crucial commentary on the work of Shapin and Schaffer), modernity, as propelled by the seventeenth-century paradigm which I have labelled 'disenchanted transcendence', is caught in an *aporia* as to whether 'everything is natural', such that, as for Hobbes, even our thoughts and even our political and social constructions are in reality but the a priori calculable motions of the atoms of the world-machine (the assumption undergirding his political theory), or whether, instead, 'everything is artificial', such that, as for Robert Boyle, we can only reckon with nature,

138 Owen Barfield, *Saving the Appearances: A Study in Idolatry* (New York: Harcourt, Brace and World, 1972); Berman, *Reenchantment of the World*, 136, 140–2, 146.

139 Aristotle, *Metaphysics*, 1039b20–1040a8.

140 Feser, *Aristotle's Revenge*, 23–24; Aristotle, *Physics*, 192b8–193b22.

141 Jessica Riskin, *The Restless Clock: A History of the Centuries-Long Argument over What Makes Living Things Tick* (Chicago: University of Chicago Press, 2016), 11–76.

as with human society, through the experimental construction of *our machines*, which in either case may reveal the regular operation of unknown forces: whether human fluids and emotions, or the mysterious 'spring of air' to fill a vacuum, besides the operations of multiple 'natural spirits' as taught by the Bible and confirmed by alchemical practice.[142]

It is then very striking that it is the thesis that all is natural because mechanical (even if this suppresses the truth that this projects the human fiction of mechanism) that, as with the more French-influenced and a prioristic Hobbes, *precludes* the need for experiment, whereas it is the thesis that all is artificial that, while sustaining the need for experiment, also sustains the hinterland of mystery on which Anglican natural philosophy, whether that of Fludd, More or Boyle, often so strikingly insisted: the ultimately unknown imperatives behind both human making and God's. This shows us that the linking of nature to artifice is *not*, as we might suppose, the core of disenchantment, just because the doctrine of Creation *ex nihilo* itself renders nature a work of art, and as such linked to the mysteries of inspiration and intentional purpose.

So the more that mechanism triumphs, the more motions are inexplicably separated from mind (undoing original participation) and the more an alternative ensues between explanation by the natural machine or explanation by the artificial machine. By contrast, the *blending* of the artificial and the natural which lies at the core of experimentation (yet does not claim to read all of nature as being exhaustively at one with our devices) just by *not* totally collapsing the one to the other, but sustaining them in an *analogical* fusion, and so precluding aporetic oscillation between the one and the other, preserves also our ability formally to know and to operate with (yet not entirely control) regular and yet unknown forces in the natural world which somehow resonate with our mental and even our emotional powers.

In the latter respect, Ficino had placed a much greater stress, when compared with medieval scholastic norms, upon magical practice as an important aspect of healing the soul through a heightened attunement with created powers, angelic intelligences and God himself.[143] None of this was necessarily an aberrance in Christian terms, but was rather an extended paraliturgical and curatively directed renewal of the theurgic outlook derived by Dionysius and Maximus from Proclus, besides pre-

142 Shapin and Schaffer, *Leviathan and the Air-Pump*; Bruno Latour, *We Have Never Been Modern*, trans. Catherine Porter (Cambridge, MA: Harvard University Press, 1993).

143 I am indebted to discussions with Laura McCormack here.

existing Christian sources.[144] (Ficino, like Nicholas of Cusa before him, was very close to the Greek-inclining Camaldolesian order outside Florence, preaching in their chapel once a week.)

In the theurgic tradition, all prayer is a contemplative practice, like the Eastern Jesus prayer, which through its concentrated performance of *theoria* channels the divine (under an assumed providential destining) precisely without manipulation or appropriation. There is arguably a strange sense in which this notion of 'magic' is exactly the opposite (and *the only possible opposite*) of magic in the usual sense of a wilful and controlling act of conjuration. For there is no illusion involved here of trying to change God's mind, and yet prayer so conceived does not succumb to the opposite danger of a narcissistic concern with mere self-therapy.

4.9 The Orthodoxy of Esotericism

All this matters, because it is not possible to respond to the arrival of 'science', especially in terms of the new 'ergetic knowledge', merely by going back to Aristotle, the Fathers or Aquinas. Instead, we should look to people like Thierry, Bernard Silvestris, Alan of Lille and Achard (in the twelfth-century Renaissance),[145] besides Cusa, Pico della Mirandola, Ficino, Paracelsus and Robert Fludd (in the early modern Renaissance) or later Berkeley, Coleridge and the German Romantics such as Novalis, Von Baader and Friedrich Schlegel, who tried to rethink the Patristic vision in yet more theurgic, paradoxical, sympathetic and vitalistic terms.

It can be noted here that writers like Fludd and Henry Vaughan (twin brother of the metaphysical poet Thomas) stood somewhat between enchanted immanentism and enchanted transcendence, insofar as they were nearer (somewhat under Paracelsian influence) than the Cambridge Platonists to grasping the paradox that perfect transcendence is also perfect immanence. Thus, for them, it is less a matter of the operation of a plastic principle as an 'under-worker' (a notion in danger of drifting in Arian, 'Deistic' and theodicist directions) than of the divine uncreated Sophia also present as created Sophia in the guise of a fully-fledged *anima mundi*.[146]

[144] See Gregory Shaw, *Theurgy and the Soul: The Neoplatonism of Iamblichus* (Kettering, OH: Angelico, 2014).

[145] See Brian Stock, *Myth and Science in the Twelfth Century: A Study of Bernard Silvester* (Princeton, NJ: Princeton University Press, 1972).

[146] For Fludd and Western Sophiology in general, see Michael Martin, *The Submerged Reality: Sophiology and the Turn to a Poetic Metaphysic* (Kettering, OH: Angelico, 2015). Thomas

Of course, as earlier suggested, the truth is more that the Cambridge Platonists were *not* fully committed to an enchanted transcendence (though Cudworth, the superior philosopher, to a much greater degree than More).

Let me explain a little more why I think we have to attend to these 'alternatively modern thinkers' and not just to the 'pre-modern classics'.

Once nominalism had shown how analogy, participation, universals and real relations *do* seriously compromise the law of non-contradiction (this is the kind of thing that the more strait-laced Thomists, and even the brilliant ones like Erich Przywara will try to deny), it became *necessary* to see these things in a more 'occult' fashion, whether in the idiom of Cusanus or that of the natural magicians and alchemists. Similarly, a kind of 'post-nominalism', both in his case and in that of Lefèvre, contended that all our ideas, including of universals, are, indeed, linguistically constructed, and yet that such 'making' is truly a kind of mystical work that intimates the full reality and universal ideas of things that are at once generated and contemplated in the mind of the Trinitarian God.[147]

These are two reasons why one gets the rise of 'esotericism', besides, as its greatest scholar Antoine Faivre has pointed out, a return to the traditional neoplatonic concern to hold together physics and metaphysics and cosmology and ontology – which in the wake of the Terminists were coming ever further adrift, as we have seen.[148] Apart from a by no means contemptible (because ecumenical) commitment to the hidden unity of all ancient knowledge, there is nothing sheerly strange or entirely secretive (for all the mystique surrounding the complexly ironic Rosicrucian writings, etc.) about this stuttering current, which strongly resurfaces in the mid-eighteenth century with figures like the great Lutheran pietist and theosophist F. C. Oetinger, in whose case it was linked to attempts to articulate an interesting vitalist 'electrical' physics and theology.[149]

Browne also affirmed the reality of the world-soul. Its role was ambivalently allowed by Augustine and later affirmed by Thierry and Cusanus, amongst many others. I am indebted to discussions with Alison Milbank here.

147 Milbank, '*Mathesis* and *Methexis*'; Oosterhoff, *Making Mathematical Culture*, 102–3, 201–9. One can note here after Oosterhoff, himself following Marten Hoenen, that both realism and nominalism were themselves *viae* of technical method, at least as much as of theoretical argument or assumption. Lefèvre's mystical and pictorial constructivism, after Cusanus, is a new way of synthesis, in terms of both craft and conclusion.

148 Antoine Faivre, *Theosophy, Imagination Tradition*, trans. Christine Rhone (Albany: State University of New York Press, 2000).

149 Ernst Benz, *The Theology of Electricity*, trans. Wolfgang Taraba (Eugene, OR: Wipf and Stock, 1989).

Indeed, some of what I have just adumbrated may be the lurking reason why Renaissance Hermeticising theology was for a time endorsed at the very highest Papal level, as with the authorisation of Johannes Reuchlin's Cabbalistic project. In resisting nominalist positivism, there was also at work here a new sense of admitted Christian constitutive eclecticism, more openly able to confess its debts both to Judaism and to paganism, as with Giles of Viterbo's interweaving of mythological allegory into his *Sentence Commentary* (the last that was ever to be written).[150] There is continuity besides change at work here in relation to the Patristic legacy: the Fathers of course had to stress the break with the past; now it became conceptually necessary still more to admit and develop their allowed 'spoliation of the Egyptians' (as they named the plundering of pagan wisdom, in an allegory of the Israelite thefts from their masters, at the outset of their Exodus from the land of the Pharaohs).

4.10 The Modern Return of 'Natural Magic'

My contention then, is that the battle between the three different visions of nature never went away and has never been decisively resolved. In particular, that 'natural magic' did not truly depart, even where it was no longer named such, but merely mutated, re-emerging strongly in the Romantic period and with much influence on later science.

The intermittent emergence and today the dominance of a *fourth* model of 'disenchanted immanence' (a dead cosmos with no God, immanent or transcendent)[151] certainly does not overtake or end the inherited triple conflict. For the evidence of vital forces at work in the cosmos, plus the difficulties of explaining life and conscious intelligence, besides the emerging dominance of ecological concerns, ensure that today enchanted immanentisms are once more emergent.[152] They remain in tension both with the disenchanting impulse of today's internationally widespread and largely Protestant tendencies to undergird capitalism and technocracy with a voluntarist, individualist and sentimentally affective theology, and with

150 Giles was very mainstream, the head of the order to which the heresiarch Martin Luther belonged. See Giles of Viterbo, *The Commentary on the Sentences of Petrus Lombardus* (Leiden: Brill, 2010); Francis X. Martin, *Friar, Reformer and Renaissance Scholar: Life and Work of Giles of Viterbo 1569–1532* (Villanova, PA: Augustinian Press, 1992).

151 Thomas Hobbes foreshadowed this, but he retained a *material God.*

152 Moreover, many early twentieth-century vitalist ideas later got baptised as 'field theories' in an attempt to make them sound more respectable. See Rupert Sheldrake, *A New Science of Life* (London: Icon, 2009).

the rarer yet crucial voices (of varying religious affiliation) seeking to renew an enchanted transcendence.

What is more, it is clear that the science espoused by disenchanted transcendence gradually failed, as has already been indicated. In a very simple fashion, the book of nature just refused to be read that way. As already mentioned, if, by the mid-eighteenth century, one has a renewed attempt to account for even human existence scientifically, then this is not the same as the initial attempt of Hobbes, because by now nature has itself been understood more humanly as continuous with us in terms of vitality and sympathetic resonance. This is just how David Hume has to be read, against all the prevailing misreadings.[153]

And eventually electromagnetism, born in this epoch, proved with the Scottish physicist James Maxwell and others in the nineteenth century to be more comprehensive than mechanism; actions at a distance were now regarded as ineliminable and as applying (in accord with Newton's best surmises) to bodies at every level – an analogy between gravity and electromagnetism being assumed, though not fully understood, right up to the present day.[154]

Physics gradually came to view everything in terms of ever-shifting relations and fields of forces. Sometimes the language of 'analogy' was even returned to, as with Niels Bohr. Any idea of an ultimate cosmic container was abandoned. For contemporary physics, even our entire universe is regarded as some sort of enormous writhing whale coterminous with its own sea. There are, after all, no isolated 'things' wandering randomly in a uniform darkness, for even the most ultimate context, so far as we can know it, turns out to be itself one gigantic thing: Leviathan at large in its own mythical ocean[155]

But neither, perhaps, does pure immanentism fare so well either: if there are *only* things, only interlinked items in overlapping waves unto infinite horizons, whose 'laws' are really just their own habits, then it would seem that relative totalities continuously come to be and vanish in the course of

[153] Gaukroger, *Collapse of Mechanism*; on Hume, see 438–52. Through the influence of Shaftesbury on Frances Hutcheson, some of the concerns of the Cambridge Platonists with the cosmic and human character of sympathy, from Benjamin Whichcote onwards, were maintained by the Scots thinkers.

[154] James T. Cushing, *Philosophical Concepts in Physics: The Historical Relation between Philosophy and Scientific Theories* (Cambridge: Cambridge University Press 2000), 181–222.

[155] Carlo Rovelli, *Seven Brief Lessons on Physics*, trans. Simon Carnell and Erica Segre (London: Penguin, 2015), 37–48; Gribbin, *Six Impossible Things*. Of course, we have no warrant to identify our universe with nature or Creation as such.

an ineffable time.[156] There is no immanent 'whole', even in continuous dispersion, which could be put up as a candidate to displace the old dethroned Urizen or 'God'.

Ever since Newton, physics gradually became itself a part of natural history: any energetic system was proved destined to irreversible entropy, as everything moves towards increasing disorder and inexorable heat death .[157] At the most ultimate micro quantum level (on the conventional 'Copenhagen interpretation'), there are not even causes in the sense of efficiency, only spontaneous, mutually linked motions of diverse and obscurely linked indeterminate or 'superposed' elements of potential force and shape.[158]

This returns us somewhat to the neoplatonic view that every cause exceeds its effect and every effect its cause – for the *aitia*, or 'sufficient ground of donation', really indicates a mutation whereby it is the case that both an original something stays the same and yet something emanatively new, something else, emerges.[159] Everything is fundamentally *modal*, such that essence cannot be thought apart from its modes or 'ways' of expression, nor the individual thing apart from the individual 'ways' in which it has come to be. Perhaps modern physics encourages the articulation of a Trinitarian ontology (though not one implying a heretical modalism) in this respect.

If cause were only the mechanical impact of one thing on another, then (as with the case of motion broken up into a series of fully actual phases not being any longer motion) there would be no causality, only an inexplicable occasioning, since any force passing over into a new condition is really the original force transfigured. All real causation then paradoxically involves a transgression of causal priority – as Buddhist philosophy frequently realised.[160] The cause neither reaches nor touches its effect, nor does not do so (as with the candle and its flame), rendering what we soothe ourselves by naming 'cause' in fact an incomprehensible, but everyday, magical effect.[161]

[156] Cartwright, *Nature: The Artful Modeller*.

[157] Newton himself anticipated this, as he had not arrived at the later supposed laws of the conservation of motion and energy: Burtt, *The Metaphysical Foundations*, 267. But they only apply within an ordered system: it turns out that there is a long-term tendency to disorder and decay.

[158] Cushing, *Philosophical Concepts in Physics*, 271–344. The Bohr–Heisenberg view has been challenged by David Bohm's more causal, though also holistic account of quantum observations, seemingly favoured by Cushing. But this still remains a minority report and might be construed as another manifestation of the continuing but dubiously seductive lure of Newtonian unity, which I consider below.

[159] See Andrea Bellantone, *La Métaphysique possible* (Paris: Hermann, 2012), 223–58.

[160] See *Nāgārjuna's Middle Way*, trans. Mark Sideris and Shōryū Katsura (Somerville, MA: Wisdom, 2013).

[161] Timothy Morton, *Realist Magic Objects, Ontology, Causality* (London: Open Humanities, 2013).

It is not even, as for Aquinas, that all motion experientially traces back to something unmoving, but rather that there is never anything lying beyond motion and development (beyond the modal or the processive, even if one allows for the equal role of the essential and the individuated) within the traceable, finite world. This world therefore does *not* suggest to us any ultimacy of a monadic unmoved first mover who would not, after all, be the Christian God. Yet every finite vertical and horizontal emanation can nonetheless be seen by theology as grounded in and ultimately conditioned by the infinitely resting dynamic and equally perfectly resting motion of the Trinity.

The more that modern science regards with an infinitesimal increase the micro level, and the more that it expands exponentially to the macro, then the more it seems that 'ordinary' (but actually themselves not very coherent, as we have just seen) mechanical notions of causal priority break down in favour of spontaneous actions, reactions, prehensions and inherent tendencies which appear (as Gabriel Tarde once argued in the case of the microscopic level)[162] more akin to life and intelligence than do the surface manifestations of the pre- or primitively organic.

It is therefore, once more, just as if, in the microcosmic 'middle' of physical reality, the 'initial' and most 'all-encompassing' macrocosmic phenomena of the transfinite margins (great and small) reappear in conscious manifestation in higher animal, and supremely human life, as though the 'astrological' and the 'alchemical' resonated with the psychic, as indeed often even for the initial shapers of modern cosmology and mechanical science like Kepler and Boyle.[163] This can be seen as being in keeping with the most crucial insights of Whitehead and Henri Bergson.

Such a perspective might, however, appear to downgrade the dignity of settled form and substance, which is surely required in addition to the repeated operation of efficiency in order to account for the relative stability and regularity of the more ordinary, observable world. It is difficult to account for this stability – just as it is equally hard to account for the self-renewing creative power of alteration as with embryonic development – save by appeal to a participation in the eternal, which Whitehead described as 'ingression'.[164] One can (beyond Whitehead) ascribe the instance of

[162] Gabriel Tarde, *Monadology and Sociology*, trans. Theo Lorenc (Melbourne: re.press, 2012).

[163] On Kepler's psychic vitalism, see Patrick J. Boner, *Kepler's Cosmological Synthesis: Astrology, Mechnaism and the Soul* (Leiden: Brill, 2013). I am indebted to discussions with Conor Cunningham about the centrality of the middle or of mixture (*mixis*), with its ancient and modern chemical resonance.

[164] Whitehead, *Process and Reality*, 23, 149 and passim.

substantial stability in this world ultimately to the lure of ideas in the Mind of God, without denying that such stability is at least relatively instanced by worldly things themselves, thereby somewhat qualifying Plato with Aristotle (yet perhaps in accord with Plato's real intentions). If one affirms an ultimately creative divine source for all of reality, then one can allow a kind of equal primacy to both 'process' and 'thing' within immanence. Rupert Sheldrake has shown how the irreducibility of form goes *together* with the primacy of a habit-forming creative process, as opposed to a Newtonian dominance of 'law' which suppresses the reality of both.[165] And this conjunction requires an equal primacy to be granted also to 'relation', which we experience all the time as real, yet is puzzlingly irreducible to either the internal monism of process or the externality of mere accidental attachment to things.

It would seem that our human intelligence synthesises this dynamic stability with the more chaotic and unpredictable margins of the physical world, in its capacity to generate a flexible but ordered reality which is human culture, and all the modified geography which is human as well as physical.[166] Thus if the micro and macro levels rather curiously exhibit evidence of ontological 'life' and 'psychic intelligence', then it is equally the case that they exhibit a kind of shapeless and elusive lack of anything we can grasp as full reality, as quantum physics and post-Einsteinian cosmology have increasingly revealed.

In the face of this circumstance, more than one metaphysically reflective scientist has suggested that quantum chaos (and also macro-nullity?) is after all somewhat equivalent to Aristotelian matter, or to Thomist designated, quantified matter, which is a pre-condition for individuation, but does not fully explain the phenomenal formed level of things that we perceive to have its own formal and substantive integrity.[167] However, only Scotism viewed prime matter as a 'form in itself'; for Aristotle and Aquinas there is never any unformed matter. It therefore follows that the random, mysteriously entangled and contradictorily superimposed elements (manifesting as at once both waves and particles) of quantum physics cannot be assimilated to prime matter. It is far more as if, at the infinitesimal margins or 'the minimum', where finite fades into the transfinite, the law of non-contradiction indeed breaks down, in the manner indicated by Cusa,

[165] Sheldrake, *A New Science of Life*, 73–96.

[166] I am again indebted here to discussions with Conor Cunningham about his idea that reality lies 'in the middle' rather than either 'at the bottom' or 'at the top'.

[167] Bernard d'Espagnat, *On Physics and Philosophy* (Princeton, NJ: Princeton University Press 2003), 443–64; Wolfgang Smith, *The Wisdom of Ancient Cosmology: Contemporary Science in the Light of Tradition* (Oakton, VA: Foundation for Traditional Studies, 2013), 19–48.

Lefèvre and many alchemists.[168] On the other hand, it is correct to say, with Aristotelian commentators like Feser, that quantum physics suggests that the most atomic level is no longer 'basic', but is rather a generative source for everyday finite realities which are equally 'real' and indeed more so at the finite level. These realities include mediating, secondary qualities which are no more plausibly placed somehow inside our brains than in external things, besides consciousness and spiritual being. But it should also be noted that the idea that quantum inconstancy intrudes only at the level of the very small is misleading, and quantum mechanics increasingly shows that it can intrude at the level of any size in which inconstancy becomes manifest.[169] And this fits with the idea that the quantum level exceeds ordinary finitude: since it is incommensurable with it, it can be manifest on any plane of finite reality.

It follows, beyond Gabriel Tarde, that if instigating, infinitesimally divisible monads of all kinds (from quarks to genes to cells) somehow have an onlook towards greater wholes (as his Leibnizian nominalism, in an attempt to avoid Leibnizian pre-established harmony suggests, but cannot explain), then we cannot allow with him that parts altogether precede wholes and relations, or in consequence that manifest wholes and connections are just epiphenomenal, somewhat illusory effects of concealed micro (or macro) processes.

And all this tends to support some version of the Anthropic Principle, because the instance of the human, metaphysically (and physically, for all we know?) in the middle of cosmic reality, would then seem to concern a synthesis of the unpredictable and energetic, fluxional margins, with the more shaped and coherent manifest surfaces that lie 'in between'.[170]

4.11 The Radical Irreversibility of Time: Against the Conservatism of Relativity

Can one not wonder whether some recent (and often exorbitantly speculative) physical theories are attempts to escape from all these radical

[168] Berman, *Reenchantment of the World*, 49–65. Berman notes how the 'mystique' of crafts tended to lapse with the decline of the guilds and guild secrecy. This then mutated into a more self-conscious and deliberate esotericism, as in the case of Freemasonry.

[169] Gribbin, *Six Impossible Things*, 67–78.

[170] It is just not clear that 'science' explodes pre-modern cosmological assumptions like the centrality of the Earth or the microcosmic character of the human. Similarly, it does not really explode the understanding of colours and feelings as objectively real qualities, nor even the theory of the four elements. Does it not, after all, remain true that everything, everywhere, is variously composed of solids, liquids, vapours and burning light? The fact that they support life could reasonably suggest that somehow our earth, water and air are truly the optimum and most normative modes of the solid, liquid and vaporous. See Spike Bucklow's chapter in this volume and his *The Alchemy of Paint: Art, Science and Secrets from the Middle Ages* (London: Marion Boyars, 2009).

implications of modern science? Is not, for example, loop quantum gravity, that tries to reconcile quantum physics with relativity, integrating the quantum account of electromagnetism and strong and weak nuclear forces with the neo-classical relativist account of gravity, as in the case of Einstein's most ambitious theories, an attempt to avoid the absoluteness of irreversible time, which is a crucial mark of all post-classical physics (beginning before quantum theory)? This physics breaks with the causal and geometric symmetries of action within time and space, as always in principle reversible, of the Newtonian universe.[171]

Surely, there is a sense in which *either* time or space must be absolute, with no third, theoretically available alternative? For if space-time is absolute, then this is really a kind of fixed hyperspace, a container after all, in exacerbation of the lurking Parmenideanism of classical physics, as identified by Feser. It is time more than space which is here relativised, as talk of a fourth dimension indicates. Yet should we not agree with Bergson versus Einstein, that one cannot relativise time in the most genuine sense, as opposed to its measurability? Time, if it really exists, is irreversible and its moments are not external to each other, or convertible into each other, or fillable by a different content, like the positions of space. Nor, as Aristotle and Augustine already realised, can time be adequately thought of either as flow or as a succession of points: it includes and yet exceeds quantification.[172]

In consequence, Bergson argued, in a direct encounter with the great scientist (at a time when he was the more famous person!), that the recorders of simultaneity like clocks do not actually establish this property, so as to render it relativisable, but rather assume it as an absolute metaphysical principle, coordinated with some assumed negative presence of absolute rest, in contrast to the assumptions of Newtonian mechanics, which already tended to get rid of temporal passage by relativising all motion in terms of purely geometric variables.[173] For where fundamental motion is assumed to be undisturbed passage in a void, motion is paradoxically reduced to the instance of a static line, as now lacking its constitutive Aristotelian contrast with that 'rest', which any movement disturbs and interrupts.

171 Rovelli, *Seven Brief Lessons on Physics*, 37–48; Gribbin, *Six Impossible Things*.

172 Henri Bergson, *Durée et simultanéité* (Paris: PUF, 2009); Milbank, 'Confession of Time in Augustine'.

173 *Durée et simultanéité*, and see also Lee Smolin, *Time Reborn: From the Crisis in Physics to the Future of the Universe* (Boston: Houghton Mifflin Harcourt, 2013), 12–53, 154–71, 227–39.

As Lee Smolin argues, quantum physics in fact favours the return of time, absolute simultaneity and rest. For in apparent flouting of the principles of special relativity it has regularly recorded the instance of simultaneous changes between linked particles in terms of 'quantum entanglement' – as with the effect called 'contrary'[174] – taking no measurable time whatsoever and occurring more rapidly than the speed of light which is the supposed fixed constant that also allows general relativity to operate.

Equally, quantum physics reveals the constant emergence of unprecedented novelties which then affect the future course of events. This not only implies an 'absolute' character to time, albeit linked, as for Aristotle and Augustine, to material motion (as not for Newton), but also strongly suggests that physical laws are not transcendent to their instances, but themselves get constituted through the processes of time as habitual processes – as already suggested in the nineteenth century by both Charles Sanders Pierce and Félix Ravaisson, and today by Lee Smolin, Rupert Sheldrake and Nancy Cartwright.[175]

All the same, the evidence for the existence of black holes may indeed suggest that they vanish into singularities, where neither time nor space abide: perhaps this is the 'maximum' instance of a Cusan passing of the finite into the incomprehensible transfinite.[176] The refusal, without experimental confirmation, of Stephen Hawking, and others, to allow the reality of such singularities, and to try to keep black holes within a sheerly given spatiotemporal framework, appears to be yet another example of a finitist concern to evade the specifically modern recognition since Cusa, and before him Grosseteste, as hyper-confirmed by Cantor, that finite really is aporetically constituted of the infinite (both the infinitely great and the infinitely small, as Pascal understood), which we can only finitely register as nothing.

In this respect, a more valid invocation of the counter-intuitive continues, as with pre-modern thought, to lead us upwards to transcendence, as well as in a newly modern fashion to the aporetic margins, whereas classical physics deployed it only to discover a mythical spatialised container operating as a neutral background for isolated particles in motion

[174] This is the effect whereby, if one separates a pair of linked particles within a quantum system and looks at a particle in one place and it has the property x, one can be sure it will turn out to have the opposite property y in the other.

[175] Cartwright, *Nature the Artful Modeller*; Milbank, 'Confession of Time in Augustine'; Sheldrake, *A New Science of Life*, 1–24.

[176] Rovelli, *Seven Brief Lessons on Physics*, 49–62.

(like liberal Lockean individuals contracting within an ahistorical milieu) and to sustain the supposed tyrannical freedom of God.[177]

One can note here that Einstein deployed Hume to suggest the nullity of our everyday, bodily rooted apprehensions, whereas Hume's point might be rather that these 'feelings' can never be escaped, and can perhaps after all be trusted if they are in sympathetic continuity with nature itself, whose entities may themselves be the coagulations of 'feelings', ontologically completed as 'enjoyment' and 'satisfaction', as Whitehead argued.[178] This suggests a necessary limit to the operation of counter-intuition, and I have already suggested that quantum uncertainty can be read as implying the ineliminability and indicative reliability of the more phenomenally apparent 'middle' of reality.

Reverting to the question of time, if space and measurable time really do vanish down singularities, then we still have to allow for their inexplicable rebound, or 'bounce', suggesting the inexhaustible vitality of heat and light (in keeping with older neoplatonic light metaphysics, as with Grosseteste) as the material ground of everything.

To speak of a vanishing and a rebound is unavoidably and transcendentally to speak of a before and an after. That could be just on account of the structures of our subjectivity, but as we are wholly natural creatures, it is more plausible to suppose that each single thing, including human things, as Augustine taught, is composed of tensional 'time spans' more primarily than of 'space spans' – of aporetic compressions of a recalled past and projected future into substantive 'presences', whose only real content must (as Kierkegaard re-realised with his Platonic account of the 'moment', after the *Parmenides*)[179] be a participated fragment of eternity.[180]

For Augustine, this was also the presence of divine 'life' and (implicitly, one can argue) to a degree of 'soul' in every single created thing, since temporal process is indeed non-separable from the psychic (but not just the human psyche).[181] Yet it is not merely (as Tarde wanted) reducible to its monadic unfolding. While time assumes psychic substance, the latter

177 On this contrast, see Funkenstein, *Theology and the Scientific Imagination*, 23–201.

178 See John Milbank, 'Hume versus Kant: Faith, Reason and Feeling', *Modern Theology*, 27 (2011), 276–97; Alfred North Whitehead, *Process and Reality* (New York: Free Press, 1978), 236–65.

179 The influence of Kierkegaard on Niels Bohr is surely significant.

180 See Catherine Pickstock, 'Music: Soul, City and Cosmos after Augustine', in *Radical Orthodoxy: A New Theology* (London: Routledge, 1999), 243–78.

181 Milbank, 'Confession of Time in Augustine'.

inversely assumes the unfolding of time – whether the time of the universe or the other time of the angels.

All this may be perfectly in accord with Niels Bohr's ideal-realist and relational ontology, bringing together mind and matter as two facets of one reality, such that observers are themselves fully parts of what they observe and are co-constituted by relational processes that include ones of observation and experimentation.[182] Karen Barad has successfully shown that Bohr was not really an idealist, nor a pure operationalist (as so many popular science commentators seem to think),[183] even if one needs to bring out more the latent ontological dimension that he accorded to uncertainty against Heisenberg, and to add a stronger 'post-humanist' insistence on the co-constitution of the human observing subjects themselves, along with their habitual environment, by ongoing and ultimately unsoundable natural processes. Both the experimental apparatus and the observer are themselves parts of a dynamic and relational reality, and the cancelling, one way or the other, of superposition, whenever a quantum phenomenon is observed, is simply at one with its passage into the finite sphere where the non-contradictory holds good. This cancelling then holds no necessary implication of the positive subjectivity of scientific truth.

It is sometimes suggested that the phenomenon of later observation acting as a 're-bounding' wave to alter past quantum events implies either an impossible idealism or the surpassing after all of quantum assumption by ones of time/space relativity.[184] But this may perhaps be better understood in terms of both the teleological anticipation of the future exercised by any moving reality (see earlier) and the way in which, because the past has always already passed into the future, later interpretation always does really and actually alter the past in our everyday experience: the storming of the Bastille truly did become the inauguration of the French Revolution.

Therefore, one should sustain the requirement of quantum physics for an irreversible, 'classical' (but not Newtonian absolute) time as the framework for relative and changing observations of always shifting and changing things, as well as for the recording of entanglements whose simultaneities appear to be irreducible and independent of any changes in the positions of observers or recording devices.

[182] For a very good account of this, see Karen Barad, *Meeting the Universe Halfway: Quantum Physics and the Entanglement of Matter and Meaning* (Durham, NC: Duke University Press, 2007), 97–131.

[183] For example, Gribbin, *Six Impossible Things*, 27–40.

[184] Ibid., 79–90.

The supposed 'alternative readings' of quantum physics to the Copenhagen model are all in fact evasions, ideologically driven by the need to restore disenchanted immanence, or sometimes disenchanted transcendence. The theory of an ultimate wave behind all apparent particles suppresses radical indeterminism and contradiction at an irreducible level of fact-event. And all the other alternatives engage in experimentally unsupported fantasies of infinite plural worlds, infinite plural histories (somewhere else the wave is still a wave, etc., even if it has inexplicably become a particle when we look at it here and now) or the total algebraicisation of space as well as time, as already intimated by Einstein in response to Bohr, such that no 'elsewhere' really exists any more than a 'here' does, or a 'before' and an 'after'. Everything, according to this hypothesis, including our observations, has been absolutely determined in 'an instant' according to a cosmic dice throw whose intricate yet finite mechanisms we cannot fully grasp, and so supposedly we resort to hypostasising the indeterminate equal chances of an 'ensemble' – as when we say a dice throw or a sequence of dice throws has equal chances, in ignorance of the micro-determining forces that always in reality determine one outcome: a five or a three, and so on. This hypothesis, therefore, only 'accounts' for quantum phenomena of superposition and entangled action at a distance by denying also all normal physical reality, whose observation led us to these realities in the first place.[185]

By contrast, the 'fixity' of time is the absolute precondition for radical quantum uncertainty and constitutive relationality, where Einsteinian relativity removes it, in favour of a non-temporal 'relativism' that is in reality a new version of classical absolute stability, allowing in principle, as we have just seen, a perfect deducibility of every physical reality, based on a principle of efficient causal priority that the Copenhagen model, and its still more radicalised variants, call into question. Between the two 'relativities', one surely has to decide?

As Lee Smolin argues, the successful predictions of general relativity can be alternatively accounted for in terms of shape dynamics, which posits a more extreme expansion and shrinkage of the same objects in far-removed contexts (replacing relativised moving observers in far-removed contexts) in keeping with the notion, which he also endorses (as for Augustine), that it is, if anything, space rather than time which is 'emergent'.[186]

The already listed alternatives to the quantum implication of the primacy of time all involve various theories of quantum gravity and the 'block

[185] Ibid., 41–106. [186] Smolin, *Time Reborn*, 164–92.

universe'. These, first of all, seek implausibly to apply to the whole cosmos quantum principles which of their very nature apply only experimentally to variables *within* the cosmos, or at its margins. Second, they can only compensate for this by arbitrarily postulating, as we have already seen, that our universe is but one of many possible universes, in order to consider our own in terms of contingently determined quantum variables. In this way a reconciliation with Einsteinian relativity is sought, but at the cost of sheerly untested, and therefore not 'scientifically' validated, speculation.[187]

Instead of isolating our universe, so that one can speak of it pseudo-scientifically, as if it were a testable singular 'thing', in terms of a postulated unmoving and unchanging spacetime framework, it is more plausible, as Smolin suggests, to isolate it in terms of time and its emergence from other, previous universes (out of black holes and preceding 'big bangs'), such that the laws of our current universe were established both at its explosive outset and in the process of its emergence. The advantage of this approach is that it *is* in principle, according to Smolin, experimentally testable (though so far has not been, at least uncontrovertibly), in terms of the possible traces of echoes of previous universes that we might be able to record.[188]

Smolin has admirably contended that the most predominant effort of modern physical science, from Galileo and Newton onwards, which I would say is linked to the programme of 'disenchanted transcendence', has been to 'spatialise' reality in terms of a quasi-eternity, that would eliminate all real change in the name of supposed reason.[189] In this context, as we have seen, the work of much modern physics in the wake of Einstein does not escape this paradigm, even though the main revisionary thrust of physics modifying Newton tells against it.

Nonetheless, one could argue that Smolin himself is too wedded to an alternative, Leibnizian version of rationalism, that explicitly and dubiously accepts the ultimacy of the principles of sufficient reason and the identity of indiscernibles. For this reason, he supports the algebraic dissolution of space and time already considered, in a way that echoes both Leibniz's monadology and his *characteristica universalis*.

In consequence, he curiously seeks to combine his suspicion of Einstein's account of relativity with an endorsement of Einstein's own suspicion of Niels Bohr's account of quantum physics. Thus, he broadly

187 Ibid., 95–102, 226–51. 188 Ibid., 213–39.

189 This accords with the philosophical genealogy of the same drift, as diagnosed by Catherine Pickstock in *After Writing* (Oxford: Blackwell, 1998), 47–118.

argues in favour of 'the hidden variables' qualification of Bohr, after Louis de Broglie and later David Bohm, according to which apparent uncertainties, relativities and inconsistencies at the quantum level are to be accounted for at the level of the cosmic totality in terms of the more regular and predictable operation of unknown but finite determining factors.[190]

He rightly argues that if as for Bohm, the particle with its momentum is always first borne by the wave with its fluctuation, then the function of absolute time seems to be irreducible. But as he himself indicates, just the same conclusion applies, and perhaps a fortiori, to Bohr's variant, which requires no priority of wave over particle, nor vice versa. Smolin's priority of time does not therefore require this quantum revisionism, which will, indeed, ultimately threaten it.

Moreover, the hidden variables interpretation seems to have been somewhat experimentally disconfirmed by the team working under John Stewart Bell, as Karen Barad argues: seeking to introduce more definite framing variables of observation under our control to the quantum situation does not seem to alter the instance of inexplicable and uncanny quantum phenomena.[191] And the same verdict may apply to Smolin's endorsement of a finite universe: an infinite or transfinite one need not imply any primacy for spacetime, nor deny its birth in the course of time, in keeping with the inherited Christian philosophical speculations on actual indefinite (or 'contractedly infinite') space of Alan of Lille, the anonymous twelfth-century *Book of the Twenty-Four Philosophers*, Robert Grosseteste and Nicholas of Cusa.[192]

Smolin hopes that we might discover meta-laws for the periodic emergence of different laws of nature, which would (rather implausibly) resemble Darwinian natural selection, and (rather more plausibly) the growth of precedence within common law (yet that is *not* really a meta-law). But these would be subject to the same objection of an extra-physical externality that he raises in the case of supposed natural laws at a more basic level.

[190] Smolin, *Time Reborn*, 154–63. [191] Barad, *Meeting the Universe Halfway*, 289–92.

[192] Alan of Lille, *Sermon on the Intelligible Sphere*, in *Literary Works* [bilingual edition], trans. Winthrop Wetherbee (Cambridge, MA: Harvard University Press, 2013), 2–19; *Liber XXIV philosophorum*, II; *Le Livre des XXIV philosophes* [bilingual edition], trans. Françoise Hudry (Grenoble: Jerome Millon, 1989), II, pp. 93–6; Robert Grosseteste, *De luce*, trans. Julian Lock in Iain M. Mackenzie, *The 'Obscurism of Light': A Theological Study into the Nature of Light* (Norwich: Canterbury Press, 1996), 25–33; Nicholas of Cusa, *De docta ignorantia*, 112–16.

Instead, one can abandon the requirement of sufficient reason in relation to the 'whole', and of the identity of indiscernibles as precluding infinite copying of the same, by suggesting instead, with Bergson and Whitehead, the ultimacy of a vitally creative but not thereby anarchic process.[193] Indeed, Smolin fails to see the complicity of closed reason *with* the sheerly arbitrary, since such closure lacks any grounds for its totality, whereas Bergson and Whitehead suggest those of intuition and feeling.

A transcendental and participated creativity, as already invoked by Eriugena, Cusanus, Ficino, Pico, Lefèvre and Comenius, would seem to be more in keeping with the quantum revelation of irreducibly 'occult' and *discontinuous* features of reality: of inexplicable affinities and resonances, of regular phenomena that have established themselves beyond the reach of mathematics and logic, and even in contradiction of their most basic principles. It is not Blake's Urizen that the Creation would seem to bear witness to, but the creative God who has sophianically imbued the world with his own poetic power.

Just in terms of this vision, Bergson was able to revive the ancient instinct that it is indeed the poet who is most in tune with, and who most discerns the fundamental shaping processes of nature herself.[194]

The primacy of time therefore suggests the irreducibility, beyond the grasp of experimental science, of beginnings and endings, and of contingently established habitual processes, in line with the thinking of Maine de Biran, Samuel Butler and Bergson's teacher, Félix Ravaisson. The entirety of reality certainly does not and could not show evidence of its own absolute 'commencement' (or transcendental dependency) as Creation, yet perhaps the evidence of physics, honestly appraised, at least does not contradict our experienced sense of continuous divine creation, of a ceaseless miraculous arrival and vanishing in every 'causal' instance, which allowed the biblical legacy fully to acknowledge a metaphysical primacy of the temporal event.

193 Smolin, *Time Reborn*, 227–39. Does a spatial infinite imply the infinite repetition of the same things, as Smolin argues? In a sense yes, but then this would always be rivalled and overtaken (though overtaken again in turn by similitude) by infinite variation. One should surely be open to the idea that the identity of indiscernibles breaks down in the infinite, after Paul Cohen and others. And why do bad ethical consequences follow from this, as Smolin seems to think? Any evil once done may be infinitely repeated, but if it is redeemed, then it is also infinitely redeemed. And how do we know that any singular item is not in fact already, and always of itself, all of its infinite instances?

194 Pierre Hadot, *The Veil of Isis: An Essay on the History of the Idea of Nature*, trans. Michael Chase (Cambridge, MA: Harvard University Press, 2006), 201.

4.12 The Ergetic Version of Enchanted Transcendence as the Way Forward

The contemporary alternatives to enchanted transcendence are now (apart from the intellectually negligible, yet culturally significant, influence of disenchanted monotheism) rival immanentisms.

On the one hand, there is Quentin Meillassoux's extreme aleatory version of a 'disenchanted immanentism' which is even prepared to countenance the chance arrival in some possible world to come of enchantment – of 'resurrection' and 'God' and so forth. His ontology of contingent eventual arrival from nothing beyond even the chances of probability (an entirely lawless throw of the Mallarmean dice upon the deck of reality) constitutes a kind of Cartesianism without God.[195]

On the other hand, there is Gilles Deleuze's ontology of a self-engendering and equally lawless vitality, whose ultimate logic must therefore be obliteration.

Or, again, there can arise a combination of the two, as with Iain Hamilton Grant's mooted revival of the dark romanticism of the German *naturphilosoph* Lorenz Oken, writing around 1800, who proposed a vitalism based upon the modern ontological primacy (which can be Platonically questioned) of the mathematical zero.[196]

Yet in either case, it is more implausible to subordinate particulars to nothingness, or single process, than it is to subordinate them to the transcendent God, which subordination alone saves their appearance of shaped particularity and consistent habituation. And if the most decisive conclusions of modern physics suggest that relation is as fundamental as substance and process as a self-consistent fixity, then only the primacy of time, as Augustine saw, guarantees the ultimacy of relation and movement; for otherwise they both collapse into subordination to a spatialised totality that would be more ultimately real, whether as primary static substance (single after Spinoza, or monadically plural after Leibniz), or as primary becoming.

Instead, we can venture that within the primacy of time all is moving, all is responding, all is anticipating and thereby participating in the act of

[195] See Quentin Meillassoux, 'Appendix: Excerpts from *Inexistence Divine*', trans. Graham Harman, in Graham Harman, *Quentin Meillassoux: Philosophy in the Making* (Edinburgh: Edinburgh University Press, 2011), 175–238.

[196] Iain Hamilton Grant, 'Being and Slime: The Mathematics of Protoplasm in Lorenz Oken's "Physio-Philosophy"', *Collapse*, 4 (2008), 286–321; Lorenz Oken, *Elements of Physiophilosophy*, trans. Alfred Tulk (London: Ray Society, 1847), 5–19.

absolute creative emergence. In the case of human beings, this is our conscious feeling of our own feelings, as Whitehead realised:[197] our poetic, technological and scientific remaking and fulfilling of reality in anticipation of the eschaton. We should not simply abandon the Baconian legacy, which with people like Hartlib, Evelyn and Ray, besides Comenius. was often noble and inherently ecological, contrary to myth.[198] Was not something irreversibly disclosed to us, as a further unfolding of the Boethian and Chartrian legacy (profoundly rooted in the Patristic writings of both East and West) in the Renaissance and early modern period, including the validity of a new concern with natural magic in the widest sense? Adhering to enchanted transcendence becomes thereby not a matter of nostalgia but of renewal.

Similarly, we cannot save the planet by denying the human role as shepherd and steward, which is surely intended by both God and that nature of which we are entirely part. Nor by denying the intertwining of nature with culture, and the reality that only by 'enculturing' the climate and the variety of species, as we once encultured fire and water, will we now save both ourselves and nature. Merely wilded and neglected forests simply kill the undergrowth. No, we have instead to exercise this guarding role responsibly, humbly and wonderingly – as Tom Mcleish suggests, in the spirit equally of Plato's *Timaeus* and the book of Job.[199]

For if we make the reverse voyage from Mallarmé to Coleridge, then we can see that the entirely lawless and unhabituated dicing takes place only the deck of the ship of death, not on the deck of eternally living, created reality.[200] Here, instead, our slaying of the Albatross, of the unfathomable resonances and harmonies that 'magically' sustain nature in its constantly varying and readjusting being, indeed deliver us to a 'painted ocean' of sterile chances (where even the happy chance on board the deck of the 'painted ship' would witness to this infertility and so would prove *unenjoyable*).[201] Yet it remains possible, as for the guilty and doomed Mariner, to make the evangelical gesture beyond even the wisdom of Job: namely, to banish the wilfully ignored gothic spectres of our previous ruinings of nature by simply loving the incomprehensible but grotesquely beautiful 'sea-snakes' that surround us (Coleridge's multiplication of Job's

[197] Whitehead, *Process and Reality*, 188.

[198] For example, John Evelyn, *Sylva: A Discourse of Forest Trees and the Propagation of Timber* (London: Echo, 2009).

[199] Tom McLeish, *Faith and Wisdom in Science* (Oxford: Oxford University Press, 2014), 102–65.

[200] Howard Skelton's effectively restrained musical setting of *The Rime of the Ancient Mariner* is worth listening to in this context. I am indebted to discussions with Peter Larkin here.

[201] This has to be the answer to Meillassoux.

Leviathan) and thereby blessing them 'unaware'. This can still benignly deliver us to the shore of that other abandoned gothic realm of liturgical penitence, due shriving and yet (for the modern 'gothick' retrospect of redoubled regret in relation to nature and the social order) of ever-renewed re-narration of our escape from metaphysically ecological disaster by means of a new super-infused habitus.[202]

In order to achieve this, we need a new sort of integration of physics, the other natural sciences, philosophy and theology. Not one repeating the errors of natural theology rooted in univocity and concurrence, but rather one rooted in analogy, emanation, teleology, and participation in divine creativity. For such a perspective, theology does not supplement or complete science, but instead ascends from the limited physical and particular, through the mathematically general, to the theological and metaphysical dimension that fuses both and surpasses even the general through its integrating of concrete particulars, available to every ordinary apprehension.

In terms of the specifically modern incorporation of the ergetic, 'naturally magical' and theurgic, this means an advance from the technological to the poetic, to the mystical merging with the divine Father's generation of us through the womb of the Spirit as his children in his Son.

For such a perspective, the sole ineliminable mark of science remains tautologously its success – its proof by apparently identical repeatability, which is its always latent confirmation through technological application. Nonetheless as we have seen, one 'success' can hide from view other possible successes, and the neutrality of success is always inseparable from non-neutral contexts that are ethical, aesthetic, social and metaphysical.

In such a purview, reliable and apparently disinterested new observations of the stars count as 'scientific' just by virtue of their emerging from the application of the same procedures, deploying the same instruments and the same observations carried out in exactly the same relevant circumstances. A useful 'application' of these observations may not as yet be emergent, but it is always in the likely offing, always half-anticipated. Therefore, it is naïve simply to talk, as so often, about the pure satisfaction of this or that 'scientific curiosity' often later yielding an unexpected usefulness. For specifically scientific curiosity is already inherently defined by the desire of the curious to have the results of their inspective inquisitions confirmed with absolute reliability.

[202] See Alison Milbank, *God and the Gothic: Religion, Reality and Romance in the English Literary Tradition* (Oxford: Oxford University Press, 2018).

The dubious link of such a desire to a solitary control or detached fascination (often with the tragic or horrific) as diagnosed by Augustine, is only salved within 'science' (precisely as Paracelsus and Bacon advocated) by its charitable onlook towards the 'relief of man's estate'. The other needed salve of truly theoretical wondering and contemplation is achieved only when mere 'science' is elevated back into 'natural philosophy', within which it should always remain embedded.

This inherently technological definition of the specificity of modern science need not involve a purely instrumental account of its success. It can also admit a limited realism, in terms of which ergetic knowledge knows something surely but superficially, as when the outcome of cooking reveals in its new product certain properties and capacities of the natural (eggs can scramble!) yet but little of its entire reality.[203] We have the recipes for making mayonnaise and soufflés (which tells us something indeed about eggs by showing us something of which they are capable) but not the complete divine recipe for laying eggs in the first place.

In Bruno Latour's terms, a limited realism adheres to science insofar as our observations and experimentations incite certain actions of natural things or *actants* (whose scope beyond this local incidence we can never be entirely sure of) also upon us.[204] All that we strictly know is this incidence and event of relating, and yet just because physical reality is inherently relational and every constitutive relation is inherently a relation 'to' something (at once 'internal' and 'external'), the knowledge of a certain instance of relationship has to be taken as also a limited disclosure of what lies beyond that one mere relational instance or set of instances.

This circumstance holds good at every humanly cognitive level. But experimentation remains explicitly limited – as the price of its more precise probing – by the perimeter of questions (always linked to theoretical speculation and social purposes) not posed or excluded, and so, as we have already asserted, by experiments not performed or thought of. Indeed, quantum physics in particular suggests the possibility that a successful experimental working may disguise from us other and sometimes alternative or even contradictory workings which we have not had the time, the resources or the funding to carry through.[205]

[203] See again Barad, *Meeting the Universe Halfway*, 128–9 and 132–85.

[204] Bruno Latour, *Pandora's Hope: Essays on the Reality of Science Studies* (Cambridge, MA: Harvard University Press, 1999).

[205] See Isabelle Stengers, *Another Science Is Possible: A Manifesto for Slow Science*, trans. Stephen Muecke (Cambridge: Polity, 2018).

Thus ergetic knowledge never occurs in an extra-ergetic theoretical vacuum, as was not sufficiently acknowledged by Francis Bacon. Questions to be posed arise from a non-ergetic and therefore extra-scientific hermeneutical horizon, and 'successful' results equally get construed in different theoretical ways which success alone does not dictate. Even though there is a sense, as already affirmed, of the 'neutrality' of working – such that believers and atheists, idealists and empiricists, reactionaries and radicals scarcely argue about how to drive a car – this does not mean, for a reflexive consideration of working, such as science involves (including how it is that a car is drivable by us and the way in which it should be driven), that we can ever entirely isolate the ergetic from theoretical and wider practical factors.

For this reason, it is not so much that we should in this new project 'demand' that science become re-embedded in natural philosophy, as point out how it always is, but mostly chooses to ignore this circumstance. Such ignoring must be considered the source of a complicity between scientism and ecological damage: for without the onlook of the ergetic to both contemplation and discriminating charity, a de facto reductive natural philosophy pertains, for which the manipulable and the surveyable discloses the whole of being as inert and objective, even though this contradictorily obscures the constitutively limiting perspective of subjective manipulator and surveyor.

However, the more explicit embedding of maker's knowledge in theory is also, for an alternatively modern outlook, as I have already argued, an embedding within a wider and deeper sense of *poesis* (including *praxis*), for which the internal lure of the 'makeable' towards its own true end is not confined to the identically repeatable and to guaranteed re-performance, as most paradigmatically holds in the case of the mathematical operation. Instead, human creativity here submits to a more singular and aesthetic lure, whose truth lies entirely in its own manifest disclosure during or at the end of an 'artistic' process, itself, seen as 'fitting' its circumstances, as a building might its surroundings – rather than in an always further result that it infallibly delivers.[206] Turner's painting *The Fighting Temeraire* is true in itself and not just because of what it might indeed further and unpredictably engender, whereas the number 'two' is 'exactly' true because of its absolutely consistent functional operability: when added to 'three' it always makes five and so forth.

[206] See Rowan Williams's Gifford Lectures, *The Edge of Words: God and the Habits of Language* (London: Bloomsbury, 2014).

All merely scientific or ergetic operations and their technological applications require a subordination to this broader poetic context, which in its widest extent coincides with those singular patterns and habits that compose a culture, and which we collectively judge to be desirable. If they are displaced in their primacy by the pursuit of merely repeatable means, as if that were the main goal in itself, then inevitably science becomes (despite its inherent but minimal innocence) complicit in processes of control for the sake of control, or even in processes that exist for the sake of mere process. And process without goal is by definition a process of alteration, which in default of the pursuit of ends understood as desirable can only be an exercise of endless rearrangement or, in other words, of ceaseless destruction or else of building only in order to later turn down: a sheerly negative narrative compulsion.

This 'ceaseless destruction' or permanent revolution, which is neutral from its own vantage point, is nonetheless an iconoclastic destruction of the valuable and sacred for those still committed to the traditional cultural priorities of contemplation, charity and *poesis*.

At the widest cultural circumference, one could say that the collective 'art', that is a specific culture as such, is judged 'right' insofar as its event and incidence are seen 'sacramentally' to disclose and elevate its pre-given surroundings, just because it is not (and here the new Renaissance and Romantic insights seem vital to our understanding of the primordial) itself just pre-given or 'found', as a certain illusory notion of the contrast of 'culture' with 'nature' might suggest. Instead, nature as 'Gaia', or as an 'open All' that is governed by the world soul, or by immanent Sophia, continuously arrives or theurgically descends from a transcendent height beyond all the naturally immanent.[207] This height must equally be invoked and conveyed by the continuous 're-attuning' of all natural and artificial reality in its shifting configurations, such that both its processes and its individual substances escape instrumental sacrifice to an illusorily closed totality, or a final future that can never arrive. Instead, in their increasingly sustained harmony, they exist aesthetically to proclaim the Glory of God.

Within the transformation of 'art' into 'liturgy', an increasing coincidence of *theoria* with *poesis* gives way to a more radical passivity which renders paradoxically receptive even energetic motions, and even our own actions in relation to a transcendence which gives all and itself receives

[207] See Bruno Latour's Gifford Lectures, *Facing Gaia: Eight Lectures on the New Climatic Regime* (Cambridge: Polity, 2017).

nothing. Precisely at this point, technology can be radically embedded within ritual. As, perhaps, in the case of technically highly advanced ancient China, our technological deployment of signs and tools which inversely shapes us (since we are not human without them)[208] need not so leach away our spirit as to render us mere subhuman (and no doubt genderless) cyborgs. Our openness to be shaped by natural *actants* in the mode of mere process for its own sake is here prevented by our countervailing, well-attuned openness to the aesthetic reception of sacred shapes and modes as they arise to us through our own reshapings.

And yet our active induction into this transcendental passivity itself provides a clue to a final reversal even of this reversion from a Christian viewpoint. For in actively receiving God we are gradually incorporated into the receptively active life of the eternal work and self-giving love of the Divine Tri-unity.

4.13 Conclusion: Re-embedding Natural Science in Metaphysics and Theology

In conclusion, it can be suggested that the advocacy of a truce between religion and science is often predicated primarily upon the squeezing out of what we may legitimately and unabashedly term 'magic'. Religion is to be concerned with the spiritual, science with the material; any obscure spiritual influencing of the material or vice versa is to be disallowed – even though our most constant and daily, psychically embodied experience consists in these 'magical' transfers.[209]

But the truce does not really work, and especially does not work because it covertly repeats a specific historical genesis by which what we think of as 'religion' and 'science' got dubiously constituted in the first place. This genesis is bound up, as we have seen, with the questionable paradigm of disenchanted monotheism.

The supposedly safe, doubly buffered culture which has resulted, hopes to deal only in purely intended thoughts of which we are in command, and in purely mechanical, predictable motions, which we can also hope to master, even if such motions exist only mythically within the human sphere, now the last redoubt of the positivist mechanical philosophy, just as it was from the outset linked to the onset of capitalism and bureaucratic

208 Bernard Stiegler, *Technics and Time I: The Fault of Epimetheus*, trans. Richard Beardsworth and George Collins (Stanford, CA: Stanford University Press, 1998).

209 Again, I am indebted to the doctoral work of Laura McCormack here.

governance. But an increased autonomy for motion, in terms of a 'disenchanted immanentism', always threatens the integrity of the psychic, in the absence of any metaphysical mediation which lies more perilously close than we care to admit to the realm of inscrutably 'occult' linkage.

Our disenchanted attempts at control have proved ever more arid and dangerous, both cosmically and psychologically. Yet at the same time, it has proved impossible to sustain pure mechanism, just as a nominalistically inclined philosophy has found itself unable to understand how anything holds together, or is causally connected, whether by logic, efficiency or 'field'.[210] In the absence of God, the shadow of a dark magic therefore hovers, of obscure forces and impulses, of returning superstition at every level, and of an urge to disintegration.[211] We know and continue to know their Dionysiac political manifestations all too well. Enchanted immanentism therefore retains its allure and this appeal has grown ever more nihilistic.

Enchanted transcendence remains the option closer to reality, to common experience, to sanity and to Christian orthodoxy. It is able to realise, in the wake of the Christian Renaissance, that a certain allowance of 'natural magic' is the proper ground of mediation between religion and science, in a way that also allows the specifically modern sense of mutability and the human capacity to change things to merge with an increased sense that religion, and most of all the religion of the Incarnation, involves a dynamic and 'alchemical' cooperation of natural and human forces in the sacramental process of an active reception and eliciting of the divine.

Through such a recognition, we are able to see that it is ultimately liturgical practice and theology that can seal the alliance between experimental science and natural philosophy in terms of the embedding of the former in the latter, without a suppression of the arrival of the new to which experimental science partially attests. At the same time, this arrival can itself be further embedded, expanded and contained in terms of a fuller ethical, aesthetic and religious experience of the continuous new arrival of grace.

The book of nature and the book of the Bible would seem to be in accord: reality is a great poem, composed under the lure of a transcendent end which it further glimpses through the process of composition itself. Its

[210] See Graham Priest, *One: Being an Investigation into the Unity of Reality and Its Parts, Including the Singular Object Which Is Nothingness* (Oxford: Oxford University Press, 2016).

[211] See the discussions of Paul Tyson in his *Seven Brief Lessons on Magic* (Eugene, OR: Wipf and Stock, 2019).

poetic and 'magical' linkages are ultimately constituted more through ineffable feeling than through logic or comprehensible number. Thus it reveals itself most to the human creative imagination, whether scientific or more ultimately artistic.

This is not fantasy: it is rather what experimental science itself has tended to suggest all the way from the twelfth century till now, but that a scientific ideology, acting in the interests of both a false theology and an enterprise of spatialising secular, bureaucratic and capitalist rule through measurable control, still seeks to deny.[212] Magic alone unites science with religion; otherwise, they are allied only within processes of dangerous sundering and yet simultaneously complacent collusion.

[212] Although he is anti-theological and anti-metaphysical, and confuses modern immanentised spatialisation with the Platonic contrast of eternity with a time we *cannot* for now escape, Lee Smolin gives an acute summary of the cultural and ecological implications of spatialisation at the end of his *Time Reborn*, 252–71.

CHAPTER 5

Science, Beauty and the Creative Word

Janet Soskice

Most of the contributors to this volume share the view that there is something not quite right about contemporary understandings of the relationship between science and religion. Perhaps the most doubtful ruling assumption, over past thirty years at least, has been that the default relationship is one of conflict, and that this is largely responsible for a mental atmosphere of reductive materialism, at least in the English-speaking world. But what conflict? And which scientists? Even brief attention to the history of what we call scientific enquiry, not to say the lengthy attention given by Peter Harrison in *Territories of Science and Religion,*[1] and even a glance at the portraits on the walls of many Cambridge colleges will reveal that many, probably most, scientists in Britain of the seventeenth to early nineteenth centuries were Anglican clergyman.

My own doctoral thesis, written over thirty years ago and published as *Metaphor and Religious Language*, was supervised by a philosopher of science and drew on scientific theory construction as ally to theology in defending the use of metaphors and models to speak of that which we know we do not, and even cannot, fully understand – metaphor having been summarily dismissed from critical thought by Hobbes, Locke and the logical positivists.[2]

There are set piece controversies, but in what does the so-called conflict of science and faith actually consist? And who or what is 'science'? Peter Harrison has done us a service by calling attention, in *Territories*, to the fact that 'science' as we use the term is of very modern usage and 'theology' only slightly less so. 'Theologia' in Aquinas's *Summa theologiae* is literally 'words about God', and in that sense Aristotle and Plato wrote theology. What we call 'theology' Aquinas called 'holy teaching' (*sacra doctrina*) and

[1] Peter Harrison, *The Territories of Science and Religion* (Chicago: University of Chicago Press, 2015).
[2] Janet Martin Soskice, *Metaphor and Religious Language* (Oxford: Clarendon, 1985).

it is this and not 'theologia' which is the concern of the *Summa*, based on God's own self-revelation in scripture and to the Prophets. It was 'sacra doctrina', not 'theologia', that Aquinas called a 'scientia'. Other sciences were optics and mathematics. Much of what we call 'science' today would, I imagine, have been considered '*techne*' by medievals, something more like crafts (glassmaking, metallurgy, medicine).

When we ask, 'Who are the scientists?', I note that, while I'm surrounded by scientists at my Cambridge college, few identify themselves like this. If asked, they say they are biochemists, physicists, neurologists, geneticists, metallurgists, or geologists – mostly nineteenth-century titles. These individuals, in my Cambridge experience, are as likely to be religiously observant (or not) as their colleagues in the arts. If anything, it is the social scientists who are least likely to favour religion. It seems to me, then, that the proposition 'there is a conflict between science and religion' is a weakly grounded empirical claim. Yet the many scientists with religious commitments whom I regularly come into contact with invariably report that conflict is the default assumption of their non-religious colleagues. What are religious believers meant to be offended by: antibiotics, heart surgery, digital radios?

There are elements of a convenient 'urban myth' here, though not for that more readily dismissed. It is undoubtedly the case that religious observance has declined rapidly in post-war Europe, but is 'science' the culprit or the fall guy? Is there, in the United Kingdom at least, a powerful, cultural conviction that science has – what word should we use? – 'proved' that there is no God? That science is thought to have 'rubbished' religion I have no doubt, and give two examples.

First, the Leverhulme Lecture (1 November 2017) delivered by Sir Paul Nurse, a former President of the Royal Society, to an entirely professorial body of Electors to the various fellowships (about 250), on the topic 'Research and the Public Good'. Paul Nurse (who is not, I think, antagonistic to religion at a deep level: he's very helpful at Westminster Abbey Institute), in what was admittedly a chatty lecture, began by listing all the enemies to scientific advance – a list which included religion. Later, speaking of the importance of intellectual freedom, he mentioned in passing that when Galileo challenged the Church's cosmology they 'shook the chains of the Inquisition at him'. This is clichéd stuff, but the point is that it passes unchallenged. Surely, this shouldn't trouble us? Yet at the dinner afterwards I found myself seated next to a person involved with a large science research council that dispenses many million pounds a year in grants. He was utterly astonished, first that he should be seated next to a professor of theology and then that I should have had a theology doctorate supervised by a philosopher of science – what possible connection should there be?

Another example from the physicist and television presenter Brian Cox, filmed in a Hindu seminary in south India where he is told by students that their sacred literature says that the world was made before the gods: 'At last, a truly scientific religion!', says Cox. No need for the BBC to edit that out apparently. All evidence of the methodological materialism of modern naturalism.

Some kind of materialism (crudely, matter is all there is, though what 'matter' itself is is far from clear) is the default metaphysics of western modernity. God is dismissed as an unnecessary entity. And this is entirely the point. The default metaphysics of modernity has a notion of God but it is an idolatrous notion of God – as another 'thing' amongst 'things', an entity alongside other entities. This may be a deistic notion of God, but it is not the Christian or Jewish or Muslim one, as most contributors to this volume have been quick to point out. The classical Christian doctrine of Creator God is not that God made everything in six days of twenty-four hours, but *creatio ex nihilo*. In this teaching God made everything, including space and time (heavens and earth) and thus God is not another 'thing' in the world as, seemingly, in the imagination of Brian Cox (and, I find, many ex-churchgoers), but the One who holds all that is in being at every moment. Aquinas and others did not hesitate to say that God is Being Itself ('I Am Who I Am', and the source of all being.

In this degradation of modern metaphysics the churches and their controversies are not blameless (see Simon Oliver's chapter).[3] The post-Reformation dismissiveness of metaphysics in the study of theology laid waste to sophisticated accounts of creation and divine action. Later, in the eighteenth and nineteenth centuries, the adoption of simple 'natural' theology was easily dismissed, even at the time, by David Hume and subsequently devastated by Charles Darwin. Many arguments used to attack religious belief itself were first deployed by one side or the other in internal religious disputes. The propositionalism of the early modern period to which Peter Harrison refers has roots not only in the rise of and admiration for science but in the need to lay down battle lines between

[3] These views resonate with those of Michael Hanby in his observation that 'the advent of modern science coincides with a radical reimagination of being, nature, reason, and truth which forms the *a priori* starting point, and not merely the conclusion of scientific inquiry'. This seems to be historically the case, but was it inevitably the case?

contesting post-Reformation cohorts – not just Catholic and Protestant but various other subsets.

Two other terms to trace, if we want to look at the development of the conflict of science and religion, are 'natural' and 'supernatural', and a good deal of work has been done on this by those here amongst others. How did 'supernatural' go from describing 'faith, hope and love' as the graces of God to our human being, to meaning something entirely outside normal experience?

We should not forget the weight, in English-language philosophy, of 'histories' which took the inevitability of atheism (casting off superstition of early mankind) for granted. An example is Hume, in the *Natural History of Religion*, but other pioneers of intellectual history argued in similar ways.[4] Not all Christians held simple and deistic beliefs, but enough did to make an energised and atheistic 'Darwinism' in the hands of popularisers like Thomas Huxley seem convincing to many. The intellectual and theological roots, we could say, were shallow, and thus the appeal of the 'methodological materialism of modern naturalism'.

Many are worried by this – and not just religious believers. The philosopher Raymond Tallis, an atheist, begins in an (again excellent) discussion with Rowan Williams by admitting his opposition to a 'scientistic naturalism that says we are essentially explicable as biological organisms'.[5] Marilyn Robinson, herself a Christian, is outspoken in her criticism of this tilt of the western mindset. Charles Taylor and Alasdair MacIntyre are powerful voices that speak of the need for a 'metaphysics of value', of a need to counter a reduction to utilitarian criteria – we could also speak of the disenchantment of the Universe and of the dissolution of 'Man'.

I do not, however, think it is science as such which has disenchanted the Universe – science sees a world brimming with order, wonder and beauty – but a reductive materialism which has its origins and anchorage in a number of places (one being poor theology).[6] Let me move into a different key, by first considering a case of reductive materialism, and then some constructive ways forward by means of a discussion of Nietzsche, Ruskin

[4] See Jonathan Rée's essay 'Atheism and History', in Anthony Carroll and Richard Norman (eds.), *Religion and Atheism: beyond the Divide* (London: Routledge, 2017). This book of essays has a lot in common with this present volume.

[5] 'Science, Stories and the Self: A Conversation between Raymond Tallis and Rowan Williams', in Carrol and Norman, *Religion and Atheism*, 3–25.

[6] Fiona Ellis cites Thomas Nagel as saying that 'among scientists and philosophers who do express views about the natural order as a whole, reductive materialism is widely assumed to be the only serious possibility'. Fiona Ellis, 'Atheism and Naturalism', in Carrol and Norman, *Religion and Atheism*, 72. She goes on to list a number of variants of reductive materialism.

and beauty, and some concluding remarks on the Incarnation and the integrity of creation.

Nietzsche rejoiced that the death of 'God', hastened, as he thought, by Darwinian science, meant the end of 'truth'. Both God and 'truth' were, to his mind, mirages. Nietzsche nevertheless wished, somewhat inconsistently, to retain a belief in beauty, at least as a consolation to make human existence bearable. Nietzsche's great contemporary, John Ruskin, was not so confident beauty could be retained. Ruskin's early art criticism rested on a form of natural theology familiar since the eighteenth century and virtually ubiquitous in English intellectual life in the early nineteenth century. He believed at this time that the certainties of the Evangelical faith of his childhood were in perfect consort with the new findings of the scientists, especially, at this time, the geologists. God had delivered sermons in stone. Nature and its beauty were 'God's second book' and the beauty of the natural world was a 'moral' beauty.[7] But, after Darwin, the water lily, with its exquisite cup, could no longer be seen as devised for godly instruction but was exposed as a sexual organ in a new and unlovely drama of survival and propagation. The finely structured lily pads, we would have to say, 'merely appeared' to us to be beautiful. Bees alighting on flowers are mere pimps and panders. As the art critic Peter Fuller records in his book on Ruskin's crisis, *Theoria: Art in the Absence of Grace*, the early Ruskin 'begged the "gentle and happy scholar of flowers"' to 'have nothing to do with "the obscene processes and prurient apparitions" of the secular biologists'. Fuller continues: 'To us, such sentiments sound absurd: but Ruskin was drawing attention to the fact that the advance of one way of looking at nature had meant the loss of another. Behind his prudery lay another and deeper fear – that of the loss of enchantment of the world.'[8] We might say, though, that something of a hangover remains: the fear that all that we value is 'mere appearance'. That not only our ethical systems but even human persons are 'mere appearances', illusions we impose on what is really a substrate of continuous evolutionary flux.

Nietzsche could delight in 'mere appearance'. He praised the Greeks for stopping at surfaces. 'Those Greeks were superficial', he says in the *Gay Science* – '*out of profundity*'.[9] Are we, however, content to be superficial out

[7] See Peter Fuller's insightful study, *Theoria: Art in the Absence of Grace* (London: Chatto & Windus, 1988), 33ff.

[8] Ibid., 78.

[9] Friedrich Nietzche, author's preface to the second edition of *The Gay Science*, trans. Walter Kaufmann (New York: Vintage Books, 1974), 38.

of superficiality? Have we indeed taken superficiality to new depths? For, while we have always been concerned about our appearance in the age of Instagram, we don't conceal but openly acknowledge that our images are selected, edited and digitally altered. We are each our own curator. If I appear to my followers to be happy and successful, maybe that's all there is to happiness and success? In short, we are content not just with appearances but with the appearance of appearances. Are we swindling ourselves out of the older insight that we are made to seek the truth and to behold beauty? This, I think, is what it means to think in terms of a 'value-discriminating metaphysics'.

However, not all religiously informed aesthetics depends on the argument from design that underwrote Ruskin's early writings. The artistry of Gerard Manley Hopkins was as a poet, not of appearances, but of 'appearing' – epiphanies of individual things: a coal falling gashed and glowing into the grate, the mossy rim of a well, the flash of a dragonfly's wings, stones seen through clear water. Hopkins, like Cézanne, wrestled beauty from mere appearance to think instead of the world's astonishing capacity to appear.

Surely, this so with both beauty and truth? The best reply to Nietzsche's dismissal of truth, which he had, in the end, to extend to the claims of science as well as other putative truths, is the success of science itself. If 'truth' is in every sense a mere human construct and tissue of illusion, then the success of modern science is a miracle. Instead, we find that science proceeds in the belief that there is a given, a world which has been disclosed to us through generations of arduous and patient attention. And what is wrong with metaphor and human constructs, and even with 'mobile hosts of metaphors'? Scientific theory frequently proceeds by means of them. We construct theories about how our world works, just as we must contrive laws and systems of government. That we do so shows us to be anchored in the world of givens, not at a remove from it. At the same time, there is no 'contextless' claim, no view from nowhere, and nor need there be.

Elaine Scarry, in her essay *On Beauty and Being Just*, observes that while beauty has been banished in the language of the humanities for the last few decades, it is 'openly at play in those fields that aspire to have "truth" as their object – math, physics, astrophysics, chemistry, biochemistry – where every day in laboratories and seminar rooms participants speak of problems that are "nice", theories that are "pretty", solutions that are elegant and simple'.[10] Beauty goes on in its durable way – and in common speech people freely speak of a beautiful goal in football, a beautiful shot in tennis or a beautiful soufflé. There is something there of accuracy, of fittingness, of appropriateness to an end. We could say there is something 'given'.

Although beauty has the reputation of being merely subjective, we must all have had the same experience of being inducted into beauty. Most of us recognise daffodil shoots breaking though the soil, but when you walk through the deadness of a winter garden with a gardener they can see that this will be a foxglove, and that unpromising stump a peony. We can be schooled in sight and apprenticed in disclosure – of a winter garden, a flock of birds, a cluster of cells, or the beauty of a mathematical puzzle.

The experience of beauty can startle us as something that comes unbidden. Elaine Scarry wants not to equate beauty and truth but to say that they are allied. Beauty ignites the desire for truth; it amounts to something of a disclosure, she says, of that 'which is'. Maybe we could say that we have to love first in order to attend to something as it is. Aquinas said, 'Loving draws us to things more than knowing does.'[11]

It is around this matter of 'appearing' that, perhaps strange to relate, the practice of science not only points to beauty but brings us to a moment where we may consider what it means to say that *God is not only beautiful but Beauty itself, not only truthful but Truth itself, not only good but Goodness itself.*

In the light of creation *ex nihilo*, everything is gift. Creation has its being at every moment and at every now – and not just at some 'beginning' of time – from a loving God.

If God is the creator of all that is, including space and time, the moment of creation is not 'a long time ago', but now. And it is equally foolish to ask, as Augustine sharply remarked, what God was doing before the world was created. There was no 'time' when there was no space or matter (as even the astrophysicist today can agree). God as creator of time and space is equally present to all time and space. God is thus nearer to me, as Augustine would say, than my own breath, creating and holding me in being.

Another implication of *creatio ex nihilo* is that the 'fundamental distinction' is not between spirit and matter – as though God and soul were on one side and rocks and goldfish and subatomic particles on the other – but between God and Everything Else – that is, 'Creation', and all creation is

[10] Elaine Scarry, *On Beauty and Being Just* (Princeton, NJ: Princeton University Press, 1999), 53.
[11] Paraphrasing *Summa theologiae* 1a2ae. 28, 1.

held in being by God. This means that the unity of the world is preserved (the 'causal order', if you prefer). God is not one cause amongst causes but the Cause of all that is. Aquinas and others developed fine arguments about this and how, for instance, 'miracles' might happen, prayers answered, or a man raised from the dead. There is no conflict between holding that there is a source of all which is Being Itself, and integrated study of the beings that populate our world. On this note, while I personally do not object being classed as an 'animal', some Christians do. But surely no Christian could take issue with the confession that we human beings, like earthworms, rocks and subatomic particles, are 'creatures'.

Indeed, a truly incarnational theology (or aesthetics or ethics) should delight in this. *Creatio ex nihilo* makes room for a truly embedded and incarnational notion of the human being – one that realises there is a metaphysics of matter and even of energy.

In an excellent session of the Heidelberg Templeton Symposium (25–28 October 2012) led by the biologists Gunter Wagner (Yale) and Simon Conway Morris (Cambridge), both speakers, when in elaborating their research, used self-consciously auditory imagery – they spoke of the 'language' of cells, of the mysterious ways cells can 'talk' one with another, and how this obliges us to think very differently of the natural world. I was reminded of Evelyn Fox Keller's biography of the Nobel Laureate Barbara McClintock, *A Feeling for the Organism.* In a scientific career during which she was largely overlooked by more aggressively interventionist, male scientific colleagues, McClintock developed a research strategy of 'listening' to what is given to us by what we study.

This idea of a 'speaking' Universe has recently been a theme of Rowan Williams' Gifford Lectures, now published as *The Edge of Words.*[12] Fulfilling the Gifford Lecturer's brief for developing a 'natural theology', Williams asks what we may deduce about God from the fact that we are speaking beings. What can we make of the fact (an empirical fact and not a philosophical or religious speculation) that our Universe is such that it generates, through whatever processes are natural to it, creatures not only of intelligence but of speech? Intelligence cannot be alien or an add-on to the natural world or it would never have arisen. But plainly intelligence has arisen, or I wouldn't be writing this and you wouldn't be reading it. Contemporary science, indeed science for the last hundred years, has been

[12] Rowan William, *The Edge of Words* (London: Bloomsbury, 2014). See also his contribution to the debate with Tallis, already mentioned.

unable to consider the world as the collision of inert billiard balls. Instead, all that is, materially speaking, is energy. And indeed it appears that the Universe is a network of energy and communication.

There are interesting parallels here with Galen Strawson's defence of panpsychism – the view that consciousness in some sense goes all the way down. This is interesting in a hard-nosed way, because Strawson is an analytic philosopher and atheist. His argument is that the mind/body problem dissolves once we see that the physical world just does give rise to consciousness. We cannot rest in the dualism he ascribes to Daniel Dennett 'where the experiential and the physical are utterly and irreconciliably different'.[13] Williams is on similar grounds when he says we need to move beyond the lazy Cartesianism which sees the world as a crude dualism between 'pure structure and mindless stuff'.[14]

For any theologian who is broadly Augustinian, Thomistic or both, and also has an interest in modern, or even just post-Newtonian, science – the idea that the world is itself a kind of 'speaking' has marvellous Johannine resonances. What might it mean for religious apologetics if not only the Prologue to John's Gospel but the advance of scientific understanding should suggest that the Universe/Creation is itself a communication of which we are wholly, fully and physically a part?[15]

Not just biologists but physicists now speak of needing to attend to the primary 'given' of the Universe and of a profound communication that unites, in ways we often do not yet understand, one biological process in the body with another, one species of animal with another, one human being with another,[16] and even the organic to the inorganic. If modern physics has taught us anything, it is that 'matter' is far from obvious. Theologically conceived, we may be nearer now than for many centuries to the conceptuality of the Prologue of John's Gospel where the Universe is made through the communicative agency of a living Word, by Light for Life. If so, then it may be that attending to that Life in love is the proper activity of both science and religious faith.

[13] Galen Strawson, 'Realistic Monism', in Strawson et al., *Consciousness and Its Place in Nature: Does Physicalism Entail Panpsychism?* (Exeter: Imprint Academic, 2004), 5.

[14] Theologically, there can be no ultimate binary, despite persistent gnostic drifting, because mind and matter are both 'creatures'.

[15] 'In a nutshell, what we need is a metaphysics that thinks of matter itself and invariably and necessarily communicative – not as a sheer passivity moulded by our minds into an intelligible structure.' Williams, *Edge of Words*, xi.

[16] Rowan Williams' book has some interesting reflections on autism.

Let me return to beauty. The poet, carver, calligrapher and painter David Jones, in an essay entitled 'Art and Sacrament', makes this barbed observation:

> Were we trying to discover what it meant to say 'nature is beautiful' we'd be best advised to consider the patterns made by germ cells of a formidable disease than by considering the female torso, the green hills, or the dog rose.[17]

Jones, a boy from a modest background, had his art school studies interrupted by his time in the trenches during the First World War. In cautioning against too easy a resort to the beauties of nature, he may have in mind the vulnerability of the 'Sermons in Stone' approach to beauty which informed the young Ruskin, when faced with the cruelty and rapacity of the actual workings of Mother Nature, and of ourselves. But I believe that Jones, an artist who above all thought of himself as a craftsman, believed there to be theological deficiency in the suggestion, implicit in the 'Book of Nature' approach, that the human being, or the artist, is the passive recipient of this kind of divine teaching. As though God were somehow customising the created order by hiding in it uplifting tales of beauty, coded messages of which human beings, somehow suspended between God and the animals, were the intended beneficiaries.

Weak as this approach to beauty is on the doctrine of God and of the human being, it entirely lacks any doctrine of Christ. And here, it must be said, there is paramount difference between the Christian understanding of God as the source of all and that of the antique philosophers where the Good is an impersonal fecundity from which everything emanates. The biblical 'I Am Who I Am, the 'I AM' who is Being itself, *spoke to* Moses. And, in Christian understanding, this same I Am, the Word through whom all things were made, is the Word which, in the Prologue to John's Gospel we read became flesh and dwelt amongst us. It is no accident that the Gospel of John has Jesus repeatedly identify himself with the creative I AM who spoke to Moses. 'Before Abraham was, am' (John 8:58)

In John's Gospel Christ is the Creative Word who becomes incarnate and human like us and every way but sin in a world of harsh realities.

Indeed I think it is this balance between the glory of the Creative Word made flesh and the sometime painful actualities of fleshly existence that

[17] David Jones, 'Art and Sacrament', in Harman Grisewood (ed.), *Epoch and Artist. Selected Writings by David Jones* (London: Faber and Faber, 1959), 159.

saves good Christian art from being a 'motherhood and apple pie' celebration of beauty. Think only of Piero della Francesca's *Baptism of Christ* in the National Gallery. The order and balance of the painting, its stillness and seeming moment of eternal calm, is there, yes, but so too is the sense of movement, uncertainty, as John the Baptist lifts one foot to pour the water of the head of Jesus. Those familiar with the story know that Jesus will go from this scene to the temptation in the wilderness. Jesus's bare, open chest is vulnerable. The pink cloak, calmly held by an angel, is a pastel anticipation of the purple garment in which Jesus will be cloaked when is he mocked by the soldiers as King of the Jews. It is the same cloth that Piero puts in a companion painting, which clothes the resurrected Christ when he emerges from the tomb.

The Incarnation is a profound endorsement of the fundamental good of material reality and of being human, bodily, corporeal. John Ruskin was horrified to think the mollusc might be the ancestor man, and many Victorian Christians were scandalised that human beings should be classed as animals. David Jones, by contrast, delighted in his belief that we are, as he termed it, the 'animal-who-is-the-artist', always firmly anchored in our fleshly, bodily existence. The Christian doctrine of the Incarnation does not release us from the body and the complex natural world of our bodies are part, but affirms God's intimacy with us and all creation.

In conclusion, one fear that scientists may have is of a 'supernaturalism' of agencies (gods, demons, souls, ghosts) that is outside the natural order. But the Christian God is not an agent alongside the 'natural order' as in this picture, but the very source at every moment of its being and integrity.[18]

[18] Hence David Schindler's question, 'What would be the implications for the self-understanding and practice of science if it were conceived as a study of being in a certain respect?'

CHAPTER 6

Questioning the Science and Religion Question

Michael Hanby

The relationship between science and religion as forms of knowledge or as contingent historical practices is a secondary question, and perhaps even the wrong question, which seems to take quietly for granted and against many of our expressed theological and philosophical judgements the modern assumption that epistemology is first philosophy. It is a question the very asking of which tends to make empiricists – and therefore inadvertent atheists – of its askers, since it abstracts both questioners and their observed phenomena from their constitutive relation to God and the totality of conditions characterising their actual existence in order to construct an indifferent 'empirical' sphere, before adding these relations back in as hypothetical, second-order phenomena.[1] Obviously, these are not metaphysically theologically neutral positions, nor for most of us, desirable ones. Needless to say, this is not the question that I will be addressing in this essay.

Any formulation of this question presupposes and makes operational answers to still more basic questions: Who is God? What is the world? What is truth? This essay has more to do with *these* questions and with the way that science tends to answer them in advance of their being asked, though it is more an effort to clarify this point and a plea to put these questions first than an attempt to answer them. What follows should therefore be understood as a *speculative* attempt to *understand* the 'essence' of the problem in a very limited way and *not* as a historical attempt to situate its emergence amidst other possibilities in the history of ideas. Neither should this reflection be taken as a moralistic rejection or denunciation of science. For better and worse, science is so deeply integrated into the structure of our imaginations and into the built world in which we live

[1] See Michael Hanby, *No God, No Science? Theology, Cosmology, Biology* (Chichester: Wiley-Blackwell, 2013), 9–48, 375–415; D. L. Schindler, 'The Gift as Given: Creation and Disciplinary Abstraction in Science', *Communio: International Catholic Review*, 38 (Spring 2011), 52–102.

and move and have our being that a simple denunciation of science could hardly be meaningful or honest.

The human world, as Hannah Arendt and many others have recognised, is very much the 'built world', a product, to some degree, of human *techne*. There is thus (at least) a double sense in which nature and artifice are inseparable. They are inextricably intertwined in our lived experience, and this seems to follow as a matter of course from the fact that *homo faber*, if not the content of human nature, is apparently an immediate consequence of it.[2] Artifice, in short, is included *in* human nature and conditions both our understanding of nature and how it manifests itself.

Nevertheless, our inability to *separate* nature and artifice does not preclude our ability to *distinguish* validly and meaningfully between them. Indeed, the distinction between nature and art is as old as human thought about either, and therefore as old as philosophy itself.[3] The canonical form given to this distinction by Aristotle in the maxim 'art imitates nature' has both a positive and a negative sense. Positively, what art and nature have in common, and what distinguishes both from chance and necessity, is that the end, the perfected product, if you will, is somehow the reason for the steps that produce it – though a great deal hinges on the meaning of this 'somehow'. It can nevertheless be said of both natural and artificial things that the last end is somehow a first cause in both instances. This similarity undoubtedly helps explain both their inseparability in our lived experience and what Hans Jonas calls the 'irresistible tendency' to interpret human functions and artifacts in terms of each other, the information systems of the twenty-first century having now replaced the clocks of the eighteenth in our scientific and cultural imaginations as paradigmatic mirrors for our self-understanding.[4] Yet the fact that art is said merely to *imitate* nature means, negatively speaking, that a thing existing by nature possesses something that an artifact lacks, or better, *is something* that an artifact is not. From the very beginning, a thing existing by nature (*physei*), has its own 'reason' within it as the principle and source of its unfolding and

[2] For a discussion of *homo faber* as the consequence (*Folge*) and not the content (*Inhalt*) of the *imago dei*, see David L. Schindler, 'The Meaning of the Human in a Technological Age', *Anthropotes*, 15, no. 1 (1999), 31–51.

[3] Robert Spaemann, 'What Does It Mean to Say That "Art Imitates Nature?"', in D. C. Schindler and Jeanne Heffernan Schindler (eds.), *A Robert Spaemann Reader: Philosophical Essays on Nature, God, and the Human Person* (Oxford: Oxford University Press, 2015), 192–210.

[4] 'There is a strong, and, it seems, almost irresistible tendency in the human mind', writes Hans Jonas, 'to interpret human functions in terms of the artifacts that take their place, and artifacts in terms of the replaced human functions.' Hans Jonas, *The Phenomenon of Life: Toward a Philosophical Biology* (Evanston, IL: Northwestern University Press, 2001), 110.

therefore has a unity – *ens indivisum*, being undivided, Aquinas calls it – which it actively maintains.[5] A thing thus existing 'by nature' has an interior horizon that an artifact lacks. It has, or rather *is*, its own project, though the 'shape' of this project is given with its being and thus *ontologically* precedes its unfolding in time or any free decision on its part, even as the very being of the thing and the undertaking of its project temporally coextend. Aristotle and the scholastics called this interior principle substantial form, and its precedence over what subsequently develops in accordance with it entails some sort of distinction between the ontological and historical orders analogous to similar distinctions in the orders of knowledge and action. What is first in being (or first in intention) is typically last in development, knowledge, or execution. The form of an artifact, by contrast, does not precede its production except perhaps in the mind of its maker, who imposes it from without on parts to which it bears only an incidental and accidental relation. Its unity is not given with its existence, but rather comes about as the end result of its piece-by-piece assembly. It is therefore not a whole, except in an analogous sense, but a humanly contrived aggregate. And though it is possible to attribute even to 'merely' useful artifacts something analogous to self-hood, such that it would be wrong or even violent to *misuse* them just as it would be to deface a beautiful work of art, nevertheless *its* project is not its own, but its maker's. '*We* are the end of artificial things,' says St Thomas.[6] The distinction between nature and art is thus ultimately a distinction between two different ways of being a thing – of possessing or standing in relation to one's own being and 'essence'.[7] This difference is frequently obscured by the fact that when we moderns envision nature in its paradigmatic instance, we most likely imagine what would have heretofore been regarded as the least intelligible, and least 'natural' of things: a Newtonian inertial mass hurtling through space or the immortal words that seem to launch every high school biology textbook – in the beginning was the cell – a testament to the power that a mechanistic ontology still exercises over our imaginations. But on a traditional understanding, the paradigm for nature is its *highest* instance, the living and indeed the *human* being, who presupposes the myriad relations that constitute the human being's *actual* existence in the fullness of *esse commune* and exemplifies what is merely inchoate or partially realised in its lowest instances.

[5] See, e.g., *Aquinas*, ST 1,11,1. [6] Aquinas, *Commentary on the Metaphysics*, lect. 4, 173.

[7] For more on this difference, see Robert Spaemann, *Persons: The Difference between 'Someone' and 'Something'* (Oxford: Oxford University Press, 2007).

The scientific revolution which commenced in the seventeenth century and has not ended was a revolution against any metaphysics that would make form, mind, *logos*, or meaning intrinsic to reality from its foundations and any concept of nature that made 'wholeness an autonomous cause with respect to its component parts'.[8] At its root was a new notion of matter, liberated from its relation to form, and conceived, albeit with variations, as some sort of dimensive and hence measurable quantity, fully positive and actual in its own right.[9] The abolition of substantial form meant the elimination of *esse commune* as well, which then enabled natural philosophers to premise the actual world on a counterfactual world of inertial singularities abstracted through analysis hastening the ascent of physics to the position of first philosophy. This inversion of potency and act, we shall see, that remains endemic to scientific cognition and scientific forms of explanation. This eliminated the distinction between ontological and temporal orders, thereby paving the way for the conflation of being and history which was soon to follow. But it also evacuated natural things of just that a priori and indivisible unity, interiority, and intrinsic intelligibility which heretofore distinguished them from artifacts, qualities that would henceforth be invisible to the eyes of a science which conceals its continued dependence upon them and exempts itself from its own endemic reductionism by retreating to an Archimedean point outside nature in the moment of its theorising.[10] As the depth dimension conferred on things by form and *esse* recedes from sight, natural things become artificial and *superficial*, that is, comprised of a concatenation of 'surfaces', variously conceived, susceptible to endless analysis and synthesis but no interior intellectual *penetration*, for the interiority of being is now conceived in the image of the exteriority of spatial and temporal distention. As the indivisible unity of *ens indivisum*, the measure of a thing's 'imperfect' participation in the simplicity of God is reduced to the complex unity of aggregation it had always exhibited in the historical order; natural things become *plastic*, limited in their functions and transformations only by 'the bounds of the possible' which science perpetually transgresses.[11] For 'the

[8] Jonas, *Phenomenon of Life*, 201.

[9] Whether the unit of measurement be extension, mass, corpuscles or energy is largely a matter of indifference.

[10] 'In the experiment man realized his newly won freedom from the shackles of earth-bound experience; he placed nature under the conditions of his own mind, that is, under conditions won from a universal, astrophysical viewpoint, a cosmic standpoint outside nature itself.' Arendt, *The Human Condition*, 2nd ed. (Chicago: University of Chicago Press, 1998), 265.

[11] Bacon, *Novum Organum*, II.1.

task and purpose of human power', according to Bacon, 'is to generate and superinduce on a given body a new nature or natures' within those bounds.[12]

The seventeenth and eighteenth centuries conceived of this reduction principally in terms of *natura naturata*, the finished artifacts issuing forth from the gracious hand of a 'contriving' God who imposes laws extrinsically upon inert matter, already a truncated, mechanistic understanding of God and creation that never arrives at real theology.[13] The Romantic reaction of the nineteenth century replaced the gracious hand of God by the gracious hand of history or natural selection, thereby shifting the accent to *natura naturans* and nature as a dynamic process, whose products are finally only provisional: compromises in the aggregate actions of matter and energy that temporarily defy entropy.[14] This wasn't the intent, of course. The Romantic reaction attempted to counter mechanistic reduction and abstraction by introducing a vital principle: Blumenbach's *Bildungstrieb* or Goethe's archetypal *Urpflanze* are prominent examples, responsible for the self-organisation of matter.[15] Or perhaps it would be better to say that they simply sought to acknowledge and incorporate those intractable dimensions of being and experience, 'the remainder' excluded by but always intruding upon mechanistic analysis – and thus to recover a sense of the self-transcendence of both the living organism and the perceiving scientist.[16] Yet there seems to be less here than meets the eye in the end, inasmuch as the conflation of nature and art was destined to terminate in the conflation of being and history conceived *as* the linear series of causes and effects culminating in the construction of the present.[17] The rapidity with which ontogeny was subordinated to phylogeny in Romantic biology, and a vitalism with roots in Goethe, Schelling, and Oken was eventually transformed into its materialist, reductionist antithesis, is an indicator of this destiny, which partly explains why a figure like

[12] Ibid. [13] See Hanby, *No God, No Science?*, 107–85.

[14] See David J. Depew and Bruce H. Weber, *Darwinism Evolving: Systems Dynamics and the Genealogy of Natural Selection* (Cambridge, MA: MIT Press, 1995), 169–91; Lenny Moss, *What Genes Can't Do* (Cambridge, MA: MIT Press, 2003); Hanby, *No God, No Science?*, 250–96.

[15] Hanby, *No God, No Science?*, 250–96.

[16] On the priority of synthesis to analysis, an echo of the medieval priority of *intellectus* to *ratio*, and its relation to the priority of unity over parts, see Goethe, *Goethe's Botanical Writings*, tr. B. Mueller (Woodbridge: Oxbow Press, 1989), 76–88, 239.

[17] 'The shift from the "why" and the "what" to the "how" implies that the actual objects of knowledge can no longer be things or eternal motions but must be processes, and that the object of science therefore is no longer nature or the universe but the history, the story of the coming into being, of nature or life or the universe.' Arendt, *The Human Condition* (Chicago: University of Chicago Press, 1958), 296. See Hanby, *No God, No Science?*, 107–249.

Charles Darwin could plausibly be claimed by the mechanists and the Romantics at the same time.[18]

Corresponding to the conflation of nature and art in the ontological order are two further, interrelated reductions in the order of cognition: the conflation of *techne* and *logos*, knowing and making, on the one hand, and of truth and utility or functionality, on the other. As a result, traditional theoretical and contemplative reason would henceforth be obsolete, both because these reductions deprive contemplation of its objects and because the new conflation of truth and possibility makes such speculation superfluous.[19] The new technological manner of knowing is a knowing-by-doing that 'takes experience apart and analyses it', abstracting the intelligible wholes that present themselves to our experience from the totality to which they actually belong, breaking them down in thought if not indeed by instruments so as to reduce them to their simplest components, and reconstructing them as the sum of those abstracted components and their interactions and the antecedent causes that produced them.[20] This harassment of nature *by* art completes the reduction of nature *to* art, as ontological identity – *what things are* – is dissolved into how they work and the history by which they came to be. This is the meaning of the famous Baconian maxim, 'knowledge is power'. It is not simply that we now know the phenomena of nature *for the sake of controlling them*; it is, rather, that we know natural phenomena *by means of* controlling them. This is ultimately why Bacon says that truth and usefulness come to the same thing: because the 'truth' of this kind of knowledge is precisely *identical* to our power, to our *success* in replicating experimental results, predicting or retrodicting the behaviour of natural phenomena to reconstruct or redirect their genesis, producing new experiments and manipulating these phenomena to our own ends.[21] To put the matter crudely, if nature is essentially a machine or a mechanical process, then the knowledge of nature is essentially engineering. And if knowledge is essentially engineering, then *truth* is essentially whatever is technically possible. But since the ultimate limits of possibility can be discovered only by perpetually transgressing the present limits of possibility, this mechanical or technological

[18] See Robert J. Richards, 'Darwin's Romantic Biology: The Foundation of His Evolutionary Ethics', in J. Mainschien and M. Ruse (eds.), *Biology and the Foundations of Ethics* (Cambridge: Cambridge University Press, 1999), 113–53; Depew and Weber, *Darwinism Evolving*, 57–140.

[19] See Hans Jonas, *The Imperative of Responsibility: In Search of an Ethics for the Technological Age* (Chicago: University of Chicago Press, 1984), 6. See Arendt, *Human Condition*, 289–94; Jonas, *Phenomenon of Life*, 188–210.

[20] Francis Bacon, *The Great Instauration*, praef.

[21] Francis Bacon, *Novum Organum*, I.124.

conception of being, nature, and truth issues in an interminable war against antecedent limits of every kind.[22]

It is not accidental that modernity and liberal order are distinguished as modern and liberal in distinction from all the ages that preceded them by their culmination in a technological society and a distinctive scientific culture, characterised, in Stephen Gaukroger's words, by 'the gradual assimilation of all cognitive values to scientific ones'.[23] The tendency of technology to take on a life of its own as a comprehensive and progressive social *system* follows of necessity from its metaphysical 'essence'. The conflation of truth and possibility means that scientific truth is essentially incomplete, provisional, and public, and so its pursuit by nature will require what Dewey called 'organised intelligence', spanning generations, that 'attacks nature collectively' in a Baconian society 'organised for inquiry'.[24] It is this vision that inspired the creation of the Royal Society of London in the seventeenth century and Académie des sciences in Paris, as well as Franklin's American Philosophical Society in the eighteenth, dedicated to the promotion of 'useful knowledge' and boasting Washington, Jefferson, Madison, Hamilton, Marshall, and Paine among its members. 'Like the republic of letters', Jefferson wrote, the sciences 'form a great fraternity spreading over the whole earth, and their correspondence is never interrupted by any civilised nation.'[25] Expertise acquired in one branch of this great scientific fraternity is taken up into the system of 'organised intelligence' where it then contributes to unforeseeable and uncontrollable results in a second and third field. So, advances in assisted reproductive technologies, for example, lead to advances in genetic engineering unanticipated and unintended by the original researchers, and examples can be multiplied across other fields, such as information technology.[26] Dewey's 'organised intelligence' might thus be better characterised as *self-organising* intelligence, insofar as 'organisation' is

22 John Dewey, *Reconstruction in Philosophy* (London: Forgotten Books, 2012), 37.

23 Stephen Gaukroger, *The Emergence of a Scientific Culture: Science and the Shaping of Modernity 1210–1685* (Oxford: Oxford University Press, 2006), 1.

24 Dewey, *Reconstruction in Philosophy*, 37.

25 Thomas Jefferson, 'To John Hollins, February 19, 1809', in Merrill D. Peterson (ed.), *Thomas Jefferson: Writings* (New York: Library of America, 1984), 1201.

26 Or as biotech entrepreneur Gregory Stock puts it, 'The coming possibilities will be the inadvertent spinoff of mainstream research that virtually everyone supports.... Researchers and clinicians working on in vitro fertilization (IVF) don't think much about future human evolution, but nonetheless are building a foundation of expertise in conceiving, handling, testing, and implanting human embryos, and this will one day be the basis for the manipulation of the human species.' Gregory Stock, *Redesigning Humans: Our Inevitable Genetic Future* (New York: Houghton Mifflin, 2002), 5.

more of an emergent property from below than a structure imposed from above. Even this is too simple, however. For such achievements actually generate multiple, overlapping systems, and the artifacts of modern technology are not simply monumental, static objects imitating nature as *natura naturata*. Increasingly, technology introduces into the stream of history artifacts that are *themselves* dynamic processes and that therefore elude control by their very nature *as* historical processes. This is true even of what Jonas calls 'dead matter engineering', things like the internet or the air traffic control system. But it is especially true of *living* artifacts; for as Jonas says, you cannot recall scrap populations.[27] And the cause and effect trains set in motion by these dynamic processes do not proceed in a linear chain reaction but rather multiply 'virally' in multiple directions at once, like an organism increasing its bulk in three dimensions.[28]

It is also not accidental, therefore, that this system, whose dynamic exigences determine the conditions of our thought and action and therefore govern us more deeply than the rule of law, increasingly seems impervious to human political agency, that technocracy, emerging as a *post*-political system with a life of its own, seems to be our *fate*. 'Control', Jonas explains, 'by making ever more things available for more kinds of uses, enmeshes the user's life in ever more dependencies on external objects. There is no other way of exercising the power than by making oneself available to the use of the things as they become available.... Tasks for theory are set by the practical results of its preceding use, their solutions to be turned again to use, and so on.'[29] As these results accumulate and extend themselves irreversibly across time and space, agents continually find themselves in unprecedented situations for which the past provides no guidance, a sure sign, Jonas says, that we live in perpetual revolution. The novel situations generated for later subjects and their choices of action by these cause and effect trains, though they be progressively different from the initial agent, will nevertheless be 'ever more the fated product of what was done before'.[30]

[27] Jonas, *Philosophical Essays* (Englewood Cliffs:, NJ Prentice Hall, 1974), 146.

[28] See Arendt, *Human Condition*, 230–6; Jonas, *Imperative of Responsibility*, 7.

[29] Jonas, *Phenomenon of Life*, 193, 209. C. S. Lewis echoes this same idea: 'The last men, far from being the heirs of power, will be of all men most subject to the dead hand of the great planners and conditioners and will themselves least exercise power upon the future.' Lewis, *The Abolition of Man* (New York: HarperCollins, 1974), 58. I trust, that in referring to the 'last men', the echoes of Nietzsche are more than fortuitous. See Friedrich Nietzsche, *Thus Spoke Zarathustra* (New York: Viking, 1966), Pt. 1, §5.

[30] Jonas, *Imperative of Responsibility*, 7.

I do not pretend that this hasty and impressionistic sketch is adequate to the reality of modern science and technology in all their historical and philosophical complexity. We have only begun to grasp the nature of science in its guise as a post-political social system that sets the conditions for our thinking about it. I *do* hope it suffices to cast some light on the overwhelming power of this system and on three fundamental obstacles in engaging critically with it. Clarity on these points is essential if we hope to articulate some basic principles for future engagement.

The first obstacle and the corresponding principle have to do with the nature of this engagement and the level at which it should occur. The notion of a 'pure' science, indifferent to and uncontaminated by metaphysical and theological judgements, is and must be a fiction – both historically and as a matter of principle. Moreover, the metaphysical judgements endemic to modern science are not merely extrinsic, presupposed at the logical and historical origins of scientific inquiry, but otherwise safely 'bracketed out' from the strictly scientific work of testing hypotheses by empirical and experimental methods. Rather, they are intrinsic to the method itself, which determines the conditions under which the phenomena of nature are allowed to appear and which aspects of its manifestation are to be regarded as evidentiary. They thus determine to a great extent *what the object is* for all practical intents and purposes, though this question will soon cease to be intelligible or relevant. Metaphysical and theological judgements, therefore, do not stand opposite 'the empirical', to be invoked or evaluated in a second moment after science has done its job. Rather, these judgements are inherent in the very identification of 'the empirical', which is always an abstract and highly stylised form of experience, bringing some elements of that experience into the evidential foreground while other aspects of the total actuality, which do no cease to be operative simply because we cease to think about them, recede into the background.[31] These judgements are operational in the very enactment of scientific cognition, determining what does and does not count as a scientific question, and how God can then be thought – what God *must be* if nature is really like this – even if this God is thought not to exist or is posited only in order to be rejected or contained.[32] To come to a critical philosophical and theological engagement with the

[31] See Michael Polanyi, *Personal Knowledge: Towards a Post-Critical Philosophy* (Chicago: University of Chicago Press, 1974), 340–6; *The Tacit Dimension* (Chicago: University of Chicago Press, 1996), 29–54.

[32] A perfect example of this can be found in Stephen Jay Gould, *Rock of Ages: Science and Religion in the Fullness of Life* (New York: Ballantine Books, 1999).

sciences only after science has done its work is therefore to have arrived too late. A philosophical and theological engagement with the sciences should be *philosophical and theological*: critiquing the notions of God, being, nature, knowledge, and truth presupposed, operative within, and perpetuated by the sciences, thereby helping science to realise, to the extent science has any interest in the question, the true nature of its own act. One would hope, in other words, to help the sciences attain a deeper philosophical self-knowledge, though we have already hinted at science's built-in disincentives to acquiring it. Nevertheless, it is only by recognising scientific cognition as a certain kind of abstraction from the fullness of *esse commune*, and by science coming to a deeper philosophical *self-knowledge* consistent with this understanding, that we might hope for science to be reintegrated within the more comprehensive order of reason and being that its activity simultaneously presupposes and denies and that we might hope to acquire some degree of freedom from – or rather freedom *within* – our technocratic fate.

However, the very substance of these judgements, which I described by the conflations of nature and art, truth and function, militate against this engagement from the side of science. This is the second obstacle. Nothing succeeds like success. If by manipulating variable *x*, I can produce or inhibit result *y*, and if *y* supplies an 'inference ticket' to experiment *z*, then it is simply superfluous to ask what being, or nature, or cause, or truth is, or even *what x*, *y*, and *z* are. Indeed, insofar as these conflations transform the very meaning of 'is' so as to make thought itself functional, as Henry Veatch once showed, then questions in the 'what is?' form can no longer even be intelligibly posed: for 'is' no longer explicates the 'what' of something but merely functions as a copula conjoining two extrinsically related terms – be they mathematical terms, concepts, or historical events.[33] The conclusion is astonishing: our dominant form of reason – and therefore the one we *all* partake of to some degree – is uninterested and indeed incapable of thinking about or saying *what things are*. As Dewey put it, they are 'what they can do and what can be done with

[33] As Veatch provocatively put the matter, 'Has it never struck anyone as passing strange that the logic of *Principia Mathematica*, for all its elaboration, provides no means either for saying or thinking what anything is? And if we not only cannot claim to know what things are, but if our very logic debars us from even stating or formulating propositions as to what this, that or the other thing is, then the very idea of what a thing is, or the very conviction that each thing is what it is, that things are what they are, or indeed that anything is anything becomes simply impossible, or at least logically improper.' Henry Veatch, *The Two Logics: The Conflict between Classical and Neo-Analytic Philosophy* (Evanston, IL: Northwestern University Press, 1969), 26.

them'.[34] With contemplative reason lost to us – and whatever the 'forgetfulness of being' means, it surely means this – all that is left to us are the various species of functional questions – 'how many?', 'how far?', 'under what influence?', 'by what means?' and 'to what effect?' – that govern our engagement with phenomena a priori and entail their own pragmatic conception of truth. The relationship between the dominance of science in modern culture and its anti-intellectualism is not accidental. They are proportionally and not inversely related. There is a massive disincentive to understanding, an inducement to thoughtlessness, at the heart of our prevailing form of reason, so that even where the will to understand is present, we no longer understand understanding.

This reduction of truth to function brings us to a final obstacle that we all no doubt have heard many times, namely, science *works*, a sure sign, whenever you hear it, that the Baconian vision is still in effect. Now we may wish to contest this by insisting that science has never fully succeeded in escaping the world of classical metaphysics. Indeed, escape would be futile if this metaphysics is *true*. Reality would continue to impose itself on thought after all; principles intrinsic to thought and being but excluded by the method would return in other guises. Form would be tacitly affirmed in the very attempt to dispense with it. There is ample evidence to suggest that this is the case, both as a matter of principle and in the history of scientific development. Objectively, the experimental abstractions of modern science are still parasitic on things being what they are, doing what they do in virtue of what they are. Subjectively, scientific inquiry still commences by taking leave from the world of intelligible experience, and it advances by taking constant, if tacit recourse back to it. As Michael Polanyi once put it, a mathematical description of a frog is intelligible only by continual tacit reference to the frog from which the description is abstracted. The form long banished by mechanism continues to be invoked anew, albeit in degraded fashion, as the formal*ism* of law or as information to compensate for the remainder expelled by mechanical analysis. I believe it was the developmental systems theorist Susan Oyama who said, 'When you don't know what something is, call it information.' Reductionism always bumps up against some form of the recursion argument, and so we may always ask how well any theory 'works' when, if pressed to its logical conclusion, it would force us to regard ordinary experience as epiphenomenal. The deeper and more difficult question is how to proceed once the inner pragmatism of a functional

[34] Dewey, *Reconstruction in Philosophy*, 115.

science has liberated reason from the claim of truth and the heart from the desire to know it.

Even so, there is no disputing that science has been astonishingly successful achieving the goals it has set for itself. It has produced inventions far exceeding even Bacon's prophetic imagination. It has revealed forms of order, systems, and processes, both microscopic and macroscopic, that do not translate straightforwardly into the terms of classical metaphysics – and which require a great deal of creative, speculative thought if the tradition is to be fruitfully carried forward. Under the harassments of science, nature has revealed itself to be more plastic than the tradition imagined, history more creative. Perhaps there was always a more active and productive dimension even to contemplative knowledge than the tradition had recognised.

If metaphysics and theology are the highest sciences because they pertain to *esse commune* and its source, and thus to the deepest and most comprehensive horizons *from which* the particular sciences abstract, then the astonishing power and success of science must be metaphysically and theologically comprehended and accounted for. The basic question, given my opening assumption, is: What must being *be* that this kind of truth is possible and that it can be made to show itself and behave this way? An important and intriguing proposal comes from John Milbank, in this volume and elsewhere, which I can only superficially touch on here.[35] Milbank has long sought to overcome what he regards as an inadequate 'theory/practice duality' endemic to the tradition with a conception of baroque *poesis* that includes both indissolubly.[36] Rooting his proposal ontologically in something like Nicholas of Cusa's conception of a divine *posse* transcending the Aristotelian distinction between potency and act, Milbank proposes to elevate 'makeability' to the status of a transcendental. The 'poetic' unity of knowing and making then appears as an expression and approximation of, and indeed a participation in, what is most uniquely

[35] Milbank's emphasis on baroque poesis is at least as old as his landmark *Theology and Social Theory* (Oxford: Blackwell, 1990). For a more recent development of this understanding, besides the one in this volume, see Milbank, '*Mathesis and Methexis*: The Post-Nominalist Realism of Nicholas of Cusa', in Isabelle Moulin (ed.), *Participation et vision de dieu chez Nicolas de Cues* (Paris: Vrin, 2017), 143–70.

[36] 'It never quite worked out how, if contemplation is the highest end of human life, then leisure could be the "basis of culture" for every individual as well as the whole of society. Nor did it question a theory/practice duality or come to the realization that work also can be contemplative. This was a failure to grasp its *own* reality; it took Chauteaubriand, Hugo, Pugin and Ruskin in the 19th century to point out that medieval contemplation was also the work of the church masons, the composers, and the poets.' Milbank, 'The Gift of Ruling: Secularization and Political Authority', *New Blackfriars*, Vol. 85, No. 996 (March 2004), pp. 212–238 85, no. 906 (March 2004), 219.

Christian in the history of ontology: *creation ex nihilo* as the ontological structure of reality, grounded in the self-differentiating unity of the Trinity.[37] The proposal is not just noetically and ontologically bold; it holds certain historical and practical advantages as well. First, it issues in a kind of 'horizontal' Neoplatonism that gives a new, a specifically Christian ontological valuation to the causal agency of history as such. Within this, the history of science too can be given a new valuation. From this vantage, the work of Peter Harrison and others showing the *theological* and even liturgical origins of early modern science – even and indeed especially its affinities with *magic* – acquires a new *speculative* as well as historical importance. This makes it possible to reconceive of early modern science as the flawed expression of a genuinely *religious* and indeed *liturgical* impulse, and to reconstruct an alternative modernity prioritising a Romantic and vitalistic strand of modern science which has never completely gone away, with its various life principles, teleological processes, forms, and archetypes, over the mechanistic reductionism that seems to have won the day. Christianity can then reconcile itself to the modern discovery of evolution and to the inevitability of scientific advance, and it can redeem them simultaneously, by contextualising them within an ontology of creation *in tempore* and a richer religious and liturgical culture and by redirecting human *poesis* toward the better end implicit in its beginning.

Milbank's proposal indicates the theological and ontological level at which the question of science must be adjudicated, and it may be true that the tradition never fully realised itself, that the radical novelty and gratuity of creation *ex nihilo* never quite completed its transformation of the Greek metaphysical inheritance and never fully succeeded therefore in enfolding history into ontology. It would then follow that there is indeed a greater coincidence of knowing and making, contemplation and action inherent even in the receptivity of contemplation – in the mere abstraction of intelligible species under novel circumstances, to put it in terms of the mechanics of Aristotelian cognition – than the tradition realised, that human thought and action in the event of knowledge contribute to the *making* of truth as an event that is *ever new* as well as ever ancient. Perhaps like Milbank, I suspect all of this is at least intimated in Thomas' insight that truth adds to being a relation to intellect and in the Aristotelian insight that art can bring nature to completion and that there are certain intrinsic potencies in nature, *qua* sensible, *qua* intelligible, and so forth,

[37] See Hanby, *No God, No Science?*, 299–333.

that can only be actualised transitively in being seen, known, and therefore shaped by us. It would surely complexify our understanding of evolution were we to think deeply about the remarkable fact this beautiful, colourful visible world went unseen for millions upon millions of years, that vibrations in the atmosphere always had within them the potential to become a Bach cello suite, or that carbon molecules could bear the human spirit.[38] The advent of meaning in the world and the realisation of these various possibilities are surely *ex nihilo* events; they mark the appearance of genuine novelties, irreducible to their antecedents. To take seriously the philosophical meaning of these possibilities, and the prior actuality that is their precondition, would be to consider, in Hans Jonas' words, that human beings may yet be the measure of all things through the exemplar of their 'psychophysical totality which represents the maximum of concrete ontological completeness known to us, a completeness from which, reductively, the species of being may have to be determined by way of progressive ontological subtraction down to the minimum of bare elementary matter (instead of the complete being constructed from this basis by cumulative addition)'.[39]

An adequate response to this proposal, as well as an adequate solution to the question it seeks to solve, would require a careful sifting that far exceeds the scope of this essay. Both the challenge confronting this task and the risks inherent in getting this question wrong can be better appreciated if we pause to consider why Milbank's 'alternative modernity' has remained, after all, merely an alternative. There are undoubtedly many dimensions to this question, but part of the problem surely stems from what seems like an entailment of Milbank's own proposal to elevate *factibilitas* to a transcendental attribute of being, namely, the priority of possibility and thus futurity over actuality, and the givenness of antecedent order. Subjectively speaking, the priority of possibility, when coupled with the conflation of knowing and making, ultimately obviates the need and the desire for the contemplative dimension tacit within it, while objectively speaking, it dispenses with whatever ontological principles it may ultimately depend on. There seems little, in principle, to prevent the reduction of *poesis* to *techne* in its modern sense, just as, time and again, nothing has prevented the reduction of nature to artifice and the reduction of romantic biology in its various forms to mechanism. Mechanism may not

[38] Simon Conway Morris' treatment of 'convergence' can be read along these lines. See Morris, *Life's Solution: Inevitable Humans in a Lonely Universe* (Cambridge: Cambridge University Press, 2003).

[39] Jonas, *Phenomenon of Life*, 24.

be true, but it does not *need* to be true if it works well enough to allow me to move on to the next experiment. For science, as Joseph Ratzinger observed, is founded on the *renunciation* of the quest for truth.[40]

The eclipse of truth and the eclipse of being are two facets of the same problem. One test of whether any proposal is adequate to its depth is whether it can articulate ontological reasons, as opposed to merely moralistic or religious reasons, for objecting to the brave new eugenical world that is already upon us. In other words, is it possible to object intelligibly to human self-design and the redefinition of fundamental human realities as acts of violence against the integrity of human nature? Does the proposal allow one to mount a defence of the *humanum* based on *what humans beings are*, and not merely on how they function or on the dystopian consequences of these actions? What are the ontological preconditions for thinking 'what things are', and are these still available to us? To put the point positively, the challenge which science and a scientific culture poses to the Christian conception of the world as creation cannot be overcome simply by shaking incense at science – recovering its lost liturgical dimensions – or 'referring' science to higher ends as if the problem were merely a matter of intention. For what is fundamentally in dispute between the Christian vision and the metaphysical and theological vision of modern science is the truth of the world, indeed, the truth of truth itself.

To put the matter in terms of 'overcoming a challenge', however, is to risk conceiving this challenge in the same functional and consequentialist terms that define it, a risk, perhaps, which reveals just how difficult it is to escape the instrumental thought forms that dominate the modern mind. The fundamental question is the one with which we began: attaining an apprehension of the world adequate to its reality, recognising that 'adequate' means comprehensive but not exhaustive, if being is not the 'kind of thing' that can be exhausted. However 'creative' an endeavour this turns out to be, and however much the object of that apprehension, being a creature, bears an *ex nihilo* structure and is thus 'serially' novel as it emerges anew from nothing, I am convinced that there can be no such apprehension that does not preserve and protect that which the Aristotelian distinction between nature and art sought to protect, namely, the 'in-itselfness' of an order of being anterior to our action upon it, whose givenness provides the context and occasion of our action. Human making is always first a receiving, and what is received, which of course includes the makers

[40] Joseph Ratzinger, *Introduction to Christianity*, tr. J. R. Foster (San Francisco, CA: Ignatius Press, 2004), 66, 77.

themselves, must be more than raw material or an assemblage of elements for creative synthesis. Acknowledging this entails the further, thoroughly traditional acknowledgement of the analogical difference between the divine 'art' of creation *ex nihilo* which gives the totality of a thing's being, from the inside out, as it were, and every other form of making which simply alters existing structures and is only properly 'creative' by way of participation in the *ex nihilo* structure of *esse creatum.*

Any ontology of creation that would be true to the intrinsic goodness and intelligibility of creation and that does not wish simply to baptise technology and or to acquiesce in our technological fate will have to preserve some form of the distinction between the nature and art, the born and the made, whereby it is possible to claim that nature is more than simply whatever happens and is irreducible to a dynamic historical process, however 'creative'. It will have to apprehend and articulate an 'all-at-once' unity and completeness in things that proceeds their temporal development and the realisation of historical possibilities and thus an antecedent order, that is true and good prior to our activity upon it, a givenness that precedes our activity as its condition of possibility. All this, in turn, will require the rediscovery of a truth that is irreducible to function, that is more than mere possibility, a truth that is *not* of our own making though we may be its midwife, and a corresponding form of reason capable of contemplating once more what things are and of awaiting their answer to that question. It is upon the rediscovery of this truth, the truth of being, and a form of reason that is adequate to it, that a real engagement between theology and science depends.

CHAPTER 7

Truth, Science and Re-enchantment

Catherine Pickstock

Representations of the seventeenth-century 'scientific revolution' as a departure from a supposedly 'pre-scientific' era, encompassing most of what went before, apart from a few heroic 'anticipators', are very common. Such a view often goes hand in hand with an account of seventeenth-century 'science' which emphasises its new commitments to mechanical causation and an attitude of empirical detachment.

But there are several aspects of this presentation which are problematic. First, despite new emphases upon systematic experiment and the application of mathematics to physics, the 'science' of this century remained within the scope of 'natural philosophy', and no straightforward division was made between physics, metaphysics and theology. Some natural philosophers indeed abandoned the older Platonic-Aristotelian inheritance and favoured reductively mathematical and mechanical accounts of physical reality. Second, this did not mean that theological concerns had been abandoned, and indeed these drained views of the cosmos were often favoured for specifically theological reasons. In the terms of John Milbank's threefold classification, in this volume, they upheld a 'disenchanted transcendence'. But, third, it is by no means the case that the new penchant amongst many for mechanism, linked with philosophical nominalism and theological voluntarism (re-invoking late medieval currents), suppressed earlier Renaissance naturalist and vitalist momentum. These currents can also be regarded as belonging to 'the rise of science' (if one wishes to speak in such a misleading way), since they were also connected with mathematically informed cosmologies, the use of experiment and an interest in practical application, often linked with millenarian expectations. Again, to invoke Milbank's terms, they involved either 'enchanted immanentism' or 'enchanted transcendence'.

A continuing, if minority-report Renaissance was manifest in European thinking during this period, but a continued revived 'Platonism' was especially apparent in England. Eventually, it came to be grouped around the University of Cambridge, but the thinkers I will consider in this essay preceded or succeeded that geographical concentration. They were all three of them philosophers, rather than primarily 'natural philosophers'; but their philosophy was nonetheless imbued with the natural philosophical concerns of their contemporaries, especially with respect to cosmology, with transformative processes both natural and artificial and with the relationship of human understanding to the physical world.

In this third respect, a reflection on their writings enables us to see that 'epistemological' interests, either supporting the 'new science' or seeking to apply it to psychological experience, mental awareness and cultural phenomena, were not just a phase subsequent to the 'scientific revolution', beginning with the work of John Locke. Rather, as one can see in the case of Descartes, they were concurrent with it.

It is striking that, in the writings of Herbert of Cherbury especially, and later in those of Anne Conway (who blends immanent with transcendent enchantment), we see a continued pursuit of roughly Platonic-Aristotelian approaches (with Stoic admixtures) to accounts of perception and understanding, albeit in a recognisably new key that is no less to do with 'scientific revolution' than the work of philosophically more subversive and supposedly mainline thinkers such as Bacon, Hobbes and Boyle.

In their writings, a central and traditional concern with Truth as an eternal but participated reality is pursued in an idiom no less 'modern' than that of those whom we regard as 'modernisers'. This suggests that even today they may hold out to us a different way to be modern and to be 'scientific'.

7.1 English Platonism

Truth is not to be found exclusively in things or in the mind. If it were only in things, it would filter back invisibly into being, and the term 'truth' would be disquotable, or redundant. Were it only in the mind, one could not be certain that a supposed truth was not one's contingent perspective. The same conclusion applies if it were suggested, following what I have called 'fancy' realism, that subjectivity, mind and feeling are diffused variously amongst all things. If truth were objective, there would be no truth, only the inertness of reality. If truth were subjective, there would again be no truth, only the myriad ways in which some things happen to take other things to be.

For there to be truth, three things are requisite. First, there must be an inherent connection between objects and subjects, between things and spirits, between things known and knowing minds. As Quentin Meillassoux argues, one cannot escape the appearance of such a connection. And yet, as he continues, one appears to have no insight into it; rather, there seems to be no way to avoid an arbitrary correlation, and in turn, no way to avoid modes of idealism or empiricism, which come to the same thing, because they confine one within one's subjective awareness, for whose correlation with reality, no account may be given.

One could describe Meillassoux's proposed solution, using William Desmond's phrase, as an example of 'counterfeit theology', or parodied traditional metaphysics. One happens to live in a world in which an inexplicable correlation holds good, a world determined not by God but by the rule of chance, beyond even the laws of probability. This is Meillassoux's one truth, but it is the truth of no meaning, and no significance. Being displays itself randomly, and without truth, in any meaningful sense of that term.

In order for there to be truth, the connection between things and spirits must be more than arbitrary. Truth must, in some sense, be *supposed* to be there. It must be analogical, really relational, horizontally participatory and teleological. To know must be an event in the life of that which is known, bringing it to fruition. Otherwise, for the reasons which we have explored, there exists no truth. To speak of 'truth' becomes a *façon de parler*, which one might translate into philosophical idioms such as 'justified true belief' or 'the essence of phenomena as they appear to us'. But if there is truth, if things and spirits are connected, then one need no longer speak of a strange 'correlation', but of a mysterious but not exactly baffling 'conformation', to use the term of the Anglo-Welsh philosopher Edward Herbert, Lord of Cherbury, brother of George the poet, in his *De veritate* of 1624.[1]

If, however, conformation is to be distinguished from correlation, then a second thing is also requisite. The intrinsic order between thing and mind, object and subject, cannot be exhausted as contingent, subject to endless change and ultimate dissolution. It must somehow reflect the eternal, participate in it. In the same way that if there is no inherent link between reality and spirit, there is no truth, so it is the case that if there is no ultimate stability, there is no truth. Not everything can be stable, in fact, nothing finite that one knows of. And yet, one appears to know many truths, indeed, an unlimited number of truths. However, they are only

[1] Edward Herbert, *De veritate*, trans. Meyrick H. Carré (London: Routledge-Thoemmes; Tokyo: Kinokuniya, 1992).

scintilla, glittering shards of actual truth, to the degree that they participate in the eternal and reflect what abides.

One could argue, after Spinoza, that it might be the case that conforming reality, as immanence, is the eternal. But, as we have seen, if this is so, then reality is a dominant single process into which all else resolves, or it comprises endlessly isolated single realities, which are random and perhaps empty. In the latter case, one is dispatched into disorder and so to the absence of truth. In the former case, an inert single reality is a blind and non-teleological process, or a single monadic being or monolith, after Parmenides, lurking behind the illusion of change. Such a being is self-contained, does not express itself, and there is no truth.

It is after considering the impasse of these conclusions that the third requisite comes into view. It is not enough that truth should be eternal, and that participation in this truth should engender an order of conformation between reality and spirit, a kind of vertical correlation which spirals into everything. If this conformation participates in the eternal, the eternal cannot be a matter of ineffable being. It must, to use Plato's term, be *dynamis*. It must be one with self-expression, and one perforce does not know of any existence which does not manifest itself. Phenomenology may not exhaust ontology, but there cannot be an ontology without phenomenology. To be is to show and to express oneself, and so potentially to relate oneself to a third factor. If the finite conformation of object and subject participates in the eternal, or *conforms* to it, then one must conceive the eternal, or the infinite, as *itself* an eternal correlation between being and its expression or manifestation. This expression is eternal truth.

It was in building to this insight that both Plato and Aristotle departed from pre-Socratic monism, in order to welcome both truth and subjectivity within the scope of ontology. Reality is no longer seen as unity, nor as the flux of change, nor as an all-dissolving element such as water. Rather, reality as both being and motion, one and many, unity and expression, may be seen as order or *logos*, the coherence of the One and the Two (or Many), which is a matter of aesthetic judgement, and so inseparable from mind. The idea that mental expression belongs to the absolute is more consistent with the elaboration of the Christian theology of the Trinity, which is also a philosophical thesis. To this point, we will return.

We see that there are three requisites for truth: the conformation of finite things with finite spirit; the conformation of the same with the eternal and infinite; the conformation within the infinite of being with spiritual expression. With these three requisites, one has an ontological account of truth, but also an ontology or metaphysics in which truth plays a central role. Without these three, one is confined to a nihilistic ontology without truth, or to a theory of truth as epistemological, of whichever kind, which is not to acknowledge truth's reality.

In order to explore how one might expand upon such a metaphysics of truth, or the truth-metaphysics implied by these three requisites, let us proceed by considering three seventeenth-century English treatises which have recourse to a pre-modern approach to truth as enshrined in this threefold requirement, but do so in a post-Renaissance manner which offers us 'alternatively modern' possibilities, somewhat in keeping with those described in the tradition of French spiritual realism.

Edward Herbert, Robert Greville, and Anne Conway are writers who belong to what the philosopher J. H. Muirhead argued was the majority report of Anglo-American philosophy, rather than empiricism as is often supposed. He describes this current as 'Platonic' and 'idealist', but which one might today more accurately characterizes as, in its original inception, 'Platonic-Hermeticist', with a strong continuing admixture of Scholasticism.[2] The rival current to this philosophy in England was Baconianism, but this was perhaps more ethically pragmatic than primarily empiricist. Moreover, Baconianism could itself be 'Platonic', and the 'Platonists' included Baconian elements of modern interest in observation, experiment, conjecture and technology.

This philosophical current was by no means unique to England. Its presence was perhaps particularly marked, however, because of the politically enforced circumstances of the English Reformation, and the unease of many English intellectuals with the extremes of Protestant doctrine and its doctrinal arguments. At the same time, unease with Catholic authoritarianism was increased by the Counter-Reformation. For these reasons, these thinkers can be seen as sustaining currents of Renaissance theology, which had itself sought out a different kind of ecclesial reform. The rational quest for truth had been at the centre of this seeking, though it had not conceived reason in separation from faith, nor from grace. In continuity with the Fathers, and with Aquinas, this current problematized, against contemporary scholasticism and contemporary Protestantism, a duality of nature and grace. At its core, as for John Colet, lay a revived interest in Plato, whose corpus was by this time available, together with an appreciation of the Neoplatonic writings and associated but more enigmatic texts of the Chaldean Oracles and the Hermetic corpus. These

[2] J. H. Muirhead, *The Platonic Tradition in Anglo-Saxon Philosophy: Studies in the History of Idealism in England and America* [1931] (London: Routledge, 2018).

concerns, however, were not seen as 'Neo-pagan' in character, as they were regarded as continuing the integrating approaches of the Church Fathers.

But this integration was taken further in two respects. First, the Aristotelian separation of physics from metaphysics tended to be regarded with Neoplatonic suspicion. Cosmology was united with metaphysics, and it is notable that this is one source of the 'scientific revolution' which contrasts with later, if dialectically continuous, tendencies of a mechanical physics to 'physicalise' the metaphysical.[3] Second, the increased ethical concerns of humanism for reform and improvement encouraged a Platonic-Hermetic concern with 'natural magic' which was thought to improve people's lives, and even physical reality. This was undertaken in a prayerful spirit which was an extension of a theurgic approach to liturgy which had already entered Christianity from Neoplatonism, through Dionysius the Areopagite, who was a central point of reference for Marsilio Ficino and others.[4]

This current of thought, as we see in the case of the English thinkers, was imbued with scholastic categories, though it tended to be critical of the 'schools', by which it referred to late medieval and early modern manifestations of scholasticism. But to this sustained scholasticism was brought a distinctively modern awareness of the need to apply Aristotelian categories with caution, and in a heuristic manner, to the perplexing variety of things, and of the receding inexhaustibility of their observation, given the complexity, infinite divisibility and expandability of reality. The mutability of things, and of the human capacity to modify things, led to an increased awareness of the realm of the artificial and of the power of artifice – including an interest in the ways by which the natural and the artificial, and the physical and the mental, might interact. This interaction at times seemed to be 'magical' in character, as likewise, the human capacity for conjecture.

In the cases of Herbert, at the beginning of the English seventeenth century; of Greville, in its middle part; and of Conway, at its ending, it is no accident that these were titled nobility. For they reflect a lay, court and aristocratic unease with clerically generated squabbling which had encouraged unprecedentedly terrible civil and international wars. Their distinctive interest in truth and in reason was born of a concern with peace and

[3] Antoine Faivre, *Western Esotericism: A Concise History*, tr. Christine Rhone (Albany: State University of New York Press, 2010).

[4] See Brian P. Copenhaver, *Magic in Western Culture: From Antiquity to Enlightenment* (Cambridge: Cambridge University Press, 2015).

mediation. One would be mistaken, however, if one read their work as 'proto-enlightenment', unless one were to take into account the at times 'esoteric' character of the Enlightenment itself. These thinkers were concerned to think through truth in wholly religious terms, and to propose faith and grace as part of the integral concern of reason.

But it would also be a mistaken reading if one presented the Platonic-Hermetic-Scholastic current as if it were one united front. Rather, it is because this current was pervasive that it was fraught by many divisions: between Calvinists and Arminians, Puritans and Anglicans (but in either case often Hermetically and magically inclined), and between those who were more Aristotelian in their leanings, such as Nathaniel Culverwell of Emmanuel College, and those, such as Peter Sterry, also a Fellow of Emmanuel College, who were more Platonic in tendency. Cambridge was only one focus of this current, and there was no united front of 'Cambridge Platonism' (indeed, there were also 'Platonists' at Oxford),[5] though those who wish to deny a shared Platonic-Hermetic-Scholastic sensibility most markedly present in that University are also wide of the mark.[6] As we shall see in relation to our three writers, Herbert was opposed to Calvinist predestination; Greville, like his Parliamentarian army chaplain and possibly unacknowledged co-author Sterry, defended it; Culverwell criticized Greville's extreme version of Platonic recollection, which was fused with his Calvinism, but supported Herbert's subtle fusing of the mental and empirical contributions to knowledge. Anne Conway eventually broke with Henry More's – and implicitly Ralph Cudworth's – attempt to blend Cartesian mechanism and Gassendian atomism with vitalistic notions of the 'plastic' principle, which were partly derived from Herbert,[7] by embracing a more 'left-wing' alchemical and Kabbalistic programme of spiritual atomism, strongly influencing Leibniz, which cleaved to the esoteric, as found in earlier writers such as Robert Fludd and Thomas Vaughan. In such a way, she insisted that conformation, as the site of truth, requires a non-duality of bodies and spirits, and of God and the Creation, if they are to be capable of wielding an analogical connection. In this, her thinking was in keeping with the positions of

[5] See, e.g., Douglas Hedley and David Leech, 'Introduction', in Douglas Hedley and David Leech (eds.), *Revisioning Cambridge Platonism: Sources and Legacy* (Cham: Springer, 2019), 1–12.

[6] This is the position of Dmitri Levitin in *Ancient Wisdom in the Age of the New Science: Histories of Philosophy in England, c. 1640–1700* (Cambridge: Cambridge University Press, 2015). His selective criteria are too narrowly focussed.

[7] R. D. Bedford, *The Defence of Truth: Herbert of Cherbury and the Seventeenth Century* (Manchester: Manchester University Press, 1979), 105–10.

Herbert and Greville, lying, respectively, before and slightly outside 'Cambridge Platonism'.

7.2 Herbert's Theory of Conformation

The theory of conformation in the writings of Edward Herbert is not put forward as an epistemological theory, nor as a theory of representation. In these respects, one could hazard that it possesses features which anticipate postmodern critique, though it is necessarily rooted in a pre-modern and Renaissance sensibility.

In *De veritate*, Herbert is not arguing that the mind must 'conform' to things in their given evidence, and be merely constrained by it. Nor is he saying that the evidence which one receives through one's senses must be 'conformed' to the way in which one's mind works, or to a priori categories of understanding. Rather, by 'conformation' he is referring to a phenomenon of the Platonic *metaxu*, or of what William Desmond calls 'the between'. Truthful understanding is possible because there is a natural relation, analogy or harmony between things and mind, a kind of occult or sympathetic echo or affinity. One's understanding is an instance of the general analogy which pertains between one thing and another, of their inherent connectedness which cannot be understood in terms of mechanism, but rather of secret 'affinities', 'emanations', foreshadowings, and the construals of the 'signature' of one thing by another.[8]

The inclusion of knowing as conformation within a wider metaphysics of analogy is confirmed by Herbert's central and seemingly strange doctrine of the indefinite number of faculties.[9] Such faculties had otherwise been considered to be restricted in number, and were construed in terms of one's general mental powers to sense and to understand. In such terms, the five senses constituted five different faculties of sensing; similarly, the will, the power to reason, the power to judge, the imagination and the memory were often taken to be faculties or capacities to understand. The Platonic-Hermetic current of thought often criticised this 'scholasticism', as when Cudworth mocked the idea that the lute is played by the musical faculty, rather than by a musician. Similarly, he says, it is not the will that wills, nor the reason that thinks, but a man that does both. Here he implies a unity

[8] 'The goodness of a thing lies in its eternal character [*signatum*]': Herbert, *De veritate*, 191. One might substitute 'signature' for 'character' (*signatum*). On this aspect of Herbert, see Giorgio Agamben, *The Signature of All Things: On Method*, tr. Luca di l'Isanto and Kevin Attell (New York: Zone, 2009), 65.

[9] Herbert, *De veritate*, 75–114.

and integration of faculties, while specifically allowing that the soul is composed of varying capacities.

On the face of it, Herbert had already entertained the very opposite. In an almost 'postmodern' fashion, he favoured plurality and difference. There are not only five senses, he says, sounding somewhat anticipatory of Gilles Deleuze: there are as many senses as things sensed; as many ways to smell as there are perfumes, and as many hybridisations of the five senses as coincide with one's manifold synaesthesic experiences. Likewise, there is not a limited number of general truths: there are as many truths as there are things, and the number of things is infinite. The diversification of truths, according to Herbert, diversifies and transforms the knower, in such a way that every time a new knowledge arises, it is known by a newly emergent faculty, tailor-made for this task and no other. A postmodern delirium and fragmentation of the unified self appears to beckon.

In the face of such a diversification, many thinkers of the age were fascinated but aghast. John Locke responded that many different things can be known or done by a single power; one does not need to diversify the power itself.[10] This seems to make good sense, until one realises that Herbert does not mean by 'faculty' a pre-given, a priori mental capacity. As the Aristotelianising Culverwell discerned, he means, rather, an *arising facility*.[11] That is to say, the faculty to know a wasp is not fully present, is not fully shaped, until a wasp comes buzzing within one's purview, or perhaps until one has been stung by one.

This notion of an arising facility is an extension, as Herbert indicates, of the Aristotelian and scholastic theory of knowledge as occurring by transfer of form, or of *species*, from materialised form in the thing to a form that is spiritualised in the mind. One has the power or faculty to know a wasp because one's mind literally becomes to a degree wasp-like in its inner configuration. But Herbert developed this doctrine in two ways. First, he had recourse to a somewhat Platonic construal of the active and creative capacity of the mind: a new faculty arises whenever one sees an animal, an insect or a wasp, because one is to a degree rehearsing its creation, or its coming to be. Thomistic actualization of the form can indeed be seen as a subjective bringing-about of a thing within one's mental universe. Second, notions of *species* are, for Herbert's theory, diversified. It is not just that

[10] John Locke, *An Essay Concerning Human Understanding* (Oxford: Oxford University Press, 1979), II, xix, §§16–20, 242–4; Bedford, *Defence of Truth*, 78–80.

[11] Nathaniel Culverwell, *An Elegant and Learned Discourse of the Light of Nature* (Indianapolis, IN: Liberty Fund, 2001), 93–6, 160.

one becomes spiritually animal- or insect-like, but that one becomes specifically wasp-like, or even this wasp-like. For the Aristotelian and Thomistic legacy, knowledge was primarily of universals; now, for Herbert, knowledge is of intuited particulars. One cannot subsume the wasp, nor any one of the number of rare curative flowers Herbert mentions, such as elecampane and euphorbia,[12] under a general faculty for knowing things, nor even for knowing animated things. Rather, to know a wasp modifies the nature of one's knowing. Now one can know a wasp; one could not have known a wasp before. Now one's knowing is a waspish kind of knowing, as it becomes now earth-like, water-like, kingfisher-like or pike-like, and so forth.

This contagious diversification implies that knowledge is a work of occult fusion, an instance of the natural magic which Herbert's *De veritate* acknowledges to be at work in all things and in all places. Material evidence does not constrain thought; thought does not draw in and constrain this evidence into its own mould. And no moment of imaging 'representation' takes place in either direction. Rather, thought arises, as it were, as a silent electrical explosion of the meeting of the nonetheless incommensurate forces of matter and spirit, body and mind, in their imponderable fusion. In this fusion, an event occurs, from which something new arises. It is altogether new, but in continuity with everything, both material and spiritual, which has gone before, and is expressive of a secret affinity which was always latent or secretly promised. For if the wasp flies in such a way that it may be known, then its flying and existence always contained a kind of proto-understanding. The implications of Herbert's position are both vitalist and somewhat pan-psychic. One might also say that, for the mind to develop the faculty of knowing, the wasp shows a certain sustaining of corporeal definition within the mental realm. This is a point later insisted upon by Conway. Herbert's ontological vision, therefore, is non-dualist in character.

Knowledge, for Herbert, is an occurrence: a further weaving together of the density of the real with the luminosity of spirit, in the event of their fusion. It follows from this, as later for Greville, that there is little distinction between intelligence and truth. Intelligence is a further fullness of that 'dynamic' manifestatory power which is intrinsic to things as things. When intelligence is operating as it should, it simply *is* the truth. As I have argued in more detail elsewhere, there is no 'non-psychological'

[12] Herbert, *De veritate*, 227.

truth, unless it is in an ontological realm of Intellect lying above that of Soul, as for Neoplatonism.

Truth, for Herbert, is not a matter of evidence, of logic or of rational discourse. It is, rather, immediate and intuitive. This does not mean, however, that it is merely diverse or heterogeneous in a nominalist fashion. For Herbert does not say that there is only an arising faculty for each particular; he *also* says that there is an arising faculty for each universal reality, and that these are equally real and equally apparent. A faculty for wasps, and another one for their flight, and another one for their flight this early June morning, and yet another one for their settling on that branch of that tree, and another for their stinging me, and so on, but *equally* a new and arising category for wasps in general, insects in general, animals in general, flight in general, branches of trees in general, and so on. There is no more bias here to the specific than to the general, to 'nominalism' more than to 'realism'. Indeed, without the reality of the universal at every level, there could be no analogical harmony or operation of vital 'plastic principles' at work, for example, in the unifying and then dispersal of food through the process of digestion.[13]

It is, rather, that Herbert has added to an inherited realist outlook a new modern concern for the particular, and for continuous alteration without dispersal into monolithic flux. And whether one is speaking of universal patterns or of novel instances, the same reconstrual of truth as arising identity of thing with mind pertains: to know coincides with the capacity to know, because the latter is a *joint* product of that which comes from without, and that which arises from within. It is a work of emergent coming-together, enabled by the reality of mysterious and slumbering sympathies throughout all of existence: 'The relations of all things are limited by their analogy. Goodness of appearance is the emanation of its internal character which becomes explicit through its analogy with the internal faculties.'[14]

Herbert's approach to truth is of a piece with his account of the real and of intellect. He does not propose criteria for truth, nor a method or ontological apparatus for locating it. Truth is immediately apparent to the intuitions of rightly functioning mind. There is, he says, a truth of things – of their self-sustaining coherence – a truth of their emanations, a

[13] '... that plastic power which reduces different kinds of food to one form ... Thus the pike, the cat and the human being will each form their limbs in the same manner as does a gudgeon, and according to the knowledge proper to their species, direct the food to the proper points.' Ibid., 169.

[14] Ibid., 191.

truth of concepts and a truth of intellect. The latter is the completion of this series, and includes all the other truths. The intellect will arise variously as the indefinitely many truths, and as the elusive truth of their unity, when all these truth-events occur in an unimpeded fashion;[15] that is, when the thing can emanate properly, when nothing impedes one's vision, when one is in the right situation for observing and construing things, when one escapes the lures of shadows and distractions, including those which are generated by one's own fallen mind.

Herbert's emphasis upon intuition, designed to overcome argument and conflict in a manner that was not so unlike Descartes, whom Herbert read with critical interest,[16] does not mean that Herbert found no place for discursive reasoning. Indeed, *De veritate* includes a section entitled *zetetica*, which is, as it were, his own 'discourse upon method'.[17] Its purpose, however, significantly for the often curative and medicinal concerns of the Platonic-Hermetic-Scholastic current, overlapping with Baconianism, is primarily therapeutic. It was not, as for Wittgenstein, designed to purge the mind of metaphysical delusion, but rather to orientate it towards the true, naturally intuited metaphysical human stance. It is offered as a systematic guide to help one clear away the occlusions which impede the natural occurrence of truth. It is concerned with purging the means and the medium of understanding, not directly with things understood, nor with the human understanding in isolation.

Such things appear, for Herbert, 'automatically', as it were, in the register of a Platonic-Hermetic metaphysics, as continuously intuited by rightly orientated intelligence. The *zetetica* offers a complementary, scholastic and Aristotelian ontology in terms of categorial classifications: whether a thing is, what its essence is, what qualities and quantities it possesses, in which relations its stands, what its place and time may be, and so on. However, this inherited ontology is recast in a methodical, heuristic and experimental idiom which betokens modern conjectural, philosophical and natural scientific developments. The critique of 'the schools' which is implied in this recasting suggests a view that their categorial classifications are somewhat too fixed and certain, too general and, at the same time, insufficiently aware of the admixture in known reality of the metaphysical, physical and artificial.

15 Ibid., 83–89.
16 For Descartes' and Gassendi's responses to Herbert, see Bedford, *The Defence of Truth*, 46–60.
17 Herbert, *De veritate*, 232–88.

One can instance this with examples. First, for Herbert the Humanist, he notes that the schools failed to divide reality between the natural, the artificial and 'a combination of both'.[18] In a passage later cited by Giambattista Vico, he describes one's perfectly comprehensive reach into the works of artifice as like that of a shoemaker, but not the wearer of the shoes, who perfectly knows the shoe. As Vico later understands, one applies the same rule of Herbertian *facultas* to understand what is meant by this analogy.[19] It is not that the shoemaker perfectly pre-models the shoe in their mind, nor that the shoemaker grasps the effective result through observation, when the shoe has been made, but that the manifestation and knowledge of the shoe keep pace with one another in a to-and-fro of making something from an array of pre-given materials. At the end of the process of making and knowing, the fully formed shoe and the perfected knowledge of the shoe arise together. The shoe and the truth of the shoe coincide, are as one, because the shoe is an artefact: *verum-factum*, as Vico will later say: the coincidence of truth as a transcendental with the made as a transcendental.

Only the creator God has such a knowledge of nature, His creation. However, in participating in God's creative knowledge, one's 'facultative' knowledge is tantamount to a part-creation of that which one knows, into which one obtains a partial insight: a *conscientia*, though not a full *scientia*, as Vico described it, again developing Herbert.

Herbert's notion of the active and transformative role of human beings is of a piece with his emphasis upon the way in which ontological classification cannot be separated from the admixture of artifice and nature in experimentation, artefaction and technology. In this way, one could suggest that, for Herbert, metaphysics is a continuing work. In this, he develops new perspectives of dilation, mutability, in-definition and infinitisation. That such a synthesis wielded a long-term influence through the late seventeenth century 'neo-Renaissance', exemplified in Newton and Leibniz, and later, upon eighteenth-century Romantic thought, and beyond, despite the dominant notion of disenchanted mechanism, suggests that one cannot dismiss these currents as transitional or marginal.

[18] Ibid., 247.

[19] Giambattista Vico, *De antiquissima italorum sapientia: liber metaphysicus, Opere filosofiche* (Florence: Sansoni, 1971), VII and Seconda Risposta III, p. 154 (translated): 'man with every faculty makes the object proper to it . . . following Lord Herbert in his book *De Veritate* . . . for every sensation there unfolds and manifests in us a new faculty'. See John Milbank, *The Religious Dimension in the Thought of Giambattista Vico, 1668–1744, Part I: The Early Metaphysics* (Lewiston: Edwin Mellen Press, 1991), 62–5.

One can also observe this synthesis at work in Herbert's categorisation of humanity in fluid terms. Man is not, he says, a 'rational animal', as for the tradition; he is complex, does not stay the same, and is not uniquely rational.[20] A human being, it is averred, is somewhat mineral, somewhat vegetable, as when he sleeps, and somewhat animal. Other animals possess the reason that is appropriate to their self-preservation, but human beings appear to possess religion, or the 'inner sense' of the existence of divinities, and of the supreme God. In addition, in the case of human beings, reason is coterminous with one's *conatus*. But what is to be preserved is spirit, which longs for an eternal preservation, because its range is not confined by finite purpose, while the soul aporetically exceeds itself. This religious longing for the eternal is specific to human beings, and may be seen as the 'last difference' which defines the human being. Herbert describes human facultative knowledge as seeking out in every case a scholastic 'specific difference', revealing that his pluralism is not to be mistaken for nominalistic deconstruction. He considers that, since laughter is unique to human beings, this must belong to their essence, and is – *contra* 'the schools' – more than accidental, even in the sense of an accompanying accident.

Herbert's reappraisal of classification suggests an attentiveness to the metamorphosis of things and to the idea that what is fundamental to them may not be *constantly* present – as seems to be the case for animality or reason – but rather, sporadically so, in the same way as religious ritual observances and outbreaks of mirth. Herbert also here suggests that one's animality and one's reason are not manifest at all times. This implies an investigative and experiential approach to metaphysical docketing, one that is not demarcated from the work of the natural philosopher, or as we should now say, 'scientist'.

Herbert's primary and spiritualising 'Platonic-Hermetic' metaphysics, for which the more scholastic *zetetica* is a clarifying aid, puts forward a division between human 'internal' and 'external' senses, the latter referring to the primary location of that which one would today think of as concerning basic factual truths of a 'theoretical' kind.[21] In such cases, although a sympathetic resonance between thing and mind occurs, in order for truth to arise, nevertheless the truths of things retain an external resistance to internal absorption or subsumption. The warmth of fire reaches within one, yet one does not burn. The actuality of conflagration is observed from a safe distance. Similarly, and with a Stoic hint in Herbert's Platonism, human 'troubles' remain external to one, because,

[20] Herbert, *De veritate*, 255–8. [21] Ibid., 208–31.

of itself, the mind lies within the path of the Good, and pursues the good with delight – the delight of a hunter, as Cudworth later says.[22]

One's apprehension of things through the senses and faculties which retain certain phenomena at a distance is always enabled by 'the internal senses'. One knows that fire burns because one experiences inwardly its heat and light, and indeed its burning, if one advances too close, though in such a case, natural harmonies and proprieties are disturbed.

However, in the case of the internal senses, that which lies properly without one reaches or is drawn within, without alteration, save one of augmentation or intensification of its inherent properties.[23] Light fully passes into one. Light is a mediating phenomenon between the material and the spiritual, however, and what is apprehended by the internal senses is more spiritual in character. So beauty remains what it is when it is without one, when it is drawn within one, but acquires a more intensive form. The inner senses register the good in things and the right harmony and order of the whole. Indeed, there is a faculty orientated towards this whole, in keeping with Herbert's general scheme. This same faculty has the sense of the participation of things in God and their orientation towards God, which accounts for their conveyance of an attracting or drawing of beauty. Through the operation of this faculty, one is gradually 'conformed' to God. But the link of this vertical conformation with the myriad horizontal conformations is so closely wrought that, for Herbert, where the things of this world are analogically conformed to each other and to mind, they will be also analogically conformed to God.

Within this field of the religious-ethical, Herbert speaks of the 'common notions' shared by all of humanity as to one's duties towards God and neighbour.[24] Commentators often puzzle over why this is the case; if these notions are seen as a priori and innate, why does Herbert appeal to a shared cultural consensus which spans all times and places? But, for Herbert, there is nothing innate to one's mind whose form is finished.[25] Rather, common notions *result* from the interaction of one person with another, and one society with another. Common notions emerge from the *most general* modes of conformation, not just between persons and things, but between persons and persons, and between peoples and peoples. This does not gainsay Herbert's naïveté concerning cultural disparities and historical variations. But within his philosophical schema, this would seem to imply

[22] Ralph Cudworth, *A Treatise of Freewill*, in *A Treatise Concerning Eternal and Immutable Morality* (Cambridge: Cambridge University Press, 1996), 173.
[23] Herbert, *De veritate*, 146–207. [24] Ibid., 115–45. [25] Ibid., 87–9, 120.

the idea that inter-human and inter-cultural conforming is to be seen as a horizon, a work still to be completed.

Alongside this sense of a receding horizon towards which one reaches, one must consider Herbert's hierarchy of certainty. Least certain is the domain of discursive reason, which he holds responsible for the violent doctrinal and confessional conflicts of his time. The problem is not one of religion corrupting reason, but rather the reverse. Dialectical process can readily go awry; one can fool oneself about a chain of logical entailments, or fail to see that one's prejudices have intervened. As for David Hume, the trouble with any sequence of reasoning is that a later judgement must always judge an earlier one, all the way back to the very beginning. The discursive process is perforce poorly inaugurated, and its need of supplementary revisions is never secure, and always ceding place to subsequent reassessment. Truth finds no secure berth in this ever-moving caravan, unsure of where it comes from or to where it might be going.

Herbert's distrust of institutional religion did not point him back towards detached reason, as it might for a modern agnostic or atheist thinker, but rather, towards what he took to be natural intuition within a divinely governed universe. After the lowest uncertainties of discursive reasoning, under the influence of revived antique scepticism, were the deliverances of the external senses. But far more certain were those of the internal ones: one's sense of beauty, goodness and the divine. In the case of the external senses, it is a matter of the truths in things seeking to awaken the answering truth of arising faculties. But in the case of the internal senses, it may be that case that one's dormant faculties look for things that will realise their longings, for example, perfect human love and community. It is in the sphere of religion that faculty takes the initial lead over object: God is the object of one's uttermost search and desire, but remains unknown and elusive. In either direction – of things seeking faculties or faculties seeking things – Herbert's metaphysics of sympathy and affinity assumes that no search can be in vain. One's searching for God becomes a certain proof not just of divine existence but of the beatific vision, the sustained happiness which every mind longs for, and even of divine grace, which he describes as the 'specially providential' reaching down of God towards personal contact with every spiritual being.

By reason of this hierarchy, Herbert does not first develop his theory of truth as conformation and then apply it subsequently to aesthetic, ethical and religious truths. It is, rather, the other way around: one believes in truth as conformation because one has a facultative appreciation of the conformity of each thing with everything else, all of these being gradually conformed to the mind of God. For this reason, the *primary* truths are religious, aesthetic, ethical and political, while theoretical and relatively empirical truths are more uncertain. The 'common notions' of the former must guide and assist one's uncertainties in the latter. Herbert was far from yielding to the temptation to take cultural refuge in the certainty of the physical and positive, unlike some contemporaries, such as Thomas Hobbes.[26]

By the same token, the highest truth coincides with the Good, and the lure of the Good takes precedence over the manifest presence of the True, and so the promptings of an emergent faculty over the seekings of things for mental apprehension. A spiritualizing Platonic-Hermeticism is here paramount. If Herbert's later reputation as the 'father of deism' is absurd, it is the case that he emphasized Christian features which he thought, perhaps implausibly, could be recognised in other faiths, and considered religious institutions and ceremonies as of secondary importance. Historical revelation, though certainly confessed, seems to have been little more than a confirmation of a kind of natural religion, whose shape remains overwhelmingly Christian in character.[27] Herbert, conspicuously or not, says nothing of Christology or the Trinity. And yet his sense of being as inherently manifest as truth, and of both as drawn forward by the further horizon of the good, could be interpreted as suggestive of Trinitarian intimations, of both a Platonic and a Christian kind.

Unlike later variants of Deism, his thought remains marked by a mystical sensibility which at times recalls Nicholas Cusa or anticipates Descartes and Pascal. Like Descartes, he regards human free will as being in the image of divine infinity, because of its limitless scope, and he holds that every divine attribute is echoed by a responsive human faculty, while the divine unity is echoed by one's faculty for their unification, which is the stamp of a seal of wax in one, coinciding with our unified personality.[28] In one's freedom and the unlimited scope of one's understanding, one's soul seems to exceed itself in such a way that the soul may expand or contract, while the indefinite number of one's faculties is mysteriously unified by one's consistency of self-preservation.[29] These mysteries of self-exceeding and unifying of the boundless are true of God. In a manner that again recalls Cusanus, Herbert invokes the coincidence of opposites, whereby the boundless and unified infinite in God is the supreme unity:

[26] Ibid., 332–4. [27] Ibid., 289–313. [28] Ibid., 146–207, 330. [29] Ibid., 146–207, 330.

'He transcends transcendence, and fills, informs and encompasses the infinite itself in the vastness of his unity.'[30]

This paradoxical combination of the self-contained as the self-exceeding, or, as this quotation suggests, of the uncontained as exceeding this containment towards form, can allow a potentially Trinitarian development. Herbert construes the divine paradox as reflected in a paradoxical ontology of creation:

> [I]n all that is finite we can find some trace of the infinite. Thus everything seems capable of being divided into an infinity of parts, but since it must in the end be resolved into a unity (the ultimate characteristic of the infinite), infinity and unity appear to meet.

7.3 Greville's Platonic Monism

If the mark of Edward Herbert's approach to truth was pluralism, that of Robert, Lord Greville's approach to truth, in *The Nature of Truth* (1640), is monism. Herbert, like his brother, was a royalist (though his military and courtly career with the Stuarts collapsed, and he was eventually forced to surrender Powys Castle to the Roundheads) and an upholder of free will against Calvinism.[31] Greville was a Parliamentarian general, shot dead by a sniper while besieging Lichfield cathedral – perhaps the first victim of sniper fire in history. He defended predestination, like Sterry and Culverwell but unlike Cudworth and More, and opposed the Arminian view that one could resist or lapse from grace by the exercise of free will. However, despite this, his Neoplatonism is prominent, more so than for Herbert, and includes citations of Marsilio Ficino, on whom his thinking was heavily dependent. His English style is ornately Baroque – perhaps under Sterry's influence – in contrast to the plain if knotted Latin of his fellow peer and political enemy.

The resemblances between Greville and Herbert, however, are twofold: first, their shared Hermetic emphasis upon affinities and correspondences in nature. In Greville's case, this emphasis is connected with his notion of the bias of all things not towards a unity of analogical conforming, but towards fusion:

> And this is very plain in the stillicids of water, which, if there be water enough to follow, will draw themselves into a small thread, because they

[30] Ibid., 330.

[31] Robert E. L. Strider II, *Robert Greville, Lord Brooke: Aristocrat, Puritan, Philosopher, Martyr* (Cambridge, MA: Harvard University Press, 1958).

> will not sever: and when they must disunite, then they cast themselves into round drops, as the figure most resembling unity. Whence is that sympathy in nature between the Earth and the Adamant, but from hence, that they being of one nature, desire to improve their unity by mutuall embraces.[32]

The second resemblance is an insistence that truth and intelligence are one and the same. Following Ficino and Plotinus, for Greville truth is the outgoing of the Absolute One as intelligence. One's mind cleaves to its participation in intellect, so that it remains in truth and part of truth. For truth is the conscious illumination of being, existence in its manifestatory radiance. Greville goes further than Herbert, in a way that is consistent with his Calvinism. For Herbert, intellect could freely err, ensuring a negative distance between truth and understanding. However, for Greville this is scarcely the case. For his outlook, the doctrine of evil as privation reaches such a pitch that evil, as nothing, is tantamount to illusion. One can be in truth and falsity, good and evil, at the same time, because evil as non-being is compatible with being, with which it is not in competition.[33] The human intellect does not cease its estate as being in the truth. This mode of intensified Platonism conforms to the Reformed *simul Justus et Peccator* and to the view that nothing one freely does, or appears to do, really conflicts with the irresistible will of God. In Calvinist terms, the divine will is the only real cause, which everywhere prevails. In 'Platonic' but in some ways Parmenidean terms, there is a single unity everywhere, and nothing else is entirely real. Greville refers to the participation of creatures in the divine nature, but it is so exaggerated a participation that nothing that participates really remains. There is only the participated-in, only God or Unity. One must suppose that Greville still thought that some souls had been consigned to eternal perdition, but his Platonising drift would seem more compatible with a Calvinist mode of universalism: If nothing falls ontologically outside the One, how can God have done other than predetermine all realities to eternal bliss, regardless of their willing?

Such a monistic disposition leads Greville to conflate intelligence with truth, and also the soul with both intelligence and truth, and in turn, with habits and actions.[34] Calvinism is again combined with Platonism: in the same way that all one's free actions are pre-given by God, the *entirety* of any action is merely remembered or recollected from the eternal. The only

[32] Robert Greville, *The Nature of Truth* [1640], facsimile reprint (London: Gregg International, 1969), 39.

[33] Greville, *Nature of Truth*, 89–107.

[34] Ibid., 1–59.

truth appears to be unity, and one is never outside it. In contrast to Herbert, analogy is overtaken by identity. To be in the truth is to return to the One.

This monistic doctrine is compounded by Greville's articulation of a series of aporias, somewhat anticipatory of those articulated by Graham Priest, writing in the wake of Nagarjuna.[35] Nothing is within its own bounds, including the soul. This is because its boundaries undo the unity which is all in which it consists. Nothing is 'in a place', because there is no constant unified place residing outside the flow and flux of things, which of themselves lack unity. Time is illusory, because it consists in present moments, which are not present at all.[36] For Greville all opposites coincide, including causes and effects. Indeed, we have already seen how he resolves the implication of a coincidence of good and evil.

It is interesting to recall that such metaphysical monism is issued in response to war and the crisis of the seventeenth century. In contrast to the response to generalised aporia, which can be construed as the affirmation of the reality of the real, outside logic and the Principle of Non-Contradiction, in Greville we find something more akin to non-Western responses to the puzzles of gluons, motion, place, time and totality as with the mid-battle song of the Bhagavad Gita.

The one reality of the One, for Greville, is nonetheless a plenitude and not a void. The One to which he apparently resolves all things in their ultimate reality is a Trinitarian reality, which contains truth and unity, abiding eternally. For Greville the Father is 'the fountain commencing', the Son is 'the channel entertaining', and the Spirit is 'the waters' impulse'. Unuttered truth is the Father, the Intellect is the Son, and the Soul is the Spirit.[37] In this Trinitarian fashion, Greville seems to restore basic differences, and difference as such, which he has been at pains to resolve. Intellect stands unitedly apart from that truth of being, which it discloses, and the psychic life, which moves this disclosure and moves beyond it to allow motion in general, also remains distinct. If there is such a distinction in God, it would seem that created minds and created living or moving things are somewhat real in their own right, as participating entities.

[35] J. L. Garfield and Graham Priest, 'Nāgārjuna and the Limits of Thought', *Philosophy East and West*, 53 (2003), 1–21.

[36] Greville, *Nature of Truth*, 89–114. For Culverwell's disparagement of these passages, *An Elegant and Learned Discourse*, 85–96, 145–6. By 'Platonism', which he refuses, Culverwell seems to refer to the extreme doctrines which Brooke espoused. One cannot necessarily read this refusal as opposed to a more tempered Platonic current.

[37] Greville, *Nature of Truth*, 6, 25.

A tension can be observed between Greville's Calvinistic Platonism and his Trinitarian Platonism. However, he sees the fountain, channel or flow structure as evidenced in created ontology. It is this structure which allows there to be transcendental truth, in addition to transcendental unity, within finite reality.

If Herbert's pluralism was qualified by a measure of monism, and his analogical mediation of being and truth pointed anonymously towards a Trinitarian metaphysics, the same is confessedly true for Greville, but from a reverse direction. His monism is pluralistically qualified by Trinitarian difference. In both cases, it would seem to be triadically structured processes of conformation which allow an ontological reading of truth, and an ontology for which truth is not subordinate to being.

7.4 Conway's Trinitarian Monism

Such a theological framework for a Platonic-Hermetic-Scholastic theory of truth is provided by Anne, Lady Conway, who also gives a non-dualist rationale for the continuous association of mind and spirit within a participatory finitude. Her treatise *The Principles of the Most Ancient and Modern Philosophy* was written around 1690, at a time when there was a certain 'neo-Renaissance' revival, in the face of a perceived failure to explain aspects of natural and human reality in material or mechanistic terms.[38] This perception was in part the work of the Cambridge Platonists, and Conway was indebted to Henry More and his mediation and critique of Descartes. However, in the face of her chronic cranial and nervous complaints, she sought the advice of Francis van Helmont, an alchemical and Christian Kabbalist thinker, who stayed with her for long periods at her Warwickshire seat and steered her thoughts in a radical direction, before she joined the sect of the Quakers, who offered her spiritual comfort. Her treatise was written up in Latin by Van Helmont, from her fragmentary notes, and has been translated into English in recent times. Its English preface is attributed at the head to Henry More, but is signed by Van Helmont, as if to indicate the double genesis of her thinking.

For Conway, there can only be truth and goodness in created things if nothing whatsoever is dead matter. This is because deadness, hardness and fixity are the results of finitude, and do not in these characteristics

[38] Anne Conway, *The Principles of the Most Ancient and Modern Philosophy* (Cambridge: Cambridge University Press, 1996).

exemplify anything of God. If things are created, therefore, they must be constituted not by the divine existence but by the divine life, the divine mind and the divine realisation of the ends of goodness.[39] Pure matter is a fiction, as it were, a kind of blasphemy. Since all things derive from the divine *logos* and spirit, all things in some sort live and think.

This theological contention is supported by various arguments. One never encounters empty matter, space or time; each thing that exists must be assumed to be divisible, or expandable to infinity, in the same way that time, though absolutely created, reaches infinitely backwards and has only a metaphysical, and no temporal beginning. With Henry More, Conway argues that spirits enjoy a certain extension and embodiment, because they are limited, while inversely, bodies, like spirits, are to a degree penetrable. But *contra* More, she denies that spirits can be distinguished from bodies by an absolute simplicity and indivisibility: this seems to be an unwarranted claim, because spirits are, in the same manner as bodies, set off from one another, so why should they not likewise be divisible?[40] On the other hand, Conway asserts that there is a sense in which any cohering body, precisely as such a body, is, like any spirit, indivisible and irreplaceable. No individual *qua* individual can turn into any other individual, and no species *qua* species can turn into any other. A wasp as wasp cannot become an elephant, nor this wasp metamorphose into this elephant.[41]

Because all things that exist as created are constituted by the divine being, thought and life, and so are as themselves also living and thinking, in some sense and in certain degrees, everything that exists is true and good. And because any being in order to exist also expresses itself, and relates to other things, everything that exists is in some sense a spirit, though material things are lesser spirits, as darker and more hardened. Higher spirits may be ethereal, but they possess subtle bodies; embodiment and limitation are as one, for Conway. Materialised things, though they are lesser, are not of themselves evil; any degree of reality which falls short of the infinite, which is unbounded, perforce exhibits some limitation, in order to be at all. This degree of limitation belongs to its truth, as does it sprightliness, while at the same time testifying to its participation in God, insofar as it does not encompass the whole of truth.

Conway's monism opens the way to a perpetual communication between matter and spirit, body and soul; they are differing degrees of the same medium. The role of motion is here especially significant: motion is the beginning of mind, and mind is a kind of faster perfected motion, as

[39] Ibid., 28–55. [40] Ibid., 56–62. [41] Ibid., 28–40.

for Plotinus and later for Bergson.[42] Motion is not here seen in mechanical terms; as for Aristotle, Ravaisson and Bergson, motion is an indivisible action and communication. It is not confined by local chronotopic coordinates. Like existence, life and thought, motion is directly ascribed to God, though it is mysteriously instigated by finite mediators. One might describe this view as a kind of semi-occasionalism. Indeed, for the contemporary philosopher Timothy Morton, it is possible to construe motion as an occult connection between things.

Non-duality is for Conway witnessed in several ways. The clearest water, it turns out, contains tiny stones; apparently solid crystals may be liquefied; the hardest crystal substance is spiritually transparent to light; to be cruel is to undergo a hardening of the heart, perversely to descend to a stony level.[43] One is reminded of the way in which, for Herbert, a void in nature may give rise to a sense of tedium and lack, whilst tempestuous anger is a sign of one's kinship at certain moments with storms and tempests.[44] For these thinkers, metaphor is disclosive because it has literal freight; indeed, it is this literal import which facilitates its disclosure of a connected reality.

This monistic outlook is connected with a doctrine of sympathy which is in turn linked with a profound doctrine of mutability. Although, as we have seen, an individual or a species cannot be substituted for another, nonetheless, things are capable in themselves of dramatic transformation. Conway interprets the dietary laws and provisions for animals in Leviticus as implying that divine justice and governance extend to all things within nature, and that beasts may err.[45] Following Origen, for Conway, it is through the deeds of creatures that they may be reborn in other animal forms. This is not so much a theory of metempsychosis as of metamorphosis. This is because no separation of body and soul is conceived. She suggests that one species could evolve into another during the course of time.[46]

In the light of her framework of mutability, there are only three absolute species for Conway, and these are God, Christ and creatures. This is the metaphysical truth of a system for which truth has an ineliminable ontological place, as the mental expression and active mind ingredient of every creature, since all creatures spring from the mind of God. The creation as a whole is one species and substance, in such a way that echoes Spinoza, with whom, following the lead of More, her thinking was explicitly

[42] Ibid., 56–70. [43] Ibid., 411, 56–62. [44] Herbert, *De veritate*, 146–207.
[45] Conway, *The Principles*, 35. [46] Ibid., 28–40.

engaged. Individual creatures within Creation are not regarded as substances, or combined together as species, but rather are seen as *modes* of the one substance, deploying Spinozistic terminology.[47] However, by this, Conway does not construe the modes as subordinate to the single substance of the Creation, because she does not see this substance, after Spinoza, as itself God. It has no hypostasised existence 'above' the modes which it contains, in such a way that would swallow them up, from its own perspective. Actively shaping substance, such as a single plastic principle, or a world soul, moreover, does not dissolve back into its modes, as Spinoza seems at times ambivalently to allow. Rather, under divine transcendence, substance and modes are kept in reciprocal play.

Modes are regarded by Conway as akin to limited combinations of substance and fluid process, reflecting the totality of substance, each mode being inherently connected with every other. She refers to them as monads and, like Leibniz, refers to their infinite divisibility.[48] Unlike Leibnizian monads, however, Conway's modes are not 'windowless'; they perceive and interact with one another. Conway's 'semi-occasionalism' is not suggestive of a pre-established harmony.

It would seem clear that Conway's substance/modes structure of finitude constitutes a Trinitarian ontology. In the first chapter of her treatise, she offers an account of the Trinity which appears at first to be heterodox and Sabellian: she denies that the second and third persons of the Trinity are really persons or substantive hypostases, and argues that they are modes of the One God, as His thinking *logos* and spiritual will.[49] She proffers this in part for inter-religious reasons: understood in such a way, it will be possible for Jews and Mohammedans to accept the Trinity, and to see that they already believe in it.

Conway does not, however, make a wholesale Sabellian move of saying that the modes come 'later', as economically manifest from God. Rather, they are seen as eternally inherent, not unlike the views of some Church Fathers, who at times hesitated as to what the three 'things' in God comprised. Conway's construal of the Trinity is somewhat undernourished, and she gives no account of substantive relations. However, her casting of the Creation within a structure of substance and modes places her Trinitarian conceptions in a different light. If the myriad modes in which creatures consist are not subordinate to Creation, because it is not God, or a fatally determining subordinate deity, one can infer that, for

[47] Ibid., 28–40. [48] Ibid., 20. [49] Ibid., 9–11.

Conway, the modes that constitute the Trinity are in turn not subordinate to the divine essence.

According to her Christian metaphysical picture, the world, like the Triune God, is dynamically constituted by its fluid and relational connectedness. Modes possess parity with substance, since their elusively linked totality would not be there without them. Because Creation reflects the structure of the immanent Trinity, it is constituted by an expressive thinking of everything by everything else, and a tending of things towards other things, and all things toward all things. The only unity of the Creation is its shared imperfect thinking of God, and its shared imperfect striving towards Him, which, in a Fallen world, takes the form of redemptive and purgative suffering, of the kind Conway herself experienced.

There is for Conway a third species, which we have so far only half-mentioned. This third species is Christ, the truth itself incarnate.[50] Not only does Conway offer a Trinitarian metaphysics of being, truth and goodness; she offers a metaphysics which includes a Christological dimension, belonging integrally to nature as well as to grace.

She does not fully elucidate how this Christological metaphysics works. It is indicated that there must be a mediator between any two realities, for them to be in contact with one another. If creatures are able to express the truth of God, and to reach him in some measure, there must be a mediating reality between God and Creation. This is not something which stands ontologically between them, for this would be impossible, but rather, something both divine or in contact with the divine, and something fully created.

In Christian terms, Conway affirms Christ as pre-existent and incarnate, and, as such, fully divine. In Jewish esoteric terms, however, consistent with the views of some of the Greek Church Fathers, such as Origen and Gregory of Nyssa, she invokes the figure of Adam Kadmon, the primal man who was perfectly near to the divinity, without being divine. She identifies Adam Kadmon with an eternal humanity, besides the divinity of Christ, which is arguably affirmed by St Paul, Origen and later Greek fathers. It can logically be argued that if Christ's humanity is eternally post-existent in God, it must have been pre-existent, since God does not undergo change.

For Conway, as for the Lurianic Kabbalists, as well as for Origen, the Creation was formed not just within the *Logos*, but within and through the primal Divine Man, whose function is in this way akin to that of *Sophia* in

[50] Ibid., 23–40.

Wisdom literature. It is as if he is Divinity in its pure immanence. It follows that for Conway, the Trinity is, in its outward but divine expression, God the Father, the eternal Messiah, and the Messiah as he is spiritually present in creatures.[51]

In the same way that Conway's ontology of substance and modes allows a non-dualistic mediation between being and truth in the Creation, as united, and being and truth as plural, so her Trinitarian account of Adam Kadmon or Christ's eternal humanity permits a certain unification in difference of the truth of God, and the truths of Creation. It appears that her philosophy lays emphasis upon a redemptive ascent to deified truth and goodness, in and through their becoming, as it were, more ethereal. At the same time, however, she is not denying the inherent truth and goodness of every degree of reality, however solidified it may be, unless things have become distorted, as by Adam's Fall. This remains for her a contingent matter, connected with the effects of human narcissism, as when spirit falls into the dark material glass of reflection, seeing only itself within, and not the echo of the divine.[52] In this way, the divine sparks, associated with Jewish esoteric tradition, become lost in the 'shattering of the vessels', containing the divine glory, and a Christian Kabbalistic redemption which consists in their recovery, recombining and restoration.[53] Nevertheless, God reaches expressively down into the finite, and there is, for Conway, one can infer, an appropriate, created and redeemed degree of spiritual embodiment which is proper to every creature. Creatures are capable of both good and evil, but insofar as they are united with the primal man, Christ's eternal humanity, they can only move from good to further good; while God in Himself, as Father, *Logos* and spiritual will, is the infinitely realized good,[54] who has no need to seek further attainment. Insofar as they are united to the 'Messiah', creatures are fully good and true, though they remain in a state of what Gregory of Nyssa described as *epektasis*, being able to go ever further in the Good, from glory to glory.

Does this mean that their embodied, materialized truth and goodness are inferior to that of God? How can this be the case, if the eternal humanity, and Creation, are God's external but eternal Trinitarian expression? It would seem that, as for John Scotus Eriugena, for Conway, a theological *aporia* arises. The Creation is not God, who is wholly good, but is the endless advance in goodness. On the other hand, this advance is wholly good, and wholly God, since the advance is from God. This *aporia*

[51] Ibid., 11. [52] Ibid., 38. [53] Ibid., 10, 37–46. [54] Ibid., 24.

is 'resolved' both Kabbalistically and Christologically: the core of Creation is God, where the primal man is perfectly united with the divine *Logos* which is at one with the Father.

It is, one can infer, in this way that Christ is the third, mediating species or substance between God and the Creation. He is the point at which Creation as not God, and yet as God ('created God', as for Eriugena), coincide. For Conway, the Christological mystery is the mystery that, since all is from God, there is a sense in which the finite is not inferior to the infinite, and the body is not inferior to spirit. This is in keeping with the way in which for her esoteric doctrine, no spirit is free of some degree of embodiment. For this reason, then, one can deduce that, for Conway, partial goods are not partially but fully good, equally precious in their fragility. In a similar fashion, partial truths are entirely true, irreplaceable in their very confinement.

The analogical quest for the divine, which Conway, like Herbert and Greville, delineates, is at one with the Christological quest for the perfect unity of the divine and the created. If analogy entails the paradoxical but tensional coincidence of identity and difference, beyond the Principle of Non-Contradiction, it must be the quest for the most extreme realisation of this coincidence, and so a Christological as well as a theological quest, as for Nicholas of Cusa.[55] Only God is certain and true, and yet one knows him only by faith, which is uncertain.

For this reason, Aquinas declared, theology becomes a certainly true science, when the absolute certainty of God appears before one as incarnate in time.[56] The event of the Incarnation ensures that faith is, from its certain outset, also a matter of Johannine and Pauline *gnosis*, a complete and most rational exercise, because it is a theosophical insight into the Trinitarian heart of God. In this way, Christology offers a path to the absolute truth, but only on the condition that every trivial and confined thing participates in the truth, and in one sense, is the monadic entirety of truth. In this coincidence of confinement and entirety, Conway's Christological metaphysics is kenotic in character. Here, the Eucharistic liturgy, which re-presents the event of Christ as the advent of truth, is the theurgic performance and realisation of this double vision: the bringing about and recognition of the divine truth of all things.

[55] Nicholas of Cusa, *On Learned Ignorance*, in *Selected Spiritual Writings*, tr. H. Lawrence Bond (New York: Paulist Press, 1997), Book III, 169–206.

[56] John Milbank and Catherine Pickstock, *Truth in Aquinas* (London: Routledge, 2001), 65.

We conclude that truth may be seen as a conforming to eternal reality, because reality is truth, and truth is reality, considered from one vital aspect. This is not to offer a theory about truth, nor to put forward a theory of truth, by showing that the other 'theories of truth' cannot speak of truth, but must substitute another property, whose own 'truth', outside the light of truth, cannot be ascertained.

Such conforming is not a theoretical but an existential matter. Truth is eternal reality, which includes eternity's gift of the finite and the unity of the two. To be in truth is a matter of worship, or of being in the estate of prayer. This is how Plato understood the philosophic life, at *Phaedrus* 279bc, with Socrates' rural invocation to Pan, outside the gates of the city: What are we to ask for from the truth but a state of being that is a conformity or alignment, in harmony between the 'outward things', which one may possess, and the 'spirit within me'?[57] For human beings on earth and in time, this alignment is the truth, a sufficient lightness of things 'borne', in such a way that they may harmonise, rather than conflict with one's subjectivity. Truth arises and abides as this liturgical 'contentment', which pertains between these two equal aspects of nature. Truth is not for the individual on their own, but is inherently shared, insofar as the harmony between thing and mind must be at one with the mediation through things of different human spirits. Phaedrus asks that the prayer of Socrates to Pan be made a prayer for him also, 'since friends have all things in common'. Truth, as well as all things, everything, must be held in common, but this holding in common is all of the truth, its entirety.

7.5 Conclusion

The cases of Herbert, Greville and Conway illustrate how, first, the main story in the seventeenth century continued to be the development of philosophy and theology as such, not just of 'natural philosophy', never mind 'science'.

Second, however, they illustrate how a sustained Renaissance current of thought, opposed alike to materialism and to a disenchanted transcendence, remained as hospitable to recognizably novel 'scientific' features as these other, more dominant currents. These features were notably an emphasis on experiment, on the possibilities of natural metamorphosis and on the unity of the physical realm, including, tentatively, the inclusion of the human within that realm which was not just a later

[57] Plato, *Phaedrus* 279b7-c1–5.

consideration, postdating physical concerns, as one observes with the interests of Thomas Hobbes.

We see, third, how these thinkers challenge us to ask, today, whether their eclectically Platonic approaches (which had many later successors)[58] did not do *more* justice to the new 'scientific' imperatives than did the approaches of disenchanted transcendence. Herbert contrived to show how all mental experience is 'experimental' as it undergoes perpetual and infinitesimal alteration in the course of sensory practice. Somewhat in anticipation of Condillac, he shows how not only our knowledge but our ways of knowing – our 'faculties' – are derived from without and yet that our encounter with things without is a continuous 'technological' shaping of them from within, as if one were shaping a shared *habit* with one's immediate ecosphere or 'habitat'. And yet this modern and 'scientific', ultra-empirical approach is continuous with a scholastic and Hermetic sense of the integrity of form and its transfer between material and psychic registers.

The notion of truth as 'conformation' reworks the traditional Neoplatonic and Augustinian view that truth and intelligence are the self-same thing, as otherwise neither retains any meaning. This view was reinforced in his own metaphysical idiom by Greville. One could say that the modern and 'scientific' search for a cognitive unity of all reality was supplied, without any material reduction and yet without leaving an embarrassing dualist residue, as for Descartes.

A new desire for unity of understanding *and* explanation is here achieved within the scope of a traditional desire for monism and the conforming of everything to transcendent Unity. Such a vision was articulated, in theologically metaphysical terms, by Anne Conway. In her case, but also to some degree with the two other thinkers, we see a concern for the priority of the *modal* (as with Conway's Trinitarian ontology) as mediating between universal essence and individual substance. This allows a sense of the dynamic and the transformative to be linked to a horizon of emanation and metaphysical degrees of descending 'unfolding'. Neither essence nor isolate thing comes 'first'. Rather, everything is constituted by 'ways' of manifestation, of developing truth which in the eternal Trinity is 'developed'. Beyond Spinoza, as we have seen, Conway no longer subordinated the modal to the substantive. A relational development had the final divine word of 'truth'. The pragmatically and poetically effective and

[58] See, again, John Milbank's chapter in this volume.

the experimentally habituating were conceived to be eternally achieved as 'truth', in such a way that eternal truth and intelligence are shared in by us through the effective and the experimental. Thereby, the 'new scientific' project was seen not as alien to an inherited metaphysics of participation but as being even more coherent in its traditional terms.

CHAPTER 8

Understanding Our Knowing

The Culture of Representation

Rowan Williams

8.1 Making Mistakes and Sustaining Truthfulness

To start with a very basic question: What is it to make a mistake, and how do we identify it? A rather hoary instance may help bring this into focus. A clock that has stopped is precisely correct twice per day; a clock that is losing two minutes per day over a week or so is never precisely correct during that period. Which clock is more useful? A simple algorithm that assessed the usefulness of a clock by the amount of time during which it was exactly correct would presumably deliver the verdict that the stopped clock was preferable. Why would this be an error? Largely because it would be treating the way in which the clock represented a true state of affairs as a matter of what could be called 'granular' correspondence; successful representation would be understood as whatever provided the maximal rate of precision in communicating the truth about states of affairs.

If we say, as any sensible person would, that a slow clock is more use than a stopped one, we are not abandoning the idea of a truth to which we and our instruments of calibration are accountable. And clearly a clock that was losing large and irregular amounts of time each day would not be much if any more useful than one that had stopped. But a slow clock in most circumstances offers a successful representation of a truth we need to know, to the extent that it secures enough of a shared ground for action with others to make it a credible means of coping with a given environment. It is a plausible element in a 'culture of representation', a set of shared practices and shared 'readings' of the world which creates a shared system of projection, within which we can speak intelligibly and act coherently. A mistake in this context is not so much a 'granular' failure of connection between stimulus and recording device but something which impedes that mutual intelligibility and coherent or convergent action. A mechanical 'truth-teller' like a clock, a source of dependable information, is what it is because of a pre-existing convention that the passage of time is measurable in certain ways which can be rendered visually and relatively easily learned. The mechanical process of the recording device is calibrated to reflect the process of some aspect of the world, which means that the relations between successive states of the recording mechanism are significant as well as the relations between any one state and the stimulus it registers, which in turn is why slow clocks are generally more use than stopped ones. As has sometimes been said, clocks do not know what time it is; they are systems into which certain regular markers have been introduced to correspond to the passage of time. Telling the time and building time-telling into human practice and planning are *cultural* affairs: they are to do with how we make sense of ourselves in one another's company, in both speech and action, over time. As such, they presuppose a process of learning – both learning the conventions by which this or that particular practice operates and learning in a more local way what refinements and adjustments are needed to sustain the practice in diverse circumstances, to read it with appropriate critical intelligence (so that we have ways of establishing that a clock is regularly slow). In this context, a mistake, a moment when the culture is challenged or disrupted, is an occasion for refining the practice to make it a more credible means of 'coping'. In small and almost imperceptible ways, this is what is going on in a lot of ordinary human conversation: not exactly the recognition and correction of mistakes, but a cumulative practice of adjustment, exploration of alternatives, testing of new vehicles of communication and so on.

The familiar – if now rather stale – debate about 'coherence' and 'correspondence' accounts of truth has often missed the point that the criteria for adequate (truthful) and functional representation of the environment are bound to include elements of both theories. No amount of coherence can long survive a consistent failure to respond realistically to a set of environmental stimuli and challenges over which we have no control and whose prediction is not an exact affair; no strict appeal to correspondence can survive the lack of a communal recognition of intelligibility and utility (the stopped clock again). What we recognise as truthful knowledge is in practice a capacity for the kind of *alignment* with our environment that both adjusts effectively to its demands and allows for a continued testing of its adjustments through exchange and shared projection beyond the immediate needs of the situation – in speculative or imaginative discourse that makes no claims to *be* knowledge but makes improved knowledge possible. To *know* a state of affairs in this context, then, is not just to have in the mind the correct representation of an environment in general; it is to be involved in a set of shared practices in which continued learning is possible. Mistakes, misunderstandings, ordinary 'lack of fit' in conversation and simple conversational energy all contribute to such learning. But the implication of this is that what we recognise as knowledge is significantly bound up with the taking of time. There may be cultural conventions that will give us instant access to what purports to be the representation of a true state of affairs (looking at the clock face, for example), but this accounts for a small segment of those practices by which we acquire knowledge in the more robust sense of being able consistently and corporately to manage our relation with a material and linguistic environment. While the activity of our brains undoubtedly receives and registers the stimuli that generate awareness of states of affairs, the brain's characteristic activity is what I have been calling 'projection', in which learned habits of connection and contextualisation are developed and tested in a variety of ways. If we say that their 'sustainability' in a particular shared culture is one aspect of such testing, this is not at all to reduce the claim to knowledge or truthfulness to some sort of consensual pressure, but to understand that a culture of both secure and corrigible knowledge involves the development of mutually recognisable discourse, means of identification, criteria of legitimate argument and so on. Without these, we should be left with a dangerously narrow norm of checkable, 'granular' representation that would have little to do with actual human culture and agency.

8.2 Truth-Telling as Successful Alignment

Scientific culture is a notably successful context for representation and 'alignment'. Its history is one of ever more imaginative and rigorous testing of shared models and vocabulary, and it is also – to a degree that some popular apologists would be reluctant to acknowledge – habituated to heuristic, non-granular modes of representation, accepted and utilised as a necessary framework for shaping further questions. The typical error of some forms of journalistic scientism is to imply that granular accuracy is the norm and, what is more, that this is what gives 'science' its superiority over other modes of knowing. But what we have been discussing so far implies an unavoidable 'cognitive pluralism' – 'the view that all explanation, and particularly the explanation of human action, quite properly uses many non-competing but convergent methods'.[1] If the point of what we think of as our cognitive activity is sustainable alignment with what we

[1] Mary Midgley, *Myths We Live By* (London: Routledge, 2003), 53.

encounter but do not control, scientific representation is simply one variety of this. What it is not and cannot be is a mode of access to the environment which is exempt from all elements of heuristic projection and manageable deviation or irregularity (the slow clock), so that it cannot be an exhaustive or paradigmatic model for truth-telling and dependable knowledge. For most serious forms of human understanding it is essential that we factor in the process of learning and transmission that has produced a particular claim to 'knowing', and also the ways in which continuing environmental pressures require continuing adjustment to and in what is said and imagined. A claim to knowing in this particular moment, in other words, has a past and a future; it exists within what Husserlian phenomenology calls a 'life-world'[2], a context of narrated human experience arising from a complex of processes which we are never fully able successfully to map or trace. Practices of successful representation, so far from being normatively the 'capture' of a state of affairs by means of a simple act of registering in the moment, depend on a given complex of factors and open out on to further horizons of questioning. Indeed, we can say that 'successful' representing reinforces the conviction that this specific representation is inadequate or incomplete. Merleau-Ponty notes,

> If my consciousness were at present constituting the world in which it perceives, no distance would separate them and there would be no possible discrepancy between them; it would find its way into the world's hidden concatenations, intentionality would carry us to the heart of the object, and simultaneously the percept would lose the thickness conferred by the present, and consciousness would not be lost and become bogged down in it. But what we in fact have is consciousness of an inexhaustible object.[3]

He goes on to argue that the moment of perception is one in which the body ('which is better informed than we are about the world') is making the connection that its history allows it to make, prior to any conscious act of appropriation by a 'mental' self. The reflecting mind follows and systematises as best it can, but for this to happen it needs to be aware also of its already given involvement in a temporal and material history of interaction which it will not completely systematise or conceptualise and which therefore prompts and enables further development of the articulation of the 'life world'.

The two salient points that emerge from this are these. First, there is an unavoidably complex set of implications about the nature of truthfulness.

[2] See, e.g., Hans-Georg Gadamer, *Truth and Method* (London: Continuum 1975), 236–42.

[3] Maurice Merleau-Ponty, *Phenomenology of Perception* (New York: Humanities Press, 1962), 238.

What has been said so far certainly means that any individual's claim to knowledge is 'perspectivally' marked, but this gives no ground to relativism in the popular sense. The perspectival is always already a matter of recognising the self's implication in other perspectives, for the simple reason that conceiving and imagining one's own perspective necessitates imagining something other to it: to see myself as a body presupposes a space in which my perspective is not the sole one. So my claim to true knowledge is intrinsically linked with an involvement in reciprocity and imaginative projection; the world I inhabit is one whose nature and boundaries are discovered in negotiation with the non-self, including the *active* non-self who is the other speaker and perceiver. Language maps out what is recognisable to self and other, what can therefore be the stuff of connected argument and action, social practice. A 'culture of representation' is the business of settling the terms of this practice – social and accountable, corrigible but needing to be learned/internalised in a process of formation or induction. Truthfulness is thus something like cognitive sustainability: what can cope with the different but related challenges of other participants in the culture and the repeated engagement with the unpredictability of the environment.

Second, if this is correct, there is a need to recognise that the practices that deliver 'knowledge' are embedded in a material environment in various ways that will remain obscure. In a helpful phrase of Orion Edgar's, '*nature* lies on both sides of perception'[4]; perceiving is part of our 'animality', not the work of some active, independent spiritual subject upon a passive external world. It makes sense to say that non-human organisms 'know' their environs, but rather than this being a springboard for the reduction of human knowledge to an instinctive or mechanical level, it should be a prompt to rethink intelligence itself as extending to the non-human in significant ways. Where exactly consciousness and linguistic capacity start and stop is not so easy to tie down as we once thought, but this is not by any means necessarily an anti-humanist concession. We might better see it as enabling us to define 'reasoning' as a dramatically diverse set of practices whose connecting structure is something to do with adequately and successfully adjusting to what is presented and 'projecting' serviceable maps of the environment according to the physical/cerebral capacity of the organism. In the case of human beings, that projective activity is exceptionally developed, so that the ability to modify the environment (as a consequence of tool-making and advanced linguistic

[4] Orion Edgar, *Things Seen and Unseen* (Eugene, OR: Cascade, 2016), 187 (italics in original).

skills) is uniquely extensive. But this does not mean that it is cut off from its material or (in Edgar's sense) 'natural' character. Properly understood, our reasoning skills are bound up with our materiality and our state of interdependence. To grasp what is involved in our claims to knowledge is to locate knowing within the matrix of shared materiality. Or, to put it in terms of contemporary political force, knowledge, reason and truthfulness have a clear *ecological* structure, ignored at some considerable risk.

The term 'ecological' itself carries an important charge. In referring us to a balance of interlocking agencies, none of them able to 'be itself' without the involvement of the entire system, it underlines the fallacy of looking for what the Canadian environmental writer Philip Shepherd identifies as the obsession with 'purity' in knowledge[5]. He notes the danger of re-casting our knowledge of our environment as knowledge not of reality but of 'its effects on our measuring apparatus'. Having refined a methodology of bracketing the time-and-matter context of our investigation so as to avoid distorting 'noise', we create a fictional knowing self, intrinsically isolated from interaction, and end up in the extreme paradoxical position of positing a world that is essentially static and – to use the word again – 'granular', over against an active investigating subject, yet this active investigating subject cannot, on the premises set out, be more than another recording mechanism, the computational brain. A wholly mysterious 'reader' of recording mechanisms has to be tacitly imported into the recording subject to make sense of the activity that is under way, and most exponents of this odd picture simply shy away from the metaphysical muddles implied in this. Methodological purity, the refinement of investigative technique, especially the capacity to screen out irrelevant material, is a technical triumph and a necessary aspect of what the scientific investigator does. But to suppose that this then stipulates definitively what counts as knowing involves us in a circularity of definition: the process of 'screening' or purifying for the sake of specific questions to be answered becomes a *programmatic* reductionism for which 'screened' material is effectively unreal, not strictly knowable. Shepherd has much to say about the long history of screening, the deep scepticism about the body as a source of knowledge that goes back to some strands of Platonism, and the implicit and pervasive gendered rhetoric of purified truth-telling, and there are intricate questions about cultural history to be explored there. But his fundamental point is a straightforward one: to recast it slightly in the terms we have been using in this discussion, he is noting that the *culture* of

[5] Philip Shepherd, *New Self, New World* (Berkeley, CA: North Atlantic Books, 2010), 122–8.

mechanised measurement naturally and inevitably does what any culture does, in refining the habit it inculcates and the questions it asks. It is thus vulnerable as any culture is to the assumption that its own protocols are normative and universal, that is, that they are not shaped by and involved in a 'nest' of other cultural practices. And the effect of confusion – or hubris – about the limits of any one culture is the practical disabling of effective and sustainable response to the world around: a 'knowledge' that actively impedes what we have called alignment to the real. If we are to speak adequately about a culture of representation in a wider and more comprehensive sense, we have to look harder at the actual practices, explanatory, interpretative, 'projective' or imaginative and, not least, contemplative, by which we construct the shared environment of language and action that enables effective and sustainable response to the (rest of the) world.

8.3 Reason, Practice and Taking Time

It is in this connection that some religious leaders have come to characterise the environmental crisis as a crisis of *reason*.[6] A 'pure' epistemology, elevating methodological strictness to a sort of metaphysical status, appears to have contributed to the current global irrationality that jeopardises human survival. Along with every specific practical measure needed to arrest this process, there is need for a more resourceful understanding of human locatedness, embeddedness in the global ecology, and this involves a recognition of the diversities of knowing and the revaluation of a whole spectrum of localised and hard-to-measure modes of 'alignment', the various cultures of representation that enable continued rational life – that is, life that is adequately responsive to what it encounters. This will include an assortment of pre-modern cultural habits, a range of symbolic narratives that 'project' connections beyond what is instantly measurable, religious practices which both insist on an accountability to and for our environment and inculcate serious disciplines for monitoring and detoxifying human acquisitiveness, and a good deal more. But if this is to be something other than an anxious rejection of the scientific legacy – which would itself be another form of dangerous cultural shrinkage – we have to think further about some of the sources in religious discourse of the problematic habits of scientific modernity. Taking forward a 'science and religion' conversation that is more than the negotiation of a secure border may be

[6] See Pope Francis, *Laudato si* (Citta Del Vaticano: Libereria Editrice Vaticana, 2015).

most significantly a matter of discerning what self-critical questions are prompted in both discourses as a result of the encounter.

Thus far, we have concentrated on issues around the embeddedness of knowing in a range of cultures that work to create and manage a dependable ecology of interaction with the rest of the world – the involvement of truth-telling with temporality and materiality, with narrative and habit. Religious discourse and practice at the very least offer some substantial resources for understanding our knowing in this light. The knowing of God is associated with the rehearsal of a history, and this rehearsal takes place in a context of physically enacted ritual and is normally echoed in routine habits of devotion. In several traditions – Northern Buddhism, Eastern Christianity, Judaism – there is a highly developed understanding of the use of material objects and practices as a means of contact with the fundamental state or context of things, a means towards the knowledge of God. Early Mediterranean Christianity develops by the end of the fourth century a concept of the connection between the contemplative and receptive apprehension of the life and interrelation of things as they are (*physike theoria*) and the contemplation of the divine. Both involve a receiving of the *logos* of what is encountered, the intelligible/communicable pattern of agency that makes something what it is; in knowledge, my own *logos* is activated and informed by the *logos* of the object; the disciplines simultaneously of self-awareness and self-forgetfulness allow me to apprehend with increasing truthfulness, and this process is part of what opens the way to the contemplation of God. It is a structure that assumes a sort of developing convergence between the subject's awareness and the agency of what is encountered, and as such points in a very different direction to the notion of a subject's epistemological 'purity' in Shepherd's terms. In a way that is characteristic of most 'pre-modern' thought, this posits a response to the environment that is both passive and active, both receptive to the act of an other and itself active in modifying that other. What it does not accommodate is any notion of an individual intellect probing and manipulating a passive object.

For the Christian spiritual tradition in which this pattern was articulated, the task of a responsible and truthful process of coming-to-know is inseparable from regular scrutiny of how our mental approach to the object can be affected by the question of how the object can be fitted to my needs or desires. Ultimately, an object is de-realised by such a concern; I cease to see what is actually there. To put it slightly differently, this is another way of stating both the unreasonableness of erecting a methodological technique into a universal norm and the self-subverting nature of constructing the mind's object in terms of the mind's supposed individual agenda. Scientific practice is properly an ascetic habit, to the degree to which it separates out questions of the intrinsic workings of its object from questions of practical utility; only if the first is observed will the second even make sense. But if the second prevails, with little or nothing beyond close-focus questions about utility, the results will be of limited value, even in relation to utility. The challenge is not to silence or shame questions of utility – which arise naturally and inevitably – but to maintain habits of thought that keep them apart from the primary investigative enterprise. And so one of the areas in which the conversation between scientists and reflective religious believers needs to develop is to do with keeping under scrutiny the precarious balance of interest in the processes of investigation, identifying the ways in which undue and persistent narrowing of the questions ends up eroding the reality of what is investigated, and what is immediately measurable by conventional means becomes the only matter of intellectual interest.[7] To return to the language used at the beginning of this enquiry, a 'culture of representation' in which what mattered was essentially the recording of a set of determinate effects on our means of measurement would represent something significantly less than the object in its full *involvement* in the 'life-world' of which the observer is also part. The contamination of pure recording by contextual factors is not a disaster. It is wholly right and intelligible to seek to minimise irrelevant output when specific questions are in view; it is neither if the solution of those questions silences other issues or obscures other horizons. The life of an object always involves an aspect which we could call the face that is turned away from the observer, and arguably the very idea of an object entails the recognition of this. Insofar as the religious perspective necessarily involves such a recognition, it becomes a potential partner in any attempt at longer-term, less formal, habit- and practice-focused responses to problems that cannot be reduced to one set of questions only. The religious perspective importantly steers attention to the particular and to particular cultures of coping, which is why effective responses to ecological crisis, to take the obvious example, need to build in what is learned from local and informal strategies for managing an environment. And the fact that so many spiritual traditions present means of learning how to bracket self-interested questions, how to attend to and take unpressured time with what is seen and sensed provides a context for understanding how and why this is intrinsic to what we have called sustainable knowing or truthfulness.

[7] Iain McGilchrist, *The Master and His Emissary* (New Haven, CT: Yale University Press, 2019).

8.4 Material Knowledge and the Mapping of Resistance

At the same time, the critical challenge has to run both ways. As we have noted briefly, there are aspects of a religiously inflected metaphysical tradition that have their own issues around purity. The stubborn vulgarised Platonism which insists that *only* a knowledge of immaterial structure counts as knowing haunts a good deal of Christian metaphysics, as does its even more problematic corollary, that God is known only when the material world is not, when physical and temporal actuality are absent. Behind these ideas is the obstinate myth of a rivalry between finite and infinite, physical and spiritual, temporal and eternal. The infinite/spiritual/eternal is configured as that which stands at the opposite end of a spectrum from the finite/physical/temporal, so that the two terms cannot be applicable in a single context. There is ample argument to show that this is a fundamental distortion of the Christian theological project,[8] but it recurs consistently, obscuring the various resources in the tradition for understanding the universal presence at the root of the finite of infinite activation, and the exploration of the inseparability of formative intelligible action and materiality in the particulars of a finite and temporal world. Scientific culture and practice rightly challenge a popular implicit metaphysic for which the collection of empirical data is detached from spiritually significant knowledge, with the result that self-forgetting attention to the actuality of the material world is ignored as a discipline of the spirit. It is unsurprising that the narrowness of scientistic functionalism reflects as in a mirror the narrowness of this misdirected religiosity – most damagingly at work in the indifference to material reality and the balance of the physical environment characteristic of some apocalyptically minded Christians.

Christian – and doubtless other religious – believers have their own concerns and even obsessions about purity and the preservation of uncontaminated agency, their own reasons for being suspicious and anxious about models of knowing that imply confluence, fusion, the rhythm of action and passivity. The exploration of a conversation with the sciences has the capacity to clarify the risks in some sorts of theological discourse as well as scientific, and to focus attention on those aspects of the theological legacy that reinforce the sense of the intrinsically 'ecological' character of

[8] For discussion of this, see T Kathryn Tanner, *God and Creation in Christian Theology* (Minneapolis, MN: Fortress, 2006); Kathryn Tanner, *Jesus, Humanity and the Trinity* (Edinburgh: T. & T. Clark, 2001); Rowan Williams, *Being Human: Bodies, Minds, Persons* (London: SPCK, 2018).

knowledge and truth-telling. Much of the theological language we have been revisiting assumes that habitual knowledge changes the knower – not in the crude sense of adding to their epistemological possessions, but in remoulding behaviours, even literally altering physical capacities. In his groundbreaking study *The Craftsman*,[9] Richard Sennett explores how the body itself is rediscovered and reimagined in physical processes of learning, as it encounters areas of significant and potentially productive *resistance* – boundary areas where the tension between action and passivity/receptivity generates fresh capacity. 'Thus, the tilt of the palm seems peripheral to the mental map a musician makes for a chord stretch yet turns out to be a zone for productive work with finger resistance; the palm becomes a working space.... [T]he "site of resistance"... denotes either a boundary, resisting contamination, excluding, deadening, or a border, a site of exchange as well as of separation.'[10] Knowledge as the discovery of productive boundaries to be negotiated and worked with rather than understood as metaphysical barriers between active selves and passive stuff is in this connection clearly a matter of learning to map a 'life-world'. And this mapping, as Sennett stresses, is not only the sketching of an ensemble of states of affairs to be grasped in a set of atomised recorded images, configurations of the recording mechanism, but an enterprise of actively adjusting to the flow of other agency, visualising continuities and resistances which together make up our true knowledge of any object – let alone any other subject.

Hence the importance of understanding what we mean by representation at a level more comprehensive than any suggestion that it is merely a registering of stimuli.[11] Sennett's emphasis on process and the exploring of resistance allow us to think of our cultures of representing as both accountable and in some degree heuristic, both claiming to connect us with the world we do not control and constantly self-reflexive and self-modifying. Representation becomes a moment within the wider process of apprehending and adjusting to the 'knowledge ecology' in which we are always already involved as speakers who in diverse ways represent themselves to themselves as subjects. Significantly, this understanding of our knowing offers a counterbalance to any anthropology that explicitly or implicitly uses a certain set of cognitive habits as a measure of someone's 'full' humanity. It has the capacity to be systematically charitable to various epistemologies in the sense that it encourages us to look not only for means

[9] Richard Sennett, *The Craftsman* (London: Penguin, 2008). [10] Ibid., 230–1.
[11] Rowan Williams, *The Edge of Words* (London: Bloomsbury, 2014).

by which granular correspondences can be established and measured but for sustained (and thus flexible and corrigible) practices of successful adjustment. And in the light of that, we are brought back to the question noted earlier of whether a society committed (as ours still appears to be) to a paradigm of indefinitely increasing levels of exploitation of the environment can be called 'rational' in any meaningful way.

8.5 The Naturalness of Knowing

Much of the argument of this essay could be summarised as an argument for the *naturalness* of knowledge, in the sense of Edgar's comment quoted earlier about 'nature' being 'on both sides of perception'. Edgar elsewhere in his book[12] elaborates the idea that we should be able to understand the human act of eating as a form of *perception*, because it involves a process of learning to discriminate and organise percepts intelligently, to engage transformingly with the world. The fact of hunger in the animal world signals that animal organisms need to act consistently (and thus to learn) in order to preserve life 'in the sense of the preservation of meaningful organizations of matter in biological individuals' – but therefore also prompts us to reflect on the specific kind of life that is human rather than canine or bovine.[13] We eat to live, but this eating becomes part of a culture (not only a biological process) of transformation; human eating keeps our animal nature alive but also contributes to the linguistic exchanges that make us recognisable to one another. A putatively human society which had no cultural resources or protocols around the consumption (or indeed excretion) of food would strike us as baffling, and one area of human interaction that seems unlikely to be captured by even the most adventurous developments in artificial intelligence is exchanges about food and drink. Sense experience, rather than being a sort of neutral deliverer of data, is already perception, already a cumulative process of developing skills in mapping the environment, well before language steps in, but it is also on a continuum with language, so that we can grasp linguistic exchange and linguistic recognition as an element in a far larger spectrum of activities by which we consolidate the shared and interactive character of our group life by proposing and accepting convergent 'stories' about where we physically are, constructing an intelligible habitat.

The language of ecology comes back persistently in this discussion. Truthful knowing is not the relation of an external recording device to

[12] Edgar, *Things Seen and Unseen*, chs. 2 and 6. [13] Ibid., 72.

passive phenomena but an aspect of sustainable interaction with a material world in whose processes we share, and the task of human knowing is both to share and to understand what is entailed in sharing. If the conversation between scientists and theologians in our present global context can move forward with something like this acknowledgement in place, the possibilities for intellectual and practical synergy are considerable; if such possibilities are not realised and the different kinds of purity-obsessions we have noted determine the two discourses, the consequences are disturbing. Most practising scientists know perfectly well the risks of confusing methodological reduction and focus with metaphysical claims, but a confused popular discourse in which both individualism and determinism are indulged leads to a damagingly narrow picture of the scientific enterprise and to the somewhat odd notion that there is a single 'scientific world view' with established philosophical credentials. Collaboration in clarifying categories is one area where science (and the philosophy of science) and theology have to work in harness, and in a way that does justice not only to credal theologies but to the varieties of actual religious practice that are designed to shape and illuminate the processes of finding and remaining 'in' truth. And many if not most theologians and reflective believers recognise at some level the urgency of environmental crisis, but the theological hinterland for a committed resistance to a false and misplaced detachment, a false and misplaced anthropocentrism or human exceptionalism, is still in need of further fleshing out. A certain theological nervousness about the unique vocation of the human person's God's image continues to hold back a more developed engagement with the idea that human consciousness may be seen as belonging on a spectrum of intelligent responsiveness that is pervasive in the material world. That is to say, it may be seen in ecological perspective, as one strategy among others for creating a sustainable mode of coping with phenomena beyond the will's control.

For both scientific communicators and philosophically minded theologians, it is important to recover an awareness of the collaborative and variegated nature of representation, and to see representation itself as simultaneously natural and cultural. It is most basically the act of mapping the environment in ways that preserve the 'meaningful organisation' of biological agents; but with evolving intelligence, it is also – in step with all other human behaviours – channelled into conscious linguistic cooperation, into the construction of cultures, through which skills of mapping and adjusting to an environment are dependably effective, though also open to reimagining. Intrinsic to this interweaving of sustainability and corrigibility is the habit of bringing into focus the ways in which acquisitive agendas distort and reduce the reality of what we seek to know; and in this regard, the Christian ascetical tradition has substantive things to say. To the extent that any representational undertaking goes beyond the mere registering of measurable external stimuli, there are broadly moral issues around the processes of discovery and description; the aspects of knowledge we have looked at in this essay have to do with the dangers of de-realising an object or an environment by restricting the questions we can properly ask about it with intellectual seriousness. As argued above, the ultimate effect of a reductive strategy understood in this way as a metaphysical prescription is both to isolate the knowing subject and to reduce the capacity of the world around to generate fresh questions. Our physical presence in the world we belong to is 'de-skilled' by excessive concentration on what Philip Shepherd described as the 'effects on our measuring apparatus'. And there is serious conceptual confusion around much discussion of the machine-like or computational character of the human brain: while the brain indisputably performs 'computational' operations, refining algorithms and connecting channels of informational input, there are two things that should make us pause before endorsing the popular trope that the brain 'is' a computer. One is the simple fact of the brain's interaction with changing organic systems elsewhere in the body, which apparently deal with information in ways less easily charted in the binaries of computational logic (remember the point noted earlier about eating as perception); the other is the capacity of the brain to generate new questions or new linguistic combinations in a way hard to characterise as simply the determined causal result of specific informational input. To go back to the axiom quoted at the beginning of this essay, clocks don't know what time it is; for their material processes to be interpreted as something called 'time-telling', there must be a cultural protocol by which certain mechanical outcomes are agreed definitively to symbolise the passage of time. An observed process becomes 'information' in the strict sense only when it is thus inculturated; the brain as a recording device may be stimulated to certain systematisable activities, but it is informed, it knows, to the extent that it incorporates the stimulus into a 'policy' within the life-world. This incorporation may be by way of conceptual refinement, complementary descriptive accounts, made ever more precise by scientific exploration, or by more informal conventions and traditions of behaviour. But the idea that truth is told by a recording procedure is a myth that needs dismantling, at least if we are to have anything like a coherent idea of what truth-telling means as a social practice.

We have heard Merleau-Ponty saying, in a – surely deliberately – paradoxical phrase that the body is better informed than 'we' are about the world. We might reword this to say that 'we' are informed by far more than the total of information we can consciously process or measure. The body has already begun to think for 'us', in that our habits of adjustment and environment-mapping begin long before we formulate conscious self-images. In so responding to and participating sustainably in the interactive complex that is our habitat, the body has begun to *know*. It is an odd way of recognising the distinctiveness of human linguistic and constructive sophistication to cut this off from its roots in bodily skill, on the grounds that only the conventions by which we measure correspondence constitute objective or scientifically interesting knowledge. A range of complementary perspectives, religious practice being prominent among them, makes it pretty clear that this is a self-defeating assumption. And what the religious and theological perspective in its most mature traditional shape proposes is not any kind of rival epistemology or dismantling of the conventions of defensible objectivity but a way of locating this range of practices and cultures within something like a comprehensive 'culture' of attention, silence and the sidelining of specific needs, wants and priorities; an orientation towards grace, perhaps, without which intelligence repeatedly collapses back into something rather less than the style of truthfulness that seems to be distinctively human – social, cultural, consciously critical and transformative.

PART III

Philosophical Problems with 'Science' and 'Religion'

CHAPTER 9

Consciousness, Intention, and Final Causation

Simon Oliver

With the exception of a very few schools of thought in Greece, ancient and medieval philosophers and theologians shared a remarkable consensus concerning the nature of causal explanation: an explanation is partial and incomplete, lacking full intelligibility, unless it refers to the end or goal of a substance. So, here is a mind-bending sentence from Thomas Aquinas which expresses well the foundational nature of final causes:

> Whence it is said that the end is the cause of causes, because it is the cause of the causality in all the causes.[1]

Or, to put the matter rather more neatly and succinctly:

> Every agent acts for an end: otherwise one thing would not follow more than another from the action of the agent, unless it were by chance.[2]

One way in which we commonly narrate the transition from the medieval world of a figure such as St Thomas to the modern world beginning in the sixteenth and seventeenth centuries is through an alleged rejection of final causes or purpose in favour of material and mechanical causal explanation. To put this simply, we move from explaining a beating heart in terms of the purpose of pumping blood around the body (thus ascribing a kind of agency to the heart) to explaining a beating heart in terms of electrical activity mechanically causing muscular contractions. We know, however, that the history of theology and natural philosophy (or physico-theology) in the seventeenth and eighteenth centuries is more complex; they did not banish final causes altogether. Final causes are indeed declared barren by

[1] Aquinas, *De principiis naturae* 4.22, in Joseph Bobik, *Aquinas on Matter and Form and the Elements: A Translation and Interpretation of the* De principiis naturae *and the* De mixtione elementorun *of St. Thomas Aquinas* (Notre Dame, IN: University of Notre Dame Press, 1998), 60.

[2] Aquinas, *Summa theologiae*, 1a2ae.1.2. All translations of the *Summa theologiae* are by the Fathers of the English Dominican Province, 2nd and rev. ed., 10 vols. (London: Burns Oates and Washbourne, 1920–2).

Francis Bacon in 1620, except in the case of human affairs. Yet Robert Boyle, in his *A Disquisition about the Final Causes of Natural Things* of 1688, declared that it is incumbent upon us to look for the final causes of creatures lest we neglect their usefulness and fail thereby to admire and thank the author of them. In 1728, the German philosopher Christian Wolff finally coined the term *teleologia* to name a branch of natural philosophy that studies the ends or purposes of things.[3] It might be thought that the naming of a specific discipline which explains the ends of things – teleology – points to the significance of final causation. Isolating and naming this science was, however, part of the gradual demise of such modes of explanation in the face of a very different metaphysics and natural philosophy. In identifying a particular domain of teleology, even while regarding it as part of natural philosophy, Wolff at the same time helped to identify and legitimate a non-teleological domain devoted to an alternative mode of explanation in terms of efficient or mechanical causes. In short, the science of teleology eventually came to be associated with a particular kind of natural theology focused on the supposed divine design of nature. Final causes were understood as essentially extrinsic to an otherwise mechanical nature. Purposes were thought to be applied to inert matter via the laws of nature which were in turn decreed and policed by God.

What seems to be going on in the transition from the medieval account of purposiveness to the modern mechanical cosmology is not so much the banishment of final causes as the wholesale reimagining of causation which results from profound shifts in the metaphysics of form and substance. One simple example of the change in the understanding of final causes can be found in the distinction between intrinsic and extrinsic teleology. For example, we might say that the final cause of the acorn becoming an oak is intrinsic to the acorn – it belongs to the form of the acorn to become an oak. On the other hand, the final cause of a car is not intrinsic to the car. Rather, it is extrinsic and lies within the mind of the designer and driver.

[3] 'Enimvero rerum naturalium duplices dari possunt rationes, quarum aliae petuntur a causa efficiente, aliae a fine. Quae a causa efficiente petuntur, in disciplinis hactenus definitis expenduntur. Datur itaque praeter eas alia adhuc philosophiae naturalis pars, quae fines rerum explicat, nomine adhuc destituta, etsi amplissima sit utilissima. Dici posset Teleologia.' Christian Wolff, *Philosophia rationalis sive Logica*, 3rd ed. (Verona, 1735), section 85, p. 25. [Certainly, a twofold reason can be given for natural things – one is to be found in the efficient cause, and the other in the final cause. Those which are sought in the efficient cause belong to the disciplines which we have already defined. Besides these sciences there is still another part of natural philosophy which explains the end of things. There is no name for this discipline, even though it is very important and most useful. It could be called 'teleology'.]

This is more or less Aristotle's distinction between nature and artifice – natural things have an intrinsic teleology whereas artificial things have an extrinsic teleology. There are countless reasons why that distinction is helpful until it becomes hardened into a dualism in which final causes are either exclusively intrinsic or exclusively extrinsic. For seventeenth-century physico-theologians, all final causes in nature are extrinsic, lying in the mind of God, and matter is purely passive – hence creation comes to be seen as a mechanism designed like a watch. The question of whether purposes and therefore agency lie intrinsically within nature or extrinsically in the mind of a divine designer generates significant problems for the understanding of life, problems which still concern the life sciences today. In her book *The Restless Clock*, the historian of science Jessica Riskin puts the problem in this way:

> I think that biologists' figures of speech reflect a deeply hidden yet abiding quandary created by the seventeenth-century banishment of agency from nature: do the order and action in the natural world originate inside or outside? Either answer raises big problems. Saying 'inside' violates the ban on ascriptions of agency to natural phenomena such as cells or molecules, and so risks sounding mystical and magical. Saying 'outside' assumes a supernatural source of nature's order, and so violates another scientific principle, the principle of naturalism.[4]

So the question of agency, which is intimately bound to the question of teleology, remains important for the natural sciences, particularly when addressing the question of life. Teleology is also a key fault line between theology and the natural sciences. In any doctrine of creation and providence, some kind of purposiveness in the form of an orientation to the Good will be central to an intelligible understanding of nature. By contrast, for many in the natural sciences the rejection of teleology is of the essence of science because it constitutes a turn from supernaturalism. This is more than a methodological choice or the mere bracketing of the supernatural, for many natural scientists claim that purposiveness is not seen in nature from *any* legitimate, rational perspective. Yet it could be argued that it is not seen precisely because of the way in which the ontology of nature has already been conceived a priori. One might therefore ask whether science is blinding itself to fundamental aspects of nature that we nevertheless grasp very firmly at the level of intuition and common sense. Insofar as teleology is discussed at all, it is often the kind which

[4] Jessica Riskin, *The Restless Clock: A History of the Centuries-Long Argument over What Makes Living Things Tick* (Chicago: University of Chicago Press, 2016), 6.

belongs to the field of intelligent design (ID). While the ID proponents' heroic attempts at confronting explanatory lacunae in evolutionary science might be applauded by some, it is not clear that the kind of final causes they propose are theologically or metaphysically coherent.

In addition to the question of intrinsic and extrinsic teleology in relation to agency and life, the question of teleology becomes particularly acute in the area of human consciousness and intention. This is the issue that I will explore in this chapter. As mentioned earlier, Francis Bacon himself declared that final causes are barren as explanations except in the case of human affairs because human conscious intention deliberates, identifies goals, and pursues those goals. So teleology comes to mark not only a potential fault line between science and theology, but also a fault line between humanity and nature. One can therefore also express the classic mind–body problem in terms of teleology: How can non-purposive, sottish matter give rise to the unity of intentional consciousness which rationally deliberates and seeks goals that explain action? Such is the problem addressed by, for example, Thomas Nagel in *Mind in Cosmos.*[5] This book received some hysterical reviews when it was published in 2012 because of its proposal that only a teleological account of nature, albeit an entirely naturalized teleology, would allow significant progress in some of the most challenging areas of natural science. In reintroducing teleology in this way, Nagel rightly attempts to subvert the two options most frequently available in the current debate: the alienation of the human from nature (humanity is intentional and goal-orientated, nature is not), or the elimination of the human as we intuitively grasp ourselves via the proposal that conscious intention is an illusion or merely epiphenomenal.

The most interesting proposals in this debate link intentional consciousness to wider nature by proposing a kind of goal-orientated appetition all the way through nature – mind from top to bottom, as it were. Such approaches tend to avoid locating goal-orientation merely in the human will but find it to be an expression of real natures or 'form'. Robert Spaemann, for example, writes that

> we only know the meaning of 'tending towards something' by association, that is, through our own experience; and not because we, as active beings, set ourselves goals, but because we find the direction towards goals beforehand within ourselves, in the form of a tendency. We can talk of external

[5] Thomas Nagel, *Mind and Cosmos: Why the Materialist Neo-Darwinian Conception of Nature Is Almost Certainly False* (Oxford: Oxford University Press, 2012).

> finality only because we have already experienced the 'tending-towards', as a form of the internal unity of living beings.[6]

So our experience of teleological orientation is not simply a matter of the exclusively free human will selecting its own ends in a way that is devoid of the determinations of base instinct or mechanical causes; rather, our ends are given by our natures, by our dynamic substantial form, the internal unity of the living organism.

It is in our experience of intention – of tending towards, stretching towards, striving for – that we find our most immediate experience of teleological orientation. For the phenomenological tradition of philosophy, intention is, of course, the defining aspect of mind. As David Hart eloquently puts it in *The Experience of God*, purposive intention is required even for the most basic activity of sense perception. He gives the straightforward example of picking up a cup expecting to drink beer, but instead drinking a mouthful of wine. The mental intention is met not with recognition but with cognitive dissonance. One does not immediately taste the wine; one experiences only confusion until one's intentional orientation is readjusted and one can taste the wine as wine, and as agreeable sancerre or tepid chardonnay. So David Hart writes,

> the mind knows nothing in a merely passive way, but always has an end or meaning toward which it is purposively directed, as toward a final cause. In every act of representation, the intending mind invests perception with meaning by directing itself toward a certain determinate content of experience, and by thus interpreting each experience as an experience of this or that reality.[7]

How, then, might we begin to conceive teleological mind to be present analogically throughout nature? Is there anything in the pre-modern conception of final causes that might allow us to think differently about purpose in mind and nature? I have argued elsewhere for the view that purpose is present in the form of appetition, principally through Aristotle's notion of *orexis* that arises from form even in the most basic instance of a material nature.[8] I will pursue this line of enquiry a little further with respect to Aquinas's philosophy of action and intention. We will see that

[6] Robert Spaemann, 'The Unrelinquishability of Teleology', in Ana Marta González (ed.), *Contemporary Perspectives on Natural Law: Natural Law as a Limiting Concept* (Aldershot: Ashgate, 2008), 291.

[7] David Hart, *The Experience of God: Being, Consciousness, Bliss* (New Haven, CT: Yale University Press, 2013), 193.

[8] See Simon Oliver, 'Aquinas and Aristotle's Teleology', *Nova et Vetera* 11, no. 3 (2013), 849–70.

Aquinas similarly considers nature to be intrinsically orientated to the good, but in a way that, although not deliberative in every instance, is nevertheless an expression of the divine intention.

Having examined Aquinas's view, I will turn to another Aristotelian concept, *hexis*, or habit, that is used as a mediating concept between intentional consciousness and nature in the work of the nineteenth-century philosopher Félix Ravaisson. We will see that habit is analogically present throughout nature, but intentional consciousness is, for Ravaisson, the archetypal instance of habit. On his view, the habitual nature of our intentional consciousness helps us to understand the way in which habit is present 'all the way down' through nature, like a spiral staircase descending to the bottom of the building, and therefore the way in which mind is never alienated from matter, not even the depths of matter. The point here is that the primary desire that we find in intentional consciousness and the appetition we find even in base matter – what Ravaisson calls will and nature – need some kind of mediation. I will suggest that material and mental *orexis* are mediated be *hexis* – by habit.

9.1 Aquinas on Intention and Action

For Aquinas, as we have seen, without the final cause there would be no agency, or at least no intelligible agency. The final cause is that for the sake of which an agent acts. Agency, however, is not restricted to intentional conscious subjects; it includes inanimate substances, even if only as instrumental agents. Aquinas notes that rational natures tend to an end as moving themselves to that end, whereas non-rational natures – everything from inanimate objects to lower animals – tend to an end as directed or led by another, eventually whatever gave them their form.

Ultimately, what moves things to their proper end, including the inanimate, is the divine rational art which is not exclusively extrinsic, but is also instilled within things by nature. In his *Commentary on Aristotle's Physics*, Aquinas makes clear that nature is an agent, but one that does not deliberate. However, as we will see later with habit, this does not mean that nature is an irrational agent or one that does not act for an end. Quite the contrary: nature does not deliberate for the same reason that a harpist does not deliberate when they play the harp, because the determinate means by which the act is undertaken has become second nature. So Aquinas writes,

> Hence, since nature has the determinate means by which it acts, it does not deliberate. For nature seems to differ from art only because nature is an intrinsic principle and art is an extrinsic principle.... Hence it is clear that

> nature is nothing but a certain kind of art, i.e. the divine art, impressed upon things, by which these things are moved to a determinate end. It is as if the shipbuilder were able to give to timber that by which they would move themselves to take the form of a ship.[9]

This passage indicates that primacy of the divine art over human art and their radical dissimilarity, even though the latter participates in the former. The divine art enters into the very being of things because God is the source of that being, and those things are thereby created. The divine art of creation has its source in the divine ideas. At the same time, the natures or forms of things by which they move and are moved are donated by God and are intrinsic to their being as creatures. In the case of human art, the teleology is more exclusively extrinsic, having its source in the human conscious intention which cannot infuse itself into the being of things.

The explanation of action also requires the good to indicate why action tends to some ends and not others. An action is ordered to a particular end because that end is good with respect to that which desires it. So in *De veritate* Aquinas describes inclination with respect to natural and violent motion. This extends as well to the inanimate as the animate:

> It is after this fashion that all natural things are inclined to what is suitable for them, having within themselves some principle of their inclination in virtue of which that inclination is natural, so that in a way they go themselves and are not merely led to their due ends. Things moved by violence are only led, because they contribute nothing to the mover. But natural things go to their ends inasmuch as they cooperate with the one including and directing them through a principle implanted in them.[10]

All natural things, animate and inanimate, are inclined to a certain end by the prime mover, God. So everything is inclined by nature to that which is intended by God, but the only intention appropriate to the divine will is God himself, who is by essence goodness, so everything is by nature inclined to the good. 'To desire or have appentency (*appetere*)', says Thomas, 'is nothing else but to strive for something, stretching, as it were, toward something which is destined for oneself.'[11] The notion of 'stretching' (*tendere*) is important because it suggests far more than a general inclination towards something. Rather, it implies an ecstatic striving for

[9] Aquinas, *Commentary on Aristotle's Physics*, trans. Richard J. Blackwell, Richard J. Spath, and W. Edmund Thirkel (Notre Dame, IN: Dumb Ox Books), II.14.268.

[10] Aquinas, *On Truth* ('*Quaestiones disputatae de veritate*'), trans. Robert W. Schmidt (Indianapolis, IN: Hackett Publishing, 1954), 22.1.c.

[11] Ibid., 22.1.c.

the good in which something continually exceeds itself as it moves towards actuality. Such motion is a constant ecstasis as it actualizes its form and exceeds itself through its own nature towards the good. But the source of such stretching toward the good – whether it be a plant growing or a child learning – is the divine intention, the divine mind. Mind comes first.

We should remind ourselves that what makes this intelligible is a very different notion of cause to the one that has, until very recently, dominated today's philosophy. Modern metaphysics tends to think of causes as events, and, moreover, a kind of spatial proximity is required if a causal relationship is to pertain between agent and patient. But the mover in the Aristotelian and Thomist view is not only that which is spatially proximate for the transmission of force, but that which donates something's form. For example, the mover of the boy is, in some sense, its parents. Something's motion springs from its intrinsic natural form spontaneously and immediately. Only in the case of the human person does the form – the soul – become also an efficient as well as normal cause of something's motion. The key point, however, is that the ultimate origin of all natural forms is the divine mind and its intention for the eternal good.

Before moving to Ravaisson, the final remark I should like to make about Aquinas's view of action and intention concerns power, and the fundamental character of action: the communication of form. For Thomas, to act is simply to communicate that through which the agent is in act. Power is not akin to force; it is quite simply the ability to make a likeness of oneself by the donation of form, hence 'every agent enacts its like'. Such power depends on the actuality of the agent; all agency is, for Thomas, a participation in the eternal 'agency' of the persons of the Trinity expressed in the begetting of the Word and the proceeding of the Spirit. Agency spontaneously arises from the actuality of the agent and is essentially an influx of form into another as it communicates a likeness of itself. The form is received according to the nature of the recipient. That influx of form may be reproduction or teaching a student, for example. Human artifice would be a very different example of the mind communicating a likeness of itself. So the form of deliberative calculation communicated to, say, a computer is received according to the material nature of a computer and should not be confused for that which first donated the form, a form that was originally held by nature in the consciousness of the human mind. The computer will only mimic the agency that brought it about because communication of that form remains extrinsic to the material nature of the computer. By contrast, the communication of form in reproduction is the transmission of a nature per se – a child from its parents, a plant from its seed.

What we are still lacking in this picture of the transmission of form is some account of how the forms of conscious intention are mediated to material natures. In what sense is thought and conscious intention constitutive of nature as such? Can we give an account of conscious intention as being the formal and final cause of nature rather than the accidental product of a process that is essentially inimical to teleological intention? One possibility is the philosophy of the nineteenth-century Aristotelian Félix Ravaisson, whose doctoral thesis *De l'habitude* was so influential in the thought of twentieth-century thinkers such as Heidegger and Bergson. I would like to examine Ravaisson's understanding of habit as the mediator between will and nature, between teleological conscious intentionality and material natures. What I hope we will see is that habit, for Ravaisson, is the concept that ties together Aquinas's conscious intentional agency with the agency of basic material natures.

9.2 Ravaisson and Habit

Ravaisson's understanding of habit is an extension of Aristotle's *hexis* into natural philosophy and metaphysics. [12] Habit, for Ravaisson, refers to the way something is or, literally, holds or possesses itself. A habit requires an organic unity which can both possess and acquire habit as a permanent way of being through non-identical repetition. Ravaisson is particularly concerned with how habit is 'contracted' through change, given that creatures that have habit have a settled and permanent way of being – as a tree or a person, for example. He starts his essay by remarking that, if one were to throw a ball in the air 100 times, it would still not acquire the habit of moving upwards. A photocopier does not have a habit because it is a mechanism without a unifying organic form and requires an external efficient cause for its operation. A habit seems to imply not simply changeability, but the ability to assimilate that change, which may arise extrinsically, into an intrinsic second nature.

Let us take a particularly clear and straightforward instance of acquiring a habit: learning to play the piano. To begin with, the movements of one's hands are deliberate and the focus of conscious laboured reflection at every moment. However, after some months of practice, one becomes habituated to playing the piano. The music flows easily and delightfully – it

[12] I am very grateful to Clare Carlisle for her publications on Ravaisson and the philosophy of habit, and for numerous conversations on this important topic. For an excellent overview, see Carlisle, *On Habit* (London: Routledge, 2014).

becomes 'second nature'. Yet one is not dulled to the business of playing the piano. On the contrary, the concert pianist is more aware of playing the piano precisely because this is the actualization of the pianist's potency to play the piano and becomes the expression of their nature. So as consciousness loses itself with respect to will (I do not have to deliberate when I've gained a certain expertise in playing the piano), it gains itself all the more in the awareness of its nature. To take another example, a bird does not deliberate about whether or not to fly, but flight is the expression of the bird's nature, and, in flight, it is most bird-like. Flight springs spontaneously, sweetly, and delightfully, as Aquinas puts it, from a bird's nature.[13]

One of Ravaisson's most important contributions concerns the development of what is known as the double law of habit. The double law plays on the opposition between habit's tendency to dull our sense of the world – to be passive – and its contrary ability to heighten attention – to be active. When we become accustomed to certain experiences or sensations, we are passive and fail to notice them. Alternatively, the non-identical repetition of movements – learning to play the piano, for example – becomes easier and the source of delight as the movements are active. Ravaisson explains this via the example of two people who drink rather a lot, one who gets drunk and the other who is a wine expert. Ravaisson's point is that the senses of the person who gets drunk have become dull to the wine because they drink by a passive habit – perhaps they drink while watching the television or chatting to a friend. The wine expert is active –noting the vintage, examining the colour of the wine, savouring its bouquet, discerning the various flavours. Sensation is intensified by active repetition, and the skills of wine tasting are honed and become habitual in a much more active sense: they are subject to knowledge and judgement.

> Activity increasingly reduces . . . the element of affection and pure sensation, and develops the element of knowledge and judgement. In this way, the sensations in which we seek only pleasure soon fade. Taste becomes more and more obtuse in the one who, by passion, is delivered over to the frequent use of strong liquors; in the connoisseur who discerns flavours, it becomes more and more delicate and subtle.[14]

But the key point for Ravaisson is that habit becomes a kind of mediator between conscious mental intention and the material. When I learn to play

[13] See Simon Oliver, 'The Sweet Delight of Virtue and Grace in Aquinas's Ethics', *International Journal of Systematic Theology* 7, no. 1 (2005), 52–71.

[14] Félix Ravaisson, *Of Habit*, trans. Clare Carlisle and Mark Sinclair (London: Continuum, 2008), 49.

the piano or speak a language, such habits become natural – swift and delightful. But this is not merely a mental habituation; the body is also involved in playing the piano or speaking a language. By the gradual acquisition of habit my conscious mental processes are drawing together my physical, corporeal processes. I am, in a very important sense, thinking and being intentional and teleological with my whole body. More to the point, my body is in a kind of tense engagement with my conscious intention. My hands may hurt through constant piano practice, for example. So the mind and the body are entirely one and yet dialectical in the motion towards second nature. Eventually, the two will settle under a newly acquired habit or second nature, a new formal unity or a new *energeia*. The point for Ravaisson is that habit is a mediating category in the sense that it changes voluntary, deliberative movements into involuntary or instinctive movements by tiny, imperceptible degrees. It makes thought to be corporeal and therefore reveals the continuity between the will and nature. For Ravaisson, habitual movements are intelligent or rational, by which he means they are teleological even when they cease to be voluntary. So every human function, descending to the depths of unconsciousness, is characterized by a spontaneous or unreflective intelligence – that is, it is teleological in the sense that the organism's goal is its way of being, and its way of being ecstatically more than itself in the acquisition of new habits. So he writes:

> Ultimately, it is more and more outside the sphere of personality, beyond the central organ of the will - that is to say, *within* the immediate organs of movements – that the inclinations constituting the habit are formed, and the ideas are realized. Such inclinations, such ideas become more and more the form, the way of being, even the very being of these organs.[15]

Crucially, we can note that the habituated nature of the piano player, when thought has been communicated to body via habit in such a way that activity is rational but non-deliberative, is much closer to the divine intellect precisely because *neither deliberates.*

The picture we have, therefore, is habit as present at every level of the continuum between will and nature, between conscious mental intention and the materiality of the body. It renders the whole 'rational' and 'teleological' in a fashion that cannot be reduced to mechanical causes because repetition is continually non-identical and, by tiny imperceptible degrees – *plus en plus, moins en moins* – issues in a second nature that, while

[15] Ibid., 55–7.

new, is in continuity with first nature by the mediation of habit. If habit were really mechanical, there would be no way to account for the fact that habit strengthens and fulfils nature rather than fractures or fragments nature. So the thought here is that, at one level, habit is deliberative and voluntary as one learns the piano, but the exercise of that voluntary deliberation includes the use of habits – muscle contractions, for example – that are not voluntary and are much more fundamentally settled. Habit mediates between these levels and mediates will into nature. What is true of human habituation from conscious intention to the base habits of the body is true of nature as such: intention is present all the way down.

> the final degree of habit meets nature itself. Hence nature is, as this final degree, merely the immediation of the end and the principle, of the reality and ideality of movement, or of change in general, in the spontaneity of desire.[16]

That final comment concerning 'the spontaneity of desire' is the answer to an important aporia for Ravaisson. To put the question succinctly: From where does the habit of forming habits arise? Ravaisson's answer is that is nature is suffused with a 'spontaneous desire' which is the source of the will – the intrinsic and irreducible habit of desire or *orexis*, which is nature itself.

If habit mediates between will and nature, and transmits rational thought into body through the acquisition of new form and the increasing predominance of the final cause over efficient causes, then nature itself is already animated by a *telos* that is rational – it is suffused with intellect all the way down. This is manifest in and through desire – the desire to be and the desire to be more, for nature continually and ecstatically exceeds itself in the actualisation of its potencies through motion. In the end, Ravaisson sees that this can only be a matter of grace, or the gracing of nature, because the establishment of nature's *telos* is not generated from nature itself, but is received in the act of its creation. So Ravaisson writes:

> Hence habit is not an external necessity of constraint, but a necessity of attraction and desire. It is, indeed, a law, a law of the limbs, which follows on from the freedom of spirit. But this law is a law of grace. It is the final cause that increasingly predominates over efficient causality and which absorbs the latter into itself. And at that point, indeed, the end and the principle, the fact and the law, are fused together within necessity.[17]

[16] Ibid., 61. [17] Ibid., 57.

9.3 Conclusion

The question of teleology is central to the debate concerning the relation of the natural sciences, metaphysics, and theology. It also makes evident some of the problems – one might almost say 'crises' – that confront the natural sciences today, not least the apparently irreducible nature of teleological explanations in certain fields (try explaining the immune system non-teleologically, for example), the problem of how one conceives a *uni*verse without a notion of cosmic teleological order, and the problem of unified intentional consciousness. There are, however, many teleologies; some are doubtless inimical to a rational and coherent understanding of nature or God. While the so-called scientific revolution of the seventeenth century did not do away with final causes completely, it did do away with some of the mediating and associated concepts which made teleological explanation intelligible, whether in natural philosophy or theology. Amongst those mediating concepts, one might include dynamic substantial form or habit or real natures. That is why philosophers such as Thomas Nagel are right to point to the necessity of admitting teleological explanations in our understanding of nature, particularly if we are to have a proper conception of how the unity of intentional consciousness arises from material nature. Where he might be mistaken is in thinking that such teleological accounts can be purely naturalistic – that is, purely intrinsic – with no account of transcendent intention which providentially binds the whole into a *uni*-verse. For that, we need a blend of intrinsic and extrinsic, of physical, metaphysical, and theological teleology.

CHAPTER 10

The Problem of the Problem of Scientism
On Expanding the Scope of Scientific Inquiry

D. C. Schindler

It has become common today, at least in some circles, to aspire to harmonise the conventionally opposed spheres of science and religion, and even those who do not themselves so aspire generally take this aspiration to be a worthy goal. The reasons for this are not hard to understand. Science is without question both a dominant force in the practical life of the modern world and an authority in the popular understanding that cannot be gainsaid. At the same time, the average person is reluctant to surrender the field of culture altogether to science, and wishes to retain some significance for religious faith, not only because of an anxiety about conceding absolute power and authority to any single human project, even one as impersonal and universally beneficial as science claims to be, but also because of an ineluctable sense that, without religion, the world will ultimately prove to be meaningless, perhaps all the more so the more science has managed humanly to improve it.

But in his recent book, Peter Harrison has raised a cautionary flag regarding this aspiration.[1] In addition to a general argument about the late invention of 'science' and 'religion' and the 'war' between them, which, for example, would have made little sense in the middle ages when science and religion were both internal virtues of the soul rather than delimited bodies of knowledge, he makes a couple of provocative observations that I wish to take as the starting point of my own reflections. First, at the very end of the book, he observes that 'advocates of constructive dialogue' between science and religion are often 'unknowingly complicit in the perpetuation of conflict' (198) insofar as they take for granted the commonly accepted meaning of the terms of the dialogue, which Harrison's study reveals to have been constructed already in conflict and as a result of it. Second, it is because of this literally congenital opposition

[1] Peter Harrison, *The Territories of Science and Religion* (Chicago: University of Chicago Press, 2015). Unattributed references will be to this book.

that, to speak of an 'integration' of these two is necessarily to have in mind something other than modern science (175) – not to mention modern religion, which he does not say here but is clearly implied in the argument of the book.

As a small contribution to the larger discussion, I wish to offer here a theoretical argument (rather than a historical one) in support of these particular observations, which I take to be both true and profoundly important, requiring a thorough reconsideration of the terms of any proposed dialogue between science and religion if such a dialogue is to be potentially fruitful. A common strategy used to advance the contemporary aspiration to 'consonance' is to highlight a distinction between science and scientism. According to the usual view, modern science represents a particular way of knowing the world that is founded on the language of mathematics and the rigorous application of an empirical method. Because of its method, science is restricted to the physical part of the world, and so long as it recognises this restriction (as most serious scientists do), it is perfectly justifiable. 'Scientism', by contrast, occurs when the restriction is forgotten (typically in the popular imagination more than within the practice of science itself), and this part is allowed to stand for the whole. In this case, science tends to discredit any other way of knowing the world. Thus, for example, 'scientism' is defined as 'the view that only science can provide us with knowledge or rational belief, that only science can tell us what exists, and that only science can effectively address our moral and existential questions'.[2] The problem with scientism, so it is claimed, is essentially that it exaggerates the scope and power of science, beyond what we might call its natural sphere: 'science has its boundaries and those boundaries should not be crossed'.[3] This exaggeration is especially pernicious when it encroaches on what have traditionally been regarded as spiritual or theological dimensions of reality – for example, we have neuroscience 'explaining away' consciousness and human free will, the 'scientific' reduction of human love and sexuality to biology, or most notoriously the supplanting of God, the author of life, by a thoroughly materialist mechanism in evolutionary theory. In such examples, science oversteps its proper limits and becomes 'totalitarian'. It is thus

[2] René van Woudenberg, Rik Peels, and Jeroen de Ridder, 'Introduction: Putting Scientism on the Philosophical Agenda', in *Scientism: Prospects and Problems* (Oxford: Oxford University Press, 2018), 1.

[3] Rik Peels, 'A Conceptual Map of Scientism', in *Scientism*, 28.

not an accident that scientism tends to represent the essential theoretical core of what has been called the 'New Atheism'.[4]

Two things would seem evident in light of the current state of affairs just described: first, totalitarian claims for science are incompatible with religious belief, which would at the very least require recognition of spiritual realities outside the domain of science, and, second, the response to the problem of scientism would therefore be to recall the inherent limits of science, and so restore peaceful boundaries between these domains. What I wish to propose, however, is that this strategy represents a significant example of what Harrison described as an attempt at consonance that unwittingly reinforces the problem it means to resolve. As Stephen Gaukroger has shown in his massive (and ongoing) study of the history of the scientific endeavour, there was a tendency from the earliest beginnings in the thirteenth century of what would become 'modern science' for the enquiry into the natural world to present itself not just as 'one cognitive discipline among many' but as 'the key to cognitive inquiry generally', and that that tendency became genuinely totalitarian already in the first properly modern pioneers of science, for example, in Pompanazzi, Telesio, Bruno, and Hobbes.[5] My argument will be that the historical coincidence is not accidental, but expresses something essential in the modern scientific endeavour. The problem is not what the critique of scientism, which seeks to defend genuine science as something else, might initially lead one to think, namely, that science has a constant tendency to puff itself up, for example, simply as a consequence of its obvious successes. Instead, my argument will be that the tendency to transgress its putative limits is a logical implication of the constitutive principles of modern science, and its original explicit self-understanding. If this is true, the attempt to avoid scientism by recalling science to its more original and authentic vocation is bound to fail.

Indeed, I aim to show that there is a deep irony here: what constitutes *modern* science, what specifies this particular phenomenon with respect to the broader tradition of inquiry into the natural world, is precisely a restriction of its scope, which not only turns out to be an artificial one but in fact establishes the inexorable tendency to encroach upon all other dimensions of reality, including the theological. The irony is that insisting

[4] Massimo Pigliucci, 'New Atheism and the Scientistic Turn in the Atheism Movement', *Midwest Studies in Philosophy*, 37, no. 1 (2013), 142–53.

[5] Stephen Gaukroger, *The Emergence of a Scientific Culture: Science and the Shaping of Modernity (1210–1685)* (Oxford: Clarendon Press, 2006), 472.

on restricting the scope of science as a way of enabling a harmony between 'science' and 'religion' actually reinforces a totalitarian logic, or to put the claim most succinctly: the distinction between science and scientism – which is meant to prevent science from making larger claims regarding reality as a whole – is itself the cause of scientism. To draw an analogy to help shed light on this claim, which may at first seem paradoxical to the point of absurdity: on the one hand, it has often been observed that what distinguishes modern politics from the previous tradition is a restriction of the scope of the common good, an isolation of the specifically political dimension from the larger, more comprehensive human good, a restriction that then reduces the state's jurisdiction over human existence to a more trivial aspect (say, justice as fairness), and so liberates other dimensions for a freer pursuit and private cultivation. On the other hand, this reconception of the political order has in reality turned out to lead to the absolutising of the political that has increasingly become a normal part of contemporary existence. The logic of liberalism, which separates church and state in a dualistic fashion and so isolates the political from the theological, is in reality a totalitarian logic, whether or not it intends to be.[6] In this case, one does not solve the problem by insisting more forcefully on the separation of church and state (e.g., in renewed calls for 'religious freedom'). My suggestion is that the logic at the origin of modern science is not only similar to the logic at the origin of modern politics, or more specifically of liberalism, but in fact is *the same logic*, in a different but related sphere. It is not an accident that, in fact, the advocates of the new politics have often been advocates of the new science. Liberalism and modern science belong together because they are founded on a common conception of order.[7]

In order to make the argument, it is first crucial to explain what I have in mind when using the expression 'modern science'. As Harrison and others have shown, the term 'science' was first used in English in the nineteenth century in the sense we typically mean it today; Harrison cites

[6] See, e.g., John Milbank, 'The Gift of Ruling: Secularization and Political Authority', *New Blackfriars*, 85, no. 996 (March 2004), 212–38; Michael Hanby, 'Absolute Pluralism: How the Dictatorship of Relativism Dictates', *Communio* (Summer–Fall 2013), 592–76; D. C. Schindler, 'Liberalism, Religious Freedom, and the Common Good: The Totalitarian Logic of Self-Limitation', *Communio*, 40, nos. 2–3 (Summer–Fall 2013), 577–615; Ryszard Legutko, *The Demon in Democracy: Totalitarian Temptations in Free Societies* (New York: Encounter Books, 2016); and Patrick Deneen, *Why Liberalism Failed* (New Haven, CT: Yale University Press, 2018).

[7] Consider the reflections by Pierre Manent, who claims that the two authorities in the twenty-first century are science and liberty, and these reinforce each other: *Cours familier de philosophie politique* (Paris: Gallimard, 2004), 9–22.

an otherwise unremarkable article from 1867 that offers one of the first explicit attempts to delimit the meaning of a term that was growing fairly common: 'We shall, for convenience' sake, use the word "science" in the sense which Englishmen so commonly give to it; as expressing physical and experimental science, to the exclusion of theological and metaphysical.'[8] The reason the word 'science' came, with some initial resistance, to be sure, eventually to replace the older term 'natural philosophy', according to Harrison, is that 'philosophy' was felt to be 'too lofty' to describe this new approach to the world; as a result of what he calls the 'more restrictive definition of science', Harrison explained that '"philosopher" was no longer an appropriate label [for the modern practitioner], given that theological and metaphysical concerns now lay beyond its disciplinary boundaries' (165). It may have taken until the nineteenth century for the older term to be replaced, but the *reality* that warranted the older term, namely, the genuinely *philosophical* inquiry into nature (which we will characterise further in a moment), had been eclipsed centuries earlier. Though our argument does not intend to be historical in the first place, it is important to look at this eclipse and attempt to formulate the principle at work as profoundly as we can.

It is not uncommon to speak of a 'Scientific Revolution', which occurred essentially in the seventeenth century. Assuming that, with all the due qualifiers required whenever one speaks in general terms about periods in intellectual history, the expression has an intelligible sense, we need to ask, What makes the particular kind of inquiry into the natural world in the seventeenth century *revolutionary*, given the fact that many of the particular insights and attitudes of the early 'modern scientists' can be found in the robust tradition of natural philosophy that preceded them, especially in the late middle ages?[9] I would like to suggest that the essential matter, that which represents the *specific* difference of modern science within the genus of natural philosophy, is *the very fact of its being revolutionary*. I mean this in two senses, a more superficial one and then a more profound one, concerning the substance of the matter. Superficially, I mean that the most obvious representatives of the seventeenth-century turn – we may take Galileo, Descartes, and Bacon as examples, though we

[8] W. G. Ward, 'Science, Prayer, Free Will, and Miracles', *Dublin Review* 8, no. 16 (April 1867), 255–98 (255 n.), cited in Harrison, *Territories*, 145–6.

[9] See, e.g., the classic work by Anneliese Maier, *Die Vorlaüfer Galileis im 14. Jahrhundert*, 2nd ed. rev. (Rome: Edizioni di Storia e Letteratura, 1966), and *Zwischen Philosophie und Mechanik* (Rome: Edizioni di Storia e Letteratura, 1958), but there have since been many historical studies showing lines of continuity.

do not necessarily mean to present them as historically first – understood themselves as precisely *breaking* with the tradition that precedes them,[10] introducing a new kind of standard, namely, a universally accessible method rather than any authoritative figures or inherited forms of understanding. More profoundly, they effectively brought about a new object of inquiry, no longer 'nature' in the robust sense of the previous tradition, but now what we might call the formal laws of the behaviour of natural things or the body of 'data' produced through experimental methods.[11] Nature is something *given*; traditional ways of understanding are something *given*. The new science is revolutionary in the sense that it represents a fundamental refusal of what is given *qua* given, whether this refusal be explicit and polemical or implicit and irenic. When I use the expression 'modern science' in the present context, I mean the word 'modern' not principally to designate a distinct time period but instead to indicate a particular way of thinking that defines itself as cutting itself off from its roots in the tradition, and by implications its roots in the world, and beginning to think about the things in the world as it were *de novo*, according to its own lights.

This point requires some deepening. As we saw above, modern science demarcates its particular sphere by excluding the 'theological and metaphysical'. What does this have to do with the eclipse of nature just mentioned? I would like to suggest that there is an essential connection between the exclusion of metaphysics and the impoverishment of nature, an impoverishment so complete we can speak of the elimination of nature as an operative principle for the understanding. This connection is even more crucial than the theological one, at least on one level, because the new science was in fact cooperative with all sorts of religious projects at first, as has often been pointed out,[12] though we will have to come back to

10 Something similar could be said about virtually any of the figures one might take as precursors to these three: for example, Bernardino Telesio can be characterized as having 'abandoned the Aristotelian path' and developing his own language and concepts: Martin Muslow, *Frühneuzeitliche Selbsterhaltung: Telesio und die Naturphilosophie der Renaissance* (Tübingen: Max Niemeyer Verlag, 1998), 4, and Bruno 'cut natural philosophy loose from all its traditional bearings', Gaukroger, *Emergence*, 115.

11 This is not to say, of course, that all of the founders of modern science shared the same methodology; indeed, there are fundamental differences between the methods adopted by Galileo, Descartes, and Bacon. But I will argue that they all nevertheless share a certain 'bracketing out' of the traditional concept of nature as a distinguishing feature of whatever method they promote.

12 Peter Harrison has brought to light in great detail the religious themes that dominated early scientific thought: see his *The Bible, Protestantism, and the Rise of Natural Science* (Cambridge: Cambridge University Press, 2001), and *The Fall of Man and the Foundations of Science*

this point below. But if the early scientific thinkers affirmed certain theological ideas, they rejected from the outset what we might call a metaphysical interpretation of nature. There is a certain paradox in this phrase: Doesn't 'metaphysical' mean that which lies on the *other side* (*meta*) of nature (*physis*), as it were, and so that which would lie strictly outside an inquiry into nature? But the paradox is intended. In the classical tradition – which reached a certain high-water mark in the high middle ages, though we will explain in a moment why this judgement requires qualification – nature represented the pivotal notion for thought.[13] It was a pivot not only because it was in a certain respect fixed,[14] and not only because it represented the intelligible *whatness* of things, their definable essence, but most basically because it designated the mysterious inner depth of the beings that constitute the world. The *nature* of a living thing is its *soul.* Non-living things may not have a soul, but they still possess the inner depth that is analogous to a soul to the precise degree that they are natural. Only artifacts lack such depth *qua* artifacts, though this does not preclude their having a different sort of depth.[15]

The study of nature from this perspective is properly understood to be philosophy because it proves to be essentially metaphysical and inevitably also theological.[16] Nature has an essentially *analogical*

(Cambridge: Cambridge University Press, 2007). Cf. Pietro Redondi, 'From Galileo to Augustine', in Peter Machamer (ed.), *The Cambridge Companion to Galileo* (Cambridge: Cambridge University Press, 1998), 175–210, and Stephen Gaukroger, *Francis Bacon and the Transformation of Early-Modern Philosophy* (Cambridge: Cambridge University Press, 2001), 74–83.

13 See Marie-Dominique Chenu, *Nature, Man, and Society in the Twelfth Century* (Toronto: University of Toronto Press, 1997).

14 According to Aquinas, 'Whatever characteristic a being has by nature and in an unchangeable way has to be the foundation and principle for everything else', *ST* 1.82.1.

15 By virtue of their being constituted of natural things, art objects have a certain substantial depth as it were 'by nature' (see the profound reflections on this point in Martin Heidegger, 'The Origin of the Work of Art', in *Basic Writings* [New York: Harper, 2008], 139–212). The Aristotelian principle that 'art imitates nature', moreover, implies an analogical extension of nature (and note that Aristotle makes art and nature reciprocally dependent: *Physics* II, 8, 194a, 199a). For general reflections along these lines, see Robert Spaemann, 'What Does It Mean to Say That "Art Imitates Nature"?', in *A Robert Spaemann Reader: Philosophical Essays on Nature, God, and the Human Person* (Oxford: Oxford University Press, 2015), 192–210. The priority of nature, however, does not at all exclude the possibility of the artist exceeding 'merely' natural form, as has always been recognized, not only by Aristotle but also by the Neoplatonic tradition more broadly (see, e.g., the clear statement in Plotinus, *Ennead* V.8.1), going back to Plato's insight into the divine origin of forms.

16 To be precise, the theological dimension cannot be said to be essential in the sense of being logically implicated or, so to speak, 'built into' the structure of things as created. In fact, even the metaphysical dimension, insofar as it is illuminated by being, *esse*, as 'super-essential' and therefore in that particular respect 'super-natural', is not simply governed by the principle of nature. On this, see Ferdinand Ulrich, 'Das Problem einer "Metaphysik in der Wiederholung",' *Salzburger Jahrbuch für Philosophie* 5–6 (1961–2), 263–98, here 293–4.

sense.[17] One can speak of the nature of stones, but also the nature of medicine, or the nature of angels. 'Nature' is not one fixed sphere marked off 'spatially', as it were, from others, but is the inner essence of whatever it is one wishes to think about. It is also analogical in the sense of being inwardly self-transcending. One's access to the natural world is through the senses, but these represent what we might call points of entry into nature, through which the mind travels in its desire to know. The study of nature is not the study of the totality of the sense world, the phenomena, as it is for Kant and indeed for the tradition of British empiricism. Instead, it is the study of natural *things*, the beings that have a nature, which manifest themselves in their accidents and thus to the human senses (which in fact have a certain normative role in natural philosophy[18]), but which never show their nature as such for the simple reason that substance cannot be an accident. Contrary to Heidegger's judgement, Heraclitus' saying was relevant not just for the early Greek thinkers but in some respect all the way up until the moment it was overturned in the 'scientific revolution': nature loves to hide.[19] Nature is thus radically analogical, having a *logos* that points beyond (*anō*) to what transcends it: the accidents of a thing point beyond to the substance, the substance itself is not an isolated thing, but a revelation of the meaning of being, and being is a manifestation of God. To study the nature of things is ultimately to contemplate them inside these 'nested' relations and so precisely as creatures.[20] The study of all of this belongs in *some* sense to natural

[17] An outstanding account of the pre-modern sense of nature as analogical, and the elimination of precisely this character in modern thought, can be found in Spaemann, 'Nature', in *A Spaemann Reader*, 22–36.

[18] See Aquinas, *Commentary on Aristotle's Physics*, I.1, in which he explains that natural philosophy is unique in studying all four causes (including the material cause), aiming as it does at the nature of things as matter–form composites. As he explains in the *Summa*, the senses are a necessary part of human knowing, ordered as it is to the 'quiddities of material things'. This would be paradigmatically the case in natural philosophy: see ST 1.84.7 and 1.85.1.

[19] Amos Funkenstein appears to have intended to argue (in a book left unfinished by his untimely death) that an overcoming of the 'esoteric' aspect of knowledge was an essential part of the Greek, Jewish, and Christian traditions (though he also implies that the 'exposure' of knowledge became systematic in early modern thought). See the published part of this work: 'The Disenchantment of Knowledge: The Emergence of the Ideal of Open Knowledge in Ancient Israel and in Classical Greece', *Aleph: Historical Studies in Science and Judaism* 3 (2003), 15–81. A qualifier is nevertheless in order: while it is true that these classical traditions sought to 'open' the mystery, this does not mean it ceases to be a mystery, but only that the invitations *into* the mystery are, so to speak, sent out to a broader audience. Goethe speaks beautifully along these lines of the 'holy open mystery'. According to Aquinas, 'Our knowledge is so weak that no philosopher will ever be able to investigate perfectly the nature of a single fly' (*In.symb.apost.*, 1).

[20] This is why the study was inherently moral: it is not possible to understand natures without an inward consent to the goodness inherent in them (inseparable from their truth and beauty) and

philosophy, no matter how transcendent. Even God has a nature! Even God enters into the field of interest of natural philosophy, and this implies no danger of reductionism insofar as the *analogical* character of nature is retained. The nature of God is infinitely different from the nature of a stone, and thus analogy opens the space for radically different sciences, kinds of thinking, with radically different sorts of principles, and so forth.[21] The proper object of study of natural philosophy is therefore the 'physical' world, the beings that make up the material world, but this does not exclude the analogous extension of nature beyond that world and beyond the world simply.[22] Natural philosophy recognises things in their natural habitat, so to speak, and that habitat is necessarily also spiritual, metaphysical, and theological.

Now, it must be said that the picture just painted represents a kind of simple ideal. The argument is about principles here, and is not meant to be only historical. In other words, the claim is *not* that everyone prior to the seventeenth century conceived things in the way just described, and everyone after did not. In fact, there are good grounds for the suggestion that the possibilities of natural philosophy opened up in principle by a robust Christian metaphysics of creation were never fully tapped in the middle ages, which tended to bind itself too narrowly to a non-traditional Aristotle,[23] so that the impetus for the rise of modern science may be said to have been stimulated by inadequacies on this score.[24] Nevertheless, the 'modernity' in modern science is the eclipse of nature as what sets the horizon of inquiry into the natural world, and, in so doing, the elimination of the analogical character that is *intrinsic* to nature, and so available only to thought that anchors itself, as it were, in nature. By giving a *content* to

originating in their Creator. This is why the transformation of the meaning of natural philosophy required a transformation in the meaning of its *usefulness*, away from the intrinsic transformation of the knowers: see Harrison, *Territories*, 117–44, and Gaukroger, *Emergence*, 472.

21 As we will see below, this does not make everything a branch of natural philosophy, even if natural philosophy is a study in principle *of everything*.

22 We will not enter into the classic distinction that Aristotle drew between physics, mathematics, and first philosophy, and the connection between all this and 'ens mobile'.

23 I say 'non-traditional' deliberately polemically. The notion that Aristotle's substantial thought was 'introduced' into the West through its intellectual encounter with Islam overlooks the fact that Aristotle had already been taken up into the Neoplatonic tradition, which means that the 'introduction' was actually a sort of newly explicit and to be sure fuller *re*introduction of Aristotelian notions, now, so to speak, from the outside.

24 For an account of the way a doctrine of creation opens up a radical principle of *novelty* in the created order, and so for the science of that order, beyond the Greek notion of substance (and indeed beyond the sense of nature that tended to govern thought in the pre-modern world), see Michael Hanby, *No God, No Science? Theology, Cosmology, Biology* (Oxford: Wiley-Blackwell, 2013), esp. 334–74.

the term 'modern', I mean to free it from an exclusively chronological sense (though of course this is not to make the time period simply a matter of irrelevance). Thus, not all thinking after the seventeenth century is modern in the sense of bracketing out the intrinsic sense of nature, but some instances of it are more fully modern than others, and one can raise the question of whether some of the subcurrents in the seventeenth, eighteenth, and nineteenth centuries, and some of the radical developments in the twentieth century (Einsteinian relativity or quantum mechanics, or the turn to systems biology, or to emergent properties in the various realms of evolutionary science, and so forth), are properly modern or represent an overcoming of certain modern assumptions. The key question in this regard, I would argue, is not the question, for example, of the dominance of a certain crass mechanism, which in *some* respect at least was fairly quickly surpassed,[25] but the question of whether nature, understood as the inner essence of things, their inherently analogical depth and intelligible whatness, represents the proper object of study, setting the horizon for the inquiry, or not. It is perfectly possible to overcome mechanism and yet fail to grasp the absoluteness of nature. However that may be, the point is that the proper alternative to the 'modern', from the perspective being proposed here, is not the 'pre-modern', which would take 'modern' to be principally a chronological epithet, but the 'extra-modern'. This latter term is especially appropriate because it recalls that which lies outside ('extra') the limits that modern thought artificially sets for itself, as we will explain below, and thus puts modern science in principle and whatever it may in fact discover, in its proper place, reintegrating it into a more ample whole, thus saving it from itself, so to speak.[26]

Before continuing it is worthwhile here to consider, from the perspective of the question we are raising, the taxonomy that John Milbank sets out in his contribution to the present volume. With an impressive breadth of vision, complexifying and problematising typical genealogies that draw a far too simplistic picture of the emergence of what came to be called science in the modern era, especially in the light of its continued development up until the present, Milbank argues that modern science is not just 'one thing', but can more adequately be understood as three

[25] See part IV, in particular, of Stephen Gaukroger, *The Collapse of Mechanism and the Rise of Sensibility* (Oxford: Clarendon Press, 2010), 293–383.

[26] Robert Spaemann helpfully presents the project of engaging with modernity as that of interpreting it *against* its own principles: 'The End of Modernity?', in *A Robert Spaemann Reader*, 211–29. Kenneth Schmitz shows how much of what is called 'postmodern' is simply a further extension of modern assumptions: 'Postmodern or Modern-Plus?', *Communio* (Summer 1990), 152–66.

(and eventually four) profoundly different and divergent streams, some more problematic, some decidedly less so, when assessed from the vantage of a more adequate theological vision of reality: there are enchanted and disenchanted sorts of monotheism, and then there are enchanted and disenchanted versions of immanentism. As Milbank makes clear, the question of whether one affirms or denies a God is not the most interesting one to consider in this regard, insofar as God can be conceived in either a full or an impoverished, reductive way. The most interesting question, the really decisive one, is whether one's approach to the world is enchanted or disenchanted: Is there some recognition of *magic* or not?

We will set aside here a more thorough discussion of Milbank's account of magic and the grounds he provides for distinguishing the black variety from the white. The suggestion I wish to make here in response to this proposed taxonomy is that the difference between the enchanted and the disenchanted cannot in any event be the most fundamental one, but this distinction is unintelligible at best and fundamentally destructive, not to say violent, at worst if it is not located within the more fundamental question of nature, such as we have sketched it above. Intelligibility is at issue because natural philosophy is after all a philosophy *of nature*; nature lies at the *centre* of this particular kind of thinking, as its organising principle. If this is true, the fundamental question must be whether the notion of nature that inevitably (and whether or not it is acknowledged as such) organises the thinking is an adequate one, whether a particular form of inquiry recognises and seeks to do justice to, the *nature* of things. The question of enchantment or even of God is a *secondary* question, which ought to arise indirectly as an organic implication of the central concern, which is bringing to light the intrinsic meaning of nature.[27] To make central what is essentially eccentric, namely, magic, even if this is taken in its so-called natural form, is disordered in the strict sense, and would tend to lead one to think, for example, that vitalism is a healthy corrective to mechanism, when in fact the two are flip sides of the very same coin.[28]

[27] The two questions, of enchantment and of God, are not secondary in the same way, of course, and it is crucial to see the radical difference: God is 'more interior to things than they are to themselves', we might say following Augustine, which means that in some sense the 'God question' opens up *in fact* at the center, or more precisely, at the center of the center, even if indirectly (which is why there is a radical difference between physics and theology, since theology is set on God precisely as its formal object), while magic presupposes the givenness of nature, and so remains marginal.

[28] See my critique of the origination of *Naturphilosophie* in Schelling, with his evocation of Bruno and the Neoplatonic theme of the world soul (now in a non-traditional and essentially non-analogical context): *The Perfection of Freedom: Schiller, Schelling, and Hegel between the Ancients and the Moderns* (Eugene, OR: Cascade Books, 2012), 111–237, esp. 226–37.

Indeed, *en*-chantment, and even more obviously the privative *dis*-enchantment, presupposes the givenness of the nature *into* which the magic, the unpredictable presence of higher powers and so forth, enters (or *from* which it is removed).[29] More profoundly, if we de-centre what we might call a properly substantial view of nature, as internal essence, we surrender any capacity to identify violence as such. (On this score, as we will see in a moment, it has perhaps not been sufficiently pondered how significant it is that it is precisely the type of motion which the older physics had identified as violent, namely, projectile motion, i.e., the motion that controverts a thing's natural tendency, that came to take a central and defining place in the new physics.[30]) Without such a reference point for thought, it seems we have nothing left to distinguish exploitative technology from genuine creativity apart from what is inevitably the 'merely' aesthetic category of what is 'fitting', which thus reduces to nothing more than the 'collective judgement' of a given culture.[31]

[29] This does not mean they are 'merely' subsequent; radicalizing relation does not imply the dissolution of substance and its essential priority, as Milbank seems to suggest when he writes that 'if the most decisive conclusions of modern physics suggest that *relation is as fundamental as substance* and process as a self-consistent fixity, then only the primacy of time, as Augustine saw, *guarantees the ultimacy of relation and movement*' ('The Gift of Ruling', section 34, italics added). Note how the stipulated 'equiprimordiality' of substance and relation immediately comes to mean the 'ultimacy of relation and movement'. Milbank misses the point that equiprimordiality means that each is in some sense subordinate to the other, without the reciprocity being merely symmetrical. According to what I am calling the 'extra-modern' perspective, substance has an absolute priority in the order of nature (which does not exclude the relative priority of relation). Similarly, Milbank says that for Aquinas 'there is nothing beyond motion and development within the traceable, finite world' (section 28). This is a significantly deficient interpretation of Aquinas (and indeed of the whole Neoplatonic tradition): nature is a principle of motion *and* rest; in some sense, *everything without exception*, even that which is apparently merely material, is 'beyond motion and development'.

[30] This is not to say that projectile motion must necessarily be interpreted as violent: here we see an important and potentially fruitful way of recognizing the limits of Aristotle with respect to the Christian vision, but without simply reversing or bracketing out as irrelevant his understanding of nature: being, as *esse*, transcends essence, but this does not imply the relativizing of essence, as Ferdinand Ulrich has definitively shown: *Homo Abyssus: The Drama of the Question of Being* (Washington, DC: Humanum Academic Press, 2018). As Ulrich also shows in this book, there is a basic reciprocity between the human soul and *esse*, which is in some sense constitutive of things, even in their substantial natures. This principle could be explored as a metaphysical grounding for the inseparability of mind and matter uncovered in quantum mechanics.

[31] See Milbank, 'The Gift of Ruling', section 39. Another criterion that Milbank introduces, which we do not mention here but which seems to be the most fundamental for him, is whether one makes natural magic a matter of attempted control (reducing it to what is identically repeatable) or instead approaches it through given rites and allows oneself to be surprised by the (always non-identical) outcome. While there is certainly a profoundly important point here, it must nevertheless be asked whether it is adequate to make the essentially subjective distinction between desire for control or grateful receptivity the ultimate one without seeking a more substantial basis for this distinction. The question of the givenness of nature simply cannot be avoided. Would Milbank have any

Let us return at this point to our basic thesis, which we are now in a position to articulate more fully. Natural philosophy is an inquiry into the inherent meaning of nature, which opens up, analogously and of itself, into a sense of the inter-relatedness of all things in the cosmos (not only the material world, though that one first, but eventually also the spiritual world), and ultimately of the Creator God – and as a result of this intrinsic analogy can receive in turn illumination from God's self-revelation in history, which is simultaneously and inseparably deed and doctrine, and the creative forms of human culture. Science in its modern form is simultaneously a displacement of the centrality of nature and an isolation of a (putatively more primitive) sphere of inquiry from the higher one. This is in its basic shape just what the critics of 'scientism' demand: namely, that science limit itself and not pretend to make grand philosophical or theological claims about the nature of reality simply. The implications of this move require closer examination.

We cannot enter into the historical detail, but it is illuminating to point out some relevant observations that others have made. According to Amos Funkenstein, 'From the Renaissance onwards, philosophers of nature advanced a new notion of a homogeneous, uniform nature, governed everywhere by the same forces and the same laws: Aristotle's hierarchy of "natures" became truly one nature.'[32] As Simon Oliver has shown, the ground for this development was prepared first by the *isolation* of physics from metaphysics and theology, which takes place in a decisive way in Avicenna, but then enters into the Western tradition.[33] This isolation, and the undermining of analogy it implies, is taken for granted in the thought forms that eventually led to the origin of nominalism in the fourteenth century, which is commonly recognised as providing the horizon, the basic intellectual landscape, within which modern science arises.[34] The founding fathers of modern science did not so much add anything to the

reason, for example, to object to something like the 'transformation of ourselves' through the manipulation of the human genome, as long as one performed such manipulation simply for the sake of mere curiosity, to see what happens, rather than, say, out of business interests, and as long as the surrounding culture generally deemed it 'fitting'? There must in the end be something more to guide the activities of science than, for example, Feyerabend's methodological anarchy.

32 Funkenstein, 'The Disenchantment of Knowledge', 19.

33 Simon Oliver, *Philosophy, God and Motion* (London: Routledge, 2005), especially the succinct conclusion, 138–55.

34 On the connection between Islamic thought and the rise of nominalism in Christian theology, see W. J. Courtenay, 'Necessity and Freedom in Anselm's Conception of God', in *Analecta anselmiana* 4.2 (Frankfurt: Minerva, 1975), 39–64, and 'The Critique on Natural Causality in the Mutakallimun and Nominalism', *The Harvard Theological Review*, 66 (1973), 77–94. On the connection between nominalism and the rise of modern science, see Funkenstein's chapter

inherited practice of natural philosophy, as they did take some basic things away. In other words, the creation of the scientific method occurred through what turned out to be a radical restriction of its scope. In different ways, both Francis Bacon and Galileo Galilei (to take two of the most obvious representatives) inaugurated a new way of thinking about the physical world precisely by bracketing out aspects that had previously been assumed to be *part* of natural things. Galileo, for example, confessed an incapacity to pronounce on *what* gravity is, and proposed that we would accomplish more by setting aside the ultimately occult interest in resolving this question.[35] Instead of diverting energy to a task has that has proven recalcitrant, we ought to content ourselves simply with measuring the effects of gravity, and attempt to formulate the laws governing motion. What is at issue here is nothing more than a shifting of attention to a reduced sphere, which is thus easier to manage. Bacon is well known for having dismissed the quest for final causes as fruitless,[36] but of course he, like Galileo, also displaced the object of the scholastic pursuit of formal causes from the intrinsic essence of a thing to the laws that govern its behaviour.[37] The clearest evidence that attention has shifted from the

'Divine Omnipotence and the Laws of Nature', in *Theology and the Scientific Imagination* (Princeton, NJ: Princeton University Press, 1986), 117–201; Etienne Gilson, *Christian Philosophy in the Middle Ages* (London: Sheed and Ward, 1955), 489–99; M. A. Gillespie, *The Theological Origins of Modernity* (Chicago: University of Chicago Press, 2008), 19–43; and Hanby, *No God*, 107–49.

35 See Galileo, *Dialogue Concerning the Two Chief World Systems*, 2nd ed. (Berkeley: University of California Press, 1967), 101, cited in Redondi, 'From Galileo to Augustine', 185. Cf. E. A. Burtt, *The Metaphysical Foundations of Modern Science* [1925] (New York: Anchor Books, 1954), 93. To be sure, William A. Wallace has shown that we can find all of the traditional language regarding causality in Galileo (including the distinction, crucial for our present argument, between intrinsic and extrinsic causes): 'The Problem of Causality in Galileo's Science', *The Review of Metaphysics*, 36 (1983), 607–32, but as many others have argued, Galileo often sought to clothe his new insights in the accepted language as far as possible. Wallace, too, accepts that Galileo proceeds in a radically new way. Contrary to the attempt of some to 'connect' Galileo with a Neoplatonic metaphysics, prior to the Aristotelian tradition (and thus to present Galileo as 'more traditional' than the scholastic natural philosophers), Edward W. Strong has shown that any similarity to Platonism or Pythagoreanism in Galileo is quite superficial; Galileo is much more adequately understood as eschewing metaphysics altogether and establishing 'natural philosophy' on independent grounds: 'The Relationship between Metaphysics and Scientific Method in Galileo's Work', in E. McMullin (ed.), *Galileo: Man of Science* (New York: Basic Books, 1967), 352–64.

36 'For the inquisition of Final Causes is barren, and like a virgin consecrated to God, produces nothing', from 'The Advancement of Learning', book III ch. 5, in *The Works of Francis Bacon*, vol. 4, ed. J. Spedding et al. (Cambridge: Cambridge University Press, 2011).

37 See Bacon's *Novum organum*, book II, aphorism 2. Note that Bacon affirms there the existence of the traditional four causes, and simply leaves some of them aside for the purposes of a more precise and controlled investigation. It is worth pointing out that there is a certain parallel between this bracketing out of what may be called the 'internal' causes of form and finality, in order to focus on the more measurable, 'external' causes of efficiency and matter, and the shift Harrison narrates that

nature intrinsic to things to something along the lines of calculating the interaction of forces can be seen in the already-mentioned fact that the distinction between natural motion and violent motion gets set aside (since natural motion requires knowledge of the particular nature of the thing moving) and violent motion becomes *the* focus of what is now 'science'.[38]

All of this is just a repetition of things relatively well known. The point I wish to make is that this bracketing out is not (or at least does not immediately pretend to be) a rejection of intrinsic formal or final causes simply. Instead, it is simply a suspension of judgement in their regard. It is not a positive claim that there is no such thing as an essence or intrinsic purpose, but a negative claim, or perhaps even more adequately put, a confession of incompetence about one's ability to achieve any definitive insight into the matter. It leaves untouched the reality itself, and leaves open in principle the possibility of affirming or denying formal and final causes as one might wish, after the more basic analysis has been completed, as an additional reflection. It becomes quite possible, thus, to bring God in, most often at the beginning and end (*principium et finis mundi*) but also when necessary at decisive points along the way (*deus interveniens*), and in any event as an indispensable part of the overall picture of the world. Note, again, that the confession of incompetence is not a universal proclamation, namely, that no one can ever know the essence of things, or know anything about the meaning of reality generally, or about the divine plan for history, and so forth. It is, rather, a more restricted claim regarding the particular task of (what will come to be called) science, a claim that still allows the nobler and more divine disciplines to occupy themselves with such mysteries. A kind of *modesty* lies at the very heart of this new way of approaching the things in the world.[39] I will return to this at the end, but

takes place in the meaning of science and religion, from the interior (virtue of the soul) to the exterior (sets of explicit propositions or a recognized body of knowledge). This parallel reveals that the shift concerns the nature of things more generally (and not just the human practices of science and religion). The move away from teleology seems to begin early in the middle ages. As Kristell Trego has shown, it begins already in Anselm: Kristell Trego, *L'essence de la liberté: La refondation de l'ethique dans l'oeuvre de saint Anselme de Canturbéry* (Paris: Vrin, 2010).

38 Bacon, for example, 'criticises Aristotle's account of the distinction between natural motions . . . and violent motions, not on the grounds that the distinction is mistaken, but on the grounds that Aristotle's concern is with the explanation of natural motions and states rather than violent ones. Bacon's point is that it is 'violent', and not natural, motions which are the ones of interest: They are 'the life and soul of artillery, engines, and the whole enterprise of mechanics'", Gaukroger, *Francis Bacon*, 136–7.

39 Consider Galileo's observation (variations on which can be found in many of the thinkers in early modernity): 'Practical considerations of this sort belong to a higher science than ours. We must be satisfied to belong to that class of less worthy workmen who procure from the quarry the marble out

this gesture of modesty is so common among the founding figures of modernity – not only in the field of what came to be known as science, but also and perhaps most evidently in political theory (a confession of incompetence regarding the integral common good), as well as in epistemology and metaphysics, and later in economics – that I think we would be justified in identifying it as the very essence of modernity.

So, what could be wrong with modesty? One might initially think that modesty is a precondition for harmony, since it keeps the partners in a relationship in their proper place, preventing any one partner from claiming too much for itself. It is just this modesty to which the distinction between science and scientism appeals as the principle of harmony. But modesty, as a virtue in the classical sense, is not principally a negative movement of separation but *first* a positive movement of the soul, which opens itself to what is greater; it is the internalising of a comprehensive order.[40] This gesture of modernity is not a virtue; it turns out to be the exact opposite of virtue, what I have called elsewhere a 'diabolical' substitute for the reality.[41] To see how this is so, let us consider what is involved in the self-limitation that constitutes modesty thus conceived. In general terms, we may point out that *actual* limitation is necessarily something received; it is a measure first given to the self 'from above' ('modesty' in fact comes from the word meaning 'measure'[42]): a limitation *of the self* in the sense of an objective genitive. It must be so. If the limitation is something the self does not receive from what lies outside the self, but something it *gives to itself* (limitation *of the self* in the sense of a subjective genitive: a self-ruling, 'autonomy'), it ceases to be conformity to a greater or more comprehensive order, because the boundary is now something imposed from below rather than being essentially responsive to what is actually given. This is a simple point, but it is hard to overstate its importance. Hegel rightly observed that one can neither establish a

of which, later, the gifted sculptor produces those masterpieces which lay hidden in the rough and shapeless exterior', cited in Burtt, Metaphysical Foundations, 94–5.

40 This point is evident in ancient philosophy, but often goes unremarked on in modern accounts even of ancient virtue ethics. It is worth observing, in this context, that Aristotle wrote his *Nicomachean Ethics* and his *Politics* as two parts of a single whole, and Plato developed his virtue theory only by toggling back and forth between the city and the soul (which we see in his *Republic*). One cannot order a part in itself unless that part at the same time participates properly in the order of the whole.

41 See part 2 of my *Freedom from Reality: The Diabolical Character of Modern Liberty* (Notre Dame, IN: University of Notre Dame Press, 2017), 151–275.

42 'Modestus' comes from 'modus', meaning 'measure'. The Greek equivalent, σωφροσύνη, comes from σως, 'safe' or 'whole', and φρήν, 'mind', bringing out even more clearly the 'holism' of the virtue.

boundary properly nor in fact even duly recognise it unless one is already in some important respect beyond that boundary.[43] To receive a limit is both to be beyond that limit insofar as one is acknowledging a responsibility and therefore a relation to what transcends one and to remain within the limit insofar as one responds to what lies beyond one by taking one's proper place and so positively fulfilling the role it implies. By contrast, to limit *oneself*, and thus to cut oneself off from the larger whole, is to usurp the authority of anything beyond where one – in an inevitably arbitrary way – has set the limit. It is thus a presumptuous self-imposition of its very logic, entirely irrespective of any subjective intentions.

The transcendence of the limit, which is part of any limit, in this case takes the form of the a priori and thus *principled* transgression of any possible order. The self-limited becomes the self-enclosed, or to use the language developed by William Desmond, it becomes an opaque quantity that lacks all porosity to its other, whatever that might happen to be. Such a self-limited part necessarily and incorrigibly imposes itself, and refuses integration by its very internal structure. One may not say that the part, here, substitutes itself for the whole, because in fact it cannot recognise anything like a whole, whether that be itself or any other, insofar as wholeness just is a mutual inherence of parts in relation to a principle that transcends them all and is presupposed as an intrinsic actuality to the parts' potentiality. Self-limitation in the modern sense simply eliminates all wholes. Rather than *responding* in an open and ready way to the whole greater than itself, it is logically *irresponsible*. Self-limitation is self-absolutisation, because it is an a priori 'cutting out' of the significance of whatever lies outside the self.

Consider the kind of authority it cannot but assume. Such a self-absolutised part does not consider, thoughtfully and confidently,[44] and then either accept or reject, whatever the other might present to it; this would be a genuinely royal sovereignty, which has a certain oversight over the whole, including those areas that lie beyond its own 'expertise'. Instead, self-enclosed self-limitation simply cannot hear anything other. It is a pusillanimous and ignorant bourgeois who suddenly finds himself president with a technological device for communicating every unprocessed thought immediately and indiscriminately to the whole world,

[43] Hegel, *Encyclopedia* (1830), §60, in *The Logic of Hegel*, tr. William Wallace (Oxford: Clarendon, 1874), pp. 97–102.

[44] See William Desmond's use of these terms in 'The Confidence of Thought: Between Belief and Metaphysics', in *The Intimate Strangeness of Being* (Washington, DC: CUA Press, 2012), 202–30.

and a big nuclear button at his fingertips. Is it an accident that Kant's self-limitation of reason to make room for faith made him essentially deaf to revelation,[45] that Descartes' radically modest methodology allowed to penetrate into his self-enclosed subjectivity only what measured up to an impossible criterion,[46] that Hobbes' and Locke's reduction of the purpose of political order became the tyranny of the bureaucratic state,[47] that Smith's and Ricardo's abstraction of a quantifiable dimension of wealth became the subjection of every dimension of human existence to the measure of profit and the transformation of all goods into commodities,[48] and finally that Galileo's and Bacon's retraction of the scope of natural philosophy to the merely empirical and mathematically describable would become the unbridled exploitation of the natural world and the radical redefinition of every single being within it, and indeed everything beyond it too? The problem in all these cases is not a lack of modesty, but the opposite, a pre-emptive modesty that becomes an invincible self-protection. To seek redress by separating even further different areas of competence only locks the disorder more firmly in place.

Let us focus at this point more directly on the self-understanding of science in its specifically *modern* guise, at its origin and more or less still today. We can get at this best by way of contrast with the classical, essentially Aristotelian way of distinguishing natural philosophy from the other sciences (or ways of thinking about the world). According to the classic understanding, all of the sciences concern being, which makes sense both because being is the proper object of the human intellect and because being is the most fundamental possible dimension of reality, the most basic answer to the question 'What is?' (and of course that is why it is the proper object of intelligence[49]). The reason the sciences are not simply the same is that being has an extraordinarily rich multiplicity of aspects even at the purely formal level, which are irreducible to each other even while remaining absolutely one in their foundation.[50] If there is to be a *harmony*, a consonance among the sciences, and so between natural philosophy and theology in their special senses, in the end it can only be because of the

[45] See my discussion of this implication in Kant in *The Catholicity of Reason* (Grand Rapids, MI: Eerdmans, 2013), 39–44.

[46] See Michael Hanby, *Augustine and Modernity* (New York: Routledge, 2003), 134–77.

[47] See Christopher A. Ferrera, *Liberty, the God That Failed* (Tacoma, WA: Angelico Press, 2012).

[48] See John Ruskin, *Unto This Last* (New York: Penguin, 1985), 155–228.

[49] Eric Perl shows the continuity of this theme throughout the Western tradition in *Thinking Being: Introduction to Metaphysics in the Classical Tradition* (Leiden: Brill, 2014).

[50] For a fuller treatment of what is simply indicated here, see Michael Hanby, 'Saving the Appearances: Creation's Gift to the Sciences', *Anthropotes* 26, no. 1 (2010), 65–96.

unity of being or, more adequately put, the analogicity of being (the conspicuous absence of metaphysics in contemporary discussions of the relation between science and religion is quite significant in this regard).

As we can see, what distinguishes natural philosophy from other sciences is, from the classical perspective, not first of all a method, but an object or, more specifically, an irreducibly distinct aspect of an object (since all sciences ultimately share the *same* object[51]): natural philosophy studies being, but it studies being *qua mobile*. There are three implications of this that bear on our immediate discussion, all of which are logically connected. First, the primacy of being in the conception of the object (as distinct from, but of course inseparably connected to, goodness, beauty, truth, and unity) implies a priority of actuality and so concreteness, rather than a priority of possibility or abstraction. Second, the primacy implies for that reason a priority of the contemplative, rather than the practical or productive, and a recognition of these latter as a sort of fruit of the internal perfection of things. And, third, the primacy implies that the approach that is proper and fitting in any given study is first determined by the object of that study. The method, in other words, comes *second*; it is precisely a response to the actual nature of its object, and seeks to conform to it in order to receive it properly, in a way that is adequate to its object. All of this is what it means to receive limitation 'from above', and, note, the limitation is paradoxical here because it represents a particular way of participating in the whole. There is an obvious connection between beginning with what is given, *qua actually given*, and the assumption of nature as a kind of fixed reference point for thought. Natural philosophy does not study some isolated *part* of reality; it is meant to study the nature of things as they open up concretely and analogously to the whole, and therefore to study the whole of reality, without any a priori restriction, materially speaking, from the most basic physical elements to the human soul and all the way up to God, precisely insofar as any of this is related to motion. Is this aspiration to the whole of reality 'scientism'? It should be apparent that this is a meaningless question, and the meaninglessness results from the fact that the distinction between science and scientism does not yet exist. This is why natural philosophy allows itself so naturally to be integrated with the higher sciences, or indeed why it is always already integrated. The study of the physical world in the classical sense is

[51] For a fuller treatment of this theme, see my articles 'The First First Philosophy', *Recherches Philosophiques*, 8 (2018), 101–16, and 'On the Universality of the University: A Response to Jean-Luc Marion', *Communio* (Spring 2013), 77–99.

recognised as a branch of philosophy, the love of wisdom, and thus participates in the desire to know the whole of reality as far as possible. As we have been suggesting, it is just the distinction between science and scientism, the reduction of its aspiration to a more modest scope, that separates modern science from this defining human desire, and thus divides it from the classical – or in any event 'extra-modern' – tradition. It is just this that makes it essentially pragmatic and ordered to the exploitation of possibility of its very nature.

We ought now to consider this distinction in relation to the description of natural philosophy just offered. The restriction of science to the empirical in the positivistic sense, as what can be predicted according to mathematically formulisable laws, is a *self*-limitation rather than a genuine modesty (reception of measure from above); it is the imposition from below of a boundary that divides the relevant from the irrelevant. But what determines relevancy here? It is the boundary itself that determines it. The distinction is not made in response to reality as it gives itself. Instead, it is posited a priori; the method precedes the object in this case, and the method is what determines the object, not only formally but also materially. It is to be noted that the absolutising of method not only characterises the founders of modern science, no matter how different the methods they absolutised and whether they were principally a priori or a posteriori, rationalist or empirical, but also characterises those who prepared the ground for these founders, quite literally making straight their path.[52] To the extent that this is true, the object is now required to conform to the method, rather than the reverse. What we need to see is not simply that bracketing out formal and final causality changes the nature of the object insofar as these causes are intrinsic to that nature, though this is true and indeed crucially important. The primary point I wish to make is more subtle and more basic: the methodological self-limitation does not simply exclude from its field of attention what may indeed turn out to bear on that field, an exclusion that transforms its object only to the degree that these aspects *would* have had some relevance, but are not permitted to have it; more radically, the limitation excludes a priori the very possibility that anything beyond the boundary could have relevance. This is the deep

[52] Ockham is the obvious figure here, but one might also point to the similarly 'revolutionary' transformation in the realm of rhetoric inaugurated by Peter Ramus: Walter Ong, *Ramus: Method and the Decay of Dialogue* (Chicago: University of Chicago Press, 2004). On the significance of method in the 'scientific age', see, e.g., Gaukroger, *Emergence*, 160–95. We ought to see the difference between being formed into a tradition and being taught an abstract technique which can be applied indifferently by anyone in principle.

implication of eliminating in principle a distinction between natural and violent motion. Whether or not the realities outside the limit would have had some relevance if they had been allowed in becomes altogether beside the point. The object is now positively redefined in the absence of these features, and to define is, willy-nilly, to establish an ideal norm. This is how self-limitation necessarily becomes self-absolutisation. The object, as redefined, is now changed into an isolated reality in itself that can be understood for all intents and purposes without any reference to form or finality, a self-contained unity existing in a (projected) space *outside* such things. Considerations of form and finality are now things that may or may not be added later, if that's what one should happen to like, but they do not enter *into* the object of study as such.[53] Again, there will thus be an inherent tendency for science, so conceived, to detach essentially from reality (to become purely instrumentalist), to marginalise the theoretical in a principled way and so to become essentially practical or 'technological' – 'maker's knowledge' – to transform its objects into self-subsisting realities with their own circumscribed intelligibility, and to drive 'big picture' sorts of questions to the realm outside properly public meaning, ultimately to the now necessarily dark corners of human subjectivity.[54] They thus betray an inexorable tendency to reduce to inscrutable matters of the heart and nothing more.

We may take two simple illustrations of what I mean in order to make the point a bit more concrete. Modern physics is defined, more or less, as the study of matter and motion.[55] How is this any different from natural philosophy's self-understanding as the study of *ens mobile*? To put it simply, while modern physics posits matter and motion as self-explicating objects, abstracted from all actual conditions and so formalised to such a pure degree as to render their intelligibility exhaustively translatable into quantity, natural philosophy understands matter and motion as conditions

[53] This ends up transforming the meaning of not only form and finality, but *all* of the causes, insofar as they depend intrinsically upon one another: see my 'Historical Intelligibility: On Creation and Causality', in *The Catholicity of Reason* (Grand Rapids, MI: Eerdmans, 2013), 137–62.

[54] On the one hand, this is already the case with what comes to be called the 'secondary qualities', but eventually it would include all kinds of meaning. See Burtt, Metaphysical Foundations, 231–9: 'The world that people had thought themselves living in – a world rich with color and sound, redolent with fragrance, filled with gladness, love and beauty, speaking everywhere of purposive harmony and creative ideals – was crowded now into minute corners in the brains of scattered organic beings. The really important world outside was a world hard, cold, colorless, silent, and dead' (238–9).

[55] This is an oversimplification, of course. It is interesting to note that physics appears to have increasing difficulty in defining its proper object, and typically proceeds more by appealing simply to a description of the practice of certain methods or a cataloguing of classes of objects.

or qualities or activities *of some real thing* (*ens*) in every case. It is not just that this anchoring of inquiry in real things opens up natural philosophy to deeper levels of reality, though this is true; it implies a radically different sense of what matter and motion are in the first place, as Simon Oliver has definitively demonstrated.[56] In this case, it is not enough to appeal to the science/scientism distinction and say that science is proper and good as a description of the physical world or even more restrictedly certain aspects of the physical world, but goes astray when it claims to do more. It has already reconceived God, the world, and everything else in the reductive way it has defined, and so isolated, matter and motion. While in one context, motion is inherently analogical, in another it is purely formalistically conceived and in fact gets eliminated, as Milbank has observed.

Much could, and needs to be, said about this point, but the limited context requires me to move to the second illustration. It is worth reflecting on how natural (so to speak) it has become for us to think of scientific abstractions such as atoms or quarks or, in another field, genes, as if they were real things. They are not! They are *not* real in the strict sense, but only through an analogous extension of the term 'real', which is to say that whatever reality they may have is due to their inherence in things that *are* real in the strict sense.[57] Michael Polanyi has shown that we in fact always intellectually 'indwell' a whole whenever we consider thematically a part; this whole represents the (tacit) distal pole from which we think toward the proximal pole of direct, explicit attention.[58] In an 'extra-modern' context that acknowledges being as the ultimate resting place of the mind, and at the same time sees the *nature* of a thing as the (always analogously open) place in which things like 'genes' have a place, one can in fact see what they are and what they mean, relative to what is actually real. But the abstraction of the commonly practiced scientific method and forms of experiment requires one willy-nilly and however unwittingly to accord these things an ontological status they do not and cannot have, and so to distort them in a

[56] See Oliver, *Philosophy, God and Motion*, especially the succinct conclusion, 187–90, in which one sees the transformation of the meaning of motion laid out in dramatic fashion.

[57] Wolfgang Smith's distinction between the *physical* and the *corporeal* is illuminating in this regard. See chapters 2 and 3 of *The Wisdom of Ancient Cosmology* (Oakton, VA: Foundation for Traditional Studies, 2003), 37–70. In biology, see, e.g., the recent article by Anne Siebens Peterson, 'Matter in Biology: An Aristotelian Metaphysics for Contemporary Homology', *American Catholic Philosophical Quarterly* 92, no. 2 (Spring 2018), 353–71, which argues for the need to recover the primacy of the *organism* to make sense of biological homology.

[58] See Michael Polanyi, *The Tacit Dimension* (Chicago: University of Chicago Press, 1996), 3–25; 'Faith and Reason', *Journal of Religion* 41 (1961), 237–41; and 'The Unaccountable Element in Science', *Philosophy* 37 (1962), 1–14.

fundamental way. We can see this, however, only if we recollect science as a study of being, that is, of reality, in a certain respect. Otherwise, we methodologically isolate this part as a self-contained reality in itself, and then force the reality to conform to the method: by subjecting things to such extreme conditions that they are radically and quite literally de-natured, we manage to isolate the aspect and make it a thing in itself, believing in doing so that we are getting closer to the secrets of nature. A natural philosopher would recognise such procedures as a paradigm of violence, even if (or especially if) they are carried out dispassionately as a matter of course in the daily work at the lab. To conclude: the very method, regardless of the scientist's state of grace or sincerity of belief, is a rejection of the God who created and redeemed the world. To attempt to conciliate religion and modern science *in this sense* is to reduce the possibility of religion to something that fits within the horizon set precisely by what methodologically excludes the metaphysical and theological. Conversely, to practice science as the study of being *qua mobile* is to open up the world, and therefore oneself as a scientist, to God as the origin and end of all things, regardless of one's explicit religious ideas.[59]

It is worthwhile, in conclusion, to reiterate that the critique of specifically *modern* science presented here, as a study of nature that prescinds from metaphysics and theology and thus ostensibly distinguishes itself from 'scientism', is not meant to be an inevitably sterile nostalgia for the pre-modern world for several reasons. The pre-modern world can hardly be claimed to have exhausted the infinite implications of conceiving natural philosophy as the study of *ens qua mobile*, especially in a Christian context, which radicalises and deepens the significance of motion.[60] This formulation implies that motion itself reveals something irreducibly significant about the meaning of being. It has no doubt been insufficiently recognised that, within a horizon opened up by the insight that God *is love*, and that this God both *created* the natures of the world we live in and *redeemed* them from their fallen condition, the motion that exceeds the limits of nature need not always be interpreted as ipso facto violent, but can also be seen (within conditions that would require careful formulation) as natural analogies of grace. Indeed, the developments that have occurred in the past several centuries in science and technology even

[59] This is not simply because a reflection on motion eventually leads to the concept of an Unmoved Mover, but also because the primacy of *actuality* simultaneously roots the objects of the mind in being and in history, which if studied faithfully will ultimately entail an encounter with what have been called the theologoumena of Christian revelation.

[60] On this point, there is a great deal of light cast by Milbank's essay in this volume.

in our betrayal of nature – *felix culpa*! – can be acknowledged as having opened up radically new insights into things. The point being argued here is that whatever these insights may be, they pose a genuinely radical danger of self-destruction to the extent that they are not themselves redeemed in the specific sense of being recollected, and so reintegrated, around the centre of the concept of nature.

Modern science, just like modern liberalism,[61] came into existence through a rejection of the God who created and redeemed the world; the gesture of exclusion of the 'theological and metaphysical' – what we have come to call the 'scientific method' – is the gesture of its birth, and its genesis constitutes its essence. From the perspective of the 'extra-modern' tradition, insofar as this tradition rests on and grows from the actuality of being, we can see that there is a radical self-deception and self-protection 'built into' the very structure of modern science and liberalism alike, the two modes of theory and praxis by which we most fundamentally interpret ourselves in our relation to the natural world, to each other, and to the God who is the origin and end of it all. Until we recognise the challenge being posed by the 'revolutionary' thinking of the seventeenth century to the integration of the diverse 'spheres' of inquiry and thus the integration of the human soul simply, a challenge that is only sharpened by appeals to the distinction between science and scientism, faith will simply have no meaningful light to cast, no substantial word to say, in what is improperly supposed to be the dialogue between science and religion.

[61] Harrison himself alludes to this 'parallel' in his concluding reflections (*Territories*, 189–90), but I wish to suggest the connection has a central importance, both for our understanding of modern science and for our understanding of liberalism.

PART IV

Before Science and Religion

CHAPTER 11

Lessons in the Distant Mirror of Medieval Physics

Tom McLeish

11.1 Introduction: A Twenty-First-Century Physicist Reads Medieval Science

The commonly accepted historical narrative that 'science and religion' inhabit a context of 'conflict' or 'warfare' is deeply flawed. As Peter Harrison has incisively demonstrated,[1] the meanings of the words themselves have shifted throughout history, and furthermore, alternative theological framings of the past (such as Bacon's theology of Fall and restitution that underpinned experimental science[2]) have demonstrably propelled scientific advances. But in the late modern era, questions surrounding science and theology have been largely confined to the field of apologetics, with various degrees of warmth attributed to different possible constructed relationships between the two categories (or alternative epistemologies). Addressing this problematic entrapment, and freeing the discourse of theology, as it construes the relation between science (in general, and of physics in particular) with religion, is a running theme of this collection of chapters. The assumption that one can delineate categorical relationships is, since Barbour's scheme,[3] almost genetically hardwired into the discourse. The task facing 'after science and theology' must therefore call on the huge imagination required to think into a different paradigm. Such conceptual leaps can be assisted by drawing on radically different viewpoints, removed in culture and time from one's own, yet drawing at depth on a shared theological tradition. I have attempted to outline, for example, how a 'theology of science' might be developed from the biblical Wisdom tradition, and in particular the anguished relational

1 Peter Harrison, *Territories of Science and Religion* (Chicago: University of Chicago Press, 2015).
2 Peter Harrison, *The Fall of Man and the Foundations of Science* (Cambridge: Cambridge University Press, 2007).
3 Ian Barbour, *Religion and Science: Historical and Contemporary Issues* (San Francisco, CA: Harper, 1997).

material in the book of Job,[4] whose detailed contemplation of materiality I have found to resonate with scientists, including myself, at surprising intensity. This ancient text is as far removed in its thought-world from our own times as it is possible to find such writing, but speaks from within a Semitic monotheism of covenant relationship, where sin spoils yet where there are no easy solutions, where vindication can be sought but is not cheaply won, and where a natural world in apparent chaos demands some measure of human understanding. There is distance, but also resonance with our own predicament. The natural wisdom of Job is also a source shared with the medieval thinkers discussed in this chapter. A second viewpoint from an equally fresh perspective takes and transforms an early patristic theology, focussing on the work of Origen.[5] This chapter's task is to examine, and reflect from the position of the science of our own age, the theological framing of high medieval natural philosophy. As in the other two cases, we find advantage in a focus on a major writer of the period, in this case the thirteenth-century English polymath Robert Grosseteste.

Barbara Tuchman wrote an influential book on the upheavals of the European fourteenth century which she titled *A Distant Mirror*.[6] She recognised that the political forces and currents of over half a millennium ago were very different from our own, yet claimed that the continuity of underlying human ambition and intrigue created a relevance to the distant perspective that closer history would deliver with less impact. The notion sums up well the reflective, and critically distant, perspective I suggest that we need on science and religion. In this case, a hard look into the 'distant mirror' of the twelfth and thirteenth centuries, rather than the fourteenth, might provide some much-needed perspective on our current difficulties. More than this – we might well find ingredients there from which to construct a healthy theological narrative support for our engagement with nature. It is surely here that such cultural roots must lie, when the Aristotelian transmission from Muslim Spain into northern Europe galvanised the formulation of new questions of what we might know of an ordered universe and its workings. This period in the history of science is particularly fascinating because it contains the search for questions themselves (this it shares, of course, with the ancient nature poem of *The Lord's Answer* of Job 38–42).

[4] Tom McLeish, *Faith and Wisdom in Science* (Oxford: Oxford University Press, 2014).
[5] See Pui Ip's chapter in this collection.
[6] Barbara W. Tuchman, *A Distant Mirror: The Calamitous 14th Century* (New York: Knopf, 1978).

The first-order questions posed by the great natural philosophers of this period were as concerned with the reasons, the human meaning of 'doing science', as they were with the questions themselves. What does the God-given task of understanding nature achieve? Where does it fit within the vocations of human beings, and with the linear history of a Christian theological narrative? When this level of question is on the table, fundamental issues of teleology are inescapable – in stark contrast to our contemporary intellectual scientific world, in which they are hardly ever raised. The intellectual climate of the period that saw the formation of the secular universities also generated second-order questions which fed equally from theological and biblical sources: What are the fruitful avenues of investigation that might lead to an understanding of nature, and which the more unprofitable? Is there a theological mandate to search for order in the material world, and to reimagine it? What is the role of mathematics describing the world, if any? Might an investigation of nature call on experimental manipulations as well as observation? What constitutes a complete understanding of a phenomenon? These are questions of vital importance to science itself, yet which cannot be answered within scientific methodologies, nor the narrow social framing of science in our own century. The high middle ages remind us that at great turning points in science, we need to go beyond its disciplinary boundaries for resources to reframe its direction of travel[7]. This is timely today when the ever-present need for sources for the scientific imagination is very little talked about, and swamped by a largely instrumentalist and method-based scientific education.

For these reasons, it is after all not such a strange idea to ask what we might learn, or at least what questions we might ask, by visiting the emerging scientific world of Anselm or of Robert Grosseteste and their contemporaries. In this chapter I would like to examine five ways in which this 'scientific distant mirror' can nourish the task to reframe science and religion, or to construct a theology of science, in our own times. These are the following: (1) the disruption of the damaging myth of a 'dark age', (2) a teleological narrative for science, (3) a fresh apprehension of scientific imagination, (4) a Christological and incarnational metaphysics and (5) a scientific theology of time. The first (in the following section) is best dealt with by a close scientific reading of a medieval treatise in natural philosophy, which serves as a helpful introduction to the following

[7] Thomas S. Kuhn, *The Structure of Scientific Revolutions* (Chicago: University of Chicago Press, 1962).

discussions of its metaphysical and theological framing. The chapter concludes with a reflection on some of the theologians' contributions to this volume in the light of the 'Distant Mirror' and this author's experience of scientific practice.

11.2 Undermining a Myth: A Colourful Scientific Reading over Eight Centuries

As has already been noted, a common meta-narrative of the history of science in both public media and (at the least) school education is that nothing remotely resembling science existed before the early modern period (or the late sixteenth century).[8] According to this story, before Galileo and Newton, any philosophy of the natural world was clouded with magic, alchemy, superstition and – worse of all – the dogma of theology. There are other sub-narratives that emerge – that the scientific method is entirely modern, that medieval thinkers' chief goal was in any case to recapitulate the thoughts of the classical philosophers and not to move beyond them, that the medieval church repeatedly suppressed innovative thinking in general, and that 'theology' and 'science' were indistinguishable and mutually polluting in the medieval world of scholasticism.

A direct test of this set of narratives would be to put twenty-first-century scientists into direct contact with the natural philosophy of the thirteenth. While not impossible to imagine through either a physicist unusually conversant in medieval Latin and the Aristotelian and Islamic background to the new movements in science (an early example would be Duhem[9]), or a Latinist and translator uncommonly aware of physical and mathematical ideas (Crombie[10] comes to mind), the contextual and linguistic difficulties that surround the task suggest that an active and intense interdisciplinary team approach is the most likely methodology to succeed. Fortunately, such a collaboration of Latinists, medieval historians, philosophers, theologians, physicists, mathematicians, engineers and psychologists has been working together to this end for the last ten years. The international *Ordered Universe* project[11] has focussed intently on the scientific corpus

[8] Ronald L. Numbers (ed.), *Galileo Goes to Jail and Other Myths about Science and Religion* (Cambridge, MA: Harvard University Press, 2009).

[9] Pierre Duhem, *Le Système du monde. Histoire des doctrines cosmologiques de Platon à Copernic*, vols. VII, VIII (Paris: Hermann et Fils, 1956–8).

[10] A. C. Crombie, *Robert Grosseteste and the Origins of Experimental Science 1100–1700* (Oxford: Oxford University Press, 1953).

[11] Links to project outputs, methodologies and resources are at https://ordered-universe.com.

of opuscula of the English polymath Robert Grosseteste (1173–1253). Master to the early Oxford Franciscans in the 1220s, and Bishop of Lincoln from 1235 until his death, from about 1215 to 1235 this remarkable scholar wrote detailed, imaginative and highly mathematical treatises on sound, light, colour, comets, the spheres, the atmospheric elements and more. We begin the present physicist-author's encounter with medieval science and its theological framing with an example from the *Ordered Universe* collaboration, examined through the project's central methodology of collaborative close reading.

The shortest of Grosseteste's scientific treatises, the *De colore* (*On colour*) is enough on its own to remove credence in such a fiction as a medieval 'dark age'. As the collaboration has reported in depth elsewhere,[12] the *De colore* represents a piece of work that a modern scientist would recognise as being in continuity with, though naturally distant from, questions posed and methods pursued today. Grosseteste does not allegorise or mystify colour; he does not accord any supernatural powers of transformation to it; he writes no explicitly theological material in his treatment at any point. On the contrary, he treats colour as a perceived property of the natural world with an inner structure that may be discerned by those with eyes and mind's sight.

Color est lux incorporata perspicuo – the opening line of the treatise – introduces the conjecture that colour is an emergent property of light and matter.[13] Within the context of his more substantial work on the physics and cosmology of light, the *De luce*, this initial definition identifies colour as a corollary of Grosseteste's more general theory of light. His thesis is that the material extension of all bodies (including the largest body of all – the cosmos itself – as treated in the *De luce*) depends on an active indwelling of continuously self-multiplying (propagating) light within material body. The reasoning here is that infinitesimal and indivisible atoms on their own, in no matter how great a number, cannot give rise to extensive (volumetric) bodies. The atoms must be supplemented by a form able to adopt finite – not infinitesimal – volume. Light is the candidate for this 'first form' (previously advanced by Avicenna), leading Grosseteste to expect visible effects of such indwelling light, beyond mere substantiality. And so it is – he identifies the different colours of objects as betraying the

[12] Greti Dinkova-Bruun, Giles E. M. Gasper, Michael Huxtable, Tom C. B. McLeish, Cecilia Panti and Hannah Smithson, *Dimensions of Colour: Robert Grosseteste's* De colore*: Edition, Translation and Interdisciplinary Analysis* (Durham, NC: Durham Medieval and Renaissance Texts, 2013).

[13] Ibid., 16. Trans.: Colour is light incorporated in a diaphanous medium.

activity of different qualities of light (characterised by the variation of two quantities of greatness – *multa/pauca* – and clarity – *clara/obscura*) within materials characterised along a third dimension (of purity – *purum/impurum*)[14]. There is to this day an unsolved problem in cognitive psychology of the apparent ordering, continuity and perceptive proximity of colours.[15] Grosseteste prepares the ground for an approach to this issue by creating an abstract theatre of colour space. He is also working in a highly mathematical way (though this has not always been recognised in the secondary literature on the *De colore*, even by Crombie[16]). The numbers of possible colours and their contingencies are calculated in terms of the combinatorics of his three bipolar qualities. Never explicit, but clear to mathematically equipped readers of his and Aristotle's theories of colour, is that in developing a three-dimensional colour space between the opposing poles of black and white, he is going far beyond the Philosopher.[17] For Aristotle, colours ascend from black to white in a linear, one-dimensional scale. All colours are met with at some point on a single pathway from one pole to the other. But the *De colore* describes in combinatorial clarity the higher dimensionality of the space which ascending and descending series of colours inhabit. We can deduce that the entire space envisaged by Grosseteste is three-dimensional, equivalent to a cube, and that the central meeting place of ascending and descending colours is a two-dimensional mid-plane cut between two opposite corners of the colour cube.[18] The treatise can be read as a constructive criticism and development of Aristotle's one-dimensional ascending series of colours as, by implication, an inadequate account of the phenomenon. Grosseteste insists that *per experimentum* (whether by thought or in action is beside the point here) one only reaches all possible colours by the variation of three independent quantities rather than a single quantity. The treatise does not represent a mere recapitulation of ancient thought, but goes far beyond it

14 Ibid., 48.

15 S. M. Wuerger, L. T. Maloney and J. Krauskopf, 'Proximity Judgments in Color Space: Tests of a Euclidean Color Geometry,' *Vision Research*, 35 (1995), 827–35.

16 Crombie, *Robert Grosseteste*, 111.

17 Aristotle, *De sensu et sensatu*, available in translation at http://classics.mit.edu/Aristotle/sense.html.

18 In a fascinating confirmation of this, the work to prepare a new edition of the *De colore* by the Ordered Universe project came across a mathematical issue with the earlier one by Bauer (L. Bauer [ed.], *Die Philosophischen Werke des Robert Grosseteste, Bischofs von Lincoln* [Aschendorff: Münster, 1912]). Only two Latin words were ascribed to 'black', rather than the triplet that the mathematical dimensionality of the treatise would require. Although grammatically and philologically correct, the mathematical analysis proved decisive: an earlier manuscript than those available to Bauer was identified, with the missing 'coordinate' (the word *obscura*) in the position suggested by its mathematical role.

in imaginative theory as well as in mathematical complexity and observational relationship.

Within this short text of 400 Latin words we find, in this reading, a recognisably scientific approach to the mathematical modelling of an observed physical phenomenon. Naturally it is of its own time, not of ours – we now understand the origin of the three-dimensionality of colour to have its origins in the three types of photosensitive cone cells in the human retina, not directly in the properties of light or materials. But the core characteristic of science is to be found not in the answers it holds *pro tem* but in the quality of questions it poses, in the methodologies as well as the imagination that it adopts to address them and in the direction of intellectual travel. Good science is very rarely 'correct' in an absolute sense, but 'wrong in constructive ways'. So Newtonian gravity is correct, as far as we know, in only a low-gravity, limiting sense, yet without it, Einsteinian general relativity would never have been imaginable. In this sense, the questions and methods in colour science today are in continuity with Grosseteste's thought. If that were not true, it would be hard to explain why the team of scientists encountering this work in detail within the Ordered Universe project, when making a comparison between the *De colore* and Grosseteste's related treatise on the rainbow, the *De iride*, was immediately inspired to create some new science. They recast the physical optics of the rainbow, and the perceptual framework of human colour vision, to show that even in contemporary terms, Grosseteste was correct in asserting that colour space can be both spanned and mapped by 'the space of all colours in all possible rainbows'.[19] The rainbow proved a vital experiential link to colours seen in the thirteenth century, since neither the physics of light and raindrops nor the physiology of the human retina has altered over the succeeding centuries. Remarkably, this analytic work, required originally to establish whether the colour space of the *De colore* was indeed equivalent to the perceptual space used today, led to the discovery of a new mapping for the space in which the coordinate system is inspired by the spectral characteristics of rainbows. The new coordinate system also possesses an extraordinary aesthetic quality: the coordinate constant lines that result from it appear as intersecting sets of spirals (much as the appearance of the centre of a sunflower), when projected into the standard red-green-blue colour space of today.

[19] H. E. Smithson et al., 'Colour-Coordinate System from a 13th-Century Account of Rainbows', *Journal of the Optical Society of America*, 31 (2014), A341–A349.

The interdisciplinary study of Grosseteste's 'colour corpus' enriches the history of science in more ways than re-illuminating an obscured but essential period in its development. It also challenges the assumption that science develops in linear fashion, never revisiting its past, in oft-repeated distinction to the non-linear temporal character of the arts. There are real and deep questions concerning the structure of the material world, posed in previous times, but ripe for reappraisal when other tools and ideas have come to light. Respecting the thought of his own time, it is inappropriate to decorate him, as some have done,[20] as the originator of 'experimental science', but viewing the story of science through such a distant mirror also disarms our easy hindsight – it is not obvious that as artificial and simplified construction as an experiment can act as a pathway to learning anything about the complex reality of nature. That takes three more centuries of experience, and the theological development (by Francis Bacon and others) of some of the ideas Grosseteste himself explored (see Section 11.5 below). However, the strong suggestion that observation (*per experimentum*) may be enhanced or clarified by construction stands enigmatically at the close of the *De Colore*:

> What is understood in this way about the essence of colours and their multiplication, becomes apparent not only by reason but also by experience to those who thoroughly understand the depth of the principles of natural science and optics. And this is because they know how to make the diaphanous medium either pure or impure, so that in it they can receive bright light, or dim if they prefer, and through the shape formed in the diaphanous medium itself they can make scarce light, or increase that same light at will; and so through skilful manipulation they can show visibly, as they wish, all kinds of colours.[21]

This intriguing text strongly suggests that its writer was familiar with material manipulation. A colleague familiar with glass-making, for example, was convinced that only someone who had seen the process of shaping and colouring molten glass could have written it in that way.

By the same token, even this short sortie into a text of medieval natural philosophy refutes the commonly held but misguided notion that early science was uniformly 'suppressed by the church'. We read a Christian thinker in the thirteenth century developing pagan philosophy from the fourth century BCE transmitted to him via the Islamic tradition of the earlier medieval period. In the case of the *De colore* Grosseteste drew explicitly from the twelfth-century Cordoban Muslim scholar Averroes

[20] Crombie, *Robert Grosseteste.* [21] Dinkova-Bruun et al., *Dimensions of Colour*, 19.

(Ibn Rushd), and was one of the first western masters to read and employ Averroes's *Commentary on the Metaphysics* in his own work. Such a confident and open use of sources from radically different and theologically incommensurate traditions by one charged with the care of Franciscan students does not speak of a repressive ecclesiastical milieu.

This summarised case study illustrates, finally, the invalidity of an attempt to conflate the scientific and theological disciplines even in the thirteenth century. In all the treatises on light, Grosseteste is self-consciously engaging in work that is not theology. His motivation to explore scientific topics might be consequent to a theologically derived ethic or teleology (see Section 11.3 below), but it remains nevertheless quite distinct from it. His logic is tested, at least in thought, against observation and demonstration, not against doctrine. This is not to say that his agenda, such as the motivation to consider light as a primary study, is not derived from broader considerations, including the theological.[22] Yet he derives no direct consequences for theology from his conceptualisations of colour, his geometric optics of the rainbow or his physical theory of the cosmogony of the celestial spheres. He is perfectly capable of doing this, but does so only in his theological works. So, for example, in the *Hexaemeron* he draws on the physical properties of light to make a theological point: 'Among corporal things it is light which provides the most evident demonstration, through example, of the Most High Trinity' (referring to the triple property of luminosity, splendour and heat).[23] In the scientific works he achieves detailed conceptualisations of hidden dynamics and structures that satisfy his desire for an explanation of observed phenomena (colour, the rainbow, the motions of the stars and planets), but nowhere makes explicit allusion to theological ideas such as the Trinity. Again, this is by no means to suggest that he disconnects his scientific work from all theological motivation and framing – far from it – but it is to assert that he is perfectly clear on when he is doing science, when theology, and how to employ distinct methodologies in the two endeavours.

11.3 A Teleological Narrative for Science

Perhaps the most striking contrast between Grosseteste's intellectual world and ours can be found in their differing framing teleologies. Cultural

[22] Hans-Georg Gadamer, *Philosophical Hermeneutics*, 2nd ed., tr. and ed. D. E. Linge (Berkeley: University of California Press, 2004).

[23] Robert Grosseteste, *Hexaemeron*, tr. C. F. J. Martin as *On the Six Days of Creation* (Oxford: Oxford University Press, 1996).

narratives are able to reflect, and even to generate, shared purpose or, equally, to proclaim purposelessness[24]. Grosseteste knew why he was exploring the natural world within a theological project (as he and his contemporaries also developed sub-theologies of learning, including the accommodation of pagan and Islamic thinking within a Christian milieu), and develops a strong sense of purpose in doing so. Our own time has lost any such propelling meta-narrative for science, except within highly instrumental political agendas and a niche public dissemination of mind-expanding contemplation. In a post-modern atmosphere of suspicion around all overarching stories, those framings are also withering.

Grosseteste wrote of both simple and more sophisticated motivations to engage in natural science. On a delightfully straightforward level, at one point in his commentaries on the Psalms, he reflects that, if the Bible chooses to convey truth to its readers through the illustrations of natural objects (trees, clouds, falling leaves, etc.) then it behoves us to discover as much as we are able concerning them, simply in order that we might better understand the scriptures.[25] Origen's study of physics (see accompanying chapter by Pui Ip) drew on similar motivation which, according to Gregory Thaumaturgus, his student, served as a preparation to scriptural interpretation. By practising contemplation of nature beyond the mere appearance of things, students are accustomed to look for deeper meaning beyond the surface of nature, a skill that they need to cultivate in preparation for spiritual interpretation of scripture. An application of this very direct thinking appears in an explanatory note accompanying Grosseteste's translation of John Damascene's *De fide orthodoxa*. Two chapters in the earliest manuscripts at his disposal concerned scientific topics that ostensibly had no contact with the theological substance of the work as a whole. Earlier editors had sometimes omitted them for that reason. But Grosseteste reinstates both, explaining:

> These two chapters, namely the 24th about seas and the 25th about winds, are omitted in some Greek manuscripts; perhaps because they did not seem to contain a theological subject. But according to truly wise men, every notice of truth is useful in the explanation and understanding of theology.[26]

Although he is perfectly able to distinguish between theology and science as, for example, in the first part of book one of the *Hexaemeron* (again,

[24] J.-P. Dupuy, 'The Narratology of Lay Ethics', *Nanoethics*, 4 (2010), 153–70.

[25] Giles Gasper, 'The Fulfillment of Science: Nature, Creation and Man in the Hexaemeron of Robert Grosseteste', in Jack Cunningham and Mark Hocknull (eds.), *Grosseteste and the Pursuit of Religious and Scientific Learning in the Middle Ages* (Cham: Springer, 2016), 221–42.

[26] Cf. Rome, De a.

there was no age – certainly not the thirteenth century – in which they were 'indistinguishable'),[27] he takes the two as mutually dependent. He maintains a clear distinction between theological and scientific writing, but within an implicit and deep connectivity of his whole project. So although we find no explicit theological introductions or conclusions to the scientific works, this is because their theological context is assumed.

For a detailed exposition of that context, we need to turn to the philosophical works. In the *Commentary on the Posterior Analytics* (of Aristotle) Grosseteste places a more sophisticated theological philosophy of science within the overarching Christian narrative of Creation, Fall and Redemption. Developing a Boethian metaphor of laddered intellectual faculties through a Christian theology of the Fall, he describes its effect on the higher intellectual and spiritual powers (in descending hierarchy, those of understanding, memory, imagination) as a 'lulling to sleep' by the weight of fallen flesh, maintaining that the lower faculties, including critically the senses, are less affected by fallen human nature than the higher.[28] Human understanding (*aspectus*) is now inseparable from human emotions and loves (the *affectus* – the disposition to be affected); the inward turning of the latter now dulls the former. However, there is an avenue of hope that the once-fallen higher faculties might be reawakened: engaging the *affectus*, through the still-operable lower senses, in the created external things of nature allows it to be met by a remainder (*vestigium*) of other, outer *light*.[29] So a process of re-illumination can begin once more with the lowest faculties and successively re-enlightens the higher:

> Since sense perception, the weakest[30] of all human powers, apprehending only corruptible individual things, survives, imagination stands, memory stands, and finally understanding,[31] which is the noblest of human powers capable of apprehending the incorruptible, universal, first essences, stands![32]

27 Gasper, *Hexaemeron*. 28 Crombie, *Robert Grosseteste*, 129.

29 This Latin articulation is close to the goal of the Greek tradition of *theoria physikē* (natural contemplation), climaxed in Evagrios of Pontus and Maximus the Confessor.

30 We recall Paul's categories in 1 Cor 1:7.

31 This may be an abbreviation of a five-step 'ladder, or *scala* of intelligence', detailed by Isaac of Stella: 'For the soul too, while on pilgrimage in the world of its body, there are five steps towards wisdom: sense-perception, imagination, reason, intelligence and understanding.' 'Sermon 4 on the Feast of All Saints', in *Isaac of Stella: Sermons on the Christian Year*, vol. 1, intro. B. McGinn, tr. Hugh McCaffery (Collegeville, MN: Cistercian Press, 2016).

32 Robert Grosseteste, *Commentarius in posteriorum analyticorum libros*, ed. P. Rossi (Florence: Unione Accademica Nazionale Corpus Philosophorum Medii Aevi, Testi e Studi, 1981), qtd. in R. W. Southern, *Robert Grosseteste: The Growth of an English Mind in Medieval Europe* (Oxford: Clarendon, 1992), 167.

Human engagement with the external world through the senses, necessary because of our fallen nature, becomes a participation in the *theological* project of salvation. Furthermore, the reason that this is possible is because this relationship with the created world is also the nexus at which the human seeking is met by divine illumination. As a central example, the 'physics of light' grounded in the cosmogony of the *De luce* informs a 'metaphysics of light' as a vehicle to become a 'theology of light'. The *De impressionibus elementorum* makes explicit the theological action of light that remains implicit in the *De luce* – light (following the epistle of James 1:19) is a symbol of the perfect gift that descends from the Father of Lights. The implied restorative process that begins with an alertness to nature through our senses becomes another of Grosseteste's 'critical Aristotelian' moves[33]. With Aristotle he insists that all knowledge of particulars and universals comes through the senses, but against Aristotle he allows this to be met with divine illumination.

This double move even suggests a theological motivation for novel combination of experiment and mathematics implied in his scientific works – in every case it is at the meeting point of observed phenomena and mathematical reasoning that understanding is born. The teleological employment of scientific investigation as an instrument of human participation in a reversal of the effects of sin in the Fall is an idea that itself reawakens in the early modern period, especially (but by no means exclusively) in Francis Bacon.[34] The *Novum organum*, a philosophical and theological foundation for the ascendant experimental philosophy of the seventeenth century, by no means abandons all the scholastic work of its medieval predecessors, however strident Bacon's claims may be to the effect that it does. Its justification of experimental method as avoiding worst excesses of fallen imagination and reason, and its teleology of the recovery of a prelapsarian state of knowledge of nature, are together more than just echoes of medieval articulations.

A richer teleology of science for today, which goes beyond the pure factual acquisition in education and the instrumentalism of economics in research, is of vital urgency. Although Grosseteste's far deeper and more humanly resonant framings of natural philosophy are of their own time, they are not untranslatable into our own. Remarkably, the contemplative and palliative potential of *physics* has been articulated very recently by one

[33] Crombie, *Robert Grosseteste*, 129

[34] Peter Harrison, *The Fall of Man and the Foundations of Science* (Cambridge: Cambridge University Press, 2007).

of the United Kingdom's leading (and better theologically informed) science journalists.[35] There is more to say, and to experiment with, here, including the educational advantage of developing a holistic body-and-mind approach to experimental dexterity and exploration.

11.4 A Contemplation of Visual Scientific Imagination – *Sollertia*

William Blake inveighed against the science of Newton and Boyle as reason devoid of imagination. In the Romantic period, Keats and Poe would do likewise. Some of the theological critiques of this volume (Schindler, Milbank) seem to echo this tradition of revulsion at science's perceived disenchantment of nature. This tradition is as likely to be evidence that the rare attribution of the activities of creation or imagination to the work of science is a misunderstanding that arose early in the modern period. I have attempted elsewhere to draw attention to the silent stories of imagination that must drive the task of the sciences as much as they do the arts, to reimagine the world.[36] For any working research scientist, it is obvious that imagination is the greater part of their significant work. Einstein, among others, was perfectly clear on the point: '[to the scientist] imagination is more important than knowledge; imagination encircles the world'.[37] 'Imagination', however, covers a rich and varied set of mental propensities. It may extend in visual, textual or abstract modes – all these and more are exemplified in scientific work.[38] The landmark work of Amos Funkenstein identified the theological ground of essential aspects (such as notions of cosmological homogeneity and infinity) of scientific imagination from medieval to modern reception.[39] The dominant imaginative mode in science is still, for better or worse, the visual, certainly for the physicists, a prioritisation that constitutes another inheritance from theologically framed, medieval science. In this section we continue to draw on Grosseteste to illustrate a detailed account of the visual imagination.

We might expect that, since light is for Grosseteste both the supreme physical and theological form, so among the senses his preferred

[35] Tim Radford, *The Consolation of Physics* (London: Scepter Books, 2018).

[36] Tom McLeish, *The Poetry and Music of Science: Comparing Creativity in Science and Art* (Oxford: Oxford University Press, 2019).

[37] Albert Einstein and Leopold Infeld, *The Evolution of Physics* (London: Cambridge University Press, 1938).

[38] McLeish, *Poetry and Music of Science.*

[39] Amos Funkenstein, *Theology and the Scientific Imagination* (Princeton, NJ: Princeton University Press, 1986).

metaphorical example to illustrate the result of a meeting between sense and revelation would be sight. And so it proves to be. As the higher senses become sharpened by their infusion of illumination through the lower, so a higher penetrating power, *sollertia* awakens. (Grosseteste borrows the use of the word from the translation by James of Venice of Aristotle's *Posterior Analytics* – in Greek this is *agchinoia*, which might also be rendered 'acumen'.) In the *Commentary on the Posterior Analytics* Grosseteste writes:

> *Sollertia*, then, is a penetrative power by which the vision of the mind does not rest on the surface of the thing seen, but penetrates it [the thing seen, *rem visam*] until it reaches a thing naturally linked to itself [*sibi naturaliter coniunctam*]. In the same way as [*sicut si*] corporeal vision, falling on a coloured object, does not rest there, but penetrates into the internal connectivity and integrity of the coloured object, from which connectivity its colour emerges, and again penetrates this connectivity until it reaches the elementary qualities from which the connectivity proceeds.[40]

This is his great articulation of the restorative effect of the divinely assisted contemplation of nature, but it is also a striking articulation of the experience that epitomises the work of scientific observation and imagination in any age. Any contemporary scientist would recognise the meaning as a felt experience. An enhanced form of seeing, by which not only the outer appearances of things, but also their inner logic and workings, are perceived, is arguably the prime metaphor for scientific understanding. 'Ah – I see it now!' is not an arbitrary exclamation. Grosseteste's exposition of *sollertia* also fills out in more detail the ladder (or *scala*, which we met in the last section) of restored human understanding. The penetrative power of the 'vision of the mind' as a connectivity with the object understood is preceded by a similarly patterned connectivity of the 'corporal vision' with the inner integrity of the object perceived. The *De colore* indicates that Grosseteste develops his theory of colour as a physical consequence of the metaphysical form (of light) giving extension and integrity to matter. So once more we see his metaphysics of light develop from his reading and thinking through Aristotle, towards a theory for scientific method itself. Remarkably, he manages to work in an isomorphism between the physics of light and matter, and the perception of the same light and matter by the

[40] Rossi (ed.), Grosseteste, *Commentarius in posteriorum analyticorum libros* ii, p. 281, quoted by R. Southern, tr. Sigbjørn Sønnesyn (personal communication); Aristotle's *Posterior Analytics* II.19 is also in the background here, where the emergence of general understanding from particulars of sense-perception is described: 'It is like a rout in battle stopped by first one man making a stand and then another, until the original formation has been restored.'

human intellect.[41] Colour vision becomes the vehicle by which he explains that a subjective 'connectivity' or, perhaps better, 'complex structure' is generated in our mind through sense-connection with an objective connectivity in the material world.

Grosseteste does not have to invent the extended metaphor of vision in regard to the human intellectual relationship with nature, however – it occurs both in the Church Fathers and in biblical Wisdom literature with which he is familiar. In Gregory of Nyssa's *On the Soul and the Resurrection*, his sister (and 'Teacher') Macrina defends the real activity of the soul (or mind) during a moving debate as she lies dying. She chooses the example of the phases of the moon to make her case: we do not assume that the appearance of a waxing and waning object is sufficient to describe the reality, but understand that the Moon is a sphere passing through successively different angles of illumination by sunlight as seen from the Earth. It is mind (*psyche* in the treatise) that performs this task – 'the mind that sees', seeing below the surface of phenomena, or in Macrina's words:

> You see what the eye does teach; and yet it would never of itself have afforded this insight, without something that looks *through the eyes* [my italics] and uses the data of the senses as mere guides to penetrate from the apparent to the unseen. It is needless to add the methods of geometry that lead us step by step through visible delineations to truths that lie out of sight, and countless other instances which all prove that apprehension is the work of an intellectual essence deeply seated in our nature, acting through the operation of our bodily senses.[42]

The closely parallel biblical source is the Hymn to Wisdom of Job 28. Grosseteste refers to this ichneutic search for Wisdom, humorously described in the Hymn, in developing a discussion of theology itself in the opening of the *Hexaemeron*. McEvoy points out that in this context he is distinguishing theology from the sciences by emphasising the place of divine revelation – it possesses a necessary totality that the 'wise of the world' are not able to discover, but that must be received by faith.[43] Yet, as we have already seen, he derives theological motivation for his work in the liberal arts in general, and cannot have been unmoved by the reason given

[41] Remarkably, the visual perception of depth in materials beneath a translucent surface is currently an active topic in vision research; see, e.g., R. W. Fleming and H. H. Bülthoff, 'Low-level Image Cues in the Perception of Translucent Materials', *ACM Transactions on Applied Perception*, 2, no. 3 (2005), 346–82.

[42] 'On the Soul and the Resurrection', New Advent, www.newadvent.org/fathers/2915.htm.

[43] J. McEvoy, *Robert Grosseteste* (Oxford: Oxford University Press, 2000).

at the close of the Hymn, that God himself knows the way to wisdom by demonstrating just such extended, divine, vision:

> But God understands the way to it; it is he who knows its place.
> For he looked to the ends of the earth, and beheld everything under the heavens,
> So as to assign a weight to the wind, and determine the waters by measure.[44]

Here once more is the special, enhanced way of 'seeing' that recruits other aspects of mind than perception alone, including quantitative reasoning, to the task of beholding all of creation. Furthermore, although the Hymn concludes with this description of divine beholding, no student could miss the structural sense in which this conclusion balances its opening verses, equally powerfully descriptive of the unique view of the Earth from below afforded to the eyes of human miners dangling by ropes in their deep-cut shafts. Not even the sharp-eyed falcon can claim their vision of the earth 'from beneath, transformed by fire'. It is not only God who has access to the deep perception of creation which is the Way to Wisdom – the invitation is extended to humans as well.[45]

Grosseteste draws on both biblical and patristic material to develop a cultural (and in his case, necessarily theological) narrative of science. However, the central place within his thought that he accords to his own metaphysics of light, and the detailed example of the 'physical structure' underlying colour that he develops in the *De colore* and the *De iride*, give him material to expand and develop *sollertia* as a running teleological metaphor. He is explicit in his demonstration that sense perceptions can awake the higher senses into a grasp of underlying reality (the two qualities of light itself and their intersection with a third quality of the indwelt matter) when mathematics and geometry are also summoned to the task of deeper seeing. Finally, all this is set within an overarching biblical narrative of Creation, Fall and Redemption in which humankind is invited to participate in the process of recreation.

11.5 Christological and Incarnational Metaphysics and Theology of Time

There is another purpose evident in Grosseteste's thought behind the re-engagement of the human mind with the inner structures of the cosmos,

[44] Job 28:23–2 tr. in David A. Clines et al. (eds.), *World Biblical Commentary 18A* (Nashville, TN: Thomas Nelson, 2006).

[45] The special sort of 'seeing' which is Wisdom – and also the greatest metaphor for scientific insight – is also picked up strongly by Oxford theologian and philosopher Paul Fiddes in his recent *Seeing the World and Knowing God* (Oxford: Oxford University Press, 2014).

one that is independent from the post-lapsarian invitation to reawaken fallen minds. This second strand is important to him, for one of his great theological questions concerns an alternative history – one in which there is no Fall from grace. In the *De cessatione legalium* he asks famously, 'An Deus esset homo etiam si non esset lapsus homo?'[46] The question of the incarnation in such an unfallen world has corollaries of further questions – in particular and to the current matter in hand, would we be doing 'science' in such a world? Is there, in other words, a motivation for natural philosophy that goes beyond the restoration of a mind at first perceiving nature clearly, but now, through fallen human nature, clouded and dulled? Although the text does not address this question directly, it points in very strong directions that parallel Grosseteste's conclusion that there would indeed have been an incarnation of God in an unfallen world, and that his relationship with human and non-human creation maintains a directional, temporal and teleological narrative even without its disastrous first turn.

In this, his chiefly Christological work, Grosseteste's continuous theme is unity. He points out, once again driven by a prime unifying principle of light, that the human body communicates with all corporeal natures ('*communicat in natura*') because of the way light is incorporated into all elements by its reflection from the heavenly bodies. He extends his light metaphysics of matter to living beings: the rational soul of humans, the sensitive souls of animals and the vegetative souls of plants all share in both the same indwelling of constitutive light, and the composition of the elements. He entertains a very early insight into the material way in which humankind is, literally, earthed into creation.

A related account of such material connectedness across the cosmos is found towards the end of the *De luce*. It is worth quoting in full:

> And it is clear that every higher body in respect of the luminosity begotten from it is the species and perfection of the following body. And just as unity is potentially every following number, so the first body by the multiplication of its luminosity is every following body. Earth, in contrast, is all higher bodies by the collection in it of the higher luminosities. Thus, the poets call it 'Pan' (that is, 'All') and it is named Cybele as if cubele from the cube (that is, from solidity); because it is the most compressed and dense of all bodies, it is Cybele and mother of all the gods, for although all higher luminosities are brought together [in earth], they have not come forth in it through their operations, but it is possible that the luminosity of any celestial sphere you

[46] Translation: 'Would God have become incarnate had Man not fallen?' From Robert Grosseteste, 'On the Cessation of the Laws', tr. Stephen M. Hilderbrand, *The Fathers of the Church, Medieval Continuation* (Washington, DC: Catholic University of America Press, 2012).

> please be drawn out from earth into act and operation, and so from earth, as if from a kind of mother, any god will be procreated.[47]

A modern version of this sentiment was made famous by the scientist and communicator Carl Sagan,[48] drawing a material communication between human and cosmic materiality not from light but from the atomic generative properties of stars:

> The nitrogen in our DNA, the calcium in our teeth, the iron in our blood, the carbon in our apple pies were made in the interiors of collapsing stars. We are made of star-stuff.

For both writers there are real, material reasons that connect us to even the most distant objects in the universe. For both the connectivity arises through a temporal process of emission and condensation. The difference is in the material detail: Grosseteste deduces them from the structuring properties of light, Sagan from the unique environments within the cores of stars, where alone heavy elements can be manufactured, prior to their subsequent explosion and re-condensation. In spite of the efforts of thinking such as this, deeply poetic in the connective and emotive force of its idea, the deeply relational cultural context that it suggests for science has not (yet) taken root in its modern instantiation.

The greatest unity of all, of which this material unity is a shadow and a consequence, is that of Christ with both church and world. Grosseteste's strongest reason for advocating an incarnation irrespective of Fall is that:

> It is not consistent with reason that the universe, because it is the most perfect and most beautiful, participate only in the weakest kind of unity.[49]

In contrast to the linear temporality of biblical history, the theological narrative that supports the unity of creation and Church into Christ is explicitly structured around a circular sort of time. Although Christian narrative theology is usually taken to invoke a linear concept of time, Grosseteste identifies an element of the circular (first woman is born of man without generation, last man is born of woman without generation) that resonates with the Pauline passage on Christ and creation to the Colossians (1:15–20). The perspective into material and natural structure described in the Hymn to Wisdom of Job 28 is in that tradition both a divine and a human one – or rather it takes the human perspective onto

47 Robert Grosseteste, *La Luce: Introduzione, testo latino, traduzione e commento*, ed. Cecilia Panti, tr. Neil Lewis (Pisa: Edizioni Plus, 2011).

48 Carl Sagan, *Cosmos* (London: Random House, 2002), 244.

49 Hilderbrand, *The Fathers of the Church*, 166.

creation into the divine one.[50] For this to be true, the incarnate and loving gaze onto creation described at its temporal origin becomes true at all times. One can enter the circle of creation, incarnation and re-creation at any point. From this point of view, the circular temporal structure of the world and the external, potentially detached perspective on it becomes similar to a Stoic world view,[51] except that it is Christ in Creation who says 'Yes!' to 'the universe in its totality', not humans.

In similar vein to Milbank's suggestion of a prioritisation of time in this volume, Chris Tilling has recently described this strange temporality in which time 'bends' or 'spirals' around Christ.[52] Just as a twentieth-century physicist is surprised by resonances of thought in reading thirteenth-century descriptions of the mind's sight in teasing out the play of light uniting with matter that gives rise to colour, while being delighted by the difference in thought-world, so the contortions of a circular, or ever-present, time that are theologically motivated are not so very strange in the century after we first learned that both time and space were geometrical, woven together and, in the presence of any mass or energy, curved.

11.6 Medieval Meets Modern: Towards 'Theology of Science' after 'Science and Religion'

A Christian theology of science, the declared goal of this volume's authorial team, must be relational, soteriological and Christological. It must respect both the non-ontological status of God and the narrative freedoms and constraints of humans and material creation. It must dissolve the epistemological divisions and hierarchies of the late modern world. It must also be responsive to and resonate with the lived human experience of doing science, especially when that endeavour is explored as a vocation. The medieval thinking we have encountered in this short survey exemplifies thinking that supports all these, albeit reflected in a distant mirror that can only partially furnish the vision we need for our own times. Yet it does remind us of starkly fresh alternatives to our own cultural assumptions that will surely assist in rendering them more transparent.

50 I owe to Celia Deane-Drummond the insight that this 'theological geometry of looking into creation *with* God, rather than to detect his imprint, which I articulated in *Faith and Wisdom in Science*, is antithetical to the 19th century framing of "natural theology"'.

51 As articulated by Pui Ip in the accompanying chapter in this section.

52 Chris Tilling, *Paul, Christ and Narrative Time*, in A. B. Torrence and T. H. McCall (eds.), *Christ and the Created Order* (Grand Rapids, MI: Zondervan, 2018).

When held up to my own lived experience as a scientist who attempts to pursue scientific research vocationally, and with the experience of engaging with the theological and historical material in this volume (including the pleasurable experience of engaging the authors), the Distant Mirror helps contextualise apparent conflicts and disjunctures found when reading across this volume's chapters. For example (and taking Peter Harrison's warning that the evolution of meanings leads easily to advocates in different language traditions talking past each other), I realise that for some authors, 'science' is taken to signify a single academic discipline, or a collection of them, together with an alien community of 'scientists', not as a shared 'liberal art' with a God-given purpose. So David Schindler's comparison of the totalising implications and false humility of 'science' to those of public and private spheres of late modern political liberalism makes sense only within the former meaning, identifying science with a disciplinary community of practice, to which, presumably, a 'theologian' would not belong. One cannot 'surrender the field of culture' to a liberal art in the holistic, restitutional and gifted sense that these original 'disciplines' once had. To turn the complementary methodologies into distinct communities with unique and even exclusive epistemological claims is one of the contingent harms of modernism. It gives rise to the totalising but incoherent notion, for example, as David Bentley Hart points out, of the 'causal closure of physics (CCP)'. It is the only disciplinary fragmentation that permits the amnesia of the intentional that gives breath to such an idea in the first place. Perhaps it is worth emphasising the divisive power of CCP by pointing out the considerable rancour within the physics community itself on what is meant by 'physics' here. The arbitrariness of favouring one special length/energy scale (such as the nuclear) is obvious even within a wider theoretical physics that recognises emergent fundamental structure on all scales.[53] Panning out once again across the disciplinary landscape reveals the connection between the local example of what 'P' means in CCP, the contested boundaries between sciences and humanities, and that other set of pernicious modern dualisms that divorce the 'spiritual' from the 'material'. Schindler is right to call the exclusion of metaphysics from physics an 'impoverishment of nature'.

It is very hard to drop the entrenched disciplinary fragmentation which has dogged our academic landscape for over two centuries now, together

[53] Tom McLeish, 'Soft Matter – An Emergent Interdisciplinary Science of Emergent Entities', chapter 20 in Sophie Gibb, Robin Hendry and Tom Lancaster (eds.), *The Routledge Handbook of Emergence* (London: Routledge, 2019).

with the wicked rivalries of value, perception, esteem that it has brought, but these chapters point to the obligatory status of mounting this challenge to theologians of science. I would suggest that one consequence of searching for a 'theology of science' is the recasting of these definitions. A 'ministry of reconciliation' for this task must include the recognition that one of the damaging consequences of modern 'wrong turns' has been the very transformation of a disciplinary landscape from commonly contemplated and teleological liberal arts to a campus map with boundaries, frontiers and all the apparatus of security and defence that it implies. Our task is an inherently, and radically, interdisciplinary one. Unless, for example, we can imagine identifying physics as a 'humanities discipline', we have not begun to grasp just how radical.

In answer to the call for a 'theology of science,' John Milbank has advocated a move from 'disenchanted' to 'enchanted' transcendence, within his foursquare taxonomy of relational world views of nature. This strikes me immediately as refreshingly 'boundary-free', for one thing, entertaining seriously the theological consequences of modern (especially quantum) physics. But the consequences for a scientifically coherent re-enchantment of the world stem from deeper and wider experiences of engagement with the material world than quantum field theory and general relativity. Milbank also sets any scientific reader a very serious challenge not to flee at the first mention of 'occult', 'magic', or even 'enchantment' itself. There is good confessional precedent in identifying natural philosophy as the holy gift by which Christians may not indulge in pagan fear of hidden and vicious natural forces, from at least as ancient sources as Bede and Hrabanus. Perhaps Rowan Williams' happy notion of 'the face turned away from the observer' helps to exorcise the dark associations of the 'occult', for as Grosseteste beautifully articulated in his reflection on *sollertia*, and in which Macrina rejoiced, the gift of what we would now term the 'scientific imagination' to perceive what is 'turned away from' the senses (due to distance, scale or simply non-radiation at optical wavelengths) is enough to enchant anyone prepared to venture beyond science as a minimal and cold epistemology to an exercise in contemplation, as well as in the multifaceted experience of Wonder that William Desmond unpacks.[54]

The strongest thematic resonances of the theological chapters in this volume with the experience of doing science are with those that attain an

[54] William Desmond, *The Voiding of Being: The Doing and Undoing of Metaphysics in Modernity* (Washington, DC: Catholic University of America Press, 2019), 106–20.

uncanny understanding of it through narrating the relational, immersive, liminal and aporetic. The displacement of 'truth' from a fixed locus in either subject or object to an immersed, connected and dynamic relationship, and from an aloof universality to a participative *techne*, as articulated by both Catherine Pickstock and Rowan Williams, is already the faithful experience of a scientist, however privatised and 'untravelled' (in the sense of Wordsworth's critique of scientific poiesis in the nineteenth century or Medawar's in the twentieth). It is surely the culturally sustained fear of admitting that these metaphysical choices are, operationally, the necessary ones, elicited by a false desire to maintain disciplinary difference, that has in turn provoked the reductive materialistic window-dressing of the scientific house. Michael Hanby is correct to point out that metaphysics is always intrinsic to doing science (as to theology of course) and cannot, despite the repeated insistence of many 'science popularisers' to the contrary, be bracketed out. Yet this must also imply that the 'alternatively modern' possibilities that Pickstock illustrates with her three not-quite-modern examples may require little more than an increased honesty on the part of scientific witnesses, than a revolution in how science 'makes accessible the sheer inhuman otherness of matter'. That this framing for science borrows directly from George Steiner's teleology for art might help to answer Hanby's insight that success of this project will require at least more nuance of the distinction between art and nature.

In a further example, Janet Soskice is right to draw attention to the necessary connective tissue of metaphor in the construction of scientific understanding, especially through her personal experience of comparative analysis of metaphor in both science and theology. Soskice brings us to the same Abrahamic place of epiphany where Coleridge also found the language to describe the relationship between Creator, human and nature. In science, as in poetry, as aspect of the *imago dei* is the imaginative creation by analogy of 'little I AMs' of an image of the world that was once breathed into existence by the original. The conspiratorial silence on the essentially creative and re-creative modes of science is surely one of the contributors to a perceived disjuncture between science and theology. And by thus identifying the appropriate metaphor for God's second book as one of poetry, rather than of prose, goes some way (see Milbank's chapter) to meeting Foucault's identification of 'disenchanted transcendence' as the 'prose of the world'.

In conclusion, it is perhaps surprisingly easy (and that ease must in itself be of some import) for 'modern scientists' to become 'medieval' in their theology of science, once Simon Oliver's advice to welcome a wholehearted teleology is permitted entry, once they listens to the personal experience of truth as dynamic, relational and 'in-between', rather than objective, once the myth of an extrinsic observer is seen for what it is and an immersive creatureliness acknowledged, and once they, as well as their theologian colleagues, are willing to dissolve the disciplinary walls that are more part of our problem than our solution. As for magic and enchantment, neither needs incorporation into science. Both are already there – it's time that secret got out.

CHAPTER 12

Physics as Spiritual Exercise

Pui Him Ip

In *The Territories of Science and Religion*, Peter Harrison has taught us that 'science' and 'religion' are not natural kinds. In pre-modern times, the study of nature was intimately linked to the moral and spiritual spheres of human life.[1] *Scientia* in Thomas Aquinas is situated within a framework that links the right use of reason to moral and spiritual virtues.[2] Similarly, Aristotelian physics, including the locomotion of bodies, was clearly linked to Aristotelian ethics via the notion of teleology, as Simon Oliver has insightfully highlighted.[3] These observations reveal the oddity of our current understanding of physics vis-à-vis the rest of human history. In antiquity, physics had always been supposed as integral to human moral and spiritual development. Few physicists today, however, would say that their research contributes to ethics or spirituality.[4] The renowned historian of Greek science G. E. R. Lloyd has put this emphatically: 'nothing follows from cosmological Copernicanism for interpersonal behaviour, just as

[1] Peter Harrison, *The Territories of Science and Religion* (Chicago: University of Chicago Press, 2015), 26–34. Harrison writes that 'classical Greek engagement with nature [e.g., natural philosophy = physics], while often touted as a predecessor to modern science, was so imbued with theological and moral elements that its relationship to "science" as we now understand it is at best complicated. It is not just that astronomy and natural philosophy had some additional ethical elements that were largely peripheral and have now fallen by the wayside. It is rather that the study of nature was given a role in a broader philosophical enterprise that had moral goals and, quite often, theological presuppositions. Unlike anything in the modern sciences, the study of physics or natural philosophy was an exercise directed toward the transformation of the self' (p. 33). It is my aim in this essay to explore the crucial conditions which make this possible in the ancient conception of physics identified by Harrison here.

[2] Ibid., 13. This connection is also found in Robert Grosseteste, in whom we find a complex and sophisticated approach to the restorative potential of physics in relation to the moral and spiritual condition of humanity. See Tom McLeish's chapter in this volume, especially Sections 11.4 and 11.5.

[3] Simon Oliver, *Philosophy, God and Motion* (London: Routledge, 2005), 45–50.

[4] Some, like George Ellis, have entertained the possibility that physics can contribute to ethics. See Nancey C. Murphy, *On the Moral Nature of the Universe: Theology, Cosmology, and Ethics* (Minneapolis, MN: Fortress Press, 1996). Another attempt is found in Tim Radford, *The Consolations of Physics* (London: Sceptre, 2018). I thank Tom McLeish for this reference.

nothing follows from Black Holes ... or from the Big Bang'.[5] Of course, the mismatch between modern and pre-modern conception of physics in itself need not be an issue. The significance of this mismatch might simply lie in its support for Harrison's claim that historically, the concept of 'science' has always been evolving. From a critical point of view, it might even be said that we have simply moved onto a better understanding of physics. My purpose in this chapter, however, is to challenge us to resist jumping into this easy answer. By way of an engagement with ancient philosophical and patristic conception of physics, I want to rethink the estrangement between physics, on the one hand, and the moral and spiritual spheres in human life, on the other, so prevalent in our modern conceptions.

Let me begin by outlining a preliminary motivation for rethinking the estrangement. The estrangement between physics and the moral/spiritual dimension of human flourishing in our modern conception leads to some serious impasses that characterise our thinking in modernity. First, since the seventeenth century, physics has largely been a project that sought an increasingly unified picture of the world.[6] Newton's law unified the insights of statics, astronomy, and dynamics; Maxwell's equations unified electricity and magnetism into one single phenomenon; Boltzmann's statistical mechanics unified thermodynamics with the atomic picture of the microscopic world. The standard model of particle physics subsequently unified all known forces in nature except gravity. And finally, the greatest of all, Einstein's general theory of relativity unified the phenomenon of gravity with our understanding of dynamics and motion. Modern physics is thus in a perpetual search for *unification*, and this desire is reflected in the current attempts to unify quantum physics with relativity.[7] But this search for unification in modern physics is oddly and rather arbitrarily self-limiting. Modern physics is constantly going after a unified

[5] G. E. R. Lloyd, 'Science and Morality in Greco-Roman Antiquity,' in *Methods and Problems in Greek Science* (Cambridge: Cambridge University Press, 1991), 368.

[6] A good summary can be found in Étienne Klein, Marc Lachièze-Rey, and Axel Reisinger, *The Quest for Unity: The Adventure of Physics* (Oxford: Oxford University Press, 1999). A historical perspective is offered by Helge Kragh, *Higher Speculations: Grand Theories and Failed Revolutions in Physics and Cosmology* (Oxford: Oxford University Press, 2011). Margaret Morrison, *Unifying Scientific Theories: Physical Concepts and Mathematical Structures* (Cambridge: Cambridge University Press, 2007), provides detailed philosophical reflections on the meaning of 'unification' in the physical sciences. My suggestion will be that the concept of unification in physics is arbitrarily self-limited to our picture of the material universe considered apart from humans.

[7] This is the search for the so-called quantum gravity. For a layman introduction, see Carlo Rovelli, *Reality Is Not What It Seems: The Journey to Quantum Gravity* (London: Penguin, 2017). The best technical introduction is Claus Kiefer, *Quantum Gravity* (Oxford: Oxford University Press, 2012).

world-picture, but one that has no place for the human as mental, spiritual, moral beings. What I am suggesting is that the search for grand unification in physics is not really a search for ultimate unity. Rather, modern physics is interested in a grand unification of *only* our pictures of the materialist universe. The search for grand unification in physics does not include the task to locate humans in this picture, a fact that reveals a host of problems at the heart of the nature and goal of modern physics. First, how can physics as an enterprise claim to promise a *grand* unification of our world-pictures if it simply ignores a crucial component in it, namely, ourselves? Either the unification offered by physics is not what it promises, a *grand* unification, or physics must offer a principled answer as to why its unifications should be restricted to the non-human parts of nature. This leads to a further question: Is the self-limited prospective of modern physics a rigorous approach to the study of nature? In other words, is the self-limitation to the materialistic universe a *principled* choice, or is it simply an *arbitrary* methodological choice? There is a lack of clarity in modern physics about this question.

These issues, I believe, show that the estrangement between physics and the human moral/spiritual sphere is damaging for the integrity and rigour of physics' perennial search for unification in nature. That is, modern physics has a self-consistency problem in an analogous way to a similar problem that is widely recognised today. This is the so-called mind–body problem in modern analytic philosophy. As John Searle puts it, the mind–body problem is created by the need of grand unification. On the one hand, we have a conception of the world that is purely materialistic, with no obvious place for our mental life. On the other hand, we have a clear sense that we are mental-intellectual beings. How then do these conceptions fit together?[8] I believe that the mind–body problem is a good parallel to the problem I am highlighting here. The two problems are similar because the root issue is the same: modern physics lacks a principled, metaphysical account of why there is no place for humans as mental, moral, spiritual beings in its self-limited search for unification. The mind–body puzzle arises because the picture of reality offered by physics[9] does not integrate the mental. These modern impasses, I suggest, are damaging to the self-consistency of modern physics' search for grand unification of

[8] John Searle, *Minds, Brains and Science*, reprint edition (Cambridge, MA: Harvard University Press, 1985), 13.

[9] Non-reductive versions of physicalism do have room for mental realities. So here I am mainly thinking of reductive physicalism where the mental is reducible to physical processes and realities.

our world-pictures because it seems that modern physics is arbitrarily self-limiting in setting the goal for unification as simply the unification of the physico-materialistic dimensions of reality.

12.1 Retrieving the Ancient Vision

Motivations aside, it is worth re-emphasising with Harrison that the estrangement between physics and the human did not always exist. The title of this chapter, 'Physics as Spiritual Exercise', is a reference to the work of the great French historian of philosophy Pierre Hadot, who first described the study of physics in antiquity as 'spiritual exercises'.[10] By using this term, Hadot was trying to define a kind of activity that involves the whole of human being. Spiritual exercises thus refer to activities that are certainly intellectual, as involving thoughts and thinking, and certainly ethical, as involving consequences on our moral actions.[11] But for Hadot, spiritual exercises in ancient philosophy are more than simply intellectual or ethical exercises. Spiritual exercises refer to activities that bring about an inner transformation of the person, via both the process of the exercise, and the result produced by the exercise. These exercises moreover involve a sense of self-transformation, a high point of view, which consequently re-forms and re-shapes the person's whole manner of being-in-the-world. According to Hadot, ancient philosophy can be understood as offering spiritual exercises. As such, ancient philosophy was a much more substantial site for discovering a tradition that later on has been narrowly identified with the *exercitia spiritualia* in the later tradition associated with Ignatius of Loyola. Hadot's argument turns specifically on physics. He argued that ancient schools of philosophy, whether Platonic, Aristotelian, Epicurean, Stoic, or Christian, all envisaged the goal or finality of physics in something else beyond physics itself. Moreover, this goal is intimately connected with aspects of human moral and spiritual flourishing. Two quotations will illustrate this point beautifully. First, a passage from Cicero, which sets out starkly the moral value of the study of nature:

[10] Hadot discusses this idea in various places. The clearest summary is found in Pierre Hadot, *What Is Ancient Philosophy?* (Cambridge, MA: Harvard University Press, 2004), 207–11. In the same work, Hadot also offers a helpful summary of physics as spiritual exercise in Epicureanism (117–22) and Stoicism (128–31). Hadot's discussion of Marcus Aurelius' use of physics is particularly illuminating, as it has many similarities with Origen which, due to the limited space, I cannot go into. See also Pierre Hadot, *Philosophy as a Way of Life: Spiritual Exercises from Socrates to Foucault*, ed. Arnold Davidson (Oxford: Blackwell, 1995), 179–206, especially 191–5, 196–9.

[11] Hadot, *Philosophy as a Way of Life*, 81–2.

> I do not think we need to renounce the questions of the physicists (quaestiones physicorum). The observation and contemplation of nature are a kind of natural food for the soul and the mind (Est enim animorum ingeniorumque naturale quoddam quasi pabulum consideratio contemplatioque naturae). We rectify and dilate ourselves; we look down at human things from on high, and as we contemplate the higher, celestial things, we feel contempt for human things, finding them petty and narrow. The search for the largest things, as well as for the most obscure, brings us pleasure. If something probable presents itself to us in the course of this research, our mind is filled with a noble, human pleasure.[12]

And second, a selection of fragments from Epicurus, who sets out the goal of the study of nature in terms of its benefits for the well-being of the inquirer:

> If we were not disturbed by our worries about celestial phenomena and death, fearing (because of our ignorance of the limits of pain and desire) that the latter is something dire for us, we would have no need of the study of nature (φυσιολογίας).
>
> We cannot free ourselves of fear about the most essential things if we do not know exactly what the nature of the universe is (μὴ κατειδότα τίς ἡ τοῦ σύμπαντος φύσις), but attribute some hint of truth to mythological stories, so that without the study of nature it is impossible to obtain pleasure in its state of purity (ὥστε οὐκ ἦν ἄνευ φυσιολογίας ἀκεραίους τὰς ἡδονὰς ἀπολαμβάνειν).
>
> ... There is no profit to be derived from the knowledge of celestial phenomena other than peace of mind (ἀταραξίαν) and firm assurance (πίστιν βέβαιον), just as this is the goal of all other research.[13]

These quotations reinforce Harrison's thesis that science, especially physics, is not a 'natural kind' since in antiquity, the estrangement between physics and the good life was non-existent. But for those who are puzzled and perhaps sceptical, one might ask: How could physics bring about moral and spiritual transformation, as described by Cicero and Epicurus? What did they actually mean by this? Here, I shall draw attention to two concrete examples highlighted by Hadot, both referring to an aspect of

[12] Cicero, *Lucullus*, XLI, 127 (*On the Nature of the Gods* and *Academica*, tr. H. Rackham, Loeb Classical Library (Cambridge, MA: Harvard University Press, 1933), 630–2; English translation from Hadot, *What Is Ancient Philosophy?*, 209.

[13] Epicurus, *Capital Maxims*, §§11 and 12 (= Diogenes Laertius, 10.142–3; Cambridge Classical Texts and Commentaries 50, 817); Letter to Pythocles, §85 (= Diogenes Laertius, 10.85; Cambridge Classical Texts and Commentaries 50, 782). English translation from Hadot, *What Is Ancient Philosophy?*, 118.

physics that is fairly familiar to us. The first example is Epicurean physics.[14] Strangely enough, Epicurean physics offers a very similar picture of the cosmos as the one found in Newtonian physics. According to the Epicureans, the universe is made up of atoms – tiny, indivisible, immutable bodies – and empty space in which these atoms move. Everything that we see, let it be bodies of living bodies, but also the stars and the Earth, is made up of infinite number of atoms. These atoms, according to Epicurean physics, normally fall at equal speed in a straight line in space, but by chance, they may deviate from their trajectory and collide with one another. These accidental collisions are the source of composite bodies, and so, in this way, according to chance, worlds and bodies are born as well as disintegrated. For the Epicureans, this picture of the world helps human beings to put down their irrational fears of the gods of ancient mythology and death. This is because if the universe is simply made up of atoms and space, then clearly there is nowhere for the gods of mythology to intervene in our lives. So there is no need to fear the gods, which is one of the greatest sources of unhappiness according to the Epicureans. Similarly, there is no need to fear death, because if everything we are, including the soul, is made up of atoms, then we will also disintegrate at death and lose all sensory capacity. The atomistic picture of reality thus leads to the conclusion in Epicurus' *The Letter to Menoecus*: 'death is nothing for us. So long as we are here, death is not, and when death is here, we are not.'[15]

The second example comes from Stoic physics. The Stoics actually held what is nowadays called the cyclical model of the universe, according to which the universe comes to be and collapses periodically so that the universe we live in now is simply one stage of this perpetual cycle. According to the Stoics, the cyclical model of the universe reinforces the central insight from the study of nature, where everything we see in the cosmos is rationally pre-determined.[16] In Stoic physics, humans are simply parts of one great living rational organism, which is caused by the transformation of fire – the symbol of universal reason for the Stoics – into other elements. One day, however, according to the Stoic theory of cosmic conflagration, the cosmos in its various elements will return to its original

[14] The details here are drawn from Hadot, *What Is Ancient Philosophy?*, 119–20. For further details, see the relevant sections in A. A. Long and D. N. Sedley (eds.), *The Hellenistic Philosophers, vol. 1: Translations of the Principal Sources with Philosophical Commentary* (Cambridge: Cambridge University Press, 1987).

[15] Epicurus, Letter to Menoecus, §124 (= Diogenes Laertius, 10.124). Cited in Hadot, *What Is Ancient Philosophy?*, 120.

[16] Long and Sedley, *The Hellenistic Philosophers, vol. 1*, 274–9.

state again. This, according to the cyclical model of the universe, happens again and again. According to the Stoics the cyclical model of the cosmos aids human beings to see themselves as part of the chain of cause and effect. This acceptance of fate – or determinism in modern parlance – re-orientates individuals' views of themselves. It teaches the individual to be indifferent to what one should be indifferent about, namely, the events in nature of which we have absolutely no control. Instead of fighting and worrying about that, Stoic physics teaches us to accept ourselves wholeheartedly as simply a part of the cosmos, and be attentive of each moment of life. As Hadot summarises beautifully, 'The Stoic choice of life consists precisely in being able to say "Yes!" to the universe in its totality, and therefore to want what happens to happen as it happens.... It is physics that allows us to understand that all is within all.'[17]

My two examples illustrate how physics actually worked as spiritual exercises in ancient philosophy. Atomic theory might advance our understanding of the nature of matter, but for the Epicureans, the theory's primary goal is to eliminate an irrational fear of mythological gods and death. Likewise, the cyclical theory of the universe might advance our understanding of cosmology. But for the Stoics, the theory's primary goal is to bring about an acceptance of fate, which consequently helps us to put down unnecessary worries in life about the things of nature we cannot control, and re-orientates us to see ourselves as simply part of the chain of cause and effect. Thus in both examples, an advance in understanding nature fulfils a higher goal in human moral and spiritual life. Physics, in this regard, is envisioned as the source of inner transformation for human beings.

12.2 The Metaphysical Foundation of the Ancient Vision

Hadot's analysis shows that physics as a human activity could be imagined differently. While moderns rarely think of the advances in understanding electromagnetism or gravity as effecting an existential self-transformation in humanity, nevertheless, the ancient vision offers a perfectly plausible alternative. But is this attitude simply arbitrary? In other words, is treating physics as spiritual exercise simply an idiosyncrasy of antiquity? What, if anything, makes this approach a convincing one to take? This is the question that I want to address in this section.

[17] Hadot, *What Is Ancient Philosophy?*, 211.

The ancient schools of philosophy each had a different framework for justifying its own approach towards physics. It is true that all the major schools perceived physics as contributing to the good life, but each conceived how this works in a different way.[18] So there is really no single generic approach to justify this attitude shared by all the schools. But if we dig deeper, a promising response can be found. Physics should be conceived as spiritual exercise, for the ancients, because it is grounded on a comprehensive account of reality, a metaphysics, in which an intimate link between nature and the human can be found. In Aristotle, for instance, we find a concept of nature that is comprehensive: it spans human nature as well as animals, inanimate beings (e.g., plants), and the natural elements (e.g., fire, water). Such a cosmic order, in turn, makes natural the concept of cosmic order, as Lloyd explains:

> The concept of 'good' is not confined to contexts where we can identify individuals or species whose good is in question, but is applied to the cosmos as a whole, conceived not merely as orderly but as a hierarchical whole, in which everything from the natural elements, up past plants, animals and humans, to the divine heavenly bodies and the Unmoved Mover himself has its own particular capacities and due place in the series.[19]

In a world-picture such as Aristotle's, we find an explicit connection between nature and humanity. It makes sense then to think of physics, the understanding of nature, as possessing significant implications for human moral and spiritual development. Thus physics serves as a kind of spiritual exercise, as Hadot describes it, for the ancients because they had a metaphysics of *cosmic order* according to which nature spans all levels of reality.

To illustrate this point, I shall turn to the third-century Christian philosopher and exegete Origen of Alexandria (c. 185–c. 253).[20] The case of Origen demonstrates that the deep link between physics and human flourishing, grounded on a metaphysics of cosmic order, was also taken up in a *Christian* context. As a writer, Origen was interested in developing what we might call a theological metaphysics – one that is deeply informed by scriptural exegesis, Christian tradition, as well as the latest scientific

[18] Lloyd, 'Science and Morality in Greco-Roman Antiquity', 352. Lloyd divides the different schools broadly under two 'camps': the teleogists who believed the good or a divine figure in which one finds the final purpose and end of all things, and the anti-teleologists who rejected such frameworks.

[19] Ibid., 366.

[20] Though one could have chosen any Greek patristic authors from Clement of Alexandria onwards to illustrate this point. See Joshua Lollar, *To See in to the Life of All Things: The Contemplation of Nature in Maximus the Confessor and His Predecessors* (Turnhout: Brepols, 2013), 101–59.

advancement of his times.[21] So a brief look at Origen will give us a better idea of where philosophical theology might become important in the task of rethinking physics' relation to the human.

Let me begin with some historical context. Origen was a Christian educator who lived in Alexandria, Egypt, the capital of learning at that time, for the first half of his life. Later on, he moved to Caesarea, Palestine, until his death and started a Christian learning circle there. Origen was involved with the development of a Christian *Paideia* – a culture of educated Christians who were familiar with the questions in Late Antiquity and who engaged theologically and scripturally with these questions. His teaching spans not only the Christian Scriptures but also logic, ethics, physics. Origen's educational legacy was long-lasting because he definitively shaped Christianity in the fourth century, influencing Eusebius of Caesarea, the historian who gave us the first *Ecclesiastical History*, and the Cappadocian Fathers, who defined Trinitarian Orthodoxy, Basil the Great, Gregory of Nazianzus, and Gregory of Nyssa. We are fortunate that one of Origen's students, Gregory (possibly Gregory Thaumaturgus, the 'wonder-worker'[22]) left us an account of Origen's conception of the Christian curriculum of learning, so that we have an idea about how physics fits into a third-century vision of Christian education.[23]

[21] Origen first set out his Christian philosophy in his major work entitled *Peri archōn* (On First Principles). This work is most likely to be in imitation of a well-defined genre of philosophical writing in his time. Ilaria Ramelli, 'Alexander of Aphrodisias: A Source of Origen's Philosophy?', *Philosophie Antique. Problèmes, Renaissances, Usages*, 14 (2014): 243–6. But as Brian Daley has pointed out, the *Peri archōn* was conceived primarily as a treatise setting out the principles of Christian scriptural interpretation. Brian E. Daley, 'Origen's 'De principiis': A Guide to the Principles of Christian Scriptural Interpretation', in John Petruccione (ed.), *Nova et Vetera: Patristic Studies in Honor of Thomas Patrick Halton* (Washington, DC: Catholic University of America Press, 1998), 3–21. A particularly helpful account of Origen's philosophical system is given by the comparative approach taken in Henri Crouzel, *Origène et Plotin: Comparaisons doctrinales* (Paris: Téqui, 1991). Crouzel's analysis showcases the similarity of Origen's position in relation to the neo-Platonism of his time. Mark Edwards, on the other hand, stresses the dissimilarities between Origen and Platonism. See Mark J. Edwards, *Origen against Plato* (London: Routledge, 2017). Crouzel and Edwards together offer a balanced picture of Origen's philosophical system.

[22] Scholars have continued to dispute whether the author of the *Address of Thanksgiving to Origen* should be identified as Gregory Thaumaturgus, who has been identified as the forefather of Cappadocian Christianity. See Michael Slusser (ed. and trans.), *St. Gregory Thaumaturgus: Life and Works* (Washington, DC: Catholic University of America Press, 1998), 16–21.

[23] See the helpful discussion by Henri Crouzel (ed. and trans.), *Remerciement à Origène, suivi de la Lettre d'Origène a Grégoire* (Paris: Cerf, 1976), 40–2. The significance of this account of Origen's pedagogy for understanding ancient education has begun to receive appreciation by scholars only recently. See David Satran, *In the Image of Origen: Eros, Virtue and Constraint in the Early Christian Academy* (Oakland: University of California Press, 2018).

According to this account, Origen's pedagogy centres around the goal of developing human persons who live virtuously and piously. The goal of Origen's teaching is to instil a virtuous character into his students, through teaching and modelling the art of living virtuously. As part of this educational program, students would receive a curriculum of learning roughly fitting into a three-fold division of philosophy.[24] First, students receive instructions on logic and dialectic.[25] Then they move onto physics, which comprises of subjects such as geometry and astronomy.[26] Then they move onto ethics, defined as the art of living rightly and making good moral decisions, rather than simply learning theories of moral actions.[27] Finally, as a Christian curriculum, Origen goes beyond the standard tripartite curriculum at the time by giving instructions on theology to students.[28] In Origen's case, theology most likely involves scriptural exegesis and hermeneutics, exemplified by extant works such as the *Commentary on John*. Each of the stages in the ascent towards divine matters was conceived of as having a moral and spiritual significance.[29] Logic, for instance, was envisaged as helping students to make better judgements on various opinions, so that students could live according to what is worthy, and turn away from what is vain and deceitful. In this context, it is no wonder that physics was also conceived by Origen as a spiritual exercise. According to Gregory, once the students were well trained in judging a good argument from a bad one, they were immediately led to lessons in physics, where Origen explains 'each existing thing, and analysing them with great wisdom down to their most basic elements, and then weaving them together by reason and going over the nature of the entire universe and each of its parts, and the endless alteration and transformation of the things in the world'.[30] In Gregory's words, in Origen's curriculum, physics seems to involve the study of geometry, which makes up the foundation of physics, and astronomy, which together with geometry makes 'heaven accessible for us'. What then, according to Gregory, was Origen's

[24] This programme was not invented by Origen, as it resembles the scheme of teaching in use in the Greek schools at the time. See Sandro Leanza, 'La classificazione dei libri salomonici e i suoi riflessi sulla questione dei rapporti tra Bibbia e scienze profane, da Origene agli scrittori medioevali', *Augustinianum*, 14 (1974), 651–66 (652).

[25] *Address to Origen*, VII, §§93–108.

[26] *Address to Origen*, VIII, §§109–14.

[27] *Address to Origen*, IX–XII, §§115–49.

[28] *Address to Origen*, XIII–XV, §§150–83.

[29] This theological ascent, of course, is not confined to the patristic period. The medieval curriculum described by Robert Grosseteste in *De artis liberalibus*, in Giles E. M. Gasper, Cecilia Panti, Tom McLeish, and Hannah E. Smithson (eds.), *The Scientific Works of Robert Grosseteste*, 6 vols. (Oxford: Oxford University Press, 2019), vol. 1, can be seen as developing the same approach. For a summary of Grosseteste's vision, see Tom McLeish's chapter in this volume.

[30] *Address to Origen*, VIII, §110.

intention in teaching physics in his curriculum? The answer is: to create a sense of wonder (θαῦμα) and astonishment in the student so as to replace the 'irrational one' in our souls.[31] For Origen physics teaches us to wonder at God's creation, and to use it appropriately as a path towards the loftiest learning, namely, the divine realities. This attitude replaces the irrational wonder of worshiping the visible and sensible realities, a common attitude at the time. In this sense, physics is thus conceived by Origen as a spiritual exercise. By instilling knowledge of the intricate divine fabrication of the universe in us, physics transforms the human person from a vain admiration of the sensible cosmos in itself towards developing a more truthful sense of wonder at the Creation which points the person towards the divine mysteries. This is why the study of physics, according to Origen in the *Commentary on the Song of Songs*, will form and shape its students so that 'nothing in life may be done which is contrary to nature, but everything is assigned to the uses for which the Creator brought it into being'.[32] It is only when we are students of physics that we may distinguish the useless and vain wonders at the sensible creation itself from the wonder at the Creator, a wonder that is profitable in helping humans to live uprightly according to the intention of their Creator.

This brief analysis shows that Origen's conception of physics in his Christian curriculum fits well with the ancient philosophical tradition described by Hadot. The goal of physics, for Origen, is not found in and of itself, but rather lies in its ability to transform our sense of wonder into one that aligns our lives to the purpose of the Creator. Origen's vision, however, was not an arbitrary one. It was ultimately grounded on his comprehensive account of reality. And it is in this framework where we find the rationale of Origen's understanding of physics as a spiritual exercise. Let me briefly illustrate how Origen's account of physics as a spiritual exercise is a principled one, resting on his metaphysics.[33]

According to Origen's scheme, there are generally two categories of things – things that are moved from without (ἔξωθεν μόνον κινεῖται), such as lifeless things like stones, logs, and so on, and things that have their

[31] *Address to Origen* VIII, §111.

[32] *Commentary of the Song of Songs*, Prologue 3.3. English translation from R. P. Lawson (trans.), *Origen. The Song of Songs: Commentary and Homilies* (Westminster, MD: Newman Press, 1957), 40.

[33] Here, I shall not elaborate on the connection between Origen's cosmology and his account of ethics based on his theory of human free will central to his theology of what might be called the 'drama of salvation'. For a brief analysis along the same perspective I am sketching out here, see Lollar, *To See into the Life of All Things*, 111–20.

causes of movement within themselves (ἐν ἑαυτοῖς ἔχει τὴν τῆς κινήσεως αἰτίαν).[34] For those that are moved from without, their motion is to be explained entirely according to external causes. Amongst those that are self-moved, we find a further division. There are some that are moved by a natural instinct towards certain kind of movement. Origen had in minds animals such as spiders, which by natural instincts make orderly webs. In these cases, the motion of the spider is explained not by an external cause but rather by its inner instinct to carry out these movements. However, there are others, like humans, who are rational animals. These have natural instincts too, but in addition, rational animals have the faculty of reason. Accordingly, rational animals can judge their own natural instinct by means of reason, as, for example, in the case where a human rejects the natural instinct of hunger for the sake of fasting and personal purification.[35] The motion of rational animals must be explained not simply by natural instincts, but by how reason is exercised by them. According to this metaphysical scheme, the concept of *natural motion* is thus divided into three forms. Under this framework, the human is integrated into an overarching account of nature. Thus in Origen, all parts of nature – animate, inanimate, and rational – are explicitly connected in a single metaphysics of nature according to which different parts of nature are assigned different kinds of *natural motion*. Such a unified account of nature, a cosmic order, undoubtedly provided a metaphysical foundation to Origen's conception of physics as integrally concerned with right living, as reported by Gregory.

As should by now be clear, ancient philosophers, including Christians, did not simply arbitrarily conceive of physics as spiritual exercise.[36] Rather, the vision is a principled one. The commitment to a cosmic order underlying the whole of reality was foundational for the ancient conception of physics. For the ancients, it is plausible to treat physics, and the knowledge of nature gained from it, as a way to bring about the good life because they were convinced metaphysically that nature spans the whole of reality, including humanity. Contemplating the well-ordering of nature, then, inevitably must be relevant to questions on the well-ordering of human life. Physics and ethics were integrally connected to one another by

34 *On First Principles*, III.1.2, in John Behr (ed. and trans.), *Origen: On First Principles*, (Oxford: Oxford University Press, 2017), vol. 2, p. 286.

35 *On First Principles*, III.1.3–4 (in ibid., 288–92).

36 My account here must be supplemented by the systematic analysis in Lollar, *To See into the Life of All Things*, 43–165. Given that Lollar's analysis was equally inspired by Hadot, it can be read as a detailed extension of the argument set out here.

the ancients because they were simply following the logical conclusions of their metaphysical commitments.

12.3 The Desirability of the Ancient Vision

So far, I have sketched out a case that physics has not always been estranged from the concern for human flourishing. In antiquity, physics was conceived as a spiritual exercise such that the study of nature was an indispensable source of human moral and spiritual transformation. I have argued the ancient vision did not arise due to an arbitrary subjection of science to ethics. Rather, the ancients were able to connect physics and human flourishing in a principled way, because they possessed a metaphysics of cosmic order wherein the connection between all parts of nature – inanimate, animate, and human – is explicitly sketched out. But the question remains: Is the ancient vision of physics more desirable than the one we currently possess?

One way to address this question is to say that the separation between the study of nature and the 'good life' supposed by modern physics might be morally and spiritually *deforming* in some way. On this perspective, this estrangement is detrimental for human moral and spiritual development. A return to the ancient vision of physics as spiritual exercise can then be judged desirable. But this would be an overly simplistic way to retrieve the ancient vision. For as Lloyd has successfully captured, the instinctive disease in modern readers when encountered with the ancient vision I have just sketched out here is not groundless. Is it not the case that one of the most significant legacies of modern science was to sever an unwarranted, misleading connection between science and human ideologies? Has not David Hume taught us that it is unwarranted to move from an 'is' (a fact of nature) to an 'ought' (a good way of living)?[37] If ancient physics indeed was conceived as giving instructive knowledge for human's moral and spiritual well-being, has not this tradition fallen into the error so forcefully attacked by Hume? When science and the good life are so intimately

[37] Lloyd, 'Science and Morality in Greco-Roman Antiquity', 366–7. According to Lollar, Origen and the Greek tradition he inherited intentionally violate Hume's claim. Lollar writes: 'For Clement and Origen . . . the "is" of the facts of the world are given to instruct human beings in the "ought" of virtue as elementary instruction in the Christian way of life.. . . Origen's notion of ethics is not a matter of defining the axiom of moral theory but rather of returning to the divine Origin of being through the transformation of the passions and as such, his is not a confusion but rather a refusal of an absolute distinction between ontology and praxis.' Lollar, *To See into the Life of All Things*, 118–19.

entangled, then science inevitably becomes a tool for ideological control. Lloyd highlights a concrete instance of this in Aristotle where the notion of cosmic order that structures all things hierarchically in his account of nature forms the foundation for his justification of slavery.[38] All these considerations rightly put a huge question mark above the viability of reopening the close link between physics and human flourishing that once existed in the ancient vision of physics as spiritual exercise. Despite all the impasses in modern thought caused by the severance between physics and the good life I highlighted in the beginning, the price might just be too high to pay to retrieve the ancient vision as a remedy.

One is of course right to point out all the dangers latent in the ancient vision. While physics might indeed be conceived as a spiritual exercise, such a conception might also enable it to be a tool for political control. So we cannot naively return to the ancient vision of physics wherein one was able to 'bring back, from the frontiers of knowledge, tablets of stone for the human predicament'.[39] Of course, modern physics is right that one cannot read off ways for humans to live better lives through knowledge of nanomaterials or galaxy formation. But our current conception and praxis of physics is fraught with the opposite danger. We moderns, far too easily, have dissociated any ethical or spiritual connections with our knowledge of physics. Modern physicists do not boast a glorious track record of handling our unprecedented understanding of nature with responsibility towards human flourishing.[40] This fact ought to challenge us to rethink the view that the best conception of physics should be totally free of any connections with human moral and spiritual flourishing. An absolute severance between physics and the good life will inevitably lead to irresponsible use of physical knowledge. One crucial arena in which this is becoming increasingly clear is our relationship with the environment. To what extent is our knowledge of nature gained in physics responsible for the ecological crisis? Pope Francis, in his integral ecology set out in the recent encyclical *Laudato si*, identifies the recovery of the notion of cosmic order, an account of nature that spans human, animals, plants, and everything in the world, central to the ancient vision of physics as crucial for a way forward:

> When we speak of the 'environment', what we really mean is a relationship existing between nature and the society which lives in it. Nature cannot be regarded as something separate from ourselves or as a mere setting in which

[38] Lloyd, 'Science and Morality in Greco-Roman Antiquity,' 365–6. [39] Ibid., 368.
[40] Lloyd himself highlights this fact too. See ibid., 356.

> we live. We are part of nature, included in it and thus in constant interaction with it.[41]

In other words, while it might be undesirable to return to the ancient vision of physics, the notion of cosmic order at the heart of this vision is urgently required today. This is because the recovery of this notion instils a sense that we are intimately connected to all that exists, a notion that Francis rightly highlights as crucial for a change of attitude towards the environment.[42] This analysis simply illustrates how dangerous it is to remain complacent with a concept of physics in which there is no sense of connection with human flourishing.

So where does that leave us? I have argued that the vision of physics as spiritual exercise is no less dangerous than the modern vision. The point is simply that the dangers encountered in each are *different*. In the ancient vision, there is always the danger that one is tempted to read off from nature ideals for the good life that are not justifiable upon inspection. However, the operational severance between physics and human flourishing in the modern vision is equally dangerous because it tempts its practitioners to give little thought to the responsible production and use of physical knowledge. So even if the ancient vision might posit too close a link between physics and human flourishing, it is worth pondering whether such a connection can be reopened in ways that avoid the pitfalls. Lloyd sums up this matter succinctly:

> Even though a first reflection on the issue of the connections between science and morality in the ancient world is one of the pitfalls that went with these connections remaining too close – pitfalls both from the side of the distorting effects on the science, and from that of the narrowness of the morality sometimes grounded in that science – a second point to ponder is the unwisdom of the notion that it is better for no link to remain, for rather, clearly, the *connection* is of the utmost concern. This is unlikely to be forgotten for sure, in the context of the ever-increasing problems of the morality of particular scientific investigations. But more generally, it may not be inopportune, from the perspective of what is supposed to be par excellence a discipline contributing to humane education, to insist on the relevance to such of science.[43]

This remark elucidates that one major lesson from taking a serious look at the ancient vision of physics is simply the rediscovery of a sense in which

[41] *Laudato si* §139. English translation: www.vatican.va/content/francesco/en/encyclicals/documents/papa-francesco_20150524_enciclica-laudato-si.html (accessed 15 January 2021).

[42] Ibid. §11. [43] Lloyd, 'Science and Morality in Greco-Roman Antiquity,' 370–1.

physics is, and should continue to strive to be, an activity that contributes towards humane education. My retrieval of this vision here intends to signal not a displacement of modern physics by a return to ancient physics, but rather a return of modern physics to a position where the advances in knowledge of nature we gain from it can once again be subjected to the spiritual exercise of natural contemplation (θεωρία φυσική), an activity that attends to nature for the sake of human moral and spiritual formation. In other words, physics need not become re-identified with natural contemplation, but it must become open to it.

In more concrete terms, my suggestion is that the retrieval of physics as spiritual exercise is desirable as it will enable modern physics to contribute to the 'humane education' Lloyd alludes to. But this retrieval should be conceived as the reinvention of *natural philosophy* and not as the displacement of modern physics. My contention, then, is that modern physics as it is currently conceptualised and practised is problematic only if it is devoid of an integral connection with human moral and spiritual formation. There should remain a space in physics for the methodological separation between the study of nature and the good life; but this separation should not habituate us to cease contemplative engagement with the knowledge of nature we gain from it. The remedy, I suggest, is a return to natural philosophy as an additional space for this contemplative engagement, practised by those trained and steeped in the natural sciences but who also accepted the vocation of 'thinking nature', that is, to hold nature as formative of our thinking about human moral and spiritual flourishing.[44] This reinvention of natural philosophy is desirable as it will open up a disciplinary location wherein modern physics can re-establish its integral contribution to a 'humane education'.[45]

[44] Here I borrow one aspect of a term recently used by Willemien Otten, who has argued that what joins thinkers such as John Scotus Eriugena and Ralph Waldo Emerson together is that they both desire 'to "think nature" – that is, engage in thinking in such a way that they hold nature in their minds, always reserving space for nature's ability to dictate thought, all the while recognizing the innate correspondences or links between nature and selfhood'. Willemien Otten, *Thinking Nature and the Nature of Thinking: From Eriugena to Emerson* (Stanford, CA: Stanford University Press, 2020), 5.

[45] One concrete example of an attempt to carry out the kind of 'natural philosophy' I envisaged here is David Bohm, *Wholeness and Implicate Order* (London: Routledge, 1980). While Bohm's represents a highly idiosyncratic approach, what makes his work particularly apt as an illustration of my proposal is that he takes modern physics (especially quantum mechanics) seriously as a subject matter not only for analytical philosophical reflection (as is commonly found amongst philosophers of physics today) but also for contemplation about the nature and flourishing of human life. Moreover, Bohm also attempts to offer an unified account of nature that does not suppose an artificial separation between nature and human nature.

But there is another way of framing the desirability of the ancient vision which brings me back to the start of this essay. I begin by highlighting the conceptual impasses created by the estrangement between nature and humanity in modern physics. What the retrieval of the ancient vision of physics reveals is that the tendency to separate the study of nature and the good life rests upon an implicit intuition of a metaphysical 'gap' between nature and humanity. Modern physicists do not conceive their work as spiritual exercise since in their metaphysical intuition, unlike the ancients, there is no continuity between nature and human nature, between the laws of nature and the laws of human living.[46] For the ancients, especially the Greek Fathers, the situation is notably reversed as human nature is considered as part of the meaning of the term 'nature' (φύσις), thus resulting in a basic outlook that desires to contemplate how the Logos of nature informs the Logos of human living. The ancient vision thus possesses a level of metaphysical unity – one that conceives human nature under a more general conception of nature – absent in the implicit instinct underlying modern physics. The ancient vision, I suggest, offers a desirable alternative as it provides a more unified picture of reality that is 'principled', that is, grounded in its underlying metaphysical account of nature. It is worth noting that the desirability for such a unified picture rests primarily upon a metaphysical instinct and is not entirely decidable by empirical observation. One might draw a parallel here with the project of 'grand unification' between all known physical theories that some theoretical physicists are engaged in today. In both cases, the desirability of such a 'grand unification' should be understood as primarily (though not only) driven by a metaphysical instinct that reality *should* indeed display such unity, that a unified picture of reality is more fitting than a fragmentary picture. So the question of whether a unified vision of nature is desirable would depend strictly on metaphysical considerations. And herein lies my more ambitious suggestion arising from the retrieval of the ancient vision of physics: the desirability for a unified vision of nature demands to be rigorously re-examined metaphysically once more in our times. It is only when this metaphysical task is adequately addressed will we be able to assess the wisdom of renewing the practice of physics as spiritual exercise today.

[46] This is why Philo of Alexandria, for instance, has little problem finding consonance between laws of nature and the Torah of Moses. See Johannes Zachhuber, 'Nature', in Mark J. Edwards (ed.), *The Routledge Handbook of Early Christian Philosophy* (Oxford: Routledge, 2021), 27–40 (30–1).

CHAPTER 13

Making Art
Meaningful Materials and Methods

Spike Bucklow

Making art is shaped by the frameworks that furnish artists' conditions of belief or contexts of understanding. Those frameworks and contexts include science, so the ways art can be made can throw light on scientific interpretations of our place in the world. Now, we are so familiar with the modern, Western, scientific way of understanding the world that it is difficult to appreciate how radically it differs from pre-modern and non-Western ways of understanding the world. It is perhaps easiest to get a flavour of those differences by considering specific historic episodes in the development of modern science. I would therefore like to open this essay with a brief account of the genesis of one central, and now all-pervasive, aspect of modern life.

Before the French Revolution, thousands of expert artisans were employed in haute couture and associated trades, as French aristocracy enjoyed fashions which included extravagant costumes and complex coiffures. The Revolution's industrial-scale beheading of its citizens started with those whose clothes and hairstyles identified them as members of the elite. Not surprisingly, fashions in clothes and hairstyles simplified rapidly, and legions of highly skilled Parisian dressmakers and hairdressers became unintended victims of the Revolution. Almost overnight, they lost their livelihoods and required alternative employment.

About thirty years earlier, Alexis-Claude Clairaut had predicted when Halley's comet would be closest to the Sun. He was out by thirty-one days (in a cycle of seventy-five years), but the result hardly mattered because he had created a model of the comet's trajectory that could be solved mathematically. The necessary calculations were laborious, so he recruited two friends to methodically process the numbers over nearly five months. Together, they had undertaken the world's first large-scale scientific calculation and their achievement was immediately recognised.[1] Following Clairaut's example, Gaspard de Prony, in the midst of the Revolution, used eighty unemployed Parisian hairdressers to solve complex mathematical problems, deconstructed into very simple operations that could be undertaken by the unskilled. Their work was completed in 1801.[2]

About thirty years later, following de Prony, Charles Babbage lobbied the British government for support in building a 'difference engine' to mechanise unskilled numerical work. Babbage's lobbying was unsuccessful, but, in 1835, the director of the Greenwich Royal Observatory, George Airy, used military models of standardization – employing male teenage East Enders under close surveillance in relentless factory-like conditions – to process astronomical data.[3] Later, the military needed to predict ballistic trajectories and, in the First World War, the British army set up similar operations with female 'human computers' at Girton College, Cambridge. The first digital electronic computers were made in the 1930s, about a century after Babbage's analogue mechanical computers. However, through the depression, the US Works Progress Administration provided employment and, in 1938, one WPA project employed three mathematicians to oversee the work of 125 unskilled human computers. Over the next ten years, these economically disadvantaged and often reluctant people produced twenty-eight volumes of precision mathematical tables. They directly contributed to calculations required for making the atom bomb.[4]

The French Revolution's disregard for human life was materially manifest in the technology of the guillotine, but echoes of that same disregard are deeply intrenched in almost all technologies today – from laptops and mobile phones to planes and bike lights. Of course, the French do not carry sole responsibility for the deskilling of work that is another manifestation of disregard for human life, if less graphic than the guillotine. Babbage, for example, suggested that complex mathematical calculations should be undertaken in a manner guided by 'a cotton- or silk-mill or

[1] David Grier, 'Human Computers: The First Pioneers of the Information Age', *Endeavour*, 25, no. 1 (2001), 28–32.

[2] Ivor Grattan-Guinness, 'Work for the Hairdressers: The Production of de Prony's Logarithmic and Trigonometric Tables', *IEEE Annals of the History of Computing*, 12, no. 3 (1990), 178–81.

[3] Simon Schaffer, 'Astronomers Mark Time: Discipline and the Personal Equation', *Science in Context*, 2, no. 1 (1988), 115–45.

[4] David Grier, 'The Math Tables Project: The Reluctant Start of the Computing Era', *IEEE Annals of the History of Computing*, 20, no. 3 (1998), 33–50.

similar establishment'.[5] In this, he was following Adam Smith, the Scottish economist and moral philosopher, whose deskilling of work has been openly celebrated on British twenty pound notes, from 2007 to the time of writing – 'The division of labour in pin manufacturing (and the great increase in the quantity of work that results)'.

One day, a Parisian seamstress's livelihood would have depended upon decades of experience, her fingers constantly adjusting the pull on a needle in the knowledge of a thread's strength and a fabric's tendency to pucker. The next, it depended upon repeatedly either adding, subtracting, multiplying or dividing two single-digit numbers, with no concern for honed motor control. Likewise, a hairdresser's livelihood changed from depending upon a highly nuanced understanding of social relations to being in a position of social impotence. (Individual rebellion by human computers was frustrated because self-checking systems in the organisation of tasks meant that deliberate errors could be nullified.) As far as human computers were concerned, it made no difference whether they used pencils and sharpeners or pens and ink – their materials held no meaning, and neither, by design, did their methods.

Countless other episodes in the development of modern science could be cited, but even the briefest overview of the origins of computing displays the trajectory of modern science's attitudes towards human life and work. The wholesale conversion of seamstresses and hairdressers into human computers involved viewing people as instruments and assessing their value on the immediately observable consequences of their actions. The Industrial Revolution depended upon the ability to codify those actions to the extent that deskilled people could then be usurped by machines. And the success of that enterprise encouraged a belief that the mechanical codification of tasks was an adequate representation of those tasks. The current promise, or threat, of artificial intelligence (AI) is a continuation of the same and simply depends upon more intricate representations of some tasks currently undertaken by humans. Yet it is of interest to observe that the tasks that have proved most amenable to AI are generally 'expert' tasks. This suggests that, even if they are hidden from our view, 'everyday' tasks involve complexities that are beyond the modes of representation available to digital technologies.

This essay will consider the relationship between pre-modern science and the pre-modern lived experience. The flavour of that relationship –

[5] Charles Babbage, *On the Economy of Machinery and Manufacture*, 3rd ed., 1835, 191–6, in Schaffer, 'Astronomers', 120.

which, I assert, is very different from the relationship between modern science and the modern lived experience – will be alluded to by reference to specific examples of tasks involved in the traditional creation of art. And by comparing the approaches of pre-modern and modern science, I hope to throw light on cultural choices about world views and their consequences, highlighting two factors relevant to the 'after science and religion' project.

Importantly, making art requires understandings of, and competencies in, the manipulation of both the material and the social worlds. Without such knowledges and skills, artworks could not be the 'objects of power' that they demonstrably are, and have been, across all human cultures.[6] Here, I wish to focus on the material aspects of making art in medieval, renaissance and early modern Europe and would immediately acknowledge that the traditional creative process involved many tasks that could at first sight be considered 'mechanical', in other words, physically arduous and intellectually unchallenging. Nonetheless, I would suggest that these methods need not have been meaningless, unlike the purposefully meaningless working methods of individual human computers or pin-factory workers.

Not surprisingly, technicalities in the making of art respond to cultural changes. For example, where the preparation of artists' colours was once the domain of monks, it became a task for the laity. Particularly gruelling tasks, like the rasping of New World woods to make the red pigment 'brazil', were undertaken in the sixteenth and seventeenth centuries by slave labour and then by prisoners in Amsterdam's jails until windmills proved more cost-effective.[7] However, for tens of millennia, red, yellow and brown rocks have been laboriously ground by hand by the same individuals who then adorned their bodies and cave walls and, eventually, their altarpieces and chapel ceilings with the resulting 'sienna', 'ochre' and 'umber' pigments.[8]

Yet even if grinding rock was hard work, it still involved considerable skill, and, for the Greeks, skill in the most material sense could be related to wisdom. For them, the contemplative life, *theoria*, led to *sophia*, which is timeless and unchanging wisdom. At the other extreme, the sensual life, *poesis*, involved *techne*, which is morally neutral skill, like knowing how to

[6] Elizabeth DeMarrais and John Robb, 'Art Makes Society', *World Art*, 3, no. 1 (2013), 3–22.

[7] Erma Hermens and Arie Wallert, 'The Pekstok Papers, Lake Pigments, Prisons and Paint-Mills', in E. Hermens (ed.), *Looking through Paintings* (London: Archetype, 1998), 276–80.

[8] Ruth Siddall, 'Mineral Pigments in Archaeology', *Minerals*, 8 (2018), 201–35.

grind pigments or paint flesh. However, the normal way of life, *praxis*, fell somewhere between the two and led to *phronesis*, which is the wisdom of the ever-changing political and social worlds. The biblical idea of wisdom is a broader version of the Greek *phronesis* since it is rooted in the well-being of more than just the political and social realms, but it too can be nourished by the practices of everyday and life and work.[9]

Grinding rock was undertaken by painters or their assistants, often as apprentices, and could be undertaken in formal structures, such as the medieval guild of St Luke. These were political and social structures and were perfect places for developing wisdom – whether changeable *phronesis* or timeless *sophia* – since, for apprentices at formative stages in their lives, guilds were 'schools for practice'. Now, practice is related to the Greek *praxis*, and the modern idea of a school comes from the Greek word *scholé*, which included the concept of leisure. In the modern world – thanks to radical changes in working conditions, as illustrated by the French Revolution's re-deployment of skilled seamstresses and hairdressers as unskilled human computers – the word 'leisure' means 'time off', 'free time' or 'when not working'. However, in the pre-modern world, the word described a state of mind characterised by inward calm. To be leisurely was to be free from the chatter of outside world and therefore able to hear clearly; it was to be free from pressures and therefore able to act with deliberation; it was to be free of distraction and therefore able to focus. Calling this state of mind *scholé* suggests that the ancients considered being leisurely as the best way to learn.[10]

So, when a fourteenth-century artists' manual recommended that one could grind the red pigment vermilion 'every day for twenty years', it was not intended as punishing hard labour, as preparing red pigments later became for New World slaves or Dutch prisoners. With a leisurely state of mind, grinding vermilion could have been an opportunity for an artist to learn and become 'better and more perfect' themselves, just like their pigment.[11] In fact, if a person was of a restless disposition, then a repetitive action like grinding pigment could provide rest. Today, the nature of the workplace has changed so radically that we tend not to see the repetitive acts undertaken at supermarket check-outs, for example, as particularly restful. Nonetheless, repetitive acts that are undertaken by choice can provide profound mental respite, even if they are extremely arduous. So,

[9] David Kelsey, *Eccentric Existence* (Louisville, KY: Westminster John Knox Press, 2009), 194–5.

[10] Josef Pieper, *Leisure: The Basis of Culture*, tr. A. Dru (London: Faber and Faber, 1952).

[11] Cennino Cennini, *The Craftsman's Handbook*, tr. D. V. Thompson (New York: Dover, 1960), 24.

for example, marathon runners are completely liberated from their everyday worries once 'into their stride' or 'in the zone'. A marathon typically involves 30,000–50,000 steps and takes, for most, three or four hours. Grinding rock by hand generally took thousands of cycles of a granite muller over a porphyry slab and nearly always took much longer than the process of applying the resulting paint to a panel or canvas.

The fact that today people freely undertake repetitive tasks as leisure activities makes it easy to appreciate that the repetitive tasks involved in the traditional historic processing of artists' materials need not have been considered onerous. Grinding rock could be an opportunity to be absorbed by the process, and then both the material and the method could become meaningful. The human could still be identified as an instrument when viewed by a disinterested observer, but the person who participated in the task could be engaged in the phenomena in ways that are not evident to the observer. The leisurely, or mindful, craftsperson is attuned, for example, to subtle cues such as the sounds associated with grinding, which shift imperceptibly from unpleasant screeches through a series of rhythmic hisses to a steady hypnotic song. These are easily missed by one who just passes through the artists' workshop and who has no inkling that the sounds might be meaningful. Leisurely or mindful craftspeople are also privy to subtle cues that are completely inaccessible to any outside observer, such as their sixth sense – the proprioceptive senses that enable them to judge material properties through their muscles. Proprioceptive skills include, amongst other things, the pre- or subconscious reflection upon live muscle sensations in the light of stored muscle memories, and they are the precious product of long practice. These underlie some of a traditional craft's 'secrets', and they are literally secreted within the body of the craftsperson, below the levels that are accessible to explicit conscious interrogation. Of course, these intensely personal ways of understanding the world are still necessary for navigating the modern world. For example, as an everyday task, we know whether or not a cardboard carton of milk is full by its resistance to being lifted, and, as an expert task, surgeons know how hard to pull a suture to re-join but not tear flesh. These essentially inward ways of knowing 'what feels right' have, however, been banished from the official modern scientific view of the world.

When we have acquired such proprioceptive skills, we retrospectively recognise a shift in our conscious relationship with a task and say it has been 'mastered'. This is the basis of the painter's 'masterpiece', the work of art that demonstrated to the guild that its teachings have been secreted within the individual. Likewise, so-called Old Master paintings acknowledge the embodied skills of their authors. The acquisition of proprioceptive skills occurs naturally through repetitive practice. It was the essentially natural and inward, or secret, mode of this acquisition that led to it being overlooked by those, like Adam Smith, who observed pre-industrial pin-makers but never actually made a pin.

Adam Smith eschewed pin-making because it was very obviously repetitive, involving a limited set of actions and executed by rote or habit, and, since Descartes, habit was considered to arrest and inhibit thought and freedom. However, habit has an essential role to play in the sequential acquisition of skills. For example, the detailed 'understandings', in Merleau-Ponty's use of the word,[12] that enable walking have to be assigned to pre- or subconscious habit in order to free up consciousness and allow it to attend to the detailed understandings that will enable running. Habit can be seen as an efficient 'synthesis of past events'.[13]

The creation of art involves the artist developing an extraordinary hierarchy of habits. These range from grinding pigments, which may have been undertaken with particular 'workshop styles',[14] to depicting ears, which could be executed quasi-automatically and thus constitute 'signatures' in unsigned paintings.[15] The fact that a particular distribution of sizes of microscopic particles may be indicative of a given workshop and that the idiosyncratic trajectory of a loaded brush can be used to identify a painter indicates that habits are very specific to individuals and their relationships with particular materials or circumstances. A habit is an extraordinarily personal nexus with the world, and, as it develops, it gradually attunes the subject to the object of its attention, summarising previous experiences to facilitate responses to unknown futures.

Felix Ravaisson, the philosopher and archaeologist, saw habit as an 'obscure activity' or 'unreflective spontaneity' that grew out of the conscious will but, when fully grown, resided below the reach of 'will, personality and consciousness'.[16] It thus enabled engagement with a world that was beyond the will, personality or consciousness. For Ravaisson, a 'double law' underlay habit, at once weakening passive sensations while

[12] Maurice Merleau-Ponty, *The Phenomenology of Perception*, tr. C. Smith (New York: Humanities Press, 1962), 44.

[13] Elizabeth Grosz, 'Habit Today: Ravaisson, Bergson, Deleuze and Us', *Body and Society*, 19, nos. 2–3 (2013), 220.

[14] Jan van Asperen de Boer, 'An Examination of Particle Size Distribution of Azurite and Natural Ultramarine in Early Netherlandish Paintings', *Studies in Conservation*, 19, no. 4 (1974), 233–43.

[15] Carlo Ginzburg, 'Morelli, Freud and Sherlock Holmes', *History Workshop*, 9 (1980), 5–36.

[16] Felix Ravaisson, *Of Habit*, tr. C. Carlisle and M. Sinclair (London: Continuum, 2008), 51, 53.

strengthening deeds and active perceptions.[17] It was the tendency whereby originally voluntary ideas were gradually absorbed into natural actions and, as such, could be seen as essential in the development of motor skills.[18] This view of habit therefore not only bridges the mind–body divide; it also bridges the apparent gulf between culture and nature (habits are initiated by the will and become 'second nature'). And indeed, the concept of habit as intelligent tendencies or inclinations in nature is manifest in the language that describes the animal, vegetable and mineral realms.

Animals can have 'habits', or regular behaviours that are open to adaption and therefore not instinctive. Gun dogs, for example can point, lifting a front paw to indicate the presence and direction of game (possibly using one paw to indicate hidden 'feathers' and the other for hidden 'fur'). Plants are said to have 'habits', defined as their characteristic shapes or architectures, which are the product of general inclinations and particular circumstances. For centuries, the circumstances in which oak trees grew were controlled by varying local practices of forest management to create two distinct tree habits from one type of acorn. These craft practices were coordinated across northern Europe in the late Middle Ages to source straight-grained wood (from Baltic oaks) and twisted-grained wood (from English oak) to make split-able panels and load-bearing beams, respectively. Even in the mineral realm, the word 'habit' is used to describe the shapes in which crystals grow. Responding to their immediate environments, like oak trees, carbon atoms can aggregate into structures that are laminar (in the case of graphite) or pyramidal (diamond).

Different possible crystal habits may imply that atoms have a degree of consciousness about their environment (temperature and pressure, for example), while plant habits imply greater consciousness of their environment (wind directions, water sources, the presence of neighbouring obstructions, etc.) and a will to move towards the light. But such existential or vegetative souls or self-organising tendencies need not imply an animist material world or any inherent material agency.[19] Indeed, current suggestions that inanimate materials possess agency may owe something to the failure of their authors, like Adam Smith, to physically engage with craft in a traditionally habitual and leisurely manner.

In the absence of first-hand experience, it is easy to overlook the ways in which humans who modify materials are simultaneously modified by them

[17] Ibid., 49. [18] Ibid., 71. [19] Alfred Gell, *Art and Agency* (Oxford: Clarendon, 2013).

in reciprocal relationships.[20] When an artist or craftsperson works with their material, it is as if they are the leading partner in a couple, but when the couple dances, their quality of movement depends equally on both partners. Of course, the material is better at some steps than others, so the dance can improve only if the artist is sensitive, and responds, to the material's dispositions. We do not need to assign consciousness to animals, vegetables and minerals, but their habits do, however, allow the post-rationalisation of 'affordances', or the types of behaviours that are typically associated with parts of the material world that, once absorbed, assist us in navigating or harnessing the outside world.[21] The extent to which the artist learns or the material teaches – the material possesses affordances or agency – depends upon the perception of 'obscure activities'.

For example, in terms of modern science, graphite's laminar habit, combined with the idea of slippage between layers, accounts for its use as a lubricant, whilst the pyramidal habit of diamond could be seen to underpin its hardness and account for its use as an abrasive. Of course, the atoms that underlie graphite and diamond were parts of a minority view in pre-modern science, in which, for example, gold's affordances or agency were not thought of as due to constituent atoms. In pre-modern science, gold was the only metal to survive trial by fire because of its relationship with the sun, the only luminous planet. Each of the metals corresponded to a planet as a terrestrial 'embodied intelligence' that reflected a celestial 'intelligent body'. Gold and the sun were forms of matter with similar ways of participating in their respective realms.

It was the pre-modern artist's or craftsperson's task to recognise the predispositions of their materials and hone their responses to them through repeated mutual engagement. But materials' affordances or agencies may not be obvious since they are outward signs of materials' own habits or 'obscure activities'. So, as part of the dialogue between craftspeople and their materials, the ingredients or conditions of procedures could be modified in processes of trial and error. And, just like modern scientists, artists and craftspeople were guided in the construction of their trials by the cosmological frameworks available to them.

Most pre-modern science understood the cosmos in hylomorphic terms, as matter manifest in a variety of forms. But even in modern science, matter still comes in various forms – the modern world's atoms are forms

20 Andrew Pickering, *The Mangle of Practice: Time Agency and Science* (Chicago: University of Chicago Press, 1995).

21 James Gibson, *Ecological Approach to Visual Perception* (Boston: Houghton Mifflin, 1979).

of (subatomic) matter arranged in patterns that constitute just over a hundred elements. The exact number of elements is of no great importance, as it changes whenever the conditions are achieved that enable the generation of a new element. But the supposed nature of modern science's hundred-or-so elements as the fundamental 'building blocks' of the physical universe is extremely important. The role of building blocks implies that everything we see, hear, feel, taste or smell is, or has its origins in, an assemblage of different, more or less indestructible entities. Those assemblages are unimaginably complex combinations of entities that are not only about four times as populous as the letters of the alphabet but are, moreover, also completely inaccessible to our senses.[22] Atoms – like the carbon that underlies both lubricating graphite and abrasive diamond – are therefore beyond the comprehension of any one individual and can be understood only by virtue of mediating instrumentation and collective enterprise. Modern materials are therefore inherently meaningless and any method that manipulates them is merely expedient.

In contrast, the pre-modern hylomorphic understanding of the world saw a universal 'prime matter' that manifested itself in four fundamental forms: earth, water, air and fire. These four forms of matter were also called elements, but they were ways of being or 'habits', not building blocks. The four pre-modern elements could be called the modes of solidity and fluidity, the vaporous and the consuming, respectively. And like those entities that underlie modern science, they were completely abstract. But while the modern elements are amenable only to inspection mediated by technological instrumentation and mathematical interpretation, the pre-modern elements lent themselves to direct engagement with an individual's imagination. That imagination was, in turn, guided by bodily experiences of a reality lived amongst things that participated, to greater or lesser extent, in being habitually solid, liquid and gaseous, as well as amongst things that habitually appeared to consume other things.

This pre-modern science constructed upon elemental modes of being proved incapable of manipulating the physical world with sufficient precision to make planes or mobile phones. It could not make accurate predictions, but, in combination with other expressions of the underlying pre-modern metaphysic, it could be used to post-rationalize sophisticated and detailed observations about the physical world. The traditional elements' very evident failure to provide a theoretical framework that enabled

[22] In Latin, *elementum* simultaneously meant element (in cosmology), number (in arithmetic) and letter (in grammar).

robust prediction of material behaviour would have been a very grave weakness indeed if one was seeking a universally applicable model of reality. However, the predictive failure of the four elements could also be said support the argument that universally applicable models of reality are not to be found in, or perfectly reflected by, any lived experience of the material world. The pre-modern explication of the material world in terms of any one of a number of different expressions of a metaphysic logically led to the idea of 'the exception that proves the rule'. It acknowledged that all rules – including the rules of habitual elemental behaviour – necessarily have limited scope.[23]

Yet a lived reality is, of course, facilitated by some degree of predictability. Although we cannot reliably know whether or not it will be obscured by cloud, we can reliably know, for example, that the sun will rise in the east. Repeated experience of the natural world sets parameters on our expectations of order and variation and, up to the seventeenth century, the science based on four elements evidently satisfied those expectations. Their efficacy as a framework in which to order the experience of lived reality was accepted with caveats. Their failures could be rationalised in terms of other influences – such as relationships with planets, and so on – having a role in the predisposing of behaviours in physical phenomenon. For artificial, as opposed to natural, phenomena to be repeated efficiently, the many variables that determine their outcome must be minimized. This is a practical expression of Occam's razor – identifying and controlling relevant factors while ignoring irrelevant factors. For the modern science laboratory, the positions of planets are amongst the irrelevant factors that can be ignored for most experimental purposes. On the other hand, for the pre-modern artists' workshop, the positions of planets were theoretically relevant to some material processes.[24]

The four pre-modern elements, positions of the planets, and so on, certainly did not explain everything, but they did give meanings to artists' materials. They also evidently explained enough to enable the construction of a coherent material world view that allowed the conversion of accidental discoveries into reliable technologies. In other words, they generated

[23] Of course, despite its different aspirations, this is also true of modern science – the rules that explain the behaviour of billiard balls do not explain the behaviour of an audience watching a game of billiards. However, a reductive science assumes that it is only a question of time before 'higher' phenomena can be fully explained by 'lower' phenomena.

[24] Mary Merrifield, *Original Treatises on the Arts of Painting* (New York: Dover, 1967), vol. II, 432–54.

methods that were repeatable. And, I would say, precisely because those methods were also considered meaningful, the resulting technologies were capable of making great works of art and providing support for enduring social structures.

The four elements have been theorized for millennia as manifestations of *hyle* in Greek natural philosophy, 'the waters' in the hexameral tradition and Latin *sylva*.[25] But more importantly, for the purposes of this chapter, they were also experienced. The four elements were never found pure but were always mixed in composite bodies, in which – if perfect balance was not obtained – one element predominated. The Doctrine of Signatures codified how the dominant elements could be identified in composite bodies, but no complex codification was necessary for many phenomena. The howling wind, for example, could manifest the power residing in air, and pouring rain expressed its combination with water, while the rock ledge that offered shelter and security provided the imagination with a model for earth's properties. The campfire that provided respite from the cold, as long as it was fed – or threatened life, if it got out of control – demonstrated fire's power.

First-hand, embodied, experience of the meteorological and geological 'elements' effortlessly taught pre-moderns the meaning of being predominantly earthy, watery, airy or fiery. Earth's solidity was the definitive example of dependability except, of course, when moved by fire in earthquakes and volcanoes, by water in mudslides or by air in sandstorms. Water's liquidity provided an entirely consistent pattern of changeability; tranquil when undisturbed, torrential when hurled off earth in cascades, tempestuous when whipped up by air and boiling when subjected to fire. Like earth, air was also dependable, except when the stuff of life was crushed under earth, drowned in water or consumed by fire. Like water, fire also involved change, although while water's nature was essentially passive, fire's nature was so active that it could be thought alive with an insatiable appetite, eating voraciously until starved. These behaviours established what could be taken for granted and, within this framework, all materials, as elemental mixtures, had inherent meanings.

Through the concept of the four humours, the elements were also harnessed to post-rationalise the way humans operated in their own psychic worlds. When a person's internal balance was lost, earthy melancholic tendencies could make them dull and heavy, watery phlegmatics became washed out, and airy sanguines could be vacuous whilst fiery

25 David Macauley, *Elemental Philosophy* (Albany: State University of New York Press, 2010).

cholerics were aggressive. People's internal balance was affected by the food and drink they consumed, so that alcohol, for example – which was traditionally seen as a mixture of fire and water – could make people more phlegmatic or choleric when drunk. Internal balance was also affected by the cycle of the seasons and the cycles of life, so that melancholic tendencies were more likely, for example, in autumn and old age. The internal balance of the soul was also affected by the colours that entered the eye and the sounds that entered the ears. Painting and music were therefore therapies that could help prevent 'accidents of the soul'; indeed, Aristotle saw the four elements as 'instruments of the soul'.[26]

Like physical habits, these mental structures helped reinforce links between the inside and outside worlds. The four elements aided the construction of an encompassing world view in which all matter, including human matter, resonated. The profound connection between humans and their material world could be compared to the relationship between children and their mother, since, etymologically, the word 'matter' has its root in *mater*, or mother.

Given these connections, it was widely assumed that there were fundamental dialogues between the four elements manifest in the outside world, in the physical body and in the soul. Given such intimate links between an individual's psyche and their external environment, it was recognised that the management of physical and mental health depended on what we might call lifestyle choices. Of course, the lifestyle one adopted was determined in large part by the type of work in which one was engaged. In the pre-modern world, many if not most occupations were deeply influenced by the materials habitually encountered in work, and – dance-like – those materials' own habits could 'rub off' on the people who worked with them.

For example, aspects of world views held by the original members of the Potter family were formed by their relationship with clay, the early Smiths were likewise influenced by their engagement with iron, and the Carpenters with wood. Now, moulding clay is done with gentle hands lubricated by water, whilst forging iron is done with forceful hands assisted by fire. On the other hand, carving wood is done by repeatedly gouging or chipping away at a solid block. Years of experience of working every day with clay, iron or wood – and learning the ways those materials responded to different treatments – could shape a person's expectation of how to

[26] Aristotle, *On the Soul* (II, x, 423a), tr. W. S. Hett, Loeb Classical Library (Cambridge, MA: Harvard University Press, 1964), 131.

engage with the world outside the workshop and also influence their understanding of how it might respond to them. The effect of working those materials was so profound that not only did people take their family names from their vocations, but material behaviours also shaped the language that we all now all share. They shaped familial identities and social strategies. Were the original Potters more inclined to 'mould circumstances' to their liking, did the early Smiths 'forge a path' ahead and did the Carpenters 'carve out a niche' for themselves? While these are now merely figures of speech, 'moulding' still carries an echo of massaging events, 'forging' suggests violent confrontation and 'carving' has connotations of a laborious incremental process. Each of these valid social strategies reflects a meaningful workshop method and material behaviour. Given the religious nature of much pre-modern, guild-based, art and craft practice, methods involving materials could be both models for, as well as models of, life.[27]

The religious nature of guilds was social, with a pastoral dimension, but it could also be seen as a consequence of the mode of learning they practiced and promoted. Pieper said about the acquisition of knowledge in a leisurely manner that 'effort is not the cause; it is the condition'.[28] This has obvious parallels with Ravaisson's understanding of habit in which the acquisition of skill presupposes past efforts but is not the necessary result of those efforts. Through the Greek idea of habit as *ethos*, it has been suggested that the 'ontology of habit' is linked to the 'theology of grace'.[29] This implies that craft skills, like the virtues, are gifts that are received, not achievements that have been earned, and that guilds were institutionalised manifestations of a gift exchange system.[30] The current description of artists and craftspeople as 'gifted' may be a faint recognition of the origin of skill or knowledge as a gift. Certainly, if the 'obscure activity' of habit is beyond the reach of will and consciousness, then will and consciousness cannot legitimately take credit for the fruits of habit. As such, embodied skills should not really be described as having been 'mastered' but, rather, 'followed'. This is in stark contrast with the approach taken by modern science.[31]

[27] Clifford Geertz, *The Interpretation of Culture* (New York: Basic Books, 1973), 95.
[28] Pieper, *Leisure*, 41.
[29] Clare Carlisle, 'Between Freedom and Necessity: Felix Ravaisson on Habit and the Moral Life', *Inquiry*, 53, no. 2 (2010), 126–37.
[30] Bert de Munck, 'Artisans, Productions and Gifts: Rethinking the History of Material Culture in Early Modern Europe', *Past and Present*, 224 (2014), 63.
[31] Carolyn Merchant, 'The Violence of Impediments: Francis Bacon and the Origins of Experimentation', *Isis*, 99 (2008), 731–60.

Heraclitus called receptive contemplation, which was integral to learning through apprenticeship, 'listening to the essence of things'.[32] And of course, all things have different essences. So, for example, vermilion (a particular crystal habit of mercury sulphide) may make a 'better and more perfect' red if ground for twenty years, but not all pigments behave the same. Azurite and malachite (two different habits naturally adopted by copper carbonate) lose their rich blue and green colours if ground too much, becoming insipid greys. Also, if gold leaf is ground too much it loses its glitter and becomes a very expensive way of achieving the colour of mud. If you see these changes, then you've gone too far, hence the importance of listening to the hypnotic songs sung by materials as they lie between the muller and the slab.

In order to realize the best results with their materials, artists and craftspeople had to attend to more than just a material's song, and gold leaf is a good example of the relationship that a material could demand of the whole being of its would-be dance partner. When purified to twenty-four carats, gold becomes malleable enough to beat into sheets about a hundred times thinner than a cigarette paper. These sheets, or leaves, can then be adhered to a panel and polished to create the appearance of solid gold. The gold leaf that surrounds painted depictions of Christ, the Virgin and Saints represents heaven. Now, that heaven was not achieved by force, indeed, not on any artist's terms, but only on gold's terms, as the metal that survived trial by fire. Independent leaves of gold cannot be touched because they are so thin that the least pressure between thumb and finger would rip them apart. They can be moved only by mutual attraction onto a fine squirrel-hair brush, and, once lifted, the slightest breeze will waft them away, to crumple and tear on the workshop floor. Beaten gold determines the pace of work, slowing the artist down to a rhythm in which moving the leaves has to be coordinated with shallow, gentle breathing. Laying gold leaf on a panel to represent heaven requires a relaxed, calm and meditative approach – the behaviour of the most immaterial of materials sets the conditions for the artist's behaviour and ensures a heavenly means towards a heavenly effect.

It is therefore fitting that many pre-modern works of art are anonymous, and the painter of the *Wilton Diptych*, for example, is unknown.[33] However, when viewed from the perspective of the four elements,

[32] Heraclitus, *Fragment 112*, ed. Diels, cited in Pieper, *Leisure*, 33.

[33] The National Gallery, 'The Wilton Diptych: English or French?', www.nationalgallery.org.uk/paintings/english-or-french-the-wilton-diptych (accessed September 13, 2021).

grounded in a geocentric universe, the way the painting materials have been employed in its heavenly section exactly mirrors the positions those materials would have adopted, in the ideal world, if they had been given the freedom to follow their own dispositions.[34] The *Diptych* is not a masterpiece and it is not by an Old Master. And rather than the product of 'mastering' muscles and materials, the object may derive its undeniable power as a cultural artefact from the painter 'following' the natural inclinations of their muscles and their materials. Not mastering, but following our nature is art as leisure, not labour.[35] As such, the painting may be seen as the product of physical processes that reflect mental processes which allow expression of the *intellectus* that transcends individuality – a gift that participates in the 'angelic faculty of non-discursive vision'.[36]

In conclusion, modern science recognises that humans actively seek out patterns in their environments and construct meanings by matching patterns of causes with patterns of effects. Modern science also recognises the value of habit, for example, as a means of improving signal-to-noise ratios when seeking out patterns in formally replicable laboratory experiments. As such, modern science has much in common with the pre-modern ways of making art. However, key differences are modern science's emphasis on effortful *ratio* at the expense of receptive *intellectus* and its dependence upon disembodied representations of phenomena. The modes of representation that are appropriate for modern science's mediating instrumentation have unambiguously extended the depth of its view into the world. However, they have simultaneously constricted its breadth of view.

While pre-modern science sought to engage an individual's experiences and feelings, the methodology of modern science aims to exclude them. If modern science can know only what it makes – through the laboratory experiment – then its knowledge is limited by eliminating the personal. I would suggest that the relationship between science and religion will evolve when modern science finds ways of accommodating the fact that the human instrument has access to a range of phenomena that are far beyond the reach of any mediating technical instrumentation. This is not a denial of technological efficacy or a claim that people possess X-ray vision but is instead an acknowledgement that the embodied and engaged first-

34 Spike Bucklow, *The Riddle of the Image* (London: Reaktion, 2014), 107–40.

35 Thomas Aquinas, *Summa Theologica* (II, ii, 108, 2) quoted in Pieper, *Leisure*, 40.

36 Pieper, *Leisure*, 35.

person participant has access to a range of phenomena far beyond the reach of any disinterested third-person observer, whether human or machine. It is a recognition that the mind is a mediator and that unmediated intelligences reside both in and beyond the body. It is also an affirmation, from the perspective of the unscholarly craftsperson, of statements in the biblical and hermetic traditions – 'the lowest reflects the highest' and 'as above, so below' – and of suggestions in the more recent literature.[37]

The advent of any substantially new relationship between science and religion will require the return of science from a narrow *techne* to a broad *art*, an activity in which things are 'put together or joined'.[38] However, in its current incarnation, science aims to master and work on nature, not follow and work with it. As a result, science has chosen to relinquish the insights offered by intuition, aesthetics and proprioception. Acknowledging their potential epistemological validity would seriously complicate the modern scientific enterprise.[39] It would also require of the would-be scientist a broader education and an expanded intention – not only to learn about nature but also to learn from nature, to not only bend nature to our will but also to bend our will to it. It would, however, go some way towards healing the official division between subject and object, and it has already been profitably embraced by the tiny minority of individuals who have effected paradigm shifts in the so-called hard sciences, and also, institutionally, in some of the so-called soft sciences. By considering different styles of 'knowing through making' – such as painters' practices – and re-evaluating its own relationship with personal imagination, social norms and skilled labour, science might change from a *techne* into an *art* and thus be in a position to find a new relationship with religion.

[37] Michael Polanyi, 'Life Transcending Physics and Chemistry', *Chemical and Engineering News*, 45, no. 35 (1967), 54–69.

[38] OED, online version.

[39] A first step might be to consider the differences between the practice of science in the English-speaking world with the tradition of *Wissenschaft.*

Conclusion

Peter Harrison

Providing the historical background to contemporary debates and discussions is often regarded as just that – background. History is seen as setting the context, perhaps offering an interesting account of how we got to where we are today, but beyond this not much more. When stronger, normative claims are made on history's behalf, they are often dismissed as sentimental gestures towards an idealised past that could never realistically be recovered. The contributors to this volume have taken a different view, seeking to show how historical considerations can significantly shape contemporary discussions and move the conversation forward in novel ways. The 'how we got to where we are today' question turns out to be of vital importance to how we might move beyond modes of science–religion interaction that are largely unproductive. Beyond this, history can also show the potential of paths that were not taken (or were taken by only by the few) by pointing to alternative models of the relationship that were possible because the cultural territory was differently divided in the past, but which nevertheless have some prospects of success in the future.

One the key developments in the 'how we got to where we are today' story was the 'great reversal' of the nineteenth century to which Lightman refers in his chapter. What transpired in this reversal was that religious understandings of the meaning and purpose of nature gave way to naturalistic ones that were underpinned by the success of the sciences. This was not a simple matter of science finally triumphing over religion, however. Since the birth of modern science in the seventeenth century, the Christian narrative had co-existed quite happily with burgeoning scientific activities. Even in the first half of the nineteenth century, natural theology had provided the matrix within which the sciences were communicated to general audiences. For this reason, Liberal Protestant thinkers had happily accommodated their theology to the findings and ethos of the sciences. So it was that the scientific naturalists, whose activism is described in

Lightman's chapter, received a measure of support from sectors of the theological community. The longer story behind this transition, moreover, stretches back much further than the distinctive forms of rationalistic deism and higher biblical criticism launched in the eighteenth century. Indeed, the origins of this development might be traced as far back as late medieval philosophy and reformed Christian theology. The point to notice here, however, is just how different were connections between theology and knowledges of nature prior to the reversal. Early modern science was deeply informed by a range of seventeenth-century theological assumptions. The nineteenth century 'out growing' of that original embedding and then the interpretive reversal of their original relationship contributed powerfully, by the late twentieth century, to the dominance of a naturalistic understanding of the world that was fundamentally at odds with traditional religious worldviews.

This reversal gave a particular shape to science–religion discourse, with respective territories set out for science and religion, and along with them a necessarily lopsided power relation. At its simplest, this development placed science in the driving seat, with the onus being placed on the religious side to make the concessions and compromises. The much-touted dialogue model of science–religion interactions – and this tends to be the favoured option for religiously sympathetic participants in the conversation – finds itself in this unenviable position.[1] In practice, while 'dialogue' is suggestive of a conversation between two equal partners, the reality is that the 'conversation' has often consisted in one-way traffic (Lightman, Harrison). There are few, if any, instances that we can point to in which the content or conduct of science has changed significantly as a consequence of this kind of interaction.[2] This is dialogue in name only.

An alternative strategy in the wake of the great reversal is simply to keep science and religion separate. One simple version of this would be the assertion that science deals with facts, religion with morals and meaning. This 'non-overlapping magisteria' option, to use the well-known expression of Stephen Jay Gould, has a certain appeal, not least because it seems

[1] There are a number of typologies of science–religion interaction, most of which feature some version of dialogue. Best known is Ian Barbour's four-fold typology: conflict, independence, dialogue, integration; the first three are typically regarded as live options for the present. See Ian G. Barbour, *Religion in an Age of Science* (San Francisco, CA: Harper and Row, 1990), ch. 1.

[2] Fine-tuning arguments may seem to offer an example, but anthropic reasoning was first deployed by British astronomer Fred Hoyle, a self-declared atheist. A better case could perhaps be made for convergent evolution, which although a generally known feature of evolutionary history, has been championed by Christian evolutionists like Simon Conway Morris in *Life's Solution: Inevitable Humans in a Lonely Universe* (Cambridge: Cambridge University Press, 2003).

obviously true that science and religion are not competing explanatory frameworks, and that areas of significant overlap are fewer than commonly assumed.[3] Again, however, because of the social and epistemic prestige of science, what happens in practice is that science gets to choose what territory it occupies, with the consequence that it can gradually encroach upon the ever-shrinking domain of theology and religion. We see instances of this in attempts to ground morality in the natural sciences, and in reductionistic social scientific accounts of religious belief that seek to act as debunking arguments.[4] In short, the independence model can often just amount to an unsatisfactory truce (Milbank) in which one party makes all the adjustments.

The stark alternative to dialogue and independence is conflict. As Lightman's chapter so lucidly illustrates, late nineteenth-century religious thinkers found themselves having either to make significant concessions to the sciences in the name of dialogue or independence or to resort to the conflict position. This option might have preserved something of the integrity of some long-held religious beliefs and ways of life but at a significant cost. For the dominant culture, 'religion' in this mode could easily be dismissed as a reactionary and irrational holdover from a pre-scientific era.

The historical analysis that informs this collection suggests that contemporary science–religion discourse is constrained by the circumstances of its history and the categories in which the relationships are expressed. The constraints give rise to the equally unsatisfactory options of a one-sided dialogue, a false peace, or an inevitable conflict. But this same analysis also points towards ways out of this 'trilemma'. In this volume, two have predominated. The first involves looking back to the origins of modernity, when the pioneers of modern science made a break with the dominant medieval synthesis of theology and Aristotelian philosophy, and opted instead for the alternative that has underpinned much of modern science. What we see at this historical juncture is that there were then (as there remain) alternative potential philosophical partners for the sciences. The second move involves an exploration of the pre-nineteenth-century categories 'natural philosophy' and 'the natural philosopher' as offering

[3] Stephen Jay Gould, *Rocks of Ages: Science and Religion in the Fullness of Life* (New York: Ballantine, 1999).

[4] Mikael Stenmark has described this as 'scientific expansionism'. *How to Relate Science and Religion: A Multidimensional Model* (Grand Rapids, MI: Eerdmans, 2004), xi–xii. This shades into conflict.

different models for the relationship between science and religion, and for the persona of the modern 'scientist'.

Regarding the first option, we can say that early modern figures, in the wake of the challenges to traditional authority unleashed by the Protestant reformation, found themselves freed from obeisance to Aristotle. They were able to ask anew what kind of philosophical partner would best do justice to both their theological commitments and scientific ambitions. There were several options on the table: live versions of the traditional Aristotelian synthesis, Platonism and Neoplatonism, Scepticism, Natural Magic (often linked to Neoplatonism), Neostoicism, and, finally, Christianised Epicureanism. While many combinations were trialled, the last of these was to provide the most enduring partner for an emerging new natural philosophy (although, arguably, it was less successful in the sphere of natural history and, subsequently, biology). Christian Epicureanism offered a corpuscular matter theory that drained nature of all its inherent virtues and powers, and this turned out to be perfectly matched with a voluntaristic Deity who, through his arbitrary will, imposed laws of motion on a world now made up of inert particles distributed in space. While this partnership yielded a powerful and predictive physics, its incipient materialism and atheism never really went away. Fatefully, then, it was this partnership that laid the foundations for the 'great reversal'. For its seventeenth-century proponents, laws of nature were God's laws, and the only genuine causal power in the natural world was God. All that nineteenth-century naturalists had to do was to redescribe God's ubiquitous causal activity in the world, along with his laws, as 'natural'. Laws of nature that had once been divine edicts now became brute facts about the natural world that were not capable of further explanation, and questions about the ultimate nature of causation were passed over in silence.

The science–religion discussion that largely takes the official, if often implicit, metaphysics of modern science for granted tends to be locked into a tight range of restricted possibilities for the relationship between science and religion. This is the 'trilemma' problem. This position also inherits a set of quite specific and potentially intractable difficulties. One of the central legacies of the nineteenth-century transformation of laws of God into laws of nature was the entirely new conundrum of how divine action was possible in a world that was now described as 'casually closed' (Hart, Milbank, Schindler). On the one hand, this apparent problem has been celebrated by naturalists as a vindication of their commitments; on the other, it has exercised and tested the ingenuity of those theistic scientists and philosophers who accept the terms in which it is stated.[5] The clear implication of a number of the contributions to this volume is that this 'problem', as typically understood in much science–religion discourse, is the artefact of a set of metaphysical assumptions about causation that are regarded either as indispensable presuppositions of modern science or as necessary implications of its findings. The mistake, on this analysis, is to address the problem of divine action in the implicit metaphysical terms in which it initially presents itself (Soskice). History provides a rich repository of other ways of looking at this question. While the alternatives proposed by a number of our contributors may appear to some as nostalgic attempts to revive esoteric and obsolete metaphysical doctrines that have been lost in the mists of time, in fact they are simply re-asking the question that confronted early modern thinkers and which helped drive the scientific revolution: Which set of philosophical commitments best does justice to both the practices of science and perennial questions of ultimate meaning and value? The available metaphysical alternatives have never really gone away, moreover, and a more careful and historically informed excavation of the foundations of our scientific practices will reveal the extent of their survival (Hart, Milbank).

The goal here is not simply that of finding a metaphysics that is congenial to Christian theology while being indifferent to science and its fundamental questions. Some of the alternatives to the regnant disenchanted transcendence may turn out to be more consistent with the actual findings of the contemporary sciences (Hart, Milbank).[6] Another way of thinking about this is to enquire whether there might be an inconsistency between the official version of materialistic, mechanistic philosophical underpinnings of science and what must actually be true for the modern sciences to work in the way they do (Hart). We can similarly ask whether

[5] A key example here would be the long term 'Scientific Perspectives on Divine Action' project, which ran from 1998 to 2005 and was sponsored by the Vatican Observatory and Berkeley Centre for Theology and the Natural Sciences. For an analysis of the metaphysical commitments of this group, and their implications, see Ignacio Silva, 'Revisiting Aquinas on Providence and Rising to the Challenge of Divine Action in Nature', *The Journal of Religion*, 94 (2014), 277–91; and 'A Cause among Causes: God Acting in the Natural World', *European Journal for the Philosophy of Religion*, 7 (2015), 99–114. Another symptom of this way of framing the problem is the emergence of 'Intelligent Design', which similarly buys into a Deistic conception of the operations of the Deity, while implicitly subscribing to a mechanistic understanding of the operations of nature.

[6] For recent statements of this principle, see Edward Feser, *Aristotle's Revenge: The Metaphysical Foundations of Physical and Biological Science* (Neuenkirchen-Seelscheld: Editiones Scholasticae, 2019), and William M. R. Simpson, Robert C. Koons, and Nicholas J. The (eds.), *Neo-Aristotelian Perspectives on Contemporary Science* (London: Routledge, 2017).

certain features of the world – consciousness, for example – could even be scientifically explicable without recourse to an alternative metaphysics – one, for example, that is more open to teleology (Oliver).[7]

Beyond this, a reconsideration of the question of suitable metaphysical partners may potentially progress our scientific investigations in novel and fruitful ways. The scientific revolution of the seventeenth century was at least in part a revolution in the philosophical and theological underpinnings of natural philosophy, and to a large degree it was motivated by theological questions.[8] While 'normal science', to use Thomas Kuhn's term, might happily trundle along indefinitely with a business-as-usual approach to its assumed philosophical premises, the potential for 'revolutionary science' calls for a re-evaluation of those premises. There is potential here, then, for a new and genuinely two-way conversation that involves not just taking science as it is and making theological adjustments, but exploring possible new metaphysical foundations that will move the current sciences in productive new directions.

The second option that has been explored in this volume, which overlaps the first, has been to look carefully at the category of natural philosophy and consider the ways in which it differs from modern science and how it might provide a resource for contemporary discussions of science and religion (McLeish, Ip, Bucklow). The most obvious payoff from such a study is that the idea of an essential tension between science and religion is, from a historical perspective, very odd. Natural philosophy, while formally distinct from theology, nonetheless included God and his creation within its scope. This was not merely the case for the Middle Ages, moreover. In the eighteenth century, Isaac Newton could still maintain that God-talk was integral to natural philosophy.[9] So the historical trajectory that establishes how God got to be removed from the study of nature – and this can be tracked by looking at when and how the nineteenth century notion of 'science' comes to displace the traditional

[7] Again, teleology is not to be confused with design (see the preceding note).

[8] The classic study is E. A. Burtt, *The Metaphysical Foundations of Modern Science* [1925] (New York: Anchor Books, 1954). But also see Amos Funkenstein, *Theology and the Scientific Imagination* (Princeton, NJ: Princeton University Press, 1986). Funkenstein refers to early modern scientific thinkers as 'secular theologians' on account of the way in which they drew upon theology in their natural philosophical speculations.

[9] '. . . to discourse of [God] from the appearances of things does certainly belong to natural philosophy'. Isaac Newton, *Mathematical Principles of Natural Philosophy*, tr. Andrew Motte with a preface by Roger Cotes (London, 1729), General Scholium. Historian Andrew Cunningham has suggested that natural philosophy was fundamentally about 'God's achievements, God's intentions, God's purposes, God's messages to man'. 'How the Principia Got Its Name; or, Taking Natural Philosophy Seriously', *History of Science*, 28 (1991), 377–92.

idea of 'natural philosophy' – is an obvious place to look if we are to rethink the present relations between science and religion, and ponder whether that nineteenth-century transition was necessary and irreversible.

Another feature of the practice of natural philosophy was that it enabled the study of nature to be combined with deep philosophical reflection. One consequence of the transition from natural philosophy to the modern sciences, then, was a separation of questions of utility from matters of truth and intelligibility (Hanby).[10] These are routinely conflated in many present discussions of science on account of the mistaken assumption that utility – 'science works' – is a sure sign of the truths of theoretical models that underpin its workings or its naturalistic assumptions.[11] But that is not so (Pickstock). However, this easy equivalence of utility and truth gives the naturalistic operating assumptions of the sciences a 'free pass' as it were, as science comes to assume the role of a comprehensive philosophical outlook that establishes the ultimate truth of things (Schindler).

In addition to attending to natural philosophy, several contributors have also looked at natural philosophers themselves, noting that natural philosophy as a *practice* (as opposed simply to a specific area of study) called for a particular kind of moral or spiritual deportment. Modern science, by way of contrast, is typically thought of as value-free or morally neutral; that is to say, the methods of science can be followed irrespective of the moral or religious commitments of its practitioners. Sociologists Max Weber and Robert K. Merton have spoken in this context of 'moral equivalence', which they regarded as integral to the professionalisation of science.[12] As it relates to religious interests in the contemporary conduct of science, this principle is represented by the adoption of methodological naturalism, which stands in for a kind of neutrality. That, at least, is how it is meant to work in theory. But perhaps the moral equivalence of modern science has been overstated, and there may be a sense in which elements of moral or intellectual formation have been carried across from the persona of the natural philosopher to that of the modern scientist. Science may still

[10] For an elegant account of these two aspects of science, see Pete Dear, *The Intelligibility of Nature* (Chicago: University of Chicago Press, 2006).

[11] On the complex connexions between utility, truth, and naturalism, see Peter Harrison, 'Naturalism and the Success of Science', *Religious Studies* 56 (2020), 274–91.

[12] See Steven Shapin, *The Scientific Life: A Moral History of a Late Victorian Vocation* (Chicago: University of Chicago Press, 2008), ch. 3. See also the classic papers by Frank M. Turner, 'The Victorian Conflict between Science and Religion: A Professional Dimension', *Isis*, 69 (1974), 356–76, and Sydney Ross, 'Scientist: The Story of a Word', *Annals of Science*, 18 (1962), 65–85.

be regarded as a kind of spiritual practice (Williams, Ip). Thinking along these lines opens up the possibility that science and religion might represent complementary (or conflicting) 'devotional' practices or trajectories of intellectual and moral formation. On the complementary side, we might speak of shared intellectual virtues and an orientation towards truth. But it is also worth considering whether some of the formative practices of modern sciences, insofar as they involve the adoption of methodological naturalism, reductionism, or a purely utilitarian interest, might be in tension with the modes of formation operative in both traditional natural philosophy and the religious life.

The lesson in relation to the modern category of 'religion' is that the religious life is not exhausted by the propositions to which the faithful adhere, as if these could be separated out from the practice of religion and presented for comparison and analysis alongside scientific propositions that had similarly been severed from the context in which they had been generated. In both cases, the deeper question is whether there can be a genuine alignment between the respective forms of life. In relation to scientific practice, for example, a fundamental issue is whether naturalism is a genuine metaphysical commitment, linked to a deeper form of life, or a conditional strategy adopted for the quite specific purpose of developing techniques for operating upon the world. More generally, we can ask whether the naturalism that tends to dominate twenty-first-century intellectual discourse (and which was the outcome of the transitions described in Lightman's chapter) points to a fundamental incompatibility between religious sensibilities and the metaphysics associated with the modern sciences. If that is true, the strategy of methodological naturalism turns out to be a makeshift work-around for a deeper problem that will be fully resolved only by a radical shift of metaphysical commitments.[13]

To conclude, these essays do not represent the last word on science and religion. On the contrary, they are intended to offer a starting point for a new set of discussions. Whatever the reader may make of the arguments, it is hoped that this volume provides something of a template to be followed, or improved on, in thinking about what science and religion themselves

[13] Alvin Plantinga has challenged the concept of metaphysical naturalism, suggesting that it is a stance that theistic scientists should not adopt. See, e.g., 'Methodological Naturalism', *Perspectives on Science and Christian Faith*, 49 (1997), 143–54. However, without a more radical approach to the underlying metaphysics, this tends to point in the direction of the halfway house of intelligent design. This is not what is being advocated here.

'are' in new ways, and in taking a fresh look at the tacit philosophical underpinnings of contemporary science. More ambitiously, we hope that some in the scientific community itself – in addition to our short list of present conscripts – will see opportunities for reflection on the meaning and significance of the remarkable scientific achievements of the modern age, and perhaps even envision new possibilities for the sciences themselves.

References

Primary Sources

Alan of Lille, *Sermon on the Intelligible Sphere*, in *Literary Works*, tr. Winthrop Wetherbee (Cambridge, MA: Harvard University Press, 2013).

Anon., *Liber XXIV Philosophorum*, II; *Le Livre des XXIV philosophes*, tr. Françoise Hudry (Grenoble: Jerome Millon, 1989).

Aristotle, *Complete Works of Aristotle*, 2 vols., ed. Jonathan Barnes (Princeton, NJ: Princeton University Press, 1984).

On the Soul. Parva Naturalia. On Breath, tr. W. S. Hett, Loeb Classical Library (London: Loeb, 1964).

Bacon, Francis, *The New Organon*, ed. Lisa Jardine and Michael Silverthorne (Cambridge: Cambridge University Press, 2000).

The Works of Francis Bacon, 14 vols., ed. James Spedding, Robert Ellis, and Douglas Heath (Cambridge: Cambridge University Press, 2011).

Birks, Thomas Rawson, *Modern Physical Fatalism and the Doctrine of Evolution* (London: Macmillan, 1876).

Boethius, *De trinitate*, in *Theological Tractates* and *The Consolation of Philosophy*, tr. H. F. Stewart, E. K. Rand, and S. J. Tester, Loeb Classical Library (Cambridge, MA: Harvard University Press, 1973).

Cicero, *On the Nature of the Gods and Academica*, tr. H. Rackham, Loeb Classical Library (Cambridge, MA: Harvard University Press, 1933).

Conway, Anne, *The Principles of the Most Ancient and Modern Philosophy* (Cambridge: Cambridge University Press, 1996).

Cudworth, Ralph, *A Treatise of Freewill*, in *A Treatise Concerning Eternal and Immutable Morality* (Cambridge: Cambridge University Press, 1996).

Culverwell, Nathaniel, *An Elegant and Learned Discourse of the Light of Nature* (Indianapolis, IN: Liberty Fund, 2001).

Darwin, Charles, *The Origin of Species by Means of Natural Selection*, 6th ed. (London: John Murray, 1873).

Diogenes Laertius, *Lives of Eminent Philosophers*, 2 vols., tr. R. D. Hicks, Loeb Classical Library (Cambridge, MA: Harvard University Press, 1972).

Drummond, Henry, *Natural Law in the Spiritual World* (London: Hodder and Stoughton, 1883).

Evelyn, John, *Sylva: A Discourse of Forest Trees and the Propagation of Timber* (London: Echo, 2009).

Fairbairn, A. M., *Studies in the Philosophy of Religion and History* (London: Strahan, 1876).

Flint, Robert, *Theism*, 9th ed. (Edinburgh: William Blackwood and Sons, 1895).

Francis, *Laudato si 'On Care for Our Common Home'* (Vatican City: Vatican Press, 2015).

Giles of Viterbo, *The Commentary on the Sentences of Petrus Lombardus*, ed. Daniel Nodes (Leiden: Brill, 2010).

Gregory Thaumaturgus, *Address of Thanksgiving to Origen*, in *St. Gregory Thaumaturgus: Life and Works*, ed. and tr. Michael Slusser (Washington, DC: Catholic University of America Press, 1998).

Greville, Robert, *The Nature of Truth* [1640] (London: Gregg International, 1969).

Grosseteste, Robert, *Commentarius in Posteriorum Analyticorum Libros*, ed. Pietro Rossi (Florence: Leo S. Olschki, 1981).

On the Cessation of the Laws, tr. Stephen M. Hilderbrand (Washington, DC: Catholic University of America Press, 2012).

La Luce: Introduzione, Testo Latino, Traduzione e Commento. ed. Cecilia Panti, tr. Neil Lewis (Pisa: Edizioni Plus, 2011).

On the Six Days of Creation: A Translation of the Hexaëmeron, tr. C. F. J. Martin (Oxford: Oxford University Press, 1996).

Die Philosophischen Werke des Robert Grosseteste, Bischofs von Lincoln, ed. L. Baur (Aschendorff: Münster, 1912).

The Scientific Works of Robert Grosseteste, 6 vols., ed. Giles E. M. Gasper, Cecilia Panti, Tom McLeish, and Hannah E. Smithson (Oxford: Oxford University Press, 2019), vol. 1.

Hegel, Georg Willhelm Friedrich, *The Logic of Hegel*, tr. William Wallace (Oxford: Clarendon, 1874).

Herbert of Cherbury, Edward, *De veritate*, tr. Meyrick H. Carré (London: Routledge-Thoemmes; Tokyo: Kinokuniya, 1992).

Huxley, Leonard (ed.) *Life and Letters of Thomas Henry Huxley*, 2 vols. (New York: D. Appleton, 1900), vol. 1.

Huxley, Thomas Henry, 'The Evidence of the Miracle of the Resurrection', in Catherine Marshall, Bernard Lightman, and Richard England (eds.), *The Papers of the Metaphysical Society 1869–1880: A Critical Edition* (Oxford: Oxford University Press, 2015), vol. 2, 366–72.

Science and Hebrew Tradition (London: Macmillan, 1893).

[Huxley, Thomas Henry], 'Science and Religion', *The Builder*, 18 (1859), 35.

Imperial College, Huxley Papers, Huxley to James Creelman, June 11, 1894, Volume 12, 343.

Isaac of Stella, *Sermons on the Christian Year*, vol. 1, intro. B. McGinn, tr. Hugh McCaffery (Collegeville, MN: Cistercian Press, 2016).

Iverach, James, *Theism in the Light of Present Science and Philosophy* (New York: Macmillan, 1899).

Jefferson, Thomas, 'To John Hollins, February 19, 1809', in Merrill D. Peterson (ed.), *Thomas Jefferson: Writings* (New York: Library of America, 1984).
Kingsley, Fanny (ed.), *Charles Kingsley: His Letters and Memories of His Life* (London: Henry S. King, 1877), vol. 2.
Locke, John, *An Essay Concerning Human Understanding* (Oxford: Oxford University Press, 1979).
Martineau, James, *Essays, Reviews and Addresses* (London: Longmans, Green, 1891), vol. 3.
Matheson, George, *Can the Old Faith Live with the New? or, The Problem of Evolution and Revelation* (Edinburgh: William Blackwood & Sons, 1885).
Moore, Aubrey L., *Science and the Faith: Essays on Apologetic Subjects* (London: Kegan Paul, Trench, 1889).
Morris, F. O., *All the Articles of the Darwin Faith* (London: Moffatt, Paige, 1875).
Nāgārjuna, *Nāgārjuna's Middle Way*, tr. Mark Sideris and Shōryū Katsura (Somerville, MA: Wisdom Publications, 2013).
Newton, Isaac, *Mathematical Principles of Natural Philosophy*, tr. Andrew Motte with a preface by Roger Cotes (London, 1729).
Nicholas of Cusa, *Coniectura de Ultimis Diebus*, tr. Jasper Hopkins, in *Nicolai de Cusa Opera Omnia*, vol. IV (Opuscula I), ed. Paul Wilpert (Hamburg: Felix Meiner, 1959)
De docta ignorantia, 3 vols., ed. and tr. P. Wilpert, H. G. Senger, and R. Klibansky, *Philosophische Bibliothek*, vols. 264a–c (Leipzig-Hamburg: Meiner, 1994–9),
On Learned Ignorance, in *Selected Spiritual Writings*, tr. H. Lawrence Bond (New York: Paulist Press, 1997).
Opera Omnia jussu et auctoritate Academicae Litterarum Heidelbergensis (Leipzig-Hamburg: Meiner, 1932–2007).
Nietzsche, Friedrich, *The Gay Science*, tr. Walter Kaufmann (New York: Vintage Books, 1974).
Thus Spoke Zarathustra (New York: Viking, 1966).
Oken, Lorenz, *Elements of Physiophilosophy*, tr. Alfred Tulk (London: Ray Society, 1847).
Origen, *On First Principles*, ed. and tr. John Behr (Oxford: Oxford University Press, 2017).
The Song of Songs: Commentary and Homilies, tr. R. P. Lawson (Westminster: Newman Press, 1957).
Pascal, Blaise, *Pensées*, tr. W. F. Potter (London: Dent, 1910).
Patrologia cursus completus, series Latina, ed. J.-P. Migne (Paris, 1857–1912)
Plato, *The Collected Dialogues of Plato*, ed. Edith Hamilton and Huntington Cairns (Princeton, NJ: Princeton University Press, 2005).
Plotinus, *The Enneads*, ed. Lloyd P. Gerson, tr. George Boys-Stones, John M. Dillon, Lloyd P. Gerson, R. A. King, Andrew Smith, and James Wilberding (Cambridge: Cambridge University Press, 2018).
Ruskin, John, *Unto This Last* (New York: Penguin, 1985).

Temple, Frederick, *The Relation between Religion and Science* (London: Macmillan, 1884).

Thomas Aquinas, *Commentary on Aristotle's Physics*, tr. Richard J. Blackwell, Richard J. Spath, and W. Edmund Thirkel (Notre Dame, IN: Dumb Ox Books, 1999).

Commentary on Metaphysics, 2 vols., tr. John. P. Rowan (Green Bay, WI: Aquinas Institute, 2020).

On Truth ('Quaestiones disputatae de veritate'), tr. Robert W. Schmidt (Indianapolis, IN: Hackett Publishing, 1954).

The Summa Theologiae of St. Thomas Aquinas, 2nd ed. rev., 10 vols. (London: Burns Oates and Washbourne, 1920–2).

Tyndall, John, *Fragments of Science*, 8th ed. (London: Longmans, Green 1892), vol. 2.

Vico, Giambattista, *De antiquissima italorum sapientia: liber metaphysicus, Opere filosofiche* (Florence, Sansoni, 1971).

On the Most Ancient Wisdom of the Italians, tr. Jason Taylor (New Haven, CT: Yale University Press, 2010).

von Goethe, Johann Wolfgang, *Goethe's Botanical Writings*, tr. B. Mueller (Woodbridge: Oxbow Press, 1989).

Westminster Sermons (London: Macmillan, 1874).

[Wilberforce, Samuel], 'Darwin's *Origin of Species*', *Quarterly Review*, 108 (July 1860), 225–64.

Wolff, Christian, *Philosophia rationalis sive Logica*, 3rd ed. (Verona, 1735).

Wordsworth, William, *The Prelude: The Four Texts (1798, 1799, 1805, 1850)* (London: Penguin, 1995).

Secondary Sources

Agamben, Giorgio, *The Signature of All Things: On Method*, tr. Luca di Santo and Kevin Attell (New York: Zone, 2009).

Albertson, David, *Mathematical Theologies: Nicholas of Cusa and the Legacy of Thierry of Chartres* (New York: Oxford University Press, 2014).

Alfsvåg, Knut, *What No Mind Has Conceived* (Leuven: Peeters, 2010).

Arendt, Hannah, *The Human Condition* (Chicago: University of Chicago Press, 1958).

The Human Condition, 2nd ed. (Chicago: University of Chicago Press, 1998).

Assmann, Jan, *Moses the Egyptian: The Memory of Egypt in Western Monotheism* (Cambridge, MA: Harvard University Press, 1997).

Barad, Karen, *Meeting the Universe Halfway: Quantum Physics and the Entanglement of Matter and Meaning* (Durham, NC: Duke University Press, 2007).

Barbour, Ian G., *Issues in Science and Religion* (London: Harper Torchbooks, 1966).

Myths, Models and Paradigms (New York: Harper and Rowe, 1974).
Religion in an Age of Science (San Francisco, CA: Harper and Row, 1990).
Religion and Science: Historical and Contemporary Issues (San Francisco, CA: Harper, 1997).
Barfield, Owen, *Saving the Appearances: A Study in Idolatry* (New York: Harcourt, Brace and World, 1972).
Barton, Ruth, '"An Influential Set of Chaps:" The X-Club and Royal Society Politics, 1864–85', *British Journal for the History of Science*, 23 (1990), 53–81.
'"Men of Science": Language, Identity and Professionalization in the Mid-Victorian Scientific Community', *History of Science*, 41 (2003), 73–119.
Bebbington, D. W., 'Henry Drummond', in *Oxford Dictionary of National Biography*. https://doi-org.ezproxy.library.yorku.ca/10.1093/ref:odnb/8068.
Bedford, R. D., *The Defence of Truth: Herbert of Cherbury and the Seventeenth Century* (Manchester: Manchester University Press, 1979).
Bellantone, Andrea, *La Métaphysique possible* (Paris: Hermann, 2012).
Benz, Ernst, *The Theology of Electricity*, tr. Wolfgang Taraba (Eugener: Wipf and Stock, 1989).
Bergson, Henri, *Durée et simultanéité* (Paris: PUF, 2009).
Berman, Morris, *The Reenchantment of the World* (Ithaca, NY: Cornell University Press, 1981).
Bobik, Joseph, *Aquinas on Matter and Form and the Elements: A Translation and Interpretation of the De Principiis Naturae and the De Mixtione Elementorun of St. Thomas Aquinas* (Notre Dame, IN: University of Notre Dame Press, 1998).
Bohm, David, *Wholeness and Implicate Order* (London: Routledge, 1980).
Boner, Patrick J., *Kepler's Cosmological Synthesis: Astrology, Mechnaism and the Soul* (Leiden: Brill, 2013).
Bos, A. P., *Cosmic and Meta-Cosmic Theology in Aristotle's Lost Dialogues* (Leiden: Brill, 1989).
Boulnois, Olivier, *Métaphysiques rebelles: Gènese et structures d'une science au Moyen Ăge* (Paris: PUF, 2013).
Brague, Rémi, *Aristote et la question du monde* (Paris: PUF, 1988).
Brightman, Edgar, 'An Empirical Approach to God', *The Philosophical Review*, 46 (1937), 157–8.
Brooke, John Hedley, *Science and Religion: Some Historical Perspectives* (Cambridge: Cambridge University Press, 1991).
Brown, James Robert, *The Rational and the Social* (London: Routledge, 1989).
Bucklow, Spike, *The Alchemy of Paint: Art, Science and Secrets from the Middle Ages* (London: Marion Boyars, 2009).
Bucklow, Spike, *The Riddle of the Image* (London: Reaktion, 2014).
Burton, Simon J. G., '"Squaring the Circle": Cusan Metaphysics and the Pansophic Vision of Jan Amos Comenius', in Burton et al. (eds.), *Nicholas*

of Cusa and the Making of the Early Modern World (Leiden: Brill, 2019), 417–49.
Burtt, E. A., *The Metaphysical Foundations of Modern Science* [1925] (New York: Anchor Books, 1954).
Carlisle, Clare, 'Between Freedom and Necessity: Felix Ravaisson on Habit and the Moral Life', *Inquiry*, 53 (2010), 126–37.
On Habit (London: Routledge, 2014).
Carruthers, Mary, *The Craft of Thought: Meditation, Rhetoric and the Making of Images, 400–1200* (Cambridge: Cambridge University Press, 2008).
Cartwright, Nancy, *Nature, the Artful Modeller: Lectures on Laws, Science, How Nature Arranges the World and How We Can Arrange It Better* (Chicago: Open Court, 2019).
Cashdollar, Charles D., *The Transformation of Theology, 1830–1890: Positivism and Protestant Thought in Britain and America* (Princeton, NJ: Princeton University Press, 1989).
Cavanaugh, William T., *The Myth of Religious Violence* (Oxford: Oxford University Press, 2009).
Cennini, Cennino, *The Craftsman's Handbook*, tr. D. V. Thompson (New York: Dover, 1960).
Chenu, Marie-Dominique, *Nature, Man, and Society in the Twelfth Century* (Toronto: University of Toronto Press, 1997).
Clines, David A., et al. (eds.), *World Biblical Commentary: 18A Job 21–37* (Nashville: Thomas Nelson, 2006).
Copenhaver, Brain P., *Magic in Western Culture: From Antiquity to the Enlightenment* (Cambridge: Cambridge University Press, 2015).
Copenhaver, Brain P., and Charles B. Schmitt, *Renaissance Philosophy* (Oxford: Oxford University Press, 1992).
Courtenay, W. J., 'The Critique on Natural Causality in the Mutakallimun and Nominalism', *The Harvard Theological Review*, 66 (1973), 77–94.
'Necessity and Freedom in Anselm's Conception of God', *Analecta Anselmiana*, 4, no. 2 (1975), 39–64.
Coyne, Jerry, *Faith versus Fact: Why Science and Religion Are Not Compatible* (New York: Viking Press, 2015).
Crombie, A. C., *Robert Grosseteste and the Origins of Experimental Science 1100–1700* (Oxford: Oxford University Press, 1953).
Crouzel, Henri, *Origène et Plotin: Comparaisons doctrinales* (Paris: Téqui, 1991).
Crouzel, Henri (ed.), *Remerciement à Origène, suivi de la Lettre d'Origène a Grégoire* (Paris: Cerf, 1976).
Cunningham, Andrew, 'Getting the Game Right: Some Plain Words on the Identity and Invention of Science', *Studies in History and Philosophy of Science*, 19 (1988), 365–89.
'How the Principia Got Its Name: or, Taking Natural Philosophy Seriously', *History of Science*, 28 (1991), 377–92.
'The Identity of Natural Philosophy', *Early Science and Medicine*, 5 (2000), 259–78.

Cunningham, Conor, *Darwin's Pious Idea: Why the Ultra-Darwinists and Creationists Both Get It Wrong* (Grand Rapids, MI: Eerdmans, 2011).
Cushing, James T., *Philosophical Concepts in Physics: The Historical Relation between Philosophy and Scientific Theories* (Cambridge: Cambridge Press, 2000).
D'Agostino, Fred, 'Verballed? Incommensurability 50 Years On', *Synthese*, 191 (2013), 517–38.
Daley, Brain E., 'Origen's "De Principiis": A Guide to the Principles of Christian Scriptural Interpretation', in John Petruccione (ed.), *Nova et Vetera: Patristic Studies in Honor of Thomas Patrick Halton* (Washington, DC: Catholic University of America Press, 1998), 3–21.
Daston, Lorraine, and H. Otto Sibum, 'Scientific Personae and Their Histories', *Science in Context*, 16 (2003), 1–8.
Davidson, D., 'The Very Idea of a Conceptual Scheme', *Proceedings and Addresses of the American Philosophical Association*, 47 (1973), 5–20.
Davie, George, *The Scotch Metaphysics: A Century of Enlightenment in Scotland* [1952] (London: Routledge, 2001).
Dawson, Gowan, and Bernard Lightman, 'Introduction', in Gowan Dawson and Bernard Lightman (eds.), *Victorian Scientific Naturalism: Community, Identity, Continuity* (Chicago: University of Chicago Press, 2014).
Dawson, Gowan, and Bernard Lightman (eds.), *Victorian Scientific Naturalism: Community, Identity, Continuity* (Chicago: University of Chicago Press, 2014).
de Certeau, Michel, *The Mystic Fable*, tr. Michael Smith (Chicago: University of Chicago Press, 1992).
de Lubac, Henri, *La Posterité spirituelle de Joachim de Flore* (Paris: Cerf, 2014).
Scripture in the Tradition, tr. Luke O'Neill (Chicago: Crossroad, 2001).
de Munck, Bert, 'Artisans, Productions and Gifts: Rethinking the History of Material Culture in Early Modern Europe', *Past and Present*, 224 (2014), 63.
De Vries, Paul, 'Naturalism in the Natural Sciences', *Christian Scholar's Review*, 15 (1986), 388–96.
Dear, Peter, *The Intelligibility of Nature* (Chicago: University of Chicago Press, 2006).
'Religion, Science, and Natural Philosophy: Thoughts on Cunningham's Thesis', *Studies in History and Philosophy of Science*, 32 (2001), 377–86.
'What Is the History of Science the History Of?', *Isis*, 96 (2005), 390–406.
Discipline and Experience: The Mathematical Way in the Scientific Revolution (Chicago: University of Chicago Press, 1995).
Mersenne and the Learning of the Schools (Ithaca, NY: Cornell University Press, 1988).
DeMarrais, Elizabeth, and John Robb, 'Art Makes Society', *World Art*, 3, no. 1 (2013), 3–22.
Deneen, Patrick, *Why Liberalism Failed* (New Haven, CT: Yale University Press, 2018).
Depew, David J., and Bruce H. Weber, *Darwinism Evolving: Systems Dynamics and the Genealogy of Natural Selection* (Cambridge, MA: MIT Press, 1995).

Desmond, Adrian, *Huxley: From Devil's Disciple to Evolution's High Priest* (Reading, MA: Addison-Wesley, 1997).
Desmond, William, *The Intimate Strangeness of Being: Metaphysics after Dialectic* (Washington, DC: Catholic University of America Press, 2012).
The Voiding of Being: The Doing and Undoing of Metaphysics in Modernity (Washington, DC: Catholic University of America Press, 2019).
d'Espagnat, Bernard, *On Physics and Philosophy* (Princeton, NJ: Princeton University Press, 2013).
Dewey, John, *Reconstruction in Philosophy* (London: Forgotten Books, 2012).
Dinkova-Bruun, Greti, Giles E. M. Gasper, Michael Huxtable, Tom C. B. McLeish, Cecilia Panti, and Hannah Smithson, *Dimensions of Colour: Robert Grosseteste's De Colore; Edition, Translation and Interdisciplinary Analysis* (Durham, NC: Durham Medieval and Renaissance Texts, 2013).
Dobbs, B. J. T., *The Janus Faces of Genius: The Role of Alchemy in Newton's Thought* (Cambridge: Cambridge University Press, 2002).
Dolnick, Edward, *The Seeds of Life* (New York: Basic Books, 2017).
Drury, M. O'C., 'Notes on Conversations with Wittgenstein', in Rush Rhees (ed.), *Ludwig Wittgenstein – Personal Recollections* (Totowa, NJ: Rowman and Littlefield, 1981),
Duhem, Pierre, *Le Système du monde. Histoire des doctrines cosmologiques de Platon à Copernic, tomes VII, VIII* (Paris: Hermann et Fils, 1956–8).
Dupuy, J.-P., 'The Narratology of Lay Ethics', *Nanoethics*, 4 (2010), 153–70.
Eckland, Elaine Howard, *Science vs Religion: What Scientists Really Think* (Oxford: Oxford University Press, 2010).
et al., *Secularity and Science: What Scientists around the World Really Think about Religion* (New York: Oxford University Press, 2019).
Edelheit, Amos, *Ficino, Pico and Savanarola: The Evolution of Humanist Theology 1461/2–1498* (Leiden: Brill, 2008).
Edgar, Orion, *Things Seen and Unseen* (Eugene, OR: Cascade, 2016).
Edwards, Mark J., *Origen against Plato* (London: Routledge, 2017).
Einstein, Albert, *Autobiographical Notes*, tr. P. A. Schillp (Chicago: Open Court, 1979).
Einstein, Albert, and Leopold Infeld, *The Evolution of Physics* (London: Cambridge University Press, 1938).
Elliott-Binns, L. E., *The Development of English Theology in the Later Nineteenth Century* (Hamden: Archon Books, 1971).
Ellis, Fiona, 'Atheism and Naturalism', in Anthony Carroll and Richard Norman (eds.), *Religion and Atheism: Beyond the Divide* (London: Routledge, 2017), 72.
England, Richard, 'Moore, Aubrey Lackington', in *Oxford Dictionary of National Biography*. https://doi-org.ezproxy.library.yorku.ca/10.1093/ref:odnb/19097.
Faivre, Antoine, *Theosophy, Imagination Tradition*, tr. Christine Rhone (Albany: State University of New York Press, 2000).
Western Esotericism: A Concise History, tr. Christine Rhone (Albany: State University of New York Press, 2010).

Ferrera, Christopher A., *Liberty, the God That Failed* (Tacoma, WA: Angelico Press, 2012).

Ferrier, James, *Institutes of Metaphysics: The Theory of Knowing and Being* (Edinburgh: Blackwood, 1854).

Feser, Edward, *Aristotle's Revenge: The Metaphysical Foundations of Physical and Biological Science* (Neunkirchen-Seelscheid: Editiones Scholasticae, 2019).

Feyerabend, Paul, *Against Method* (New York: Verso, 1975).

Reason, Rationalism and Scientific Method, vol. 1: Philosophical Papers (Cambridge: Cambridge University Press, 2003).

Fiddes, Paul, *Seeing the World and Knowing God* (Oxford: Oxford University Press, 2014).

Fleming, John V., *The Dark Side of the Enlightenment: Wizards, Alchemists and Spiritual Seekers in the Age of Reason* (New York: W.W. Norton, 2013).

Fleming, R. W., and H. H. Bülthoff, 'Low-Level Image Cues in the Perception of Translucent Materials', *ACM Transactions on Applied Perception*, 2 (2005), 346–82.

Foucault, Michel, *The History of Sexuality, vol. 3: The Care of the Self*, tr. Robert Hurley (New York: Vintage, 1986).

Technologies of the Self (Amherst: University of Massachusetts Press, 1988).

Freeman, R. B., *The Works of Charles Darwin: An Annotated Bibliographical Handlist* (London: Dawsons of Pall Mall, 1965).

Fuller, Peter, *Theoria: Art in the Absence of Grace* (London: Chatto & Windus, 1988).

Funkenstein, Amos, 'The Disenchantment of Knowledge: The Emergence of the Ideal of Open Knowledge in Ancient Israel and in Classical Greece', *Aleph: Historical Studies in Science and Judaism* 3 (2003), 15–81.

Theology and the Scientific Imagination (Princeton, NJ: Princeton University Press, 1986).

Gadamer, Hans-Georg, *Philosophical Hermeneutics*, 2nd ed., tr. and ed. D. E. Linge (Berkeley: University of California Press, 2004).

Truth and Method (London: Continuum, 1975).

Garfield, J. L., and Graham Priest, 'Nāgārjuna and the Limits of Thought', *Philosophy East and West* 53 (2003), 1–21.

Gascoigne, John, 'Ideas of Nature: Natural Philosophy', in Roy Porter (ed.), *The Cambridge History of Science*, vol. 4 (Cambridge: Cambridge University Press, 2003), 285–304.

Gasper, Giles, 'The Fulfillment of Science: Nature, Creation and Man in the Hexaemeron of Robert Grosseteste', in Jack Cunningham and Mark Hocknull (eds.), *Grosseteste and the Pursuit of Religious and Scientific Learning in the Middle Ages* (Cham: Springer, 2016), 221-42.

Gatti, Hilary, *Giordano Bruno and Renaissance Science* (Ithaca, NY: Cornell University Press, 1999).

Gaukroger, Stephen, *Civilization and the Culture of Science: Science and the Shaping of Modernity 1795–1935* (Oxford: Oxford University Press, 2020).

The Collapse of Mechanism and the Rise of Sensibility: Science and the Shaping of Modernity 1680–1760 (Oxford: Oxford University Press, 2010).

The Emergence of a Scientific Culture: Science and the Shaping of Modernity 1210–1685 (Oxford: Oxford University Press, 2006).
The Failures of Philosophy: A Historical Essay (Princeton, NJ: Princeton University Press, 2020).
Francis Bacon and the Transformation of Early-Modern Philosophy (Cambridge: Cambridge University Press, 2001).
Geertz, Clifford, *The Interpretation of Culture* (New York: Basic Books, 1973).
Gell, Alfred, *Art and Agency* (Oxford: Clarendon, 2013).
Gibson, James, *Ecological Approach to Visual Perception* (Boston: Houghton Mifflin, 1979).
Giedymin, J., 'The Paradox of Meaning Invariance', *British Journal for the Philosophy of Science*, 21 (1970), 257–68.
Gillespie, Michael Allen, *The Theological Origins of Modernity* (Chicago: University of Chicago Press, 2008).
Gilson, Etienne, *Christian Philosophy in the Middle Ages* (London: Sheed and Ward, 1955).
Gingras, Yves, *Science and Religion: An Impossible Dialogue*, tr. Peter Keating (Cambridge: Polity, 2017).
Ginzburg, Carlo, 'Morelli, Freud and Sherlock Holmes', *History Workshop*, 9 (1980), 5–36.
Gouhier, Henri, *Les premièr pensées de Descartes: Contribution à l'histoire de l'anti-renaissance* (Paris: Vrin, 1979).
Gould, Stephen Jay, *Rock of Ages: Science and Religion in the Fullness of Life* (New York: Ballantine Books, 1999).
Grant, Ian Hamilton, 'Being and Slime: The Mathematics of Protoplasm in Lorenz Oken's "Physio-Philosophy"', *Collapse* 4 (2008), 286–321.
Grattan-Guinness, Ivor, 'Work for the Hairdressers: The Production of de Prony's Logarithmic and Trigonometric Tables', *IEEE Annals of the History of Computing*, 12 (1990), 178–81.
Gribbin, John, *Six Impossible Things: The 'Quanta of Solace' and the Mysteries of the Subatomic World* (London: Icon, 2019).
Grier, David, 'Human Computers: The First Pioneers of the Information Age', *Endeavour*, 25 (2001), 28–32.
'The Math Tables Project: The Reluctant Start of the Computing Era', *IEEE Annals of the History of Computing*, 20 (1998), 33–50.
Grosz, Elizabeth, 'Habit Today: Ravaisson, Bergson, Deleuze and Us', *Body and Society*, 19 (2013), 220.
Hadot, Pierre, *Philosophy as a Way of Life: Spiritual Exercises from Socrates to Foucault*, tr. Michael Chase (Oxford: Blackwell, 1995).
The Veil of Isis: An Essay on the History of the Idea of Nature, tr. Michael Chase (Cambridge, MA: Harvard University Press, 2006).
What Is Ancient Philosophy?, tr. Michael Chase (Cambridge, MA: Harvard University Press, 2004).
Wittgenstein et les limites du langage (Paris: Vrin, 2004).

Hanby, Michael, 'Absolute Pluralism: How the Dictatorship of Relativism Dictates', *Communio* (Summer–Fall 2013), 592–76.

Augustine and Modernity (New York: Routledge, 2003).

'Saving the Appearances: Creation's Gift to the Sciences', *Anthropotes* 26, no. 1 (2010), 65–96.

No God, No Science: Theology, Cosmology, Biology (Oxford: Wiley-Blackwell, 2016).

Hardin, Jeff, Ronald L. Numbers, and Ronald A. Binzley (eds.), *The Warfare between Science and Religion: The Idea That Wouldn't Die* (Baltimore: Johns Hopkins University Press, 2018).

Harrison, Peter, *The Bible, Protestantism, and the Rise of Natural Science* (Cambridge: Cambridge University Press, 2001).

'Conflict, Complexity, and Secularization in the History of Science and Religion', in Bernard Lightman (ed.), *Rethinking History, Science, Religion* (Pittsburgh: University of Pittsburgh Press, 2019), 221–34.

'Experimental Religion and Experimental Science in Early Modern England', *Intellectual History Review*, 21 (2011), 413–33.

The Fall of Man and the Foundations of Science (Cambridge: Cambridge University Press, 2007).

'From Conflict to Dialogue and All the Way Back', *LA Review of Books*, December 27, 2017.

'Naturalism and the Success of Science', *Religious Studies* 56 (2020), 274–91.

'Physico-Theology and the Mixed Sciences: The Role of Theology in Early Modern Natural Philosophy', in Peter Anstey and John Schuster (eds.), *The Science of Nature in the Seventeenth Century* (Dordrecht: Springer, 2005), 165–83.

'Religion' and the Religions in the English Enlightenment (Cambridge: Cambridge University Press, 1998).

'"Science" and "Religion": Constructing the Boundaries', *Journal of Religion*, 86 (2006), 81–106.

The Territories of Science and Religion (Chicago: University of Chicago Press, 2015).

Harrison, Peter, Ronald L. Numbers, and Michael H. Shank (eds.), *Wrestling with Nature: From Omens to Science* (Chicago: University of Chicago Press, 2011).

Hart, David, *The Experience of God: Being, Consciousness, Bliss* (New Haven, CT: Yale University Press, 2013).

Hedley, Douglas, and David Leech, 'Introduction', in Douglas Hedley and David Leech (eds.), *Revisioning Cambridge Platonism: Sources and Legacy* (Cham: Springer, 2019), 1–12.

Heidegger, Martin, *'The Origin of the Work of Art'*, in *Basic Writings* (New York: Harper, 2008).

Heilbron, John, 'Natural Philosophy', in Peter Harrison, Ronald L. Numbers, and Michael H. Shank (eds.), *Wrestling with Nature* (Chicago: University of Chicago Press, 2011), 173–99.

Hermens, Erma, and Arie Wallert, 'The Pekstok Papers, Lake Pigments, Prisons and Paint-Mills', in E. Hermens (ed.), *Looking through Paintings* (London: Archetype, 1998), 276–80.
Hesse, Mary, 'Truth and the Growth of Scientific Knowledge', *PSA*, 2 (1976), 261–80.
Hoff, Johannes, *Kontingenz, Berührung, Überschreitung: Zur philosophischen Propädutik christlicher Mystik nach Nikolaus von Kues* (Freiburg: Karl Alber, 2007).
Hunter, Michael, *Boyle: Between God and Science* (New Haven, CT: Yale University Press, 2010).
Isaac Newton: The Last Sorcerer (London: Fourth Estate, 1997).
Hurd, Elizabeth Shakman, *Beyond Religious Freedom* (Princeton, NJ: Princeton University Press, 2015).
Jacob, Margaret, *The Radical Enlightenment: Pantheists, Freemasons and Republicans* (Lafayette, LA: Cornerstone, 2006).
Jaki, Stanley L., *The Origin of Science and the Science of Its Origin* (Edinburgh: Scottish Academic Press, 1979).
Jonas, Hans, *The Imperative of Responsibility: In Search of an Ethics for the Technological Age* (Chicago: University of Chicago Press, 1984).
The Phenomenon of Life: Toward a Philosophical Biology (Evanston, IL: Northwestern University Press, 2001).
Philosophical Essays: From Ancient Creed to Technological Man (Englewood Cliffs, NJ: Prentice Hall, 1974).
Jones, David, 'Art and Sacrament', in Harman Grisewood (ed.), *Epoch and Artist: Selected Writings by David Jones* (London: Faber and Faber, 1959), 159.
Joyce, James, *Finnegans Wake*, ed. R.-J. Henkes, E. Bindervoet, and F. Fordham (Oxford: Oxford University Press, 2012).
Kelsey, David, *Eccentric Existence* (Louisville, KY: Westminster John Knox Press, 2009).
Kiefer, Claus, *Quantum Gravity* (Oxford: Oxford University Press, 2012).
Klein, Étienne, Marc Lachièze-Rey, and Axel Reisinger, *The Quest for Unity: The Adventure of Physics* (Oxford: Oxford University Press, 1999).
Klein, Jacob, *Greek Mathematical Thought and the Origin of Algebra*, tr. Eva Brann (New York: Dover, 1992).
Knox, Dilwyn, 'Ficino, Copernicus and Bruno on the Motion of the Earth', *Brunoniana and Campelliana*, 5 (1999), 333–66.
Kordig, C. R., 'The Theory-Ladenness of Observation', *Review of Metaphysics*, 24 (1971), 448–84.
Kragh, Helge, *Higher Speculations: Grand Theories and Failed Revolutions in Physics and Cosmology* (Oxford: Oxford University Press, 2011).
Kuhn, Thomas S., 'Notes on Lakatos', *PSA: Proceedings of the Biennial Meeting of the Philosophy of Science Association 1970* (1970), 137–46.
The Structure of Scientific Revolutions (Chicago: University of Chicago Press, 1962).

The Structure of Scientific Revolutions, 2nd ed. (Chicago: University of Chicago Press, 1970).

Lafleur, Claude, and Joanne Carrier, *L'Enseignement de la philosophie au XIIIe siècle: Autour du 'Guide de L'étudiant du Ms Ripoli 109'* (Quebec: Brepols, 1997).

Lakatos, Imre, 'Falsification and the Methodology of Scientific Research Programmes', in Imre Lakatos and Alan Musgrave (eds.), *Criticism and the Growth of Knowledge* (Cambridge: Cambridge University Press, 1970), 91–196.

Lakatos, Imre, and A. Musgrave (eds.) *Criticism and the Growth of Knowledge* (Cambridge: Cambridge University Press, 1970).

Lash, Nicholas, *The Beginning and End of 'Religion'* (Cambridge: Cambridge University Press, 1996).

Latour, Bruno, *Facing Gaia: Eight Lectures on the New Climatic Regime*, tr. Catherine Porter (Cambridge: Polity, 2017).

Pandora's Hope: Essays on the Reality of Science Studies (Cambridge, MA: Harvard University Press, 1999).

'Visualisation and Cognition: Drawing Things Together', in M. Lynch and S. Woolgar (eds.), *Representation in Scientific Activity* (Cambridge, MA: MIT Press, 1990).

We Have Never Been Modern, tr. Catherine Porter (Cambridge MA: Harvard University Press, 1993).

Laudan, Larry, 'A Confutation of Convergent Realism', *Philosophy of Science*, 48 (1981), 19–49.

Progress and Its Problems (Berkeley: University of California Press, 1977).

Laudan, Rachel, and Larry Laudan, 'Dominance and the Disunity of Method', *Philosophy of Science*, 56 (1989), 221–37.

Leanza, Sandro, 'La classificazione dei libri salomonici e i suoi riflessi sulla questione dei rapporti tra Bibbia e scienze profane, da Origene agli scrittori medioevali', *Augustinianum* 14 (1974), 651–66.

Legutko, Ryszard, *The Demon in Democracy: Totalitarian Temptations in Free Societies* (New York: Encounter Books, 2016).

Lenoble, Robert, *Histoire de l'idée de nature* (Paris: Albin Michel, 1969).

Levitin, Dmitri, *Ancient Wisdom in the Age of the New Science: Histories of Philosophy in England, c. 1640–1700* (Cambridge: Cambridge University Press, 2015).

Lewis, C. S., *The Abolition of Man* (New York: HarperCollins, 1974).

Lightman, Bernard, 'Catholics and the Metaphysical Basis of Science', in Catherine Marshall, Bernard Lightman, and Robert England (eds.), *The Metaphysical Society (1869–1880): Intellectual Life in Mid-Victorian England* (Oxford: Oxford University Press, 2019), 252–69.

'Fashioning the Victorian Man of Science: Tyndall's Shifting Strategies', *Journal of Dialectics of Nature*, 38 (2015), 25–38.

'The Theology of Victorian Scientific Naturalists', in Peter Harrison and Jon H. Roberts (eds.), *Science without God? Rethinking the History of Scientific Naturalism* (Oxford: Oxford University Press, 2019), 235–53.

Lindberg, David, and Ronald Numbers (eds.), *God and Nature: Historical Essays on the Encounter between Christianity and Science* (Berkeley: University of California Press, 1986).

Lindberg, David, and Ronald Number (eds.), *When Science and Christianity Meet* (Chicago: University of Chicago Press, 2003).

Livingston, James C., *Religious Thought in the Victorian Age: Challenges and Reconceptions* (New York: Continuum, 2007).

Lloyd, Geoffrey E. R., *Methods and Problems in Greek Science* (Cambridge: Cambridge University Press, 1991).

Lollar, Joshua, *To See into the Life of Things: The Contemplation of Nature in Maximus the Confessor and His Predecessors* (Turnhout: Brepols, 2013).

Long, A. A., and D. N. Sedley (eds.), *The Hellenistic Philosophers, vol. 1: Translations of the Principal Sources with Philosophical Commentary* (Cambridge: Cambridge University Press, 1987).

Lorraine, Daston, and Katherine Park, *Wonders and the Order of Nature* (New York: Zone Books, 1998).

Luhrman, Tanya, *When God Talks Back* (New York: Vintage, 2012).

Macauley, David, *Elemental Philosophy* (Albany: State University of New York Press, 2010).

MacIntyre, Alasdair, 'Epistemological Crises and Dramatic Narrative', in *The Tasks of Philosophy* (Cambridge: Cambridge University Press, 2006).

After Virtue, 3rd ed. (Notre Dame, IN: University of Notre Dame Press, 2007).

Three Rival Versions of Moral Enquiry (Notre Dame, IN: University of Notre Dame Press, 1994).

Mackenzie, Ian, M., '*The 'Obscurism of Light': A Theological Study into the Nature of Light* (Norwich: Canterbury Press, 1996).

Maier, Anneliese, *Die Vorlaüfer Galileis im 14. Jahrhundert*, 2nd ed. rev. (Rome: Edizioni di Storia e Letteratura, 1966).

Zwischen Philosophie und Mechanik (Rome: Edizioni di Storia e Letteratura, 1958).

Manent, Pierre, *Cours familier de philosophie politique* (Paris: Gallimard, 2004).

Marion, Florian, 'The *exaiphnes* in the Platonic Tradition: From Kinematics to Dynamics' (forthcoming).

Marion, Jean-Luc, *D'Ailleurs, La Révélation* (Paris: Grasset, 2020).

Marshall, Catherine, Bernard Lightman, and Richard England (eds.), *The Metaphysical Society (1869–1880): Intellectual Life in Mid-Victorian England* (Oxford: Oxford University Press, 2019).

Martin, Francis X., *Friar, Reformer and Renaissance Scholar: Life and Work of Giles of Viterbo 1569–1532* (Villanova: Augustinian Press, 1992).

Martin, Michael, *The Submerged Reality: Sophiology and the Turn to a Poetic Metaphysic* (Kettering: Angelico, 2015).

McAllister, Joseph B. *The Letter of Thomas Aquinas De Occultis* (Washington, DC: Catholic University of America Press, 1939).

McCarraher, Eugene, *The Enchantments of Mammon: How Capitalism Became the Religion of Modernity* (Cambridge, MA: Harvard University Press, 2019).

McEvoy, J., *Robert Grosseteste* (Oxford: Oxford University Press, 2000).
McGilchrist, Ian, *The Master and His Emissary* (New Haven, CT: Yale University Press, 2019).
McLeish, Tom, *Faith and Wisdom in Science* (Oxford: Oxford University Press, 2014).
The Poetry and Music of Science: Comparing Creativity in Science and Art (Oxford: Oxford University Press, 2019).
'Soft Matter: An Emergent Interdisciplinary Science of Emergent Entities', in Sophie Gibb, Robin Hendry and Tom Lancaster (eds.), *The Routledge Handbook of Emergence* (London: Routledge, 2019).
Meillassoux, Quentin, 'Appendix: Excerpts from *Inexistence Divine*', tr. Graham Harman in Graham Harman, in *Quentin Meillassoux: Philosophy in the Making* (Edinburgh: Edinburgh University Press, 2011), 175–238.
Merchant, Carolyn, *The Death of Nature: Women, Ecology and the Scientific Revolution* (New York: HarperCollins, 1989).
'The Violence of Impediments: Francis Bacon and the Origins of Experimentation', *Isis*, 99 (2008), 731–60.
Merleau-Ponty, Maurice, *Phenomenology of Perception*, tr. C. Smith (New York: Humanities Press, 1962).
Merrifield, Mary, *Original Treatises on the Arts of Painting* (New York: Dover, 1967), vol. 2.
Midgley, Mary, *Myths We Live By* (London: Routledge, 2003).
Milbank, Alison, *God and the Gothic: Religion, Reality and Romance in the English Literary Tradition* (Oxford: Oxford University Press, 2018).
Milbank, John, *Beyond Secular Order: The Representation of Being and the Representation of the People* (Oxford: Wiley-Blackwell, 2013).
'The Confession of Time in Augustine', *Maynooth Philosophical Papers*, 10 (2020), 5–56.
'The Gift of Ruling: Secularization and Political Authority', *New Blackfriars*, 85 (March 2004), 212–38.
'Hume versus Kant: Faith, Reason and Feeling', *Modern Theology*, 27 (2011), 276–97.
'Manifestation and Procedure: Trinitarian Metaphysics after Albert the Great and Thomas Aquinas', in Marco Salvioli (ed.), *Tomismo Creativo: Letture Contemporanee del Doctor Communis* (Bologna: Edizioni Studio Domenicano, 2015).
'*Mathesis* and *Mathexis*: The Post-Nominalist Realism of Nicholas of Cusa', in Isabelle Moulin (ed.), *Participation et vision de Dieu chez Nicolas de Cues* (Paris: Vrin, 2017), 143–70.
'One in Three and Two in One: The Double Coincidence of Opposites in Nicholas of Cusa' (forthcoming).
The Religious Dimension in the Thought of Giambattista Vico, 1668–1744, Part I: The Early Metaphysics (Lewiston: Edwin Mellen Press, 1991).
Theology and Social Theory (Oxford: Blackwell, 1990).
'Writing and the Order of Learning', *Philosophy, Theology and the Sciences*, 4 (2017), 46–73.

Milbank, John, and Catherine Pickstock, *Truth in Aquinas* (London: Routledge, 2001).
Monod, Paul Kléber, *Solomon's Secret Arts: The Occult in the Age of the Enlightenment* (New Haven, CT: Yale University Press, 2013).
Moore, James R., *The Post-Darwinian Controversies: A Study of the Protestant Struggle to Come to Terms with Darwin in Great Britain and America 1870–1900* (Cambridge: Cambridge University Press, 1979).
Morris, Simon Conway, *Life's Solution: Inevitable Humans in a Lonely Universe* (Cambridge: Cambridge University Press, 2003).
Morrison, Margaret, *Unifying Scientific Theories: Physical Concepts and Mathematical Structures* (Cambridge: Cambridge University Press, 2007).
Morton, Timothy, *Realist Magic Objects, Ontology, Causality* (London: Open Humanities, 2013).
Moss, Lenny, *What Genes Can't Do* (Cambridge, MA: MIT Press, 2003).
Muirhead, J. H., *The Platonic Tradition in Anglo-Saxon Philosophy: Studies in the History of Idealism in England and America* [1931] (London: Routledge, 2018).
Murphy, Nancey C., *On the Moral Nature of the Universe: Theology, Cosmology, and Ethics* (Minneapolis, MN: Fortress Press, 1996).
'Religion, Theology, and the Philosophy of Science: An Appreciation of the Work of Ian Barbour', *Theology and Science*, 15 (2017), 42–52.
Theology in the Age of Scientific Reasoning (Ithaca, NY: Cornell University Press, 1990).
Muslow, Martin, *Frühneuzeitliche Selbsterhaltung: Telesio und die Naturphilosophie der Renaissance* (Tübingen: Max Niemeyer Verlag, 1998).
Nagel, Thomas, *Mind and Cosmos: Why the Materialist Neo-Darwinian Conception of Nature Is Almost Certainly False* (Oxford: Oxford University Press, 2012).
'The Sleep of Reason', *The New Republic* (October 12, 1998), 32–8.
Newman, William R., and Lawrence M. Principe, *Alchemy Tried in the Fire: Starkey, Boyle and the Fate of Helmontian Chemistry* (Chicago: University of Chicago Press, 2005).
Newton-Smith, W. H., *The Rationality of Science* (Boston: Routledge and Kegan Paul, 1981).
Nongbri, Brent, *Before Religion: The History of a Modern Concept* (New Haven, CT: Yale University Press, 2012).
Numbers, Ronald L. (ed.), *Galileo Goes to Jail and Other Myths about Science and Religion* (Cambridge, MA: Harvard University Press, 2009).
Numbers, Ronald L., 'Simplifying Complexity: Patterns in the History of Science and Religion', in Thomas Dixon, Geoffrey Cantor, and Stephen Pumfrey (eds.), *Science and Religion: New Historical Perspectives* (Cambridge: Cambridge University Press, 2010), 500–39.
Oliver, Simon, 'Aquinas and Aristotle's Teleology', *Nova et Vetera*, 11 (2013), 849–70.
Philosophy, God and Motion (London: Routledge, 2005).

'The Sweet Delight of Virtue and Grace in Aquinas's Ethics', *International Journal of Systematic Theology*, 7 (2005), 52–71.
Ong, Walter, *Ramus: Method and the Decay of Dialogue* (Chicago: University of Chicago Press, 2004).
Oosterhoff, Richard J., 'Cusanus and Boethian Theology in the Early French Reform', in Joshua Hollmann, Simon J. G. Burton, and Eric M. Parker (eds.), *Nicholas of Cusa and the Making of the Modern World* (Leiden: Brill, 2019), 339–66.
Making Mathematical Culture: University and Print in the Circle of Lefèvre D'Étaples (Oxford: Oxford University Press, 2018).
Osler, Margaret J., 'Mixing Metaphors: Science and Religion or Natural Philosophy and Theology in Early Modern Europe', *History of Science*, 35 (1997), 91–113.
Otten, Willemien, *Thinking Nature and the Nature of Thinking: From Eriugena to Emerson* (Stanford, CA: Stanford University Press, 2020).
Parsons, K. P., 'A Criterion for Meaning Change', *Philosophical Studies*, 28 (1975), 367–96.
Peacocke, Arthur, *Creation and the World of Science*, 2nd ed. (Oxford: Oxford University Press, 2004).
Peels, Rik, 'A Conceptual Map of Scientism', in Jeroen de Ridder, Rik Peels, and Rene van Woudenberg (eds.), *Scientism: Prospects and Problems* (Oxford: Oxford University Press, 2018).
Perl, Eric, *Thinking Being: Introduction to Metaphysics in the Classical Tradition* (Leiden: Brill, 2014).
Pickering, Andrew, *The Mangle of Practice: Time, Agency, and Science* (Chicago: University of Chicago Press, 1995).
Pickstock, Catherine, *After Writing* (Oxford: Blackwell, 1998).
'Music: Soul, City and Cosmos after Augustine', in John Milbank, Catherine Pickstock, and Graham Ward (eds.), *Radical Orthodoxy: A New Theology* (London: Routledge, 1999), 243–78.
Pieper, Josef, *Leisure, the Basis of Culture*, tr. A. Dru (London: Faber and Faber, 1952).
Pigliucci, Massimo, 'New Atheism and the Scientistic Turn in the Atheism Movement', *Midwest Studies in Philosophy*, 37 (2013), 142–53.
Pinch, Trevor J., 'Opening Black Boxes: Science, Technology and Society', *Social Studies of Science*, 22 (1992), 487–510.
Plantinga, Alvin, 'Methodological Naturalism', *Perspectives on Science and Christian Faith*, 49 (1997), 143–54.
Polanyi, Michael, 'Faith and Reason', *Journal of Religion*, 41 (1961), 237–41.
'Life Transcending Physics and Chemistry', *Chemical and Engineering News*, 45 (1967), 54–69.
Personal Knowledge: Towards a Post-Critical Philosophy (Chicago: University of Chicago Press, 1974).
The Tacit Dimension (Chicago: University of Chicago Press, 1966).
Polkinghorne, John, *One World: The Interaction of Science and Theology* (Philadelphia: Templeton Foundation Press, 2007).

Rochester Roundabout (Essex: Longman, 1985).

Science and Theology: An Introduction (Philadelphia: Fortress Press, 1998).

Popkin, Richard H., *The Third Force in Seventeenth-Century Thought* (Leiden: Brill, 1991).

Priest, Graham, *One: Being an Investigation into the Unity of Reality and Its Parts, Including the Singular Object Which Is Nothingness* (Oxford: Oxford University Press, 2016).

Putallaz, François-Xavier, *Insolente liberté: Controverses et condemnations au XIIIe siècle* (Paris: Cerf, 1995).

Radford, Tim, *The Consolations of Physics* (London: Sceptre, 2018).

Ramelli, I., 'Alexander of Aphrodisias: A Source of Origen's Philosophy?', *Philosophie Antique: Problèmes, Renaissances, Usages*, 14 (2014), 243–46.

Ratzinger, Joseph, *Introduction to Christianity*, tr. J. R. Foster (San Francisco, CA: Ignatius Press, 2004).

Ravaisson, Félix, *Of Habit*, tr. Clare Carlisle and Mark Sinclair (London: Continuum, 2008).

Raymond, Tallis, and Rowan Williams, 'Science, Stories and the Self: A Conversation between Raymond Tallis and Rowan Williams', in Anthony Carroll and Richard Norman (eds.), *Religion and Atheism: Beyond the Divide* (London: Routledge, 2017), 3–25.

Reardon, Bernard M. G., *From Coleridge to Gore: A Century of Religious Thought in Britain* (London: Longman Group, 1971).

Redondi, Pietro, 'From Galileo to Augustine', in Peter Machamer (ed.), *The Cambridge Companion to Galileo* (Cambridge: Cambridge University Press, 1998).

Rée, Jonathan, 'Atheism and History', in Anthony Carroll and Richard Norman (eds.), *Religion and Atheism: Beyond the Divide* (London: Routledge, 2017).

Reeves, Josh, 'After Lakatos', *Theology and Science*, 9 (2011), 395–409.

Against Methodology in Science and Religion (London: Routledge, 2020).

Reidy, Michael S., and Bernard Lightman (eds.), *The Age of Scientific Naturalism: Tyndall and His Contemporaries* (London: Pickering and Chatto, 2014).

Richards, Robert J., 'Darwin's Romantic Biology: The Foundation of His Evolutionary Ethics', in J. Mainschien and M. Ruse (eds.), *Biology and the Foundations of Ethics* (Cambridge: Cambridge University Press, 1999), 113–53.

Richie, Sara Lane, 'Integrated Physicality and the Absence of God: Spiritual Technologies in Theological Context', *Modern Theology*, 37 (2021), 296–315.

Riskin, Jessica, *The Restless Clock: A History of the Centuries-Long Argument over What Makes Living Things Tick* (Chicago: University of Chicago Press, 2016).

Rosemann, Phillip W., *The Story of a Great Medieval Book: Peter Lombard's Sentences* (Peterborough: Broadview, 2007).

Rosenstock, Bruce, *Transfinite Life: Oskar Goldberg and the Vitalist Imagination* (Bloomington: Indiana University Press, 2017).

Ross, Sydney, 'Scientist: The Story of a Word', *Annals of Science*, 18 (1962), 65–85.

Rossi, Paolo, *The Birth of Modern Science* (Oxford: Blackwell, 2001).

Roux, Sophie, 'Forms of Mathematization', *Early Science and Medicine* 15 (2010), 319–37.

Rovelli, Carlo, *Reality Is Not What It Seems: The Journey to Quantum Gravity* (London: Penguin, 2017).

Seven Brief Lessons on Physics, tr. Simon Carnell and Erica Segre (London: Penguin, 2015).

Russell, Robert, J., *Cosmology: From Alpha to Omega: The Creative Mutual Interaction of Theology and Science, Theology and the Sciences* (Minneapolis, MN: Fortress Press, 2008).

Sagan, Carl, *Cosmos* (London: Random House, 2002).

Satran, David, *In the Image of Origen: Eros, Virtue and Constraint in the Early Christian Academy* (Oakland: University of California Press, 2018).

Scarry, Elaine, *On Beauty and Being Just* (Princeton, NJ: Princeton University Press, 1999).

Schaffer, Simon, 'Astronomers Mark Time: Discipline and the Personal Equation', *Science in Context*, 2 (1988), 115–45.

'Glass Works: Newton's Prisms and the Uses of Experiment', in D. Gooding et al. (eds.), *The Uses of Experiment: Studies in the Natural Sciences* (Cambridge: Cambridge University Press, 1989), 67–104.

Schindler, D. C., *The Catholicity of Reason* (Grand Rapids, MI: Eerdmans, 2013).

'The First First Philosophy', *Recherches Philosophiques*, 8 (2018), 101–16.

Freedom from Reality: The Diabolical Character of Modern Liberty (Notre Dame, IN: University of Notre Dame Press, 2017), 151–275.

'Liberalism, Religious Freedom, and the Common Good: The Totalitarian Logic of Self-Limitation', *Communio: International Catholic Review*, 40 (2013), 577–615.

'On the Universality of the University: A Response to Jean-Luc Marion', *Communio: International Catholic Review* (Spring 2013): 77–99.

The Perfection of Freedom: Schiller, Schelling, and Hegel between the Ancients and the Moderns (Eugene, OR: Cascade Books, 2012).

Schindler, David L., 'The Gift as Given: Creation and Disciplinary Abstraction in Science', *Communio: International Catholic Review*, 38 (2011), 52–102.

'The Meaning of the Human in a Technological Age', *Anthropotes*, 15 (1999), 31–51.

Schmitz, Kenneth, 'Postmodern or Modern-Plus?', *Communio: International Catholic Review* (1990), 152–66.

Searle, John, *Minds, Brains and Science*, reprint ed. (Cambridge, MA: Harvard University Press, 1985).

Seigel, Harvey, *Relativism Refuted: A Critique of Contemporary Epistemological Relativism* (Dordrecht: D. Reidel, 1987).

Sennett, Richard, *The Craftsman* (London: Penguin, 2008).

Shagan, Ethan H., *The Birth of Modern Belief and Judgement from the Middle Ages to Enlightenment* (Princeton, NJ: Princeton University Press, 2018).

Shapin, Steven, *The Scientific Life: A Moral History of a Late Modern Vocation* (Chicago: University of Chicago Press, 2008).

Shapin, Steven, and Simon Schaffer, *Leviathan and the Air-Pump: Hobbes, Boyle and the Experimental Life* (Princeton, NJ: Princeton University Press, 2011).

Shaw, Gregory, *Theurgy and the Soul: The Neoplatonism of Iamblichus* (Kettering: Angelico, 2014).

Sheldrake, Rupert, *A New Science of Life* (London: Icon, 2009).

Shepherd, Philip, *New Self, New World* (Berkeley, CA: North Atlantic Books, 2010).

Siddall, Ruth, 'Mineral Pigments in Archaeology', *Minerals*, 8 (2018), 1–35.

Siebens, Peterson, and Anne Siebens, 'Matter in Biology: An Aristotelian Metaphysics for Contemporary Homology', *American Catholic Philosophical Quarterly*, 92 (2018), 353–71.

Silva, Ignacio, 'A Cause among Causes: God Acting in the Natural World', *European Journal for the Philosophy of Religion*, 7 (2015), 99–114.

'Revisiting Aquinas on Providence and Rising to the Challenge of Divine Action in Nature', *The Journal of Religion*, 94 (2014), 277–91.

Simpson, William M. R., Robert C. Koons, and Nicholas J. Teh (eds.), *Neo-Aristotelian Perspectives on Contemporary Science* (London: Routledge, 2017).

Smith, Wilfred Cantwell, *The Meaning and End of Religion* (London: SPCK, 1978).

Smith, Wolfgang, *The Wisdom of Ancient Cosmology: Contemporary Science in the Light of Tradition* (Oakton, VA: Foundation for Traditional Studies, 2003).

Smithson, Hannah E., et al., 'Color-Coordinate System from a 13th Century Account of Rainbows', *Journal of the Optical Society of America*, 31 (2014), A341–A349.

Smolin, Lee, *Time Reborn: From the Crisis in Physics to the Future of the Universe* (Boston: Houghton Mifflin Harcourt, 2013).

Soskice, Janet Martin, *Metaphor and Religious Language* (Oxford: Clarendon, 1985).

Soulez, Antonia, 'Conversion in Philosophy: Wittgenstein's "Saving Word"', *Hypatia*, 15 (2000), 127–50.

Southern, R. W., *Robert Grosseteste: The Growth of an English Mind in Medieval Europe* (Oxford: Clarendon, 1992),

Spaemann, Robert, 'The End of Modernity?', in D. C. Schindler and Jeanne Heffernan Schindler (eds.), *A Robert Spaemann Reader: Philosophical Essays on Nature, God, and the Human Person* (Oxford: Oxford University Press, 2015), 211–29.

'Nature', in D. C. Schindler and Jeanne Heffernan Schindler (eds.), *A Robert Spaemann Reader: Philosophical Essays on Nature, God, and the Human Person* (Oxford: Oxford University Press, 2015), 22–36.

Persons: The Difference between 'Someone' and 'Something' (Oxford: Oxford University Press, 2007).

'The Unrelinquishability of Teleology', in Ana Marta González (ed.), *Contemporary Perspectives on Natural Law: Natural Law as a Limiting Concept* (Aldershot: Ashgate, 2008).

'What Does It Mean to Say That "Art Imitates Nature?"', in D. C. Schindler and Jeanne Heffernan Schindler (eds.), *A Robert Spaemann Reader: Philosophical Essays on Nature, God, and the Human Person* (Oxford: Oxford University Press, 2015), 192–210.

Speer, Andreas, 'The Division of Metaphysical Discourses: Boethius, Thomas Aquinas and Meister Eckhart', in Kent Emery Jr (ed.), *Philosophy and Theology in the Long Middle Ages* (Leiden: Brill, 2011), 91–115.

'The Hidden Heritage: Boethian Metaphysics and Its Medieval Tradition', *Quaestio*, 5 (2005), 163–81.

Stanford, Kyle P., 'An Antirealist Explanation for the Success of Science', *Philosophy of Science*, 67 (2002), 266–84.

Stengers, Isabelle, *Another Science Is Possible: A Manifesto for Slow Science*, tr. Stephen Muecke (Cambridge: Polity, 2018).

The Invention of Modern Science, tr. Daniel W. Smith (Minneapolis: University of Minnesota Press, 2000).

Stenmark, Mikael, *How to Relate Science and Religion: A Multidimensional Model* (Grand Rapids, MI: Eerdmans, 2004).

Scientism: Science, Ethics, and Religion (London: Routledge, 2001).

Stiegler, Bernard, *Technics and Time I: The Fault of Epimetheus*, tr. Richard Beardsworth and George Collins (Stanford, CA: Stanford University Press, 1998).

Stock, Brian, *Myth and Science in the Twelfth Century: A Study of Bernard Silvester* (Princeton, NJ: Princeton University Press, 1972).

Stock, Gregory, *Redesigning Humans: Our Inevitable Genetic Future* (New York: Houghton Mifflin, 2002).

Strawson, Galen, 'Realistic Monism', in Strawson et al. (eds.), *Consciousness and Its Place in Nature: Does Physicalism Entail Panpsychism?* (Exeter: Imprint Academic, 2004), 5.

Strider, Robert E. L., II, *Robert Greville, Lord Brooke: Aristocrat, Puritan, Philosopher, Martyr* (Cambridge, MA: Harvard University Press, 1958).

Strong, Edward W., 'The Relationship between Metaphysics and the Scientific Method in Galileo's Work', in E. McMullin (ed.), *Galileo: Man of Science* (New York: Basic Books, 1967), 352–64.

Stroumsa, Guy, *A New Science: The Discovery of Religion in the Age of Reason* (Cambridge, MA: Harvard University Press, 2010).

Suppe, F. (ed.), *The Structure of Scientific Theories*, 2nd ed. (Urbana: University of Illinois Press, 1977).

Szumilewicz, I., 'Incommensurability and the Rationality of the Development of Science', *British Journal for the Philosophy of Science*, 28 (1977), 345–50.

Tanner, Kathryn, *God and Creation in Christian Theology* (Minneapolis, MN: Fortress, 2006).

Jesus, Humanity and the Trinity (Edinburgh: T. & T. Clark, 2001).

Tarde, Gabriel, *Monadology and Sociology*, tr. Theo Lorenc (Melbourne: re.press, 2012).

Theocharis, T., and M. Psimopoulos, 'Where Science Has Gone Wrong', *Nature*, 329 (1987), 595–8.

Thomassen, Beroald, *Metaphysik als Lebensform: Untersuchungen zur Grundlegung der Metaphysik im Metaphysikkommentar Alberts des Grossen* (Münster: Aschendorff, 1985).

Thorndike, Lynn, 'Some Medieval Conceptions of Magic', *The Monist*, 25 (1915), 107–39.

Tilling, Chris, 'Paul, Christ and Narrative Time', in A. B. Torrence and T. H. McCall (eds.), *Christ and the Created Order* (Grand Rapids, MI: Zondervan, 2018).

Torrance, Thomas F., *The Ground and Grammar of Theology* (Charlottesville: University Press of Virginia, 1980).

Toulmin, Stephen, *Cosmopolis: The Hidden Agenda of Modernity* (Chicago: University of Chicago Press, 1992).

Trego, Kristell, *L'essence de la liberté: La refondation de l'ethique dans l'oeuvre de saint Anselme de Canturbéry* (Paris: Vrin, 2010).

Trigg, Roger, *Beyond Matter: Why Science Needs Metaphysics* (Philadelphia: Templeton Foundation Press, 2017).

Tuchman, Barbara W., *A Distant Mirror: The Calamitous 14th Century* (New York: Knopf, 1978).

Turner, Frank Miller, *Between Science and Religion: The Reaction to Scientific Naturalism in Late Victorian England* (New Haven, CT: Yale University Press, 1974).

Contesting Cultural Authority: Essays in Victorian Intellectual Life (Cambridge: Cambridge University Press, 1993).

'The Victorian Conflict between Science and Religion: A Professional Dimension', *Isis*, 69 (1987), 356–76.

Tyson, Paul, *Returning to Reality: Christian Platonism for Our Times* (Eugene, OR: Wipf and Stock, 2014).

Seven Brief Lessons on Magic (Eugene, OR: Wipf and Stock, 2019).

Ulrich, Ferdinand, 'Das Problem einer "Metaphysik in der Wiederholung"', *Salzburger Jahrbuch für Philosophie* 5–6 (1961–2): 263–98.

Homo Abyssus: The Drama of the Question of Being (Washington, DC: Humanum Academic Press, 2018).

van Asperen de Boer, Jan, 'An Examination of Particle Size Distribution of Azurite and Natural Ultramarine in Early Netherlandish Paintings', *Studies in Conservation*, 19 (1974), 233–43.

van Woudenberg, René, Rik Peels, and Jeroen de Ridder, 'Introduction: Putting Scientism on the Philosophical Agenda', in René van Woudenberg, Rik Peels, and Jeroen de Ridder (eds.), *Scientism: Prospects and Problems* (Oxford: Oxford University Press, 2018).

Veatch, Henry, *The Two Logics: The Conflict between Classical and Neo-Analytic Philosophy* (Evanston, IL: Northwestern University Press, 1969).

Verfaegh, Sander, *The Nature and Development of Quine's Naturalism* (Oxford: Oxford University Press, 2018).

Viereck, G. S., *Glimpses of the Great* (New York: Macauley, 1930).

Waddell, Mark A., *Jesuit Science and the End of Nature's Secrets* (London: Ashgate, 2017).
Wallace, William A., 'The Problem of Causality in Galileo's Science', *The Review of Metaphysics*, 36 (1983), 607–32.
'Traditional Natural Philosophy', in Charles Schmitt and Quentin Skinner (eds.), *The Cambridge History of Renaissance Philosophy* (Cambridge: Cambridge University Press, 1988), 201–35.
Webster, Charles, *From Paracelsus to Newton: Magic and the Making of Modern Science* (New York: Dover, 2013).
Paracelsus: Medicine, Magic and the Mission at the End of Time (New Haven, CT: Yale University Press, 2008).
Weeks, Andrew, *Paracelsus: Speculative Theory and the Crisis of the Early Reformation* (Albany: State University of New York Press, 1997).
White, Michael, *Isaac Newton: The Last Sorcerer* (London: Fourth Estate, 1997).
White, Paul, 'The Man of Science', in Bernard Lightman (ed.), *A Companion to the History of Science* (Chichester: Wiley Blackwell, 2016), 153–63.
Thomas Huxley: Making the 'Man of Science' (Cambridge: Cambridge University Press, 2002).
Whitehead, Alfred North, *The Concept of Nature* (Cambridge: Cambridge University Press, 2015).
Process and Reality (New York: Free Press, 1978).
Williams, Rowan, *Being Human: Bodies, Minds, Persons* (London: SPCK, 2018).
The Edge of Words: God and the Habits of Language (London: Bloomsbury, 2014).
Wootton, David, *The Invention of Science: A New History of the Scientific Revolution* (London: Penguin, 2016).
Wuerger, S. M., L. T. Maloney, and J. Krauskopf, 'Proximity Judgments in Color Space: Tests of a Euclidean Color Geometry', *Vision Research*, 35 (1995), 827–35.
Zachhuber, Johannes, 'Nature', in Mark J. Edwards (ed.), *The Routledge Handbook of Early Christian Philosophy* (Oxford: Routledge, 2021), 27–40.

Index

CPSIA information can be obtained
at www.ICGtesting.com
Printed in the USA
LVHW082337020822
725062LV00004B/76

9 781316 517925